THOSE WILD WYNDHAMS

THOSE WILD WYNDHAMS

Three Sisters at the Heart of Power

Claudia Renton

WILLIAM
COLLINS

William Collins
An imprint of HarperCollins*Publishers*
77–85 Fulham Palace Road,
London W6 8JB
WilliamCollinsBooks.com

First published in Great Britain by William Collins in 2014

A catalogue record for this book is available from the British Library.

ISBN 978-0-00-754489-9

Typeset in Minion by Palimpsest Book Production Ltd, Falkirk, Stirlingshire

Printed and bound in Great Britain by
Clays Ltd, St Ives plc

MIX
Paper from
responsible sources
FSC® C007454

FSC™ is a non-profit international organisation established to promote
the responsible management of the world's forests. Products carrying the
FSC label are independently certified to assure consumers that they come
from forests that are managed to meet the social, economic and
ecological needs of present and future generations,
and other controlled sources.

Find out more about HarperCollins and the environment at
www.harpercollins.co.uk/green

For Mama.
Always.

Contents

THE WYNDHAMS

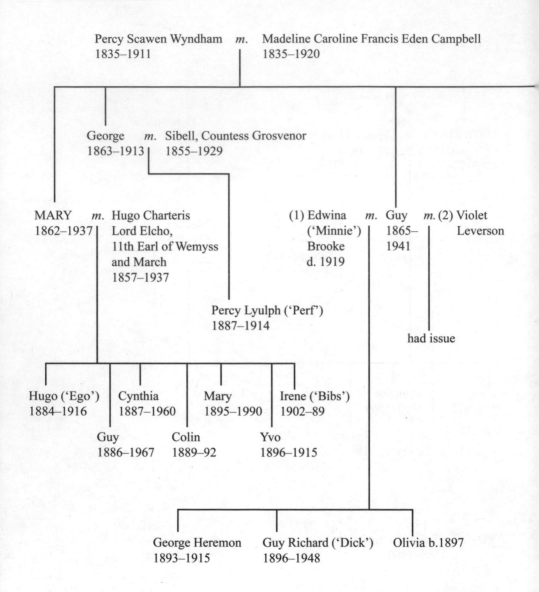

Percy Scawen Wyndham   *m.*   Madeline Caroline Francis Eden Campbell
1835–1911   1835–1920

George   *m.*   Sibell, Countess Grosvenor
1863–1913   1855–1929

MARY   *m.* Hugo Charteris
1862–1937   Lord Elcho,
             11th Earl of Wemyss
             and March
             1857–1937

(1) Edwina   *m.*   Guy   *m.* (2) Violet
('Minnie')   1865–   Leverson
Brooke   1941
d. 1919

had issue

Percy Lyulph ('Perf')
1887–1914

Hugo ('Ego')   Cynthia   Mary   Irene ('Bibs')
1884–1916   1887–1960   1895–1990   1902–89

        Guy   Colin   Yvo
        1886–1967   1889–92   1896–1915

George Heremon   Guy Richard ('Dick')   Olivia b.1897
1893–1915   1896–1948

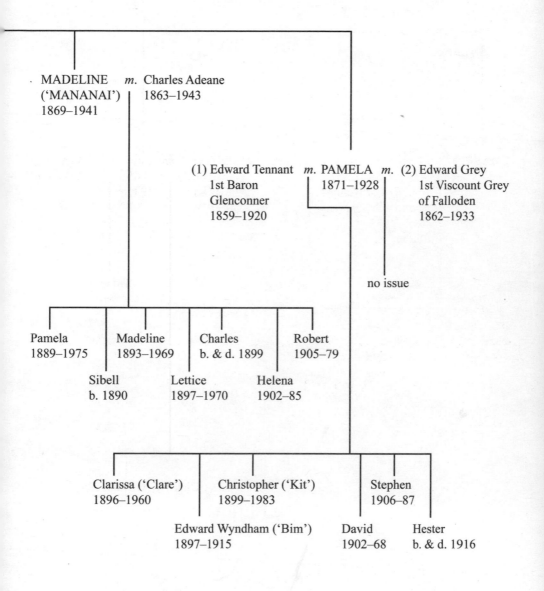

MADELINE   *m.* Charles Adeane
('MANANAI')   1863–1943
1869–1941

(1) Edward Tennant   *m.* PAMELA *m.* (2) Edward Grey
1st Baron   1871–1928   1st Viscount Grey
Glenconner   of Falloden
1859–1920   1862–1933

no issue

Pamela   Madeline   Charles   Robert
1889–1975   1893–1969   b. & d. 1899   1905–79

          Sibell   Lettice   Helena
          b. 1890   1897–1970   1902–85

     Clarissa ('Clare')   Christopher ('Kit')   Stephen
     1896–1960   1899–1983   1906–87

          Edward Wyndham ('Bim')   David   Hester
          1897–1915   1902–68   b. & d. 1916

'La Chanson de Marie-des-Anges'

Y avait un'fois un pauv'gas,
Et lon la laire,
Et lon lan la,
Y avait un'fois un pauv'gas,
Qu'aimait cell'qui n'l'aimait pas.

Elle lui dit: Apport'moi d'main
Et lon la laire,
Et lon lan la,
Elle lui dit: Apport'moi d'main
L'cœur de ta mèr' pour mon chien.

Va chez sa mère et la tu
Et lon la laire,
Et lon lan la,
Va chez sa mère et la tue,
Lui prit l'cœur et s'en courut.

Comme il courait, il tomba,
Et lon la laire,
Et lon lan la,
Comme il courait, il tomba,
Et par terre l'cœur roula.

Et pendant que l'cœur roulait,
Et lon la laire,
Et lon lan la,
Et pendant que l'cœur roulait,
Entendit l'cœur qui parlait.

Et l'cœur lui dit en pleurant,
Et lon la laire,
Et lon lan la,
Et l'cœur lui dit en pleurant:
T'es-tu fait mal mon enfant?

Jean Richepin (1848–1926)

'Do you know Richepin's poem about a Mother's Heart? It means something like this:- "there was a poor wretch who loved a woman who would not love him. She asked him for his Mother's heart, so he killed his Mother to cut out her heart and hurried off with it to his love. He ran so fast that he tripped and fell, and the heart rolled away. As it rolled it began to speak and asked "Darling child, have you hurt yourself?"'

George Wyndham to Pamela Tennant, 11 March 1912

Prologue

On a cool February night in 1900, Pamela Tennant, wife of the industrialist Eddy Tennant, was dining at the London townhouse of her brother and sister-in-law, Lord and Lady Ribblesdale. The Season had not quite started, but there was already a smattering of balls. By early summer that smattering would become a deluge, as seemingly every house in Mayfair echoed to the strains of bands and England's elite waltzed round and round camellia-filled ballrooms in what would prove to be the last year of Victoria's reign. Thus far, London seemed to have escaped the disgusting yellow smog that had blanketed the city for months the year before, and added to the misery of the swathes affected by a bad strain of influenza that year.

Pamela was not really looking forward to the Season that was to come: or to any Season, for that matter. In the five years since she had married, her refusal to play ball socially had provoked several spats with her sister-in-law. Charty Ribblesdale, one of the audacious Tennant sisters who had launched themselves on to London Society twenty years before, could not understand why Pamela should wilfully clam up when faced with new people. Pamela's refusal to play by any rules but her own mystified Charty and her sisters Margot and Lucy. They thought it alien to the ethos of the Souls: their fascinating, chattering set who affected insouciant, swan-like ease, no matter how frantically their legs paddled beneath the serene surface.

The delightfully haphazard Mary Elcho, Pamela's eldest sister, was a leading light of the Souls. Pamela, beautiful, brilliant, a master of the pointed phrase, had it in her to joust with the best of them. But she chose not to. Instead, she professed disdain for 'those murdered Summers' of the Season, and openly expressed her preference for Wiltshire, where she caravanned across the Downs in the company of her children.[1] It was a very peculiar attitude.

The burly American placed next to Pamela also seemed ill at ease among Society's hubbub. John Singer Sargent, whose *Carnation, Lily, Lily, Rose* had dazzled the Royal Academy over a decade before, was establishing himself as a society portraitist *par excellence*, but he had little time for his sitters' chatter. He preferred quiet times in the Gloucestershire village of Broadway with his sisters and nieces – incidentally not far from where Mary Elcho lived at Stanway. 'He was very nice & simple, & . . . very shy & not the least like an American,' Mary's friend Frances Horner reported to the artist Edward Burne-Jones after meeting Sargent (for Sargent, although an American by parentage, had been born and raised on the Continent), '& he wasn't very like an artist either!. . . he hated discussing all his great friends . . . & talking about his pictures.'[2]

Perhaps Charty took a certain pleasure in seating Pamela next to Sargent that evening. A taste of her own medicine – and Charty could justify the placement because Sargent was currently working on a portrait of Pamela and her sisters. It had been commissioned by their father, Percy Wyndham, who, with his wife Madeline, had built Clouds in Wiltshire, a house little over a decade old and already famous as a 'palace of weekending'.[3] Pamela, Mary and sweet-natured Madeline Adeane (who so unluckily after a whole brood of girls had finally succeeded in giving birth to a boy only for the premature infant to die the same day) had been sitting to Sargent ever since then.

There was plenty to talk about. No mention was made of the Boer War's disastrous progress, or Pamela's elder brother George, Under-Secretary in the War Office, whose triumphant speech in the House of Commons a few weeks before had singlehandedly seemed to redeem the Government's conduct of the war. All Sargent's talk was of the portrait. The first sittings had taken place over a year before, in the drawing room of the Wyndhams' London house, 44 Belgrave Square. Yet just recently, Pamela, in the thick of preparations for one of the tableaux of which she was so fond, received a letter from Percy suggesting that Sargent's portrait might still not be finished in time for this year's Summer Exhibition at the Royal Academy. What with the uncertain light at this time of year, and the fact that the Wyndhams would not be in London until after Easter, 'perhaps this is better', he concluded.[4] To Pamela's mind, this was not better. At this rate, she replied ominously, there was the danger that 'we shall all be old and haggard before the public sees it'.[5]

Pamela in the flesh made the shortcomings of Pamela in oils all too clear. Sargent told Pamela in his deep, curiously accentless voice (the legacy of his Continental upbringing) that he 'felt *sure*' that Mr Wyndham 'would not mean it to be as it is'. 'He is very anxious for some more sittings from me and enquired my plans most pertinaciously,' Pamela told Percy the next day. Her very presence had seemed to prove an inspiration: '"and now I see you oh it must be worked on" – squirming & writhing in his evening suit – "no finish – no finish" – he got quite excited'.[6]

As agreed, Pamela made her way to Sargent's studio on Tite Street in Chelsea at half-past two the following Saturday. Three or four days was all that Sargent, a phenomenally fast worker, required before she could thankfully flee London once again. 'He has not repainted the face . . . He worked on little corners of it and has much improved it I think,' Pamela said. He had remodelled her nose, taken 'a little of the colour out of my cheeks, this improves it', and transformed her hair from 'all fluffy and rather trivial looking before' to swept back, which 'has strengthened it, and made it *more* like my head really'.

There was one loss. The front of Pamela's dress, an eye-catching blue, had, Sargent said decisively, to go. It was, she explained to her parents, 'disturbing to the *scheme* . . . And much as I regret my pretty blue front I *quite* see it was rather preclusive of other things in the picture as a whole. For instance both sisters seem to *gain* by its removal – one's eye is not checked & held by it . . . My face also seems to gain significance by its removal.'[7] Mary, who had always been suspicious of Pamela's colour choice, must have been relieved: 'blue can be so *ugly* don't you think?' she had complained to their mother when Pamela had first announced her sartorial intentions.[8]

Uncharacteristically, Madeline was causing trouble. At the Ribblesdales', Sargent had been adamant that 'Mrs Adeane in particular' needed to be changed, requiring a further week of sittings. The year before, Charlie Adeane's patience with 'that blessed picture' had worn thin when Madeline had caught influenza while sitting for it. Now, with Madeline still recovering from her infant son's death, Charlie Adeane, as protective as he was devoted, might prove the spanner in the works. 'I hope you will use your influence if Charlie is against it,' Pamela implored her father; 'it seems a pity if it is so near it shouldn't be managed.'[9] Madeline Wyndham, who could never refuse anything to her 'Benjamina', as she called her youngest daughter, replied, 'I think it would amuse her – & I should trust it was *warmer* in Sargent's Studio than it is in [the] large drawing room at 44 this time of year without hot water or hot air which I am sure Sargent's studio has . . . *you* ought write to Madeline & beg her to go up for a week she can be snug as a bug in my bedroom and she & Charlie can be there.'[10]

In art, as in life, Mary was proving difficult to pin down. Marooned among the rugs, tapestries and antiques that formed the paraphernalia of an artist's studio,[11] as Sargent, muttering unintelligibly under his breath, charged to and from the easel (placed, as always, next to his sitters so that when he stood back he might view portrait and person in the same light),[12] Pamela had to exercise all her diplomatic skill when asked what she thought of Sargent's depiction of Mary. 'I *could* say honestly I liked it,' she told her parents, 'but I did not think it "contemplative" enough in expression for her.' And 'no sooner than I had said the word "contemplative" than he caught at it. "Dreamy – I must make it a *little* more dreamy!"' All it needed, apparently, was a touch to Mary's hooded eyelids, which Pamela agreed were 'a most characteristic feature of her face'; but 'of course he will not do it till she sits to him', she concluded, with not a little exasperation.[13]

Astonishingly Mary – nicknamed 'Napoleon' by her friends for her tendency to make monumental plans that rarely came to pass, and who seemed, in the view of her dear friend Arthur Balfour, 'to combine into one disastrous whole all that there is of fatiguing in the occupations of mother, a woman of fashion, and a sick nurse'[14] – got herself to London, and to Tite Street, in time for the painting to be completed so that it could be displayed at the Royal Academy's Summer Exhibition that year.

The Wyndham Sisters, to the gratification of all (and doubtless Pamela in particular) was heralded as Sargent's masterpiece. For *The Times*, it was simply 'the greatest picture which has appeared for many years on the walls of the Royal Academy'. Bertie, the elderly Prince of Wales, who had honed his eye for beauty over many years, dubbed the portrait 'The Three Graces'.

It was, crowed the *Saturday Review*, 'one of those truces in the fight where beauty has unquestionably slipped in'.[15] Though we now think of Sargent as the Annie Leibovitz of his day – intently flattering at all costs – at that time people did not see it in quite the same way. 'In all the history of painting', commented the critic D. S. MacColl in the *Saturday Review* in 1898, 'hostile observation has never been pushed so far as by Mr. Sargent. I do not mean stupid deforming spite, humorous caricature, or diabolic possession . . . rather a cold accusing eye bent on the world.' MacColl likened Sargent to 'the prosecuting lawyer or denouncing critics'. His work made the viewer 'first repelled by its contempt, then fascinated by its life'.[16] 'I chronicle,' declared Sargent, 'I do not judge.'[17] The dazzling results seduced the aristocracy, but they commissioned him with trepidation. 'It is positively dangerous to sit to Sargent,' declared one apprehensive society matron; 'it's taking your face in your hands.'[18]

One oft-repeated criticism, that Sargent did no more than replicate his sitters' glamour, is perhaps a misunderstanding of the emptiness that his brush was so often revealing. To defeat any accusation that *The Wyndham Sisters* is simply a pretty picture, one needs only to look at the sisters' hands. Pamela's fingers imperiously flick outwards as she lounges back on the sofa, in the most obviously central position as always, unblinkingly staring the viewer down; Mary's thin hands worry at each other as she perches on the edge of the sofa and gazes 'dreamily' off into the distance showing all her 'delicate intellectual beauty'. Then there is Madeline, who uses her left hand to support herself against the sofa, while her right hand, quelled by sorrow, lies in her lap, patiently facing upwards, cupped to receive the blessings that fate, in recent months, had so conspicuously denied her. Underneath the serenity is the wildness of the Wyndhams, the foreign strain from their mother's French-Irish blood, that people would remark on time and time again.

Before the sittings began, before the composition had been decided upon, Madeline and Percy Wyndham had arranged a dinner at Belgrave Square for Sargent to meet his sitters properly. Watching the family at home, Sargent had caught on immediately. Rather than paint these women in his studio, as was the norm, he set them in the drawing room of their parents' house. As one's eye becomes accustomed to the cool gloom behind the seated figures swathed in layers of white organza, taffeta, tulle, one can make out in the background the portrait of their mother that hung in that room: George Frederic Watts's portrait of Madeline Wyndham, resplendent in a sunflower-splashed gown, that had caused such a stir at the Grosvenor Gallery a quarter of a century before. Through the darkness, behind Mary, Madeline and Pamela, gleams Madeline Wyndham. So in art, as in life. Sargent had not missed a thing.

ONE

'Worse Than 100 Boys'

The eldest daughter of the portrait, Mary Constance Wyndham, was born to Percy and Madeline in London, in summer's dog days, on 3 August 1862. Percy, called 'the Hon'ble P' by his friends, was the favoured younger son of the vastly wealthy Lord Leconfield of Petworth House in Sussex. The Conservative Member for West Cumberland, he had a kind heart and the family traits of an uncontrollable temper and an inability to dissemble. It was true of him, as was said of his father, that he had 'no power of disguising his feelings, if he liked one person more than another it was simply written on his Countenance'.[1]

Percy's Irish wife Madeline was different. Known in infancy as 'the Sunny Baby',[2] she was renowned for her expansive warmth. 'She is an Angel . . . She has the master-key of life – love – which unlocks everything for her and makes one feel her immortal,' said Georgiana Burne-Jones, who, like her husband Edward, was among Madeline's closest friends.[3] Yet in courtship Percy had spoken much of Madeline's reserve – 'you sweet mystery', he called her,[4] one of very few to recognize that her personality seemed to be shut up in different boxes, to some of which only she held the key.

Percy and Madeline were both twenty-seven years old. In two years of marriage, they had established a pattern of dividing their time between Petworth, Cockermouth Castle – a family property in Percy's constituency given to them by his father for their use – and fashionable Belgrave Square, at no. 44. Madeline's mother, Pamela, Lady Campbell, came over from Ireland for the birth, and during Madeline's labour sat anxiously with Percy in a little room off her daughter's bedroom. The labour was relatively short – barely four and a half hours – but it was difficult. Lady Campbell had threatened to call her own daughter 'Rhinocera' when she was born because of her incredible size. Mary, at birth, weighed an eye-watering 11 pounds. '[T]he size and hardness of the baby's head (for which I am afraid I am to blame)', Percy told his sister Fanny with apologetic pride, had required the use of forceps to bring the child into the world. 'Of course we should have liked a boy but I am very grateful to God that matters have gone so well,' Percy concluded.[5]

Percy and Madeline's daughter held within her person the blood of Ireland and England – a physical embodiment of the vexed union between the kingdoms. Mary grew up on tales of her maternal great-grandfather, Lord Edward FitzGerald, hero and martyr of the 1798 Irish Rebellion. Her own London childhood was punctuated by acts of violence by the newly formed republican Fenian Brotherhood. In 1844 Parliament had debated, at length, the motion 'Ireland is occupied, not governed'. An ambitious young Benjamin Disraeli drew for the Commons a picture of 'a starving population, an absentee aristocracy . . . an alien church, and . . . the weakest executive in the world'.[6] While the novelist Disraeli may have been exercising a little artistic licence – certainly by 1873 only 20 per cent of Ireland's aristocracy were technically absentee[7] – fundamentally his depiction was, and remained, true. Mary and her siblings were brought up to mourn the fate of 'darling Ireland'.[8] With a Catholic strain passed down from Lord Edward's French wife, they sympathized with the Catholic masses.

Mary described herself and her younger brother George in childhood as 'the Fenians of the family'.[9]

Lady Edward – 'La Belle Pamela' – was officially the adopted
daughter of Madame de Genlis, educationalist disciple of Rousseau.
In all probability, Pamela was de Genlis' biological child, by her
lover Philippe duc d'Orléans. Orléans was Louis XVI's cousin. He
voted for the King's execution during the French Revolution, then
was guillotined himself when his royal blood rendered him
counter-revolutionary. Mary's was an exotic heritage, romantic,
royal, with a hint of disreputableness. Like all her siblings, she was
proud of it.

Mary was born at the cusp of a new age, as a myriad of developments – some welcome, others not – forced Britain and her
class to reassess their identities. She was born within five years
of the publication of Darwin's *On the Origin of Species* and the
famous Huxley–Wilberforce debate on evolution, which her father
Percy had attended;[10] the 1857 Indian Rebellion which led to control
over the sub-continent being passed from the British East India
Company to the British Crown; and Richard Burton and John
Hanning Speke's discovery of the Nile's source. When Mary was
born, the working classes (and all women) were still unenfranchised
– only one in five men could vote. Neither William Gladstone nor
Disraeli, those giants of the late Victorian political arena, had yet
formed their own ministries. Upper-class women could not appear
in public without a chaperone. During her childhood, Joseph
Bazalgette built the Victoria and Albert Embankments to cover the
new sewage system that meant the Thames was no longer the city's
chamberpot. The telephone and the first traffic light (short-lived,
it was installed outside the Houses of Parliament in 1868, only to
explode in 1869, gravely wounding the policeman operating it) were
inventions of her early youth. Mary, who as a child had fossils
shown and explained to her by her father, was born into a world
ebullient in its capacity for exploration and invention but, in post-
Darwinian terms, questing and unsure. The British were becoming,

as Charles Dilke's bestselling *Greater Britain* said, a 'race girdling the earth',[11] but within their own country the patrician male's stranglehold on power was being loosened. Mary, hopeful, endlessly curious, surrounded by novelty and change, was a child of that age.

Above all, Mary was the child of a love match – on one side, at least. It had been a *coup de foudre* for shy, crotchety Percy when as 1860 dawned he met Madeline Campbell in Ireland. Madeline was beautiful, dark and voluptuous, but she was more than that. Her earthy physicality exuded life, and enhanced it in others. 'People in her presence feel like trees or birds at their best, singing or flourishing according to their own natures with an easy exuberance . . . she has a peculiar gift for making this world glorious to all who meet her in it,' said her son George.[12]

Percy and Madeline were engaged in London in July, and married in Ireland in October. During a brief interim period of separation, as Madeline returned to Ireland, Percy gave voice to his infatuation in sheaves of letters, still breathtaking in their intensity, that daily swooped across the Irish Sea. '[D]ear Glory of my Life sweet darling, dear Cobra, dear gull with the changing eyes, most precious, rare rich Madeline sweet Madge of the soft cheeks',[13] said Percy, pouring forth his love, longing and dreams for the future. With barely concealed lust he begged Madeline to describe her bedroom so he could imagine her preparing her 'dear body' for bed, and recalled, with attempted lasciviousness charming in its naivety, their brief moments of physical contact – a kiss stolen on a balcony at a ball; a moment knocked against each other in a bumpy carriage ride. '[I]f these letters don't make you *know* how I love you, let there be no more pens, ink and paper in the world.'[14]

No corresponding letters from Madeline survive. Brief fragments of reported speech suggest she was more world-weary than her besotted swain. 'Oh Percy, Percy, I don't think you know very much about me, but that's no matter,' she told him. Some of her descendants think that there may have been a failed love affair in her past;

if so, she successfully, and characteristically, erased all trace of it.[15] Her reserve only strengthened Percy's attraction.

Madeline was well-born, if of colourful ancestry, but she had no money to speak of. Her widowed mother had brought up twelve children on an army pension. Madeline would receive just £50 a year on her mother's death.[16] The infatuated Percy persuaded his forbidding father – who succumbed immediately to Madeline's charm on meeting her – to give his blessing to the match, and to dower his bride. A month before the Wyndhams married, £35,727 16s 5d in government bonds (equivalent to around £2.75 million today) was transferred from Lord Leconfield's Bank of England account to the trustees of Percy and Madeline's marriage settlement.[17] The trust was to provide for Madeline and any younger children of her marriage. From the capital's interest Madeline would receive annually a personal allowance, known as pin money, of around £300. A provision stipulated that if the marriage proved childless, the money would devolve back to the Leconfields. Otherwise there was no indication that Madeline had not brought this money herself to the marriage.[18] A baronet's genteelly impoverished seventh daughter had been transformed, in effect, into an heiress of the first water.

The provision was never exercised. Percy and Madeline had five adored children over the course of a decade – the three girls, and the boys George and Guy. 'Ever since your birth has my Heart & Soul loved you & laughed with you & wept with you . . . sang to you to sleep – & anguished with you in all your sorrows . . .' wrote Madeline Wyndham to her youngest, Pamela.[19] She might have made the comment to any of her children, all of whom Percy deemed 'confidential', his highest form of praise.[20] Madeline Wyndham had been raised in a Rousseauesque environment of loving simplicity. The Campbell girls had no governess – doubtless partly for financial reasons – and were encouraged to educate themselves, reading whatever they chose, and making off into the fields around Woodview, their rambling house in Stillorgan, then a small village outside Dublin, to explore the natural world. Percy, raised in frigid splendour by evangelical parents who banned everything from novels to waltzing, was entranced upon first visiting Woodview. He vowed that his children would be raised in a similarly warm, loving and natural milieu. And so, despite an aristocratic lifestyle, the loving intensity of life among the Wyndhams was almost bourgeois.[21]

Mary, like all her siblings, was born into privilege's heartland. The family's life was played out against a backdrop of staff – butler, housekeeper, footmen, housemaids, cook, kitchen maids, stable boys, gardeners and the 'odd-man' who lit the house's lamps each evening as dusk fell. Only the absence of this – mostly silent – audience would have been remarkable. Madeline Wyndham never travelled anywhere without her lady's maid Easton (known as 'Eassy'), nor Percy without his Irish valet Thompson ('Tommy'). Their children's retinue included their nanny – the magnificently named Horsenail – nursemaid Emma Drake and, when a little older, governesses and tutors.

Society – of which the Wyndhams were impeccably a part – was a close-knit, interconnected group of 'the upper 10,000', four hundred or so families constituting Britain's ruling class. To outsiders it was an impenetrable, corporate mass with 'a common freemasonry of blood, a common education, common pursuits, common ideas, a common dialect, a common religion, and – what more than anything else binds men together – a common prestige . . . growled at occasionally, but on the whole conceded, and even, it must be owned, secretly liked by the country at large', said the Radical Bernard Cracroft in 1867.[22] During the mid-Victorian years, when the Queen and Prince Albert set the model of domestic rectitude, evangelism had a firm grip on the upper classes. Yet by the 1860s Darwinism had loosened that hold; and a Prince of Wales who liked a good time had come of age. Bertie's fast-living, hard-gambling Marlborough House Set became known for its sybaritic tendencies. Meanwhile, Percy and Madeline were part of a set considered markedly bohemian since, in the words of the novelist and designer Alice Comyns Carr, they 'took a certain pride in being the first members of Society to bring the people of their own set into friendly contact with the distinguished folk of art and literature'.[23]

Madeline and her female friends – aristocrats all – dressed in flowing gowns, tied their hair back simply and draped themselves in scarves and bangles. Madeline herself was reputedly the first woman in England to smoke, with a habit of three Turkish cigarettes a day, one after each meal.[24] Her friend Georgie Sumner dyed her hair red to resemble more closely 'stunners' like Lizzie Siddal, the Pre-Raphaelite muse. They read the bibles of Pre-Raphaelitism, Malory's *Morte d'Arthur* and Tennyson's poem of the same title, and, in the setting of their own family seats – Scottish castles and English stately homes – posed in medieval dress for Julia Margaret Cameron's camera. They frequented Little Holland House, home of Cameron's sister, Sara Prinsep, where G. F. Watts was literally the artist in residence (he moved in during a period of illness, and never left); and Leighton House, the creation of Frederic Leighton, later President of the Royal Academy. They considered Burne-Jones, as yet unrecognized in the wider world, to be a genius. Madeline was a talented amateur artist, particularly in the decorative arts, with a near-perfect eye. In 1872 she helped to found the School of Art Needlework with her friend Princess Christian, a daughter of the Queen. In later life, she studied enamelling under that craft's master, Alexander Fisher. All the artists Madeline knew thought she had a true artist's soul. Beauty could cause her 'thoughts that fill my heart to bursting', she told Watts.[25]

For the Pre-Raphaelites and their heirs, beauty's pursuit was not indulgence but necessity. Their dreamy art, born out of the Industrial Revolution, was intended to counteract, even arrest, the modern world's ugliness. For Burne-Jones's great friend and business partner William Morris, whose Oxford Street store, Morris & Co., was the favoured emporium of the English aesthetic classes, this philosophy led him to political activism and ardent socialism. Burne-Jones was content to improve society by feeding its soul through its eyes. The provision of art to cultivate and inspire the masses was now part of civic responsibility, reflected in the large public art galleries constructed in urban centres of the industrial north.

Mary's early childhood in Cumberland was like a Pre-Raphaelite painting brought to life. The Wyndhams lived at Cockermouth Castle, a strange, half-ruined property on the River Cocker's banks, until 1869. Afterwards they rented Isel Hall, an Elizabethan manor a few miles away. Madeline Wyndham took her children out among the heather to draw and paint, and read aloud to them Arthurian tales. At night she sang *berceuses*, French lullabies learnt from her own mother, and left them to sleep, soothed by the sound of the Cocker's rushing waters and owls hooting in the dark. She had miniature suits of armour made for George and Guy. The children played at knights and damsels with Mary dressed in her mother's long flowing skirts.[26] A portrait of eight-year-old Mary in Cumberland by the Wyndhams' friend Val Prinsep, in the flat, chalky style characteristic of their artistic circle, shows a tall, round-eyed beautiful child. In wide straw hat and loose mustard-yellow dress, she gazes directly at the viewer, bundling in her skirts armfuls of flowers.[27]

One of Mary's earliest adventures in childhood was scrambling after her father through thick heather up Skiddaw, the mountain dominating the Cumbrian skyline, with a trail of dogs in search of grouse; then sleeping overnight in a little lodge perched on the mountainside.[28] In adulthood, Mary wrote lyrically of 'the club & stag, the moss, the oak & beech fern, bog myrtle, & grass of Parnassus – Skiddaw in his splendid majesty – covered with "purple patches" (of heather) with deep greens & russet reds & swept by the shadows of the clouds – my heart leaps up – when I behold – *Skiddaw* – against the sky . . '.[29] Mary considered herself a lifelong 'pagan', fearlessly finding freedom in wildness. She attributed these qualities to her Cumberland childhood. She mourned 'beloved Isel' when the Wyndhams finally gave it up in 1876. Ever after, Cumberland was a lost Arcadia to her.

When George was born in August 1863, Lady Campbell told Percy he 'deserved a boy for having so graciously received the girl last year!'[30] In 1865 the Wyndhams had another boy, Guy. With two brothers so close to her in age, Mary was practically a boy herself. She learnt to ride on a donkey given to the children by Madeline when they were toddlers,[31] was taught to hunt and hawk by her father's valet Tommy, and was keeping up with the hounds at just nine years old, even if, on that first occasion, she told her mother ruefully, 'I did not see the fox.'[32] She kept pet rooks which she fed on live snails, and begged her mother for permission to be taken down a Cumberland coal mine by her brothers' tutor.[33] Some summers, the Wyndhams visited Madeline's favourite sister, Emily Ellis, at her home in Hyères, the French town at the westernmost point of the Côte d'Azur, which was becoming increasingly popular with the British. There Mary scrambled willingly along the narrow tunnels of the Grotte des Fées into a cavern of stalagmites and stalactites. While the other members of her party sat and ate oranges, she caught 'a dear dear little soft downy long eared bat' which, she informed her mother, in her father's absence she had installed in his dressing room: 'all day he sleeps hung up to the ceiling by his two hind legs'.[34]

High spirited to the point of being uncontrollable, the children exhausted a stream of governesses. At Deal Castle in Kent, home of the Wyndhams' friend Admiral Clanwilliam, Captain of the Cinque Ports, marine sergeants were deputed to drill the children on the ramparts to tire them out.[35] Their arrival in Belgrave Square's communal garden, clad in fishermen's jerseys, whooping and hollering on being released from their lessons, prompted celebration among their peers and anxiety among their playmates' parents. At least one couple instructed their governess not to let her charges play with 'those wild Wyndham children'.[36] In Mary's stout babyhood Percy nicknamed her 'Chang' after a popular sensation, an 8-foot-tall Chinese who entertained visitors – for a fee – at Piccadilly's Egyptian Hall. Mary grew into a 'strapping lass'. 'How well and strong I was, never tired,' she said in later life, now thin and enervated, recalling wistfully her days as a rambunctious, lanky ringleader, strongest and most daring of the three siblings. 'I was worse than 100 boys.'[37]

The fairytale had a darker side. Madeline Wyndham concealed beneath her calm, loving exterior a mind seething with dread. She had a paranoid strain capable of rendering her literally insensible from anxiety. A childhood of loss – her father's death when she was twelve, a beloved elder brother's five years after that – during the years of the 'Great Hunger', the famine that, by death and emigration, diminished Ireland's population by up to a quarter,[38] had a formative effect upon her. She was intensely spiritual, mystical and religious. Her deep foreboding of fate compounded rather than diminished that faith: 'the memory of death gave to the passing hours their supreme value for her', said her friend Edith Olivier.[39] Olivier had looked through Madeline's vellum-bound commonplace books to find them crammed with dark thoughts. 'All strange and terrible things are welcome, but comforts we despise,' reads one entry.[40] 'God to her is, I think, pre-eminently the "King of Glory",' said Madeline's son George in later years,[41] but in Madeline's mind glory came as much from darkness as from light.

When, during the Wyndhams' courtship, Madeline had confessed to bleak moods, Percy simply denied them. He did not think she was permanently in 'low spirits', he said, advising against articulating such thoughts lest 'the hearer should think them stronger than they are and permanently there when in reality they are not'. For Percy, anxieties that seemed all consuming at the time dissipated within 'half an hour', a day at most, like clouds puffed across the sky.[42] In fact, Madeline's volatile moods and her sporadic nervous collapses suggest that a strain of manic depression ran through the family – what George called the 'special neurotic phenomena of his family'.[43] The impact on her children was intense. She invested in them all her apocalyptic hopes, determined they should succeed and prove her family's merit, convinced the world conspired to bring them down. It is telling that, despite her undoubted love for her mother, Mary described Percy as 'one of the people – if not the one that I loved best in the world – who was unfailingly tender & who loved me more than anyone did and without whose sympathy I have never imagined life'.[44]

The Wyndhams' tribe naturally split between Mary, George and Guy, the trio born in the early 1860s, and the 'little girls', Madeline (known as 'Mananai', from what was obviously a childish attempt to pronounce her name) born in 1869 and Pamela in 1871.[45] As a consequence of Lord Leconfield's death in 1869 their early child-hoods were also markedly different.

Leconfield, intensely disliking his heir Henry, left everything that was not tied up in an entail to Percy. He created a trust for Percy and his heirs of a Sussex estate (shortly afterwards sold to Henry for £48,725 8s 10d),[46] land in Yorkshire, Cumberland and Ireland, £15,000 worth of life insurance and £16,000 worth of shares in turnpike roads and gas companies, and made provision for the trustees to raise a further £20,000 from other Sussex land. Percy received outright the family's South Australian estates (bought by Percy's maverick grandfather, the third Earl of Egremont, Turner's patron and three-times owner of the Derby winner, for his estranged wife); most of the household effects from East Lodge, a Brighton family property, including thirty oil paintings and all the plate; the plate from Grove, another family property; and the first choice of five carriage horses. Leconfield's will was a calculated, devastating snub to Henry. For a while, the Wyndhams continued to visit Henry and his wife Constance at Petworth, but soon enough the brothers had a spectacular row over the port after dinner. The resulting estrangement between the families lasted for almost a decade,[47] despite all the attempts of their wives, still close friends, to heal it.

Leconfield's death provoked the Wyndhams' move to Isel from

Cockermouth Castle, which now belonged to Henry; and his will made them rich. Percy and Madeline now commissioned Leighton and his architect George Aitchison to decorate Belgrave Square's entrance hall. *The Cymbalists* was a magnificent mural painted above the central staircase – five life-sized, classical figures in a dance against a gold background. Above that was Aitchison's delicate frieze of flowers, foliage and wild birds in pinks, greens, greys and powder blue. Even the most unobservant visitor could see this was an artistic house.

Shortly after Leconfield's death, Percy visited his sister Blanche and her husband Lord Mayo in India, where Mayo was Viceroy. (Mayo had previously served as Ireland's Chief Secretary for almost a decade, and it was Blanche who had introduced Percy to Madeline, when Percy visited them in Ireland.)[48] While Percy was abroad, Lady Campbell, in her seventies, was suddenly taken ill. Madeline Wyndham hastened to Ireland with newborn Mananai, Guy and Horsenail, leaving Mary and George, with their governess Mademoiselle Grivel, at Mrs Stanley's boarding house in Keswick, Cumberland. '. . . I am so sorry that dear Granny is so ill for it must make you so unhappy. George and I will try to be very good indeed so as to make you happy,' Mary wrote to her mother.[49] Lady Campbell died shortly afterwards, and Madeline made her way back to her elder children: 'so glad I shall be to see you my little darling . . . you were so good to me when I was so knocked down by hearing such sad news'.[50] Almost precisely upon Madeline and Percy's reuniting, Madeline fell pregnant. Pamela Genevieve Adelaide was born in January 1871, at Belgrave Square like all her siblings.

The little girls were born into the age of Gladstone. In 1867, Disraeli had pushed Lord Derby's Tory ministry into 'the leap in the dark': the Reform Act that gave the vote to all male householders in the towns, as well as male lodgers who paid rent of £10 a year or more for unfurnished accommodation, almost doubling the electorate. In the boroughs, the hitherto unenfranchised working classes were now in the majority. The debate over the Act was fought with passion on both sides: for most, democracy was a demoniacal prospect signifying mob rule. A series of unruly popular protests organized by the Radical-led Reform League, with hordes brandishing red flags and wearing the cap of liberty marching on Trafalgar Square, did little to dispel these fears. In a notorious incident of July 1866 – just a stone's throw from Belgrave Square – a mob of 200,000 tore down Hyde Park's railings when the Government tried to close it to public meetings, overwhelming the police 'like flies before the waiter's napkin'.[51] Contemporary theorists were concerned that *vox populi* would become *vox diaboli*. In *The English Constitution* Walter Bagehot expressed his fear that 'both our political parties will bid for the support of the working man ... I can conceive of nothing more corrupting or worse for a set of poor ignorant people than that two combinations of well-taught and rich men should constantly offer to defer to their decision and compete for the office of executing it.'[52]

The equally bleak predictions by Lord Cranborne, later Marquess of Salisbury – who resigned in protest from Derby's ministry upon the passing of the Act – seemed confirmed when the electorate returned Gladstone in the 1868 elections, at the head of the first truly Liberal ministry, a disparate band of Radicals of the industrial north, Whig grandees, some still speaking in their eighteenth-century ancestors' curious drawl, and Dissenters, the non-conformists who wanted to loosen the hold of the established Church. Gladstone immediately announced his God-given mission to 'pacify Ireland' (provoked, in part, by the Fenian bombing of Clerkenwell Prison the previous year that had killed twelve civilians and injured forty more)[53] and set about disestablishing the Irish Church, while dealing several blows to the hegemony of the British landed classes by introducing competitive exams for the civil service, abolishing army commissions and removing the religious 'Test' required for fellows of Oxford, Cambridge and Durham universities to enable non-Anglicans to hold those posts.

Percy, like his father before him, was a Tory of the oldest sort, who believed that his class's God-given duty to govern through wise paternalistic rule not just the tenantry on their estates but the country as a whole was under attack. For Percy, like most Tories, authority was 'like a sombre fortress, holding down an unpredictable population that might, at any moment, lay siege to it'.[54]

In 1867, Percy had commissioned Watts to paint Madeline's portrait. The portrait took three years to complete, partly because painter and sitter, kindred artistic souls, enjoyed their conversations so much they were reluctant for them to end.[55] In a nod to classical portraiture the statuesque Madeline, in her early thirties, gazes down at the viewer from a balustraded terrace. A mass of laurel, signifying nobility and glory, flourishes behind her; in the foreground a vase of magnolias denotes magnificence. Her gown is loose and splashed with sunflowers, proclaiming her allegiance to the world of the Pre-Raphaelites; the gaze from hooded eyes under swooping dark brows direct and forthright. The portrait, hung in Belgrave Square's drawing room, made its first public appearance – to quite a splash – some seven years later, on the opening of the Grosvenor Gallery, a private venture of the Wyndhams' friends Sir Coutts and Lady Lindsay on London's New Bond Street. It caught the eye of Henry James, recently arrived in England, reviewing the exhibition for the *Galaxy*. He told his readers of his companion's comment: 'It is what they call a "sumptuous" picture . . . That is, the lady looks as if she had thirty thousand a year.' 'It is true that she does,' said James, praising nonetheless 'the very handsome person whom the painter has depicted . . . dressed in a fashion which will never be wearisome; a simple yet splendid robe, in the taste of no particular period – of all periods'.[56]

James had seen that the aristocrat effortlessly superseded the artist. And, although it was kept well hidden beneath her friendships with artists, her undoubted talent and her air of vague, bohemian warmth, Madeline Wyndham was acutely aware of social gradations. '*You* and Papa are rather *stupid* about knowing who people are!!' she told Mary, half jokingly, half in frustration as she discussed the 'belongings' of fellow guests at a house party – by which she meant their connections and titles.[57] She assiduously cultivated the boring Princess Christian as a friend. 'She is a humbug,' declared the middle-class Philip Burne-Jones (son of Edward and Georgiana), finding that Madeline's warmth towards him as a family friend cooled rapidly when he made plain his hope that he could court Mary, with whom he had been in love since childhood.[58]

It has been said that Madeline, with her artful eye, the creator of Clouds, the exquisite Wiltshire house into which the Wyndhams moved in 1885, is the model for Mrs Gereth in Henry James's *The Spoils of Poynton*, the story of a jewel-like house created out of the 'perfect accord and beautiful life together' of the Gereths: 'twenty-six years of planning and seeking, a long sunny harvest of taste and curiosity'. Mrs Gereth is an unscrupulous obsessive who tries to manipulate her son into marrying a worthy chatelaine, then sets the house aflame rather than see it pass into the wrong hands. If Madeline Wyndham is the model, there is no clearer indication of the steel within her soul.[59]

Extravagantly generous – she kept open table at Belgrave Square, with sometimes forty people unexpectedly sitting down to lunch[60] – Madeline never spoke of the sudden change in her fortunes brought about by marriage, only fondly recollecting an Irish childhood in a 'nest of lovely sisters' visiting relations in pony and trap.[61] Her ambitions for her family were tied up with her anxiety to prove that Percy's gamble in marrying her had exalted his clan. When her daughters married, she was terrified that one might bear a child with some 'defect'.[62] It is clear that she feared what might be latent in her blood.

In the early 1870s, Madeline had an affair with Wilfrid Scawen Blunt, a handsome poet and Percy's cousin and close friend who had spent part of his childhood living in a cottage on the Petworth estate. Blunt and his wife Lady Anne spent much of their time travelling in Africa and the Middle East, and bought an Egyptian estate just outside Cairo named Sheykh Obeyd, after the Bedouin saint Obeyd buried in the grounds.[63] They spoke vernacular Arabic, and Blunt, a self-professed iconoclast, adopted Bedouin dress even in England.[64] At Crabbet Park, Blunt's Sussex estate, they founded a successful stud breeding Arab horses. The annual sale and garden party was a fixture of the Season: 'everybody who was anybody in London went in those days to Crabbet for the sale of the Arabs [sic],' wrote the journalist Katharine Tynan, recalling Janey Morris, Oscar Wilde and Jane Cobden, radical daughter of the reformer Richard Cobden, wandering through the beautiful grounds.[65]

The intrepid Arabists: Wilfrid Blunt and Lady Anne Blunt
in the late 1870s.

In the latter half of the nineteenth century Blunt was notorious
in political circles as an anti-imperialist troublemaker. Socially he
was regarded with equal suspicion as a lothario, capable of seducing
any man's wife. Yet this inveterate womanizer's diaries, in which he
recorded every conquest (albeit sometimes a little embroidered),
show him as nothing so much as a perplexed cork buffeted on the
waves of strong women's personalities. With each affair, Blunt made
grand plans for a lifelong passion. Almost invariably, his paramours
called it off, returning to their husbands enlivened by their brief
dalliance.

Madeline and Wilfrid had known each other for many years
when they tipped from friendship into 'passionate fulfilment', in
Blunt's words. He had always found Madeline seductive – 'a tall
strong woman, such as are the fashion now; no porcelain figure
like the beauties of the last century, nor yet the dull classic marble
our fathers loved'[66] – and their affair seems in large part provoked
by intense mutual physical attraction. Blunt dressed it up as a
meeting of two artistic minds. Their piecemeal dalliances – romantic
visits to Watts's studio in London and trysts among Hyères' olive
groves – provided 'something apart' from Madeline's sometimes
'overpowering' domestic life.

Blunt maintained that the affair did not affect Madeline's love
for her husband and children: 'what she gave to me was not a
plunder robbed from any other. Her tenderness was no mere weak-
ness of the heart, but its strength rather, proving its wealth . . .'.[67]
Wilfrid rarely saw things clearly, and this was no exception. Among
his papers is a photograph of Madeline with Pamela upon her lap.
Madeline is in mourning, presumably for her brother-in-law Lord
Mayo, the Viceroy, who was assassinated while visiting a penal
colony in the Andaman Islands in 1872. She wears an elaborate dark
hat that shades her hooded eyes. Her features have been refined
with age. She appears leaner and finer than Watts's voluptuous
beauty of three years before, and almost sad. Tousle-haired Pamela
sits on her lap, eyes skyward as though she is trying to glimpse her

mother's face even as Madeline grasps her daughter firmly around her stout waist. On the back of this photograph is a note in Madeline's handwriting: fragmentary, it appears to have been written in a hurry. Wilfrid must not come to look for her until later. 'I think [Percy] is not happy at finding me not alone he has not said it but I think it . . . my heart fails me . . . you *have* chosen the lowest oh it makes me so sad – I don't know why my heart is not up to it I have no courage . . .'[68]

In 1873 the Wyndhams rented Château Saint-Pierre, a neo-gothic pile near to Emily and Charley Ellis in Hyères. They settled their children there with nurse, governess and tutor, and left for several months' travel across France and Italy, sightseeing and buying art. This was the Wyndhams' longest absence – by far – from their children throughout their childhood. Undoubtedly the trip was intended as a second honeymoon to reunite them. The following year, Percy took the lease of Wilbury Park in Newton Toney, some 10 miles from Salisbury on the Wiltshire Downs. In later life, Madeline wrote her daughters impassioned warnings (scored with underlining and written in her trademark purple ink) about the dangers of drifting from their husbands. It seems she was speaking from personal experience. Wilbury, which provided easy access to London by train from Amesbury, allowing Madeline to maintain her life among the city's aristocratic art crowd, and offered excellent hunting and shooting and reasonable trout-fishing for Percy, was to arrest that drift.[69]

The affair finally ended only in 1875. Madeline asked Wilfrid to return to friendship. 'What is this prate of friendship?' wrote Wilfrid furiously in a sonnet, 'To Juliet'. In his diary, sore-pawed, he attacked Madeline as 'a pottery goddess . . . I do not think her beautiful, or wise, or good. Her beauty is a little too refined, her wisdom too fantastic, her goodness too selfish . . .'[70] Trying to forget his fantasies of a life together with her, he dusted himself off and attempted to dismiss the affair: 'it was all pleasure, of a high sensual kind, heroic in its tenderness and with no afterthought of pain. Its departure caused no unbearable sorrow. Even when it had ended finally as passion I did not grieve for her because I knew she did not grieve for me . . .'[71]

A veil was drawn over the incident. Percy never spoke of it. But between Madeline and Wilfrid there remained some friction. Despite Wilfrid's surmises, Madeline does not seem to have escaped entirely unscarred. Many years later she advised Pamela that the power 'not to fret over spilt milk is a great *faculty* it almost amounts to wisdom'. Years of '*experience* & hard toil' had taught her to let go of the regret 'that kills'.[72] Madeline did not say what that regret was. One can hazard a guess.

TWO

Wilbury

In the late 1870s, with relations once again on an even keel, the Blunts visited the Wyndhams at Wilbury. As Wilfrid left, he kissed Mary on the cheek: 'in a cousinly way'.[1] Mary blushed. Afterwards, Madeline scolded her with unusual and uncharacteristic vehemence. The incident, notable enough for Mary to remember it twenty years later, suggests that the adolescent knew something of the affair just past. It is also a rare chink in the Wyndham armour, a moment when one of Percy's 'remarkable quintette'[2] – in his words – lets slip something suggesting their family life was not so perpetually sunlit as they maintained.

Percy and Madeline's devotion to their children, and their disregard for convention, generated intense familial closeness. George spoke of 'the Wyndham-religion';[3] Mary's daughter Cynthia explained that 'Family love was almost a religion with the Wyndhams.'[4] A legendary anecdote – familiar to almost all their contemporaries – concerned Percy impatiently shushing his collected dinner guests, hissing, 'Hush. Hush! George is going to speak!' as his schoolboy son prepared to give the table his views.[5] Ettie Desborough, close friends with Mary and George, described the clan as being bred up with the pride of Plantagenets.[6] Their loyalty was fearsome. They would never listen to criticism of their own, far less give it.

At the time of Wilfrid's visit to Wilbury, Mary was in her mid-teens, awkward, lanky, childish for her age. She was devoted to her dog Crack, a thirteenth-birthday present, and her pet rat Snowy.[7] She adored the caricatures of Dickens and the romances of Sir Walter Scott. She had inherited her mother's artistic talent, and spent hours making elaborate cards and teasing cartoon sketches for her younger sisters, to whom she was known by a host of nick-names, 'Black Witch', 'Sister Rat' and 'Migs' (or 'Mogs') being just a few. She was a devotee of 'Spression' – a sort of pidgin English mixed with baby talk that she spoke with her closest friend, Margaret Burne-Jones, given somatic form by cartoons drawn by Edward Burne-Jones for the girls, endearingly shapeless animals that have been described as part pig, part dog, part wombat.[8]

An insight into Mary's character comes from one of her most vivid childhood memories, probably from the summer of 1875, which she spent at Deal Castle – a place she thought 'must be haunted by my girl spirit I was there so much'[9] – while recovering from whooping cough. She remembered sitting by the moat and, in a 'moment of cruel curiosity', feeding a live bluebottle fly to a 'huge spider [with] shining eyes'. As Mary recalled, she was imme-diately 'seized with remorse and probably killed both in righteous wrath'.[10] Mary had a delight for the gruesome (demonstrated by a zestful account to her mother of a bilious attack aged eighteen: 'I brought up *basins* of the thickest, gluest [sic] phlegm, slime, burning excruciating yellow acid with little streaks of browny reddy stuff in it, sometimes great gollops of brown fluid . . . Lastly Tuesday morning, came green bile'),[11] a curious mind and an adventurous spirit. She had a tendency to act first and think later: more accu-rately an inclination to 'choose to prefer the gratification of the present . . . to slide & glide because it was pleasant or amusing & exciting & to face & *bear* the consequences *when* they came'.[12] In adulthood, Wilfrid thought Mary sphinx-like in her inscrutability, speaking of her 'unfathomable reserve . . . her secrets are close shut, impenetrably guarded, with a little laugh of unconcern baffling the curious'.[13] Wilfrid was all too frequently baffled by women, but Pamela described her sister in similar terms, speaking of a 'deep nature' that only Mary's closest friends truly knew.[14]

As Mary entered adolescence, her life became notably more domesticated. At almost exactly the time that the Wyndhams moved to Wilbury, George was sent to prep school – the Grange in Hertfordshire – to prepare him for Eton in due course. Guy, uncontrollable without his brother, followed George after just one term. From roaming across Cumberland's hills with a pair of ragamuffin playmates, Mary found herself in a tamer Wiltshire landscape in the company of her governess Fräulein Schneider and sisters of just three and five.

A contemporary of the Wyndham children described 'an air of Bohemian quasi-culture' within the family.[15] Artistic rather than intellectual, the Wyndhams never contemplated either that Mary would attend school or that she would find her métier otherwise than in marriage. 'A woman's only hope of self-expression in those days was through marriage,' explained Mabell Airlie, a contemporary of Mary's, in her memoir *Thatched with Gold*.[16] The strides forward in women's education – the establishment of academic girls' schools, under the remarkable Dorothea Beale and Frances Buss; women's admission as undergraduates, London University being the first to open its doors in 1878 – primarily benefited middle-class daughters. Upper-class girls were educated by governesses – for the most part deliberately not too well, lest it scare off suitors. Some girls were lucky to be taught by a governess with exceptional capacities. Mary's daughter Cincie benefited in her early years from the highly gifted Miss Jourdain, one of Oxford's first female undergraduates. Bertha Schneider, or 'Bun', as she was called by the children, lacked the intellectual talents of 'Miss J'. Originally from Saxony, Bun had been poached from the Belgrave Square family who forbade their children from playing with the Wyndhams, joining the family when she was twenty-eight. A photograph of her some years later shows her to have a pleasant, somewhat clumsy-featured face, pince-nez spectacles and fashionably frizzled hair.

At sixteen Mary's day consisted of breakfast at 8 a.m., lessons from 9 a.m. until 2 p.m., 'déjeuner', some time outside – collecting ferns, blackberry picking, long walks or games of the new sport of lawn tennis – lessons from 4 until 6, dinner at 7, and reading aloud with Fräulein until bed. This was supplemented, during 'term times' (dictated by the boys' holidays), by fortnightly music lessons from a Mr Farmer in London, and art classes at the Kensington School of Art. Each autumn Bun took Mary and the little girls to a Felixstowe boarding house for 'sea air' where they rode donkeys, ate potted shrimps, paddled in the sea and read aloud, endlessly, to one another. By the time they left Eton in their late teens, George and Guy had a tolerable grounding in the basics of Latin, Greek, astronomy, history and public speaking.[17] After the same number of years of education by Fräulein, Mary was relatively well read so long as the literature was popular; spoke good French and German (with a ripe vocabulary in the latter);[18] could play the piano; and could draw proficiently, having taken exams in the subject at the Kensington School of Art ('I forget what it was now,' she said vaguely, when pressed by her mother on the subject of her exam. 'It had some sort of foliage').[19] Mary would spend much of her adult life educating herself, wading gamely through heavy tomes on esoteric subjects. In effect, she was an autodidact. Her education was rigour-free, her brain almost totally untrained.

Twenty years after she married and left home, Mary read over her adolescent diaries, thinking fondly of the 'happy life . . . that we all spent at Wilbury', laughing at copies of 'the house Annals' produced by the children, remembering their pet names for the family's twenty horses and the old blind donkey brought from Cockermouth,[20] and recalling games of sardines and nights of ghost stories, hunting and hawking in the winter, summer cricket matches

and a host of friends and neighbours near by.[21] In the memory of
the children Wilbury was merely 'a large plain comfortable house'.[22]
To modern eyes it is undoubtedly grand, with a large columned
portico and octagonal bays flanking the main section of the
building. It was set in some 140 acres of land, with amusements in
its grounds including an octagonal summerhouse and a grotto.[23]
Philip Burne-Jones remembered Wilbury as a kind of heaven, 'with
the sun pouring down upon the lawn . . . and all the magic of
youth & impossible hopes in the air'.[24]

The Wyndham children had been stage-struck since first creeping
into a performance of *Hamlet* while visiting the Crystal Palace,[25]
once home of the 1851 Great Exhibition – one of those 'huge trophies
of the world's trade'[26] in which the Victorians delighted – and now
rehoused in Sydenham. No school holiday was complete without
a trip to see the famous partnership of Henry Irving and Ellen
Terry at the Lyceum Theatre. Audiences had a voracious appetite
for novelty. By the early 1880s, at Herbert Beerbohm Tree's
Haymarket Theatre live rabbits hopped across the stage during *A
Midsummer Night's Dream*, and the storm-scenes in *The Tempest*
were so realistically staged that audience members complained of
seasickness.[27] The amateur productions at Wilbury were almost as
ambitious. Madeline Wyndham constructed elaborate sets and
costumes, but refused to take any role with more lines than could
be pinned to the back of her fan. Servants, groundsmen and stray
visitors were corralled into the hall as an audience. Mary and Philip
took the leads; Pamela and Mananai were pages and fairies. Bun
gamely took on whatever role was assigned to her – excelling herself,
in collective memory, with an enthusiastic Caliban so lovelorn that
Tommy the valet thought the character was a woman, and married
to Prospero.[28]

In London Mary and Madeline Wyndham frequently visited the
Burne-Jones family at The Grange, their house in Fulham. Mary
loved these visits where Burne-Jones amused the children by playing
wheelbarrows in the garden with Georgiana, holding her ankles

while she walked on her hands, and told them fireside stories of his youth with William Morris, Dante Gabriel Rossetti and Lizzie Siddal in Red Lion Square.[29] On occasion, Mary stayed overnight, sharing a bed with Margaret Burne-Jones, waking up in the morning to breakfast in bed and chat 'yards of nonsense' in 'Spression'.[30]

Percy's intention when renting Wilbury had always been to look for a suitable estate of his own. In 1876, the Wyndhams found the enchantingly named Clouds, a parcel of 4,000 acres of land at East Knoyle, a village a little south of Salisbury. Particulars supplied by the agents, Messrs Driver, set out the more important neighbours, and the exact distance of their seats: Longleat, Wardour Castle, Fonthill House.[31] Percy sold Much Cowarne, the similarly sized Herefordshire estate he had inherited at the age of twenty-one, and bought Clouds for just over £100,000.[32] He immediately commissioned Philip Webb, the visionary architect of William Morris's Red House, to design and build what was intended 'to be the house of the family for generations to come'.[33]

Percy was reinvesting in land at a time when it was ceasing to be the backbone of elite wealth. In the mid-1870s, the agricultural economy foundered as Britain, committed to free trade since Sir Robert Peel repealed the Corn Laws in 1846, struggled to compete with cheap grain imports from the American prairies and with refrigerated and canned goods from the Antipodes. Arable farming was particularly badly affected. Average wheat prices fell from 55 shillings to 28 shillings a quarter between 1870 and 1890. 'Land has ceased to be either a profit or a pleasure. It gives one a position, and prevents one from keeping it up,' declared Lady Bracknell in Oscar Wilde's *The Importance of Being Earnest*, written in 1895. Percy's fortune was buoyant thanks to stocks and his Australian estates. He could afford to exchange Much Cowarne (which had only a 'shooting box', and which he used purely for income – he never even seems to have visited)[34] for the slightly less profitable Clouds.[35] He played with Home Farm, carved out of the Clouds estate for his own management, like a small boy with an entrancing toy. 'He has made £184.10s by the sale of all his sheep and £146.15s by sale of wool and now has 190 lambs. His corn is in, 11 ricks of wheat, 5 of barley, 6 of oats,' Mary told her diary in 1878.[36]

As Percy retreated ever more rapidly to Tory squirearchy, his parliamentary career was stalling. In 1874, after six years in the wilderness, the Conservatives returned to power under Disraeli. 'We have been borne down in a torrent of gin and beer,' mourned Gladstone, attributing defeat to the licensing bills pushed by the non-conformist temperance supporters of his party.[37] Disraeli, half genius, half charlatan, had already put in a bid to make Conservatives the party of popular imperialism in a speech delivered at Crystal Palace in 1872.[38] Now he embarked upon an 'unwholesome political cocktail' of a foreign policy, its 'main ingredients . . . amoral opportunism, military adventures, and a disregard for the rights of others'.[39] The only guiding principle seemed to be that no action was too morally bankrupt so long as the imperial lodestone, India, was safe.

In 1875, Disraeli (with the financial help of Lord Rothschild) bought the controlling interest in the Suez Canal Company from the bankrupt Khedive of Egypt,[40] for it was a deeply embedded British belief that the Raj could be maintained only so long as the Canal was secure, in that it allowed passage to India without a long and dangerous journey round the Cape of Good Hope. In 1877, conjuror Disraeli turned a delighted Victoria from Queen into Empress, an act denounced by Gladstone as 'theatrical folly and bombast'. And as graphic details of the Bulgarian Atrocities committed by the Ottoman Turks when crushing rebellion in the Balkans consumed the international press, Disraeli stood by the corrupt Ottoman regime, as a bulwark against Russian expansion that might threaten the Raj. Yet Russia then invaded the Balkans, Britain sent warships to the Dardanelles and mobilized Indian troops to Malta, and its music halls rang to the popular refrain 'We don't want to fight, but, by Jingo if we do, / We've got the ships; we've got the men; we've got the money too!' The Conservatives were the party of patriotism, monarchy and empire; 'jingoism' was in the ascendant.[41]

Percy was staunchly pro-Turk and anti-Russian in this instance, harking back to the position Britain had held in the Crimean War, in which he would have fought but for his being invalided home from Bulgaria when he contracted pleurisy en route.[42] However, he did not by any means slavishly follow the party line. As Guy Wyndham later wrote, Percy 'held his own principles and opinions unswervingly; and they were not always those of his party' – in particular, advocating a system of protectionist tariffs when all the politicians and economists of the nation were devoted to Peelite free trade.[43] Such independent-minded action by MPs was fast dying out. The party machine was growing. The National Union of Conservative and Constitutional Associations, founded in 1867, and the National Liberal Foundation of 1877 registered voters, managed elections and chose candidates willing to toe the party line in order to deal with the challenges of the vastly increased franchise, whose votes, thanks to the secret ballot's introduction in 1872, could no longer be controlled with such ease by employer or squire, nor, after 1883's Corrupt Practices Act, influenced by bribery. It was the era of the extraordinary coincidence, in Gilbert and Sullivan's catchy lines, 'That every boy and every gal / That's born into the world alive / Is either a little Liberal / Or else a little Conservative!' Yet it has been suggested that Percy's failure to advance was also due to his ungovernable temper, which was all too familiar to his children.[44]

It is a mark of Percy's and Webb's instinctive affinity that the two difficult men never fell out during the long process of designing and building Clouds, beyond one protracted dispute over the buff colour of the glazed bricks used in the stables.[45] It took until 1881 to agree drawings and find an acceptable tender from builders. Work was not finished until 1885. The ascetic Webb asked just £4,000 for his decade of labour.[46] Through him, Percy became involved with the work of Morris's Society for the Protection of Ancient Buildings. Known fondly as 'the anti-scrape society', it tried to prevent thoughtless modern restoration, and Percy began a campaign to save East Knoyle's church. Webb became a familiar figure at Wilbury. When Mary's pet rat Snowy died, Webb provided an epitaph for the gravestone.[47]

In the early summer of 1878, Madeline Wyndham took Mary, still not quite sixteen, to Cologne to be 'finished'.[48] Mary retained fond memories of her time there, spent cramming in as many operas as possible and visiting cultural attractions like the Goethe House and the Jewish Quarter.[49] Their return to Wilbury several weeks later was welcomed. 'I am so glad glad glad glad glad that you are coming home . . .' wrote Mananai.[50] Pamela, who swore that she could not sleep when her mother was away, maintained her usual signing off: 'I love you and I've got you and I won't let you GO.'[51] A few months of Wagner was not enough to rub off the rough edges acquired over a lifetime of boisterousness: 'Mary has upset the milk over her forock [sic],' Pamela informed her parents a few weeks after Mary's return, 'but not the same one she tore yesterday.'[52]

That autumn, Mary sat entranced at the dinner table as Percy and Webb discussed the latest cause célèbre: James McNeill Whistler's libel case against Ruskin, in which the Wyndhams had more than a passing involvement. The case had arisen out of the Grosvenor Gallery's opening the year before. The Gallery – which, as advertised in *The Times*, was open daily to the public for a shilling – was effectively an artistic call to arms by Percy and Madeline's circle,[53] championing the avant-garde and challenging the nearby Royal Academy's turgid stranglehold over taste. For too long the Wyndhams' circle had seen the artists they admired being overlooked, in particular Burne-Jones, who had not exhibited publicly since a spat with the prestigious Watercolour Society almost a decade before, when he refused to cover up the genitalia of a very naked Demophoön in his work *Phyllis and Demophoön*.[54]

The Lindsays spared no expense on their sumptuous enterprise, which was all silk damask, marble columns, velvet sofas and potted palms in sky-lit galleries, and looked like a very expensive private house.[55] Many of the opening exhibition's pictures came from their friends' collections. The Wyndhams, who in some seventeen years of marriage had established themselves as discerning patrons with an excellent eye, loaned two: *Nocturne: Grey and Gold – Westminster Bridge*, a Whistler that Percy had bought some two years before on a whim when passing Piccadilly's Dudley Gallery, and the magnificent Watts of Madeline. In May 1877, the Wyndhams went to the Gallery's opening night, attending both Lady Lindsay's 'magnificent banquet'[56] for the inner circle, including the Prince of Wales and three of his siblings, and the larger reception, to which critics and lesser personages were invited, in the galleries upstairs.

That opening made Burne-Jones famous: his eight works had star position in the hundred-foot-long West Gallery, occupying an entire end wall.[57] Oscar Wilde, still an Oxford undergraduate – albeit rusticated – caused a sensation in a velvet coat embroidered to look like a cello. Soon Wilde was famous himself as the columnist informing the readership of *The Woman's World* how to adopt the aesthetic way of life, and giving American lecture tours in velvet breeches with a green carnation in his buttonhole.[58] Inspired by the Gallery, the public adopted the fashions, interior decoration and art that Madeline and her friends had cultivated for over a decade. They flocked to Liberty's department store on Regent Street for murky silks and sludgy velvets. Madeline's School of Art Needlework ('Royal' since securing Queen Victoria's patronage in 1875), which had long been producing Burne-Jones designs, moved to larger premises to accommodate demand. Sunflowers, peacocks and blue and white china, the motifs of aestheticism, appeared everywhere. Gerald du Maurier in *Punch* and Gilbert and Sullivan in *Patience* joyfully let loose on the pretensions of the 'greenery-yallery Grosvenor Gallery' and its devotees.

On that opening night, however, the great critic Ruskin was mostly struck by Whistler's effrontery in exhibiting work with so little apparent finish. 'I have seen, and heard, much of Cockney impudence before now but never expected to hear a coxcomb ask

two hundred guineas for flinging a pot of paint in the public's face,'
he wrote in *Fors Clavigera*. Whistler sued for libel, claiming *inter
alia* that since Ruskin's review he had not been able to achieve a
price comparable to that which Percy paid for his *Nocturne*. Mary,
like the art world, was agog: 'so funny', she wrote in her diary, 'the
jury going to Westminster Palace Hotel to examine the pictures,
and hearing Mr. Burne-Jones, Whistler, W. M. Rossetti and all of
them in the *witness* box'.[59]

Six months later, Madeline Wyndham took Mary and George,
home for the holidays, to Leighton House for one of Leighton's famed
chamber-music afternoons that introduced rising musical stars –
Hallé, Piatti, Joachim – to Society. Among the guests was Arthur
Balfour, in his early thirties, Conservative Member for Hertford.

Balfour, the man who once said 'Nothing matters very much,
and most things don't matter at all,' was already renowned for his
languidness. Despite six years in the Commons, he was not to make
his political name until the next ministry, as a member of the
maverick quartet known as the Fourth Party, led by Lord Randolph
Churchill, who devoted their time in opposition to harassing the
Liberal Government and their own ineffectual Leader in the
Commons, Sir Stafford Northcote.

However, Balfour was already a prime target for ambitious
Society matrons seeking to marry off their daughters. He was
impeccably connected through his mother, and the favourite
nephew of Lord Salisbury, the gloomy refusenik of the Reform
Act who was now a serious contender to take over from the elderly
Disraeli when the latter retired. From his dead father Balfour had
inherited a nabob fortune – the term used to describe those whose
riches came from working for the East India Company in the
Indian sub-continent – and the prosperous Whittingehame estate.
Balfour was not one who thought politics should govern life. He
maintained a keen interest in philosophy – the best known of his
works, *Foundations of Belief*, was published in 1895 – and held
musical concerts at his own house, 4 Carlton Gardens, for which

he had recently commissioned Burne-Jones to create a series of murals.

Above all, the tall, dark-haired, humorous Balfour was charming: 'He has but to smile and men and women fall prone at his feet,' said his close friend Mary Gladstone, who had been besotted with him for years[60] and whose father William considered him a protégé, despite their opposing political stances. Fifty years later, the Liberal MP Howard Begbie commented caustically on Balfour's undimmed charm: 'I have seen many [people] retire from shaking his hand with a flush of pride on their faces as though Royalty had stooped to inquire after the measles of their youngest child.'[61] Some years later, when Mary Wyndham was newly married, a friend would comment worriedly on her attitude towards Arthur: 'he fascinates her – her attitude is that of looking up in wonder . . . Thinks him good . . .'[62] Mary and George's shared fascination with Balfour began the day they met him. Their lives would ever after be entwined with his. And an elderly Balfour, attempting an autobiography, would put down his pen at precisely the moment he met the seventeen-year-old Mary Wyndham among the chattering crowds at Leighton House.[63]

THREE

'The Little Hunter'

At 3 o'clock on an early-summer afternoon in 1880 Madeline Wyndham presented Mary at the Royal Drawing Room in Buckingham Palace.[1] This was Mary's 'passport to Society':[2] her formal entry to her parents' world. Each spring, aristocratic households decamped, children, staff and all, to London for the Season. One year at Wilbury, Mary counted thirty-six boxes of luggage stacked up in the hall.[3] Ostensibly, the Drawing Rooms, at which presentations took place, were the most important element of the Season. In reality, Society thought them the most tedious part. Ornate carriages with bewigged coachmen and liveried footmen sat nose to tail on the Mall for hours waiting to gain entry to the Palace, traffic sometimes snaking back through St James's Park. Their occupants, stifling in their elaborate dress, were considered fair game for the crowds that thronged the Mall to watch and pass bawdy, affectionate comment.

After her husband's death in 1861, Queen Victoria had retreated into self-imposed purdah. One of her many children deputized for her as the Royal Presence to whom debutantes curtsied low before rising, waiting for their train to be draped over their arm, and then backing out of the room. Half a century on, a host of elderly memorialists dwelling long on the fragrant pot-pourri of a bygone age recalled their relief at having executed the complicated manoeuvre – which required several weeks' worth of dedicated lessons – without falling or tripping over. Doubtless Mary felt the same. The pageant along the Mall was a glorious affirmation of the social order, proving Henry James's observation that 'Nowhere so much as in England was it fortunate to be fortunate.'[4] Yet, as so often, the interplay between pageantry and power was more subtle. Over the course of a century, the traditions surrounding Britain's monarchy had become more elaborate as the reality of its sovereign power decreased.[5] The same might be true in relation to its aristocracy.

After six years of Disraeli, Gladstone stormed back to power in 1880 on the back of his Midlothian Campaign. Ostensibly the campaign was for a constituency. In reality, it was a national platform for Gladstone to inveigh against the moral iniquities of 'Beaconsfieldism' – for in raising Victoria to the rank of empress Disraeli had secured himself a peerage as Earl of Beaconsfield in token of his monarch's grateful thanks. The campaign, orchestrated by Constance Leconfield's brother Lord Rosebery, was a whistle-stop railway tour of the north. The meetings were more like religious revivals. As Gladstone, followed by a pack of press, lamented Britain's failure to act as the watchdog of weaker nations, people fainted in the crush of thousands and were handed out over the heads of those around them. Reports of his latest address rattled across the wires to Fleet Street, telegraphed across the nation in the next day's press.[6] It irrevocably altered the landscape of campaigning. Gladstone's enemies deplored his demagogic approach. But the man now popularly known as the 'GOM' – the 'Grand Old Man' – was the nation's moral compass, and his party triumphant. Queen Victoria, despite trying first to persuade the Whig Lord Hartington to form a government, was reluctantly forced to accept the inevitable and invite a man she characterized as a 'half-madman . . . mischief maker and firebrand' to be Prime Minister for a second time.[7]

The Whigs still restrained the Radical element, but the Liberal party nonetheless seemed to be lurching to the left. For the Tories the very fact that radicalism had a political voice provoked anxiety, and the parliamentary runes augured ill when Parliament, on reconvening, was consumed by the Bradlaugh Affair, in which Northampton's atheist Liberal representative asked to 'affirm' his allegiance to the Crown instead of taking the religious oath demanded of all MPs. Lord Randolph Churchill, leader of the Fourth Party, spat vitriol against Bradlaugh as a 'seditious blasphemer', bent on destroying the union of Church and State.[8] Throughout the controversy of several years – Bradlaugh was not to take his seat until 1886 – Percy stood against his party in supporting Bradlaugh, citing his belief in liberty of conscience.[9]

Gladstone's mission to pacify Ireland had only inflamed tensions, by promising reforms that did not go far enough. Ireland was gripped by a violent Land War waged by the peasantry against their absentee landlords, and masterminded by the shadowy Land League. Its head, the half-American Protestant landowner Charles Stewart Parnell, was also leader of the Irish Parliamentary Party that now dominated Irish politics, demanding land reform and Home Rule, a measure – as yet unspecified – of self-governance for John Bull's Other Island. In Britain, working-class discontent was growing as real wages, which had risen steadily throughout the 1870s, began to slump. Arable farming was year on year in greater distress. Britain was on the verge of a violent, nationwide economic depression. Calls for electoral reform were growing in volume. In 1883 Lord Salisbury, Eeyore-like in his perpetual gloom, published *Disintegration*, an essay predicting the breakdown of the social and political order as a result of mass enfranchisement. And socialism was now taking its first tottering steps into the political consciousness of the intelligentsia and the English working class.[10]

Socialism's creed of political rights and economic equality for all was inherently inimical to Mary's world. Yet for the aristocratic dowagers who, gorgon-like, lined the ballroom walls as chaperones to the young who danced before them, the more present threat came from capitalism: plutocratic fortunes from industry and finance trying to force entry into the hallowed drawing rooms of the landed elite. Throughout the 1880s the cry went up from within Society that the ruling class were losing their exclusivity, that young women were being presented at court whom nobody (by which it was meant nobody of 'birth') had ever seen. The percentage of women from the titled and landed classes presented at court fell from 90 per cent in 1841 to 68 per cent in 1871, to under 50 per cent in 1891.[11] Meanwhile the number of presentations was steadily increasing. In 1880, the year of Mary's debut, a fourth drawing room was added to the social calendar, in 1895 a fifth. 'Society, in the old sense of the term, may be said, I think, to have come to an end in the "eighties" of the last century,' said Lady Dorothy Nevill in 1910.[12] The anxiety this caused was immense. 'Let any person who knows London society look through the lists of debutantes and ladies attending drawing rooms and I wager that not half the names will be known to him or her,' thundered one dowager in 1891, inveighing against the advent of 'social scum and nouveaux riches'.[13]

These dowagers' underlying fear was that those forcing entry to their drawing rooms would use their seductive financial power to gain access to their children's beds. The Season was a marriage market for the children of the elite. Within that market, matches were 'facilitated' by careful parents, rather than expressly arranged.[14] The convention was that a young couple should be in love – but with a socially and financially suitable mate. Consequently, access to that market needed to be strictly regulated, in order to prevent young aristocrats accidentally making the wrong choice, and pure bloodlines being corrupted by plutocratic wealth.

In fact, the English elite's permeability has always been one of the key reasons for its continued survival. Its education system

– Eton and Oxbridge – could with time turn the son of 'social scum' into a gentleman apparently indistinguishable from one whose bloodline goes back centuries. Yet it required thick skin. Mary's friends Laura and Margot Tennant, the daughters of the Scottish industrialist Sir Charles Tennant, great-granddaughters of a crofter,[15] found that even after securing presentation at court, most doors were still closed to them, and, at the balls which they did attend, no men would dance with them. For Margot, social entrée came only when she managed to engage the Prince of Wales in conversation in the Royal Enclosure at Ascot. 'I felt my spirits rise, as, walking slowly across the crowded lawn in grilling sunshine, I observed everyone making way for us with lifted hats and low curtsies,' she recalled.[16] Even after the Tennant girls' entry into Society their father was always known, to their aristocratic friends, in barely concealed mockery, as 'the Bart' – a reference to the baronetcy of which he was so obviously proud and the new money that had secured it.

For the aristocratic if bohemian Mary, who had access everywhere, what feathers she ruffled were of her own making. Writing her own memoir in later life, she remembered an incident with a young Oxford undergraduate, George Curzon:

> As we were dancing we received the full impact of handsome Lady Bective's train, formed of masses and masses and layers and layers of black tulle wired and strapped, about as heavy and powerful as a whale's tail. It caught us broadside with immense force and we were swept off our feet and [hurled] to the ground and fell at my mother's feet, our heads almost under the small hard gold chair on which she was patiently sitting as chaperone.[17]

In old age, validated by decades of social success, Mary could look back on such youthful exuberance with pride. For her contemporaneous feelings we must turn elsewhere. Not to her diary: the journal that Mary kept religiously from the age of sixteen until her death was an object of record, not of confidence, and her entries generally masterpieces of pragmatism. That for 8 October 1884, by no means untypical, reads: 'Put on orange frock, went down to tea, sat in draught, rested, black'.[18] It is far better to look to her sketches. On scraps of paper she drew top-hatted men about town carrying silver canes; strolling ladies in bustles and magnificent hats by day, drooping elegantly over their fans in ballgowns by night. She drew herself in balldress, shivering with cold in the early hours of the morning; bundled up against the chill spring in an umbrella and a muff; and on horseback, elegant in her riding habit, brandishing her riding crop under dripping trees in Hyde Park's Rotten Row. On the back of an embossed thick card inviting 'The Hon Percy & Mrs Wyndham & Miss Wyndham' to one of Buckingham Palace's two Court Balls each season is a caricature of herself entitled 'Miss Parrot at the Ball'; she teased her little sisters with sketches depicting 'Pretty Mary and her plain sisters'.[19]

These sketches show the curious eye of an eager young woman getting to grips with the rules of a new, sophisticated world. Around this time Mary visited Dr Lorenzo Niles Fowler, a fashionable American phrenologist, in his Piccadilly offices. Phrenology, the art of analysing character by skull shape, is now discredited, not least for its unsavoury associations with eugenics. In the 1880s, it was Society's latest craze. Dr Fowler must have been perceptive, since his report is curiously accurate. It describes an unselfconscious young woman, young for her years, and happy to let others – particularly her mother – take the lead; combative, but quick to forgive; loyal; and easily interested in other people. Interestingly, Dr Fowler also identified a normally well-hidden element of Mary's personality. 'You are remarkable for your ambition in one form or another,' he said, commenting on her desire 'to appear well in society, to attract attention, & to be admired'. This was undoubtedly true, and something Mary herself would always disavow.[20] She visited Dr Fowler at least twice more, taking her future husband with her too. Even given her love of novelty – Mary was always enthusiastic about the latest craze – it suggests she found some merit in his analysis.

In *Thatched with Gold*, Mabell Airlie expressed the conventional expectation of a debutante: to marry as soon as possible, preferably in her first Season. Too long a delay, and 'there remained nothing but India as a last resort before the spectre of the Old Maid became a reality'.[21] A debutante's social success was certainly measured out by proposals. Mary, who declared later that 'Many wanted me to wife!',[22] received more than a few. Nonetheless, her parents did not encourage her to marry straight away. They thought eighteen far too young to take on the responsibility of a husband and household, and were anyway reluctant to lose her to a husband so soon. Still, Mary did not become engaged until her fourth Season, in 1883. The delay was longer than Madeline Wyndham – responsible for guiding her daughter towards a suitable match, determined to prove her family's worth by securing a splendid one – could have hoped for.

In the autumn of 1880 Balfour invited Mary and her parents to Strathconan, his Highland hunting lodge. The visit was not a success. Mary was tongue-tied with awkwardness: in her own words, 'a shy Miss Mog . . . feeling very stiff & studying Green's history & strumming Bach most conscientiously listening with silent awe to the flashing repartee, the witticisms & above all the startling aplomb of "grown-up conversation"'.[23] It may have been this muteness that gave rise to the story that some of Mary's circle had initially thought her a little backward.[24]

In London, Madeline and Mary invited Balfour to the Lyceum to see Ellen Terry in *Much Ado About Nothing*. Forever after the play would fill Mary with 'a peculiar kind of sadness'. Twenty years on she remembered the evening with startling clarity: 'We sat in a box and when the audience tittered at the wrong part you said savagely "I would gladly wring their necks" and I remember the sense of vague dissatisfaction when it was all over – the evening

– one of my little efforts,' she recalled to Balfour.[25] Balfour subsequently declined Madeline Wyndham's invitations to visit the family at Wilbury. By the end of Mary's second season it was clear that the affair had come to nothing.

Looking back over the abortive courtship many years later, Mary blamed her shyness and Balfour's cowardice. She could not audaciously flirt like the Tennant sisters. She, like Shakespeare's Beatrice, had needed luring. But Balfour was too 'busy and captious' to do it. 'Mama wanted you to marry me [but] you got some silly notion in your head because . . . circumstances accidentally kept us apart – you were the only man I wanted for my husband and it's a great compliment to you!. . . but you wouldn't give me a chance of showing you nicely and you never came to Wilbury and you were afraid, afraid, afraid!' she teased him.[26]

Many biographers have examined in some detail why Balfour, at whom women flung themselves, never married. It has been suggested that the 'Pretty Fanny' of press caricatures was gay, even an hermaphrodite.[27] His devoted niece Blanche Dugdale suggested that he was nursing a lifelong broken heart after the death from typhoid in 1875 of his close friend May Lyttelton.[28] In fact, Mary's analysis seems to hint at the most probable answer: Balfour was lazy, and emotion frightened him. He felt safest in a rational, logical world. 'The Balfourian manner' for which he became known 'has its roots in an attitude of . . . convinced superiority which insists in the first place on complete detachment from the enthusiasms of the human race, and in the second place on keeping the vulgar world at arm's length . . .' wrote Begbie. In Begbie's phrase, that world, which Balfour so charmed upon meeting, was never allowed to penetrate beyond his lodge gates.[29] A decade into their acquaintance, Mary pressed Balfour to express some kind of affection in his letters to her. He recoiled. 'Such things are impossible to me: and they would if said *to* me give such exquisite pain, that I could never bring myself to say them to others – even at their desire,' he explained.[30]

In December 1880, Mary visited Wilton, home of the Earl and

Countess of Pembroke. It was her first visit without her parents – she was chaperoned only by Eassy, her mother's maid – and a suitably 'safe' first foray since Gertrude Pembroke and Madeline Wyndham had been close friends for many years. The house party included two men whom Mary knew only a little, but liked – Alfred Lyttelton (brother of May), 'that nice youngest one' of the large Lyttelton clan, and Hugo Charteris, eldest surviving son of Lord and Lady Elcho, heir to the earldom of Wemyss. The house party was rehearsing Christmas theatricals in a delightfully shambolic fashion. Mary was in her element. 'We all turn our backs on the audience, we don't speak up, we laugh, we hesitate and we gabble,' she told her mother. 'Hugo talks in a very funny voice.'[31] Acerbic, witty Hugo, a talented amateur actor, was far more attractive to women than his average looks suggested (he was balding fast). He was also a complicated soul, with a morose streak and a gambling problem. His gambling was often to complicate relations with his father, whose own high-minded preoccupation – army reform – earned him the sobriquet 'the Brigadier'.[32] Two elder brothers had died in their early twenties (one an accident, the other a suspected suicide). Lady Elcho was a daunting figure even in the context of mid-Victorian evangelism, and never troubled to conceal from Hugo her feeling that the wrong sons had died.[33] 'Mums called Keems [Hugo] darling & patted him on the leg . . . neither of which has she done for years,' Hugo noted with delight (referring to himself in the third person, something he often did in correspond-ence with his wife) when he was almost thirty years old.[34]

Madeline Wyndham had known the Elchos for many years, not intimately but well. In February 1881 she invited Hugo to Wilbury. If she thought to capitalize upon interest sparked in Mary at Wilton, she was mistaken. When Madeline tried to make her daughter commit to a date, Mary professed an utter lack of interest. 'As to Hugoman, his is an indefinite arrangement. I suppose you will write to him before the time comes [although] we might have him Monday as Lily [Paulet, Hugo's cousin] comes that day,' she wrote laconically in a letter otherwise devoted to plans for rearranging balls so that her friend and neighbour Louisa Gully might attend.[35] Recalling this period a few years later, Mary gloated over her inscrutability: 'poor Mum . . . she really couldn't fathom Migs,' she said, describing herself proudly as 'the little hunter (who always hunted on her own hook & followed her own trail)'.[36] Madeline persisted nonetheless. Six months later, Hugo was posted to Constantinople as part of a short-lived stint in the Foreign Office. By this time, his acquaintance with Mary was well established. Mary wrote to him on the eve of his departure recounting her recent nineteenth-birthday celebrations at Wilbury, where she had, in accordance with family tradition, been crowned with a wreath of roses and spent the evening celebrating with songs and dancing. She had decided, she told him, that 'the [cat]' – and here she drew a little cartoon of a cat – 'believes the [hog]' – a drawing of a pig – 'to be most sage, large-minded and kind'.[37]

Meritocracy had not reached the Foreign Office. It was believed that only those with breeding could properly and confidently uphold British prestige abroad. Lord Robert Cecil commented that all a junior attaché needed was fluent French and the ability 'to dangle about at parties and balls'.[38] Several months later, bored and lonely in Constantinople, Hugo received a letter from his brother Evan, updating him on London gossip, including a nugget concerning a putative rival, David Ogilvy, heir to the earldom of Airlie:

> Apparently he [Ogilvy] came over here in the summer intending to stay for a year and a half but went back after two months as Miss *Wyndham* was too much for him. He never proposed to her but was afraid he would do so, so he retired. I suppose you keep up constant correspondence with her I daresay she has told you more about Ogilvy than I can . . .

On that mischievous note, Evan swore Hugo to secrecy.[39]

Mary most certainly had not gossiped. Hugo only discovered the truth of the matter several years later. 'I think that Mumsie

[Madeline Wyndham] proposing to Ogles for you & being refused is very funni [sic],' Hugo told Mary gleefully upon discovering the real sequence of events in 1887.⁴⁰ Mary, like her husband employing the third person, blusteringly denied all responsibility: 'It had nothing *to do with Migs*, it was entirely the old huntress's transaction . . . I didn't care a *hang* about Ogles & knew he didn't care a rap for me . . . Mumsie wanted Migs to be *clear* of Ogles (or engaged to him!!!) to "go in" for Wash [Hugo himself] with a clean nose!'⁴¹ It is quite possible that Ogles was the unnamed beau who allegedly abandoned his interest in Mary with the explanation that she was 'A very nice filly, but she's read too many books for me'.⁴²

Hugo returned to England in the spring of 1882, bearing bangles 'for Miss Mary', and determined to start a new career in politics as a member of the Conservative Opposition.⁴³ Mary was in Paris, flirting with Frenchmen and having 'a high old time'. Madeline Wyndham 'hunted' her annoyed daughter back to Wilbury and dismissed her wheedling attempts to secure an invitation for a handsome 'Musha de Deautand' whom she had met in Hyères with the excuse that there was no room. '[T]here would be no harm done just a fortnight in the *country* . . . the house is elastic you could shove somebody somewhere,' pleaded Mary, to no avail.⁴⁴ Madeline Wyndham was decided. As Mary later recalled, her mother's plan was that she was to 'go in' for Hugo and marriage 'in the summer (together with reading & music!) that makes me laugh! Hunt the arts to keep one's hand in!'⁴⁵

That summer was one of the bloodiest politically for some time. In May, Parnell and his lieutenants William O'Brien and J. J. O'Kelly were released from several months' imprisonment in Kilmainham Jail. They had been jailed for 'treasonable practices' after fomenting opposition to Gladstone's 1881 Land Act, which gave Ireland the '3 Fs' of fair rents, fixity of tenure and free sale of landholdings but which Parnell and his party considered did not go far enough. Their incarceration had thrown Ireland back into full-blown chaos:

a national rent strike by day, while the mysterious 'Captain Moonlight' terrorized landlords by night. The 'Kilmainham Treaty' released Parnell in return for his bringing his influence to bear to end the rent strike. Many thought it negotiating with terrorists, including W. E. Forster, who in fury resigned as Irish Chief Secretary. His replacement, Lord Frederick Cavendish, and his Under-Secretary Thomas Burke had barely set foot on Irish soil when they were murdered in Dublin's Phoenix Park by a gang calling itself the Invincibles. In London, men poured, hatless, out of their clubs to disseminate the appalling news.[46] Quite unjustly, Parnell and his fellow Irish parliamentarian John Dillon were blamed; arriving at the House of Commons the following day, Wilfrid Blunt was told that they were the 'conspirators'. Stoutly, Blunt refused to give credence to the rumours: 'they looked very much like gentlemen among the cads of the lobby'.[47]

Blunt was preoccupied with another devastating blow to nationalism dealt by Gladstone's ministry in Egypt. In 1882, the British occupied Egypt, in order to shore up the corrupt Khedive's unstable rule in the face of revolt by Colonel Ahmed Orabi, popularly known as the Arabi Pasha. The need to protect the interests of the 'bondholders', as those numerous Britons with investments in Egypt were now called, outweighed any nice concerns for Midlothian principles of national self-government. So firmly did the British believe that Suez must be protected that just nineteen members of the House of Commons voted against the occupation. Percy Wyndham was the only Tory to do so, vigorously opposed to what he believed to be Britain's illegal and oppressive behaviour.[48] He later made one of his increasingly rare Commons speeches on Blunt's behalf, for Blunt's fierce advocacy of the Arabi's cause – even to the extent of paying for his legal defence when the Arabi was court-martialled (the trial was abandoned, and the Arabi exiled instead) – earned Blunt exile himself. In July 1884, trying to go back to Egypt, Blunt was detained at Alexandria by British officials who, under instructions from Sir

Edward Malet, the Consul General, forbade the troublemaker entry.[49]

Access to a parliamentary seat was still easy for a young aristocrat. In January 1883, Hugo's grandfather died, and his father, now the tenth Earl of Wemyss, was elevated to the Lords. At a by-election in February, Hugo, having inherited his father's courtesy title, stepped neatly into the Suffolk seat his father had held since 1847. Seamlessly, a Lord Elcho once more sat for Haddington. At Wilbury Mary, Mananai and Pamela decorated Mary's dog Crack with yellow ribbons to celebrate – the colour of the Primrose League. The League, named after the favourite flower of Disraeli (who died in 1881), promoted working- and middle-class Toryism – the latter becoming known as Villa Toryism – largely through jamborees and summer fêtes, enticing the electorate with the promise of aristocratic proximity. It was the work of Lord Randolph Churchill, the preacher of 'Tory Democracy', an ill-defined creed that involved transferring power from the party's leadership to the National Union – the constituencies – but was really part of his own bid for power. Privately, he described it as 'chiefly opportunism'.[50]

Throughout that year Hugo sent Mary bouquets which she unpicked and made into buttonholes for him to wear; they played lawn tennis, went to the theatre, had tea and walked in the park: all under Madeline Wyndham's encouraging eye. Finally on a July night in 1883, with 'buttonhole no. 171' in his lapel, Hugo proposed and Mary said yes.[51] The next day, Hugo went to Belgrave Square to seek formally the Wyndhams' blessing. Percy gave it to him 'from my heart of hearts . . . Mary is a *great* treasure, and as I believe you know it I am very glad you have made her love you.'[52]

Mary had never properly met Hugo's parents. They were introduced the next day at tea at their Mayfair house, 23 St James's Street. Annie Wemyss took to Mary 'immensely', deeming her 'so natural, so true, so good, & so free from affectation, fastness'. '[This] is such a good thing,' wrote a mutual acquaintance to Percy, 'for as we know, she [Annie Wemyss] does not take always spontaneously to people. I confess I felt rather nervous about it . . .'[53] Madeline Wyndham was delighted. 'She will bring you all nearer together,' she told Hugo, as though her daughter were a sort of familial Elastoplast.[54]

Mary's precipitation from the Wyndhams' loving bosom into the Wemysses' chilly embrace concerned many of the Wyndhams' friends. 'Condolences' upon the loss of a daughter to marriage were conventional enough, as were the 'icy congratulations' that Mary received from Hugo's desultory rivals.[55] But many of the letters of congratulations sent to Belgrave Square were somewhat equivocal, and could not conceal a certain bemusement at her choice.[56] Rediscovering them in middle age, Mary thought it obvious that most of her relations had thought Hugo was not quite good enough.[57]

Mary did not particularly enjoy her engagement: 'six weeks of racket'[58] consisting of all the things she most disliked: endless trips 'drudging around the shops' after her mother, and being prodded and poked by crowds of people 'swarming about the house about bothering clothes'.[59] Hugo teased Mary about the new skills she was acquiring in preparation for life as a matron running a household: 'I wonder what you are doing . . . learning how many apples go to a Pie, or what butter costs at ¾ a pound . . . or perhaps you have been philosophizing over the degeneracy of modern linen . . . & regretting the halcyon days of muslins.'[60]

Both lovers expressed the sentiments expected of them. The day after their engagement, Mary told Hugo she had passed a sleepless night, contemplating the great change before her.[61] In the following days she professed herself '*completely* happy!' with her 'darling Hoggolindo . . . angel-Hoggie'. 'My bounty is as boundless as the sea,' she told 'his Lordship Hogge the Good', quoting her favourite lines from *Romeo and Juliet*. Hugo had become the very model of young Victorian manhood, swearing to 'to pray, pray with your photo before me . . . to become more deserving of my happiness, to be drawn out of my stupid narrow self to something higher, better, nearer what you are'.[62] But, all too soon, Hugo was back to his old habits, and doubts had surfaced in Mary's mind.

Barely a fortnight into her engagement, Mary had to intervene with the Wemysses on Hugo's behalf. Hugo had found his gambling poison, the Stock Exchange, and on his first flutter lost £700, the equivalent of over £57,000 today. In what would become a wearily familiar exchange, Mary persuaded the Wemysses not to tie up Hugo's inheritance in a trust, but she was worried about their future before they had even embarked on it.[63] Nor did Hugo appear to think his engagement required him to stop his constant flirting. 'I don't care how much "nonsense" you talk to everybody or *any*body at the Fisheries tonight for I do feel that you love me truly as I do you from the bottom of my heart,' Mary told Hugo in mid-July, but her stout avowals ring hollow.[64]

Around this time – perhaps precipitated by the gambling incident – Mary tried to call off the engagement. Her formal, stilted letter to 'Lord Elcho' reads like that of a slightly less tactful Elizabeth Bennet who has accidently accepted Mr Collins. She was at home in Belgrave Square, dinner was ready downstairs and doubtless her father was growing increasingly impatient, but, she declared,

> I must write this at once . . . speak straight out & tell you that I have hour by hour become more forcibly, painfully & unmistake-ably [sic] convinced that when I accepted you a fortnight ago I did *not* rightly understand my own mind . . . [I am] perfectly certain [that] I do *not* love & respect you as I feel I should . . . I feel it my duty my positive & absolute duty to break off our proposed marriage.

As soon as Mary had forced those words out, her relief is palpable: her tone becomes free and easy and her pen dashes across the page in her usual untidy manner:

I hope you will not mind much! Tho' yr pride may be shocked at first – I feel assured that you will so feel it to be all for the best for both of us & I trust you will think of me *kindly* as your *true* friend MW p.s. Please excuse my untidiness! I feel our marriage would lead to endless misery to both of us as it is. N.B. I am sure we shall always be very good friends. I know you will not take it to heart.[65]

The engagement was not broken. By the next day, Mary was writing to Hugo as though they were reconciled, but her tone remains sober and the pet-names are nowhere to be seen. Whether it was an attempt to shock Hugo into good behaviour or whether it was cold feet (thirty years later George Wyndham reminded Mary how all the siblings had 'palpitated' over their marriages – although George and his wife would also prove incompatible),[66] it was far too late for that. The Wyndhams' indulgence did not extend to engagements broken for no good reason. It would have caused a scandal unthinkable for Madeline Wyndham, and while Percy gave his children a degree of independence, he held them consequently responsible for their actions. 'Her mother had pushed her [Mary] into marrying L[or]d Elcho – so one used to be told at least,' said Maud Wyndham, daughter of the Leconfields, and Mary's first cousin, sixty years later.[67]

Arrangements proceeded as normal: the wedding presents arrived at Belgrave Square and, as customary, were displayed for inspection by family, friends and household (although some, such as Stanway, the Gloucestershire manor house given by Lord Wemyss to the newlyweds, were not capable of display). Mary began work on hundreds of thank-you letters: 'I have thanked eight presents (long elaborate letters) & August is two hours old!' she complained to Hugo.[68] Last-minute adjustments were made to Mananai's and Pamela's bridesmaid dresses and Mary's trousseau was packed in tissue paper in preparation for her honeymoon. Early on the morning of their wedding day, 10 August 1883, 'the dawn of the day which I hope through all our lives we shall look upon as a blessed anniversary', Hugo wrote to Mary anticipating their meeting in St Peter's Church in Eaton Square later that day: 'Darling God give you strength to go through it all – & make me a good Hogs worthy of the little angel Mogs . . . Goodbye my darling soon to be mine only and really.' He sketched for Mary a cartoon: a small round Mary (not entirely representative, it must be said, since Mary was tall and slender) with a tall thin bride-groom by her side shouting 'hurrah!'[69] Several hours later, as reported by *The Times*, Mary, dressed in white and decked with orange blossom, walked down the aisle of St Peter's, past relations, friends and royalty in the form of Princess Christian, towards 'Lord Elcho M.P.', and became his wife.[70]

As the assembled masses waited in the cool church for Mary to make her entrance on Percy's arm, it was Madeline Wyndham's nerves that were most frayed. 'It *was* an awful bit that in the Church before *you came* – it felt *so long*,' Madeline told Mary later, heady with relief that all had gone as planned. 'The organ played *such a tune* . . . I could *have screamed* to the man, to *stop* his twiddles . . . & then, like hot & cold or magic music, as you drew near he played louder & louder!'[71] Normally such a thing would have given Mary and her mother the giggles: this time it only gave Madeline a feeling of 'teeth on edge'.

The service was followed by a short reception at Belgrave Square. At a quarter past four, the bride and groom departed: first for Easton Lodge in Essex, lent to them by Lord and Lady Brooke, and then to Gober, in the Scottish Highlands, where Hugo was to go stalking. The Wyndhams settled in for a quiet evening at Belgrave Square. Madeline and her sisters, Julia and Lucy Campbell, alternately laughed and cried over the events of the day. Then George and Guy Wyndham went to a play. The rest of the family dined with Fräulein. After dinner, as Mananai sat and pulled apart Mary's bouquet in order to make nosegays for Mary's friends as keepsakes, her mother was reminded of her eldest daughter: 'sitting there with a melancholy face picking and pulling at all the lovely flowers!'[72] The comparison did not bode well given that all Mary's bouquets and buttonholes had been to do with Hugo.

FOUR

Honeymoon

Three years later, when the sheen of marriage had long started to fade, Mary reproved Hugo for spending their honeymoon stalking. At the time, she had seemed happy enough to yomp across the moors after Hugo, and she revelled in a sense of recklessness as the Elchos drank champagne and played piquet by night. The Wyndham family was by now summering in Hyères, and Madeline Wyndham was missing her eldest daughter desperately ('I cannot get *reconciled* to being without you,' she told Mary some two years after her marriage),[1] but Mary's letters to her family glowed with delight in her marital state. One evening, she told Guy conspiratorially, the Elchos had got so 'drunk' on champagne 'to cheer our spirits' after Hugo failed to bag a stag that Hugo fell over.[2] At this liminal honeymoon stage Mary had been freed from childhood's bonds without yet assuming matronly cares.

The little cartoons the Elchos sent one another in their marriage's early years, and coy references to 'lonely little cots' when they were apart, suggest that sexually the union was a success. Not for the Elchos the horror stories of the Ruskins, whose marriage was never

consummated, or of the young scientist Marie Stopes, who only
realized her abusive husband was impotent after six months of
study in the British Library.[3] Madeline and her daughters were
extremely frank with each other about all health matters, micro-
scopically recounting any oddities in relation to 'Lady Betsey', their
term for their menstrual cycle. Mary was enthusiastically descrip-
tive about gynaecological matters. It seems likely that Madeline
gave all her daughters some kind of warning about what a wedding
night entailed. What Mary told her mother after the event must
remain a mystery. Madeline Wyndham kept 'letter books' containing
her children's correspondence over the course of their lives. On
pasting in Mary's first letter to her following her wedding, Madeline
redacted it, so that it tells us only that Mary had 'a headache', before
the next three lines are scrubbed out vigorously with black pen.[4]

Romance was in the air at Gober. As Mary and Hugo ate their
dinner by firelight, backstage in the little hut Hugo's valet Williams
seduced Mary's maid Faivre. Prophylactics, not uncommon in the
city, were hardly readily available in the Highland wilds; perhaps
Faivre was also one of many unversed women who did not know
how babies were made. Faivre consequently found herself unmarried and pregnant – 'ruined', as Mary put it.[5] It was a highly unfortunate position for any young woman, an untenable one for a lady's
maid.

In most cases, Faivre would have found herself immediately
dismissed without a reference. When the Elchos' friend George
Curzon found out that a housemaid in his employ had been seduced
by a footman, he 'put the little slut out into the street' without a
qualm. His contemporaries considered his attitude unremarkable.[6]
Mary responded quite differently. With the help of Madeline and
Percy she helped Faivre find lodging with a tolerant North London
landlady; assisted her financially from her own pin money (Hugo's
valet had long since scarpered); and visited Faivre once the child,
a little boy, was born in the spring of 1884.[7] Most of Mary's friends
thought her admirably liberal attitude towards staff overly

indulgent. Servant troubles became a constant footnote to her daily life. Her anxiety never to hurt anyone's feelings did not serve her well as an employer.

On 14 August 1883, a few days after the Elchos had arrived at Gober, Hugo wrote a private letter to Percy. The subject was Mary's dowry. Hugo told Percy that he had proposed 'with no idea what Mary was to have or whether she was to have any[thing] at all', as unconvincing a statement as the rest of his letter was disingenuous.[8] Mary's marriage settlement had been negotiated in the weeks between the engagement and the marriage by Percy on the one hand and Hugo's solicitor, Mr Jamieson, on the other, as was the convention.[9] Mary received £15,000 (roughly £1.25 million today), the interest on which would produce an annual income of £500.[10] Hugo had thought that £100 or more of this £500 would be given to him for his own use. Now conversations with Mr Jamieson had made it clear that Percy intended the whole for Mary's use as pin money.

Hugo's frantic letter to Percy argued that Mary should not have an allowance disproportionate to the Elchos' income, lest she learn bad spending habits. His reasoning, while in line with contemporary attitudes, was both patronizing and misleading. His concern was not that Mary's spending habits should be curbed but that his own should be supported. Mary was innately frugal, and remained so all her life. She spent almost no money on clothes (far too little, her friends complained). Her eldest daughter never remembered her buying even a trinket or a bottle of scent for herself. She invariably travelled third class. Hugo, who travelled in first, and liked expensive cigars, was not otherwise extravagant in his living habits, but his gambling habit on the London Stock Exchange was improvident. 'As far as his children could make out all he wanted money for was to have plenty of it to lose!' wrote his eldest daughter Cynthia.[11]

Hugo's haste to have this issue determined while on honeymoon suggests he was in yet another financial scrape. From his sheepish tone, even he realized that his behaviour was grasping. Percy agreed that Mary should have only £350–400 a year as pin money, with the remainder going to the Elchos' common expenses.[12] From the occasional sly comment over the years it is clear that Percy knew full well why Hugo was so keen to reduce Mary's pin money. Mary knew nothing of this until stumbling across this letter years later. 'Typical', she scrawled across it in irritation, that on their honeymoon Hugo should have written to her father 'not on love but Money!', adding, correctly, that Hugo's master was 'Mammon'.[13]

From Gober the Elchos travelled to Gosford, the Wemysses' family seat just outside Edinburgh. For a century, the family had lived on another property on the estate. Now Lord Wemyss was adding two vast wings on to an Adams-built centre completed, but never lived in, a century before.[14] During the course of the works, Mary persuaded the builders to let her go up in the crane used for the building. She drew a picture for her mother to illustrate it: a tiny figure swinging high over a bare landscape.[15]

Mary hated Gosford on sight. A chill east wind whipped around the property, which looked out to the glassy grey Firth of Forth. Seagulls wheeled overhead in a 'complaining chorus'.[16] In later life she described the rebuilt house as 'like a large & gilded, dead & empty Cage'.[17] Her daughter Cynthia echoed her: 'a great block of stone that seems to me very still-born. It has no living atmosphere.'[18] Lutyens likened it to a rendition of 'God Save the King' sung flat.[19] As a newlywed, Mary dreaded the time when Hugo would succeed to the Wemyss title, requiring her to relocate to the north.

Gosford was enough to induce homesickness in anyone. Just days after they arrived, Hugo went rabbit shooting, leaving his new wife alone in the bosom of his family. He had accepted the invitation before his engagement, and claimed he could not in good conscience cancel. It was an early indication of his ability to costume selfishness as honour. In Hugo's absence, Mary attended Aberlady Church with the family, went for long solitary walks and wrote endless letters to her husband. Evan Charteris, on finding her at her writing desk once again, marvelled teasingly that she had anything further to say. Annie Wemyss visited her in her bedroom before dinner and in her own stiff way 'thimpashized' with her doleful daughter-in-law. Nonetheless Mary felt marooned in a strange place and wondered what she was doing there. 'You *must* come back soon . . . the very first instant you can . . . it is too horrid – & . . . dreary & dismal . . . everything is rainy & black & miserable & Mogs feels very sad,' she told Hugo.[20] Hugo's sympathetic replies showed no sign that he intended to change his plans.

At dinner the Wemysses lectured Mary upon the dangers of separation in marriage. Annie Wemyss noted proudly that she and Lord Wemyss had barely spent a day apart. Already, the Elchos seemed to have exceeded their tally, and Mary's solitude forced her into contemplation. 'I think *now* that Hugo & I shall always love being together by ourselves better than anything else . . . [but] the habit of living together as one cannot be acquired in a minute any more than any other habit . . . the wedding day is but the *beginning* of the marriage not the "fait accompli",' she told her mother. She had taken as her mantra 'I bide my time'. With that she could '*remove Mountains!*'[21] But Mary's brave words rang hollow. She was beginning to realize that moulding Hugo into the husband she wanted might be even more difficult than she had anticipated.

A few weeks later the Elchos returned to London. Hugo had taken a small house near his parents at 12 North Audley Street, off Grosvenor Square. The Elchos stayed at Belgrave Square while waiting for works on the rented house to be completed.[22] Both their mothers warned Mary about the dangers of city life, full of distractions to drive an emotional wedge between a young husband and wife. Once installed in North Audley Street, the Elchos made a good fist at domesticity. Sometimes they dined alone. Over champagne, Hugo practised the speeches he intended to make the next day in the Commons, speeches they both hoped would gain the attention of the party leadership and raise him out of the backbenches in due course. On other evenings Hugo read poetry to Mary as they sat by the fire.

Yet far more frequently Mary's diary recorded evenings spent in the company of others. In her journal the companions of her youth, cousins and Wiltshire neighbours, fall away. Instead she went with her sisters-in-law Evelyn de Vesci and Hilda Brodrick to watch the debates from the Ladies' Gallery in the Commons, or spent evenings at the 'New Club' (the New University Club on St James's Street) drinking champagne and 'getting lively' with Arthur Balfour, Hugo and Evan Charteris as they debated that day's point of interest with dazzling lightness and speed. With Hugo, Laura Tennant and Alfred Lyttelton, Mary passed evenings at the bachelor lodgings of Godfrey Webb where the company reclined in armchairs, played the piano and indulged in 'nice long talk'.[23] Webb was somewhat older, and had originally been a friend of Percy and Madeline's. A clerk in the House of Lords, and celebrated wit and raconteur, 'Webber' was described by some of the group as their court jester.[24] That group, of which Arthur was the undisputed king, began to refer to itself as 'the Gang'. In a few years its members would become 'the Souls'.

Marriage had established the direction of Mary's social circle. After a spat about flirtations in 1887, Hugo implied as much, telling Mary that 'me almost wishes as a punishment – though not quite! That you were now playing the part of Lady Airlie [David Ogilvy had since become Earl of Airlie] – in some provincial garrison town – jealously guarded by Othello Ogles – no Migs – no Barkin [Arthur Balfour] – NO Tommie [Ribblesdale] – NO Stanywan [Stanway] – only Ernests [babies] – soldiers wives – & tea parties of 10th Hussar Sols – with Othello Ogles pouring out the tea.'[25] Hugo's conjecture was remarkably accurate in describing the life of Ogilvy's actual wife Mabell Airlie at that time. Yet a comment by Mary in those early days suggests that the frenetic socializing for which she became notorious was partly the result of her husband's response to married life rather than her own. Two years into their marriage, Mary counted to Hugo the number of occasions that the Elchos had been 'quite alone' in the countryside, without the array of hangers-on required to keep him amused. It was just twice: the time in Gober, 'when you were stalking all day & one week at Whitsuntide at Stanway when I felt very ill – & yet you pretend to believe we are a domestic couple . . .'.[26]

In the spring of 1884, before the Elchos moved into North Audley Street, Mary had a miscarriage. She was put to bed at Belgrave Square and a doctor summoned. With fear of infections and haemorrhaging, miscarriage was considered more dangerous than childbirth, but Dr Cumberbatch said Mary's condition gave him no cause for concern. 'I suppose I have gone about it methodically in an easy going manner . . . I am as jolly as a sandgirl, or rather matron, or would be matron!' Mary reassured her mother, who had stayed in London to be near Mary for as long as she could until the stream of telegrams from Percy, left with a houseful of guests at Wilbury, grew too irate to ignore. In a quiet room, cared for by a nurse, Mary rested on a chaise longue and knitted, whiling away the days until she was allowed back into the world. Hugo drifted in and out in between stints at the Commons. She was visited by friends – Lily Paulet and Emmie Bourke (a cousin of sorts whose husband Edward was the brother of Mary's late uncle Lord Mayo) – and her sisters-in-law, who recounted their own experiences of childbearing and miscarriage. Eventually the shows of blood decreased. 'Betsey . . . from [her] kind of light out of door attire is about to put on tippet and depart,' Mary told her mother, and she was allowed to re-enter the world.

As Mary did so, she was unclear whether she was pregnant or not. Dr Cumberbatch, perplexed by the non-appearance of 'a 3 months ovum', confessed he could not tell what exactly had happened. Perhaps Mary had had a phantom pregnancy; perhaps she was still pregnant; perhaps the foetus would come away at Mary's next monthly period. If her period did not appear, 'I shan't know whether I have picked up old threads or started afresh! It's very funny,' said Mary, resolutely bright-faced, affecting nonchalance.[27] Madeline Wyndham was terrified that Mary might produce a child with some kind of 'omission': a living judgement upon the Wyndham blood and breeding. Such haziness about childbirth matters was far from uncommon. Twenty years later Mananai recounted to Madeline the story of an unfortunate girl who was told that she was to give birth in July and found herself still pregnant in September.[28] In Mary's case, 'Betsey' did not reappear. She began to feel sick and 'squeamish'. She supposed that she was either still pregnant or pregnant again.

That summer, Mary made her first visit to Stanway, the Gloucestershire house that was her wedding present from Lord Wemyss. Stanway, where the family still lives, is a magical place – a ramshackle sixteenth-century house of honey-coloured stone shouldering on to a churchyard hidden away along an alley of pleached trees. The air seems thicker and stiller there: part of the house was originally a monastery, and a sense of this seclusion remains. The Elchos arrived on 31 July 1884, met at the station by a coachman, pony-chaise and black horse all seemingly as ancient as each other. They emerged from the leafy lanes to find Stanway glowing in the evening sun, with the bells of the tiny church that stood next door pealing in celebration. '[A] sort of heavenly feeling comes over one and laps one about,' Mary told her mother of this arrival, the moment that she fell in love with the house that would be her home for the rest of her life.[29] That evening the Elchos walked up to the Pyramid, a monument at the top of a gentle hill overlooking the house that was to become the site of many a tryst and midnight escapade. Half a century later Mary could still remember the sickeningly stuffy smell of the brand-new blankets and the next day's breakfast of trout fried in oatmeal made by the housekeeper.[30]

When the Elchos arrived, the house had lain near-abandoned for half a century, kept barely habitable by a skeleton staff of ancient retainers for the rare occasions that the Wemysses used it as a shooting lodge on a foray south. Draughts whistled through cracks in the walls, cold flooded in through the latticed windowpanes. Armies of rats and cockroaches scuttled across bare floorboards, and as dusk fell bats swooped through shadowy rooms. Mary was undaunted by the state of the house and full of enthusiasm for transforming it. On pieces of rough paper she sketched out floorplans for her family, explaining the house's peculiar layout. Stanway had almost no passages: most of the rooms led on from one another and it could only sleep sixteen at a pinch – remarkably small in the context of most houses the Wyndhams visited. Mary would continually struggle with this as a hostess.

Mary's first guests – Percy, Fräulein, Mananai and Pamela – arrived on 3 August to celebrate her twenty-second birthday. Fräulein had made 'a cake with big raisins in it', and Mary had bought crackers, eagerly anticipating 'a feast & revel' with her family. Madeline Wyndham, George and Guy arrived a few days later, and work began on transforming the house. As gooseberries gently ripened in the overgrown gardens, Madeline and her daughters picked their way through dusty attics hunting for treasures. They found Chippendale chairs which they brought down to replace the early Victorian plush-and-gilt furniture already *in situ*; and they patched together lengths of embroidered materials so that they could be hung as curtains in Mary's sitting room at the end of the house that looked up to the Monument. Great pieces of furniture were trundled from room to room, old rugs laid out across floorboards.

A month later, while staying at the Wemysses' gloomy townhouse in Edinburgh, with the tick-tock of the eerie mechanical clock echoing through the rooms, Mary reported to Madeline Wyndham that 'Earnest' 'is alive and kicking!' Despite a riot of ailments ('rheumatic pains in back & tummy . . . flatulence, ript livers', insomnia and indigestion),[31] she finally relaxed. Madeline was at Wilbury, where George was waxing and waning yellow from an attack of jaundice. She seized a moment to write to her daughter before dashing into the village to 'beg borrow or steal' a hollyhock so that

Val Prinsep, seized by the urge, could paint it.[32] She sent Mary strict instructions not to travel unless she felt up to it, for 'sometimes indigestion gets such possession of one during the last months that one is only fit *for home* [where] . . . you can give yourself up to a tea gown & your sofa'.[33]

Mary did not listen. Already she carried everywhere her 'nest egg' – a wicker hand basket of unanswered letters, always full to overflowing, despite several hours spent each morning trying to reduce the Sisyphean pile. In December 1884, when she was almost to term, she hosted her first house party for 'the Gang' at Stanway, their number including Arthur Balfour, Alfred Lyttelton, Godfrey Webb, St John and Hilda Brodrick and Laura Tennant. It was a roaring success. Laura Tennant wrote, 'it's such fun here . . . we quarrel about everything – we talk up to the top of our bent – we grow hyper-sentimental and blow blue bubbles into the stars & Hugo Ld Elcho comes down upon them with jeers & in pumps & a smoking suit. We play games & the piano – we none of us open a book or write a letter – we scribble & scrawl & invent words & reasonless rhymes.'[34] The guests 'departed on the verge of tears!', Mary told Percy with pride.[35] Her diary came alive. 'Talk talk the whole time,' she recorded, scribbling down in detail all the games they played.[36] Six months later the Elchos hosted another party. 'Remember darling you are staying with very nice people. Please be careful and do not do anything to shock or annoy them,' Charty Ribblesdale warned her younger sister, Margot Tennant. 'At that moment', Mary recalled, 'Margot was walking on the church wall, pursuing Willie Grenfell with a large sponge – and astounding Hugo by her habit of talking in the passage or in her friends' bedrooms till all hours of the night or morning.'[37] It was, in the collective memory, the first house party of the Souls.[38] Mary at Stanway, in her delight, had found her métier.

FIVE

The Gang

A heavily pregnant Mary spent Christmas 1884 at Wilbury. She had planned to give birth in January, in London, but Hugo Richard Francis Charteris (later known as 'Ego' from his childish attempts to pronounce his name) appeared early, and was born at Wilbury on 28 December.[1] Thirteen-year-old Pamela was enthralled at having a 'real live baby in the house',[2] Madeline Wyndham almost sick with relief that the child was healthy. Hugo sat by Mary's side in her old bedroom as she recovered, allowing her to dictate her letters and diary to him until she was strong enough to wield a pencil herself.

Ego was born one day before Gladstone's seventy-fifth birthday. The GOM's ministry was still bedevilled by foreign policy problems. By 1884, the trouble-spot had shifted to the Sudan, where British troops had become caught up in an attempt to suppress a revolt against Egyptian rule. For almost a year, the small, fearsome General Gordon, whose piercing blue eyes burned with Christian zeal, had been besieged in Khartoum by a mysterious fanatic known as the Mahdi who had been conducting the rebellion since 1881. In fact, it was entirely Gordon's fault he was besieged. He had been sent out to effect a British withdrawal from the Sudan,[3] but on arrival he had announced his intention to 'smash up the Mahdi' and dug his heels in at Khartoum. Such was the danger of having an uncontrollable 'man on the spot', who by maverick actions could influence government policy. In the autumn of 1884, caving in to intolerable public pressure (and to an angry Queen at Windsor), Gladstone authorized relief troops to be dispatched to the Sudan. To his intense disappointment, George Wyndham, who had joined the Coldstream Guards on leaving Eton, narrowly missed out on the opportunity to form part of the rescue mission. Wilfrid Blunt, who was still keen to return to Egypt, also wanted to become involved. On Christmas Eve he addressed the Executive of the International Arbitration and Peace Association, proposing to lead a 'friendly mission' to intervene with the Mahdi on Gordon's behalf.[4] From his home at Hawarden, a weary Gladstone acknow-ledged the offer, and promised to discuss the matter with Earl Granville, the Liberal party's Leader in the Lords.[5] Blunt's offer was quietly let drop.[6]

Tucked up in bed at Wilbury, and just days into motherhood, Mary must have barely registered these matters. Her diary records only an uncharacteristic interest in food: 'pheasant and baked apples for luncheon', she noted.[7] By convention, new mothers spent a month 'lying in' after the birth. After a spell of bed-rest, and under nurse's instructions, they gradually made 'all the steps back into Life! Such as walking, [putting on] stays [corsets] & sitting on the Commode!', as Mary explained.[8] After that, they were 'churched' with a religious blessing and re-entered society.

Mary was soon bored by lying in, and frustrated by her difficulty in breast-feeding Ego, a fractious infant. As quickly as she could, she threw herself back into the social whirl. Madeline Wyndham chided her daughter for 'racketing around' at the expense of her health and her child. 'The *rule* is that one cannot possibly live in the same way for 2 or even 3 months after "*The Crisis*" as one did before.' But Mary did not listen, and before long her health gave out. In February 1885, Madeline Wyndham and Annie Wemyss joined forces, compelling a 'pale and wasting' Mary to Gosford for 'a nice quiet bit by the sea' with nothing to amuse her except long walks and her child – 'who is a most important *personage*', Madeline reminded her.[9]

Mary never really liked being by herself: 'when I'm alone my spirits go down! Down!' she said,[10] and she found Gosford as depressing as always. 'I am very low but that's not strange!' she told her mother.[11] In fact she was miserable, bursting into tears every time she heard Ego cry. On the advice of her maternity nurse, Mrs Sayers, she began bottle-feeding him, such feeding newly in vogue, as legislation curbing the adulteration of foodstuffs made cow's milk safer than before. Madeline Wyndham, fiercely opposed to the novel practice, immediately besieged her daughter with prophecies of doom: too much milk, she said, might 'fly to *ones head* & make one vy odd for a time! Go to one's leg & lay one up with what is called a milk *leg*.'[12] In her anxiety Madeline became vitriolic, and, though her anger was mostly reserved for the 'wicked' Mrs Sayers for proposing this course, Mary feared she was a bad mother and that her son was not developing as he should. Hugo had remained in London. What news he did deliver was dismal: Stanway's house-keeper had dropped dead from diabetes. Mary's initial shock and sympathy were swiftly replaced by exhaustion and alarm as she wondered how she would possibly find a suitable replacement.

The news in the wider world was just as poor. The relief troops arrived at Khartoum in January 1885 four days too late. The city had fallen. Gordon's head was impaled upon a stick under a sky as blazing as his own eyes. The news was telegraphed back to London. In the press, the GOM of the Midlothian Campaign became the MOG: 'Murderer of Gordon'. In February it was announced that a further dispatch of troops would effect the orig-inal evacuation plan. Among these troops were Hugo's jubilant brother Alan and George Wyndham, 'in the 7th Heaven of delight' at the prospect of a good old rout. 'It's like a death in ones [sic] heart,' said Madeline as she broke the news to Mary.[13] All her forebodings, poured out to Mary in letter after anguished letter, charged towards one impossible truth: George was departing to his death. Percy, who thought this intervention as wrong as all Britain's actions in Egypt thus far, was scarcely more optimistic. In a letter written on the eve of George's departure he assured him that he did not think '*for a moment* your most *precious* life is thrown away' if his son should die in combat.[14] At Gosford, Mary suffered a violent bilious attack. Madeline thought it was a direct response to her 'grief' at the news.[15]

As the troops prepared to leave, the Wemysses travelled south, and the Wyndhams congregated first at Wilbury and then in London. Only Mary was absent, forbidden by both families from making the long journey while she was still frail. She remained with Mrs Sayers and Ego, reliant upon her family's letters for updates. They were not encouraging. 'Tonight is the *awful* night when we say goodbye I never felt such a horrible feeling as it is – Poor darling Rat [Madeline Wyndham] looks so unhappy but she bares [sic] it wonderfully,' Mananai told Mary on the eve of George's departure after a day spent watching the inspection of the troops at Wellington Barracks.[16] The next day they were at the Barracks again, among the cheering crowds waving off the troops in the glittering sunshine of an early-spring day, determined – said Madeline – to show George 'no signs . . . of our sorrow but rejoice in his joy'.[17]

Madeline left London for Gosford. The visit was intended to raise her own spirits as much as her daughter's, but seems rather to have made them confidantes in each other's misery. She then returned to Wilbury 'with a distracted mind & a sad heart & eyes that have gone blind with much crying these last weeks'.[18] The house was in a state of upheaval. Final preparations were being made for the move to Clouds, which was to take place while the Wyndhams were in London for the Season. 'The packing that is going on here is terrific. 3 immense waggons came here the other day and were loaded I don't know how high & then trudged off at six o'clock in

the morning,' Pamela reported to Mary.[19] On finding that her pet
white sparrows had been left unfed and allowed to die in the chaos,
Madeline saw another augury of George's fate.[20] It was not long
before her mind would find another avenue along which to race.

In April 1885 the Gang rejoiced at the engagement of Alfred
Lyttelton to Laura Tennant, two of the most beloved of their group.
All who knew Laura praised her to the point of hyperbole. She was
possessed of 'an extra dose of life, which caused a kind of electricity
to flash about her . . . lighting up all with whom she came into
contact', said Adolphus ('Doll') Liddell, one of the many men in
love with her.[21] Laura was intensely spiritual, very flirtatious and
extremely frank. Mary considered her to be her closest friend. The
two concocted grand plans for a literary salon. Shortly after the
engagement the Elchos jaunted to Paris with Arthur Balfour, Godfrey
Webb and Alfred Lyttelton to visit Laura, who was with Margot and
Lady Tennant shopping for her trousseau. 'We form a fine representative party of Englishmen a married couple, an engaged couple,
"doux garcons" as Webber wd call it in his fine English accent . . .
& Margot does well for a sporting "mees"', Mary told Percy.[22]

In old age Mary recalled the irrepressible Tennant sisters' debut
in London as causing 'a stir indeed – one may almost call it a
Revolution . . . theirs was a plunge, a splash as of a bright pebble
being thrown from an immense height into a quiet pool . . . Many
were startled and most were delighted.'[23] The Tennant girls, unchap-
eroned by their mother, were 'of totally unconventional manners
with no code of behaviour except their own good hearts', as the
wife of Arthur's brother Eustace, Lady Frances Balfour, put it.[24] At
Glen House, the family home in the Scottish Borders, they entertained male guests in their nightgowns in their bedroom, arguing
late into the night over philosophy, spirituality, politics and
psychology. The room was known as the 'Doo-Cot' (Dovecot) in
ironic reference to their heated debates. In London – and in qual-
ification of Mary's recollection – it took them some time to achieve
entrée. Laura met Lady Wemyss – who lived not thirty miles from

Glen at Gosford – only when she married Alfred.[25] Alfred's brother Spencer described the Tennants to his cousin Mary Gladstone as a family of 'brilliant young ladies and vulgar parents'.[26] Mary Elcho, of somewhat unconventional behaviour herself, was captivated from the first.

Mary recounted this week in Paris to her parents in exhaustive, delighted detail. She told them about afternoons dozing on the sofa while Laura played the piano in their little shared sitting room; about their proficiency at lawn tennis that had roused the natives to applause; about their conversation, 'as animated as the most spirited of Frogs'. Mary complained to Percy about the stolid Lady Tennant: 'someone always has to lag & try to talk to her & she talks not at all! Except in the most commonplace manner.' She told them about drives in the Bois de Boulogne, delicious déjeuners and dinners at the Lion d'Or. They went to the Théâtre du Palais-Royal and then, Mary added in strangely bathetic phrase, they 'walked home afterwards'.[27] She did not tell her parents that the person with whom she had walked arm in arm, deep in conversation, on the winding route home was not Hugo but Arthur.[28] On their return to London Arthur dined with the Elchos. Mary was wearing a low-cut gown which startled her guest into an unexpected compliment. 'You have a jolly throat,' he told her, such an effusive comment for the reserved Arthur that Mary openly blushed.[29]

One of the Gang's defining characteristics, stemming directly from the nightgowned Tennant girls entertaining in the Doo-Cot, was their belief that men and women could be intellectual equals, and capable of intimate friendship on the mental plane. They chided scurrilous-minded outsiders, unaccustomed to seeing one man's wife deep in conversation with another woman's husband, for suspecting more earthly inclinations. Among themselves they conceded a little more. Mary described herself to Hugo as a 'little flirt . . .!'[30] but all maintained that this flirtation was innocent. Throughout the early years of their marriage, the Elchos conducted a double romance with the Ribblesdales. The two couples holidayed together in Felixstowe and the New Forest, splitting off into contented pairs: Hugo and Charty, Mary and Tommy. It was convenient, diverting and fundamentally harmless. As Mary explained, 'Migs in practice (flirtation practice) dwells on the ambiguity of implications the possibility of a backdoor or loophole that Tommy considers the word to contain. Migs thinks it doesn't matter *what* she says in her letters to men conks [admirers], provided she only *implies* it . . . for if brought to book she can say that they have misunderstood her – and nice men conks never take one to task.'[31] In essence, it was courtly love, updated: men pursued, women teased, both remained beyond reproach.

Yet Mary and Arthur's relationship was different. 'She reverences him,' said Laura. Worryingly for Laura, upon broaching the issue with Arthur it seemed that he was not 'as indifferent heart-wards to her as I at first thought – he said several things about it that gave me qualms'. Mary and Arthur's obvious mutual attraction was not beclouded by the bavardage of 'flirtation practice'. Within the context of Society this was dangerous: 'the eyesight of the world . . . is vastly farsighted & sees things in embryo', Laura warned Mary.[32] The gossips of the New Club, seeing Mary and Laura dining with Arthur alone, could cause havoc.[33]

Laura was not the only person warning Mary that summer. Shortly after the Elchos had returned from Paris, Madeline Wyndham visited Stanway and had several lengthy private talks with Mary, undoubtedly about Arthur. Afterwards, Mary wrote to thank her: 'I can't say what it was having you here & what it is to have you at all. You are the best influence in my life & stronger than myself . . . as noble healthy & cleansing as a gust of . . . mountain air removing cobwebs from one['s] moral mirror.'[34] But, despite these protestations, her behaviour did not alter at all.

Mary had boasted that her mother, in the years before her marriage, had never quite been able to 'fathom' her. Now, it seemed no one could. Laura, analysing the situation, could only conclude that Mary, in the grip of fascination, neither knew herself nor could help herself, and that moreover infatuation blended with ambition: for 'her affection for Hugo is strangely mixed up with her affection for the man she knows can, will & does help Hugo more than anyone else does'. For Laura, Mary was a woman buffeted by her emotions, and only Laura's firm hand might prevent Mary from sleepwalking into disaster. 'I never allow for a minute when I am with Mary that she is in love with A . . . were I to say "you are in love" she would believe me and poking the fire is productive of flame; & at present the conflagration is chiefly smoke,' she told Frances Balfour, further placing the onus upon Arthur, as one capable of controlling his feelings, to put a stop to things.[35]

A letter written by Mary to her mother that summer suggests otherwise. Madeline Wyndham's anxiety had been exacerbated, rather than eased, by her visit to Stanway. Shortly after leaving Mary, and while visiting her friend Georgie Sumner, she sent Mary a frantic letter. She did not directly mention the subject. Instead over numerous pages of increasingly illegible scrawl she dwelt long on the cautionary tale of Georgie, estranged from her husband, suffering 'deadly remorse', feeling she had 'sinned against God & Man . . . and would die . . . sooner than act again as she did . . .'.[36] 'I thought perhaps you might send me a wopper,' Mary replied, treating her mother to a lengthy, strangely abstract discourse on the nature of wrongdoing. It is a tortuous read, but in short it divides the world into two classes: wrongdoers too stupid or wicked to know they did wrong; and those who knew, but did it anyway, preferring to face the consequences at a later date. Mary classed herself in the latter camp. The only remedy she saw was to 'pray . . . to set one's heart & to keep it fixed in the right direction & day by day the effort will become less . . . the backsliding & driftings less frequent – to be able to make one's will want to do the right thing'.[37] Taken out of the abstract it is a startling admission. Mary's heart was not fixed in the right direction. She wanted to be with Arthur.

The following year, the Elchos and Arthur went on a walking

tour of North Berwick. Printed backwards in tiny letters in Mary's sketchbook from the trip are the words: 'How I wish I could, but you know that would be impossible.' It has been suggested that the 'impossible' thing was divorce, although it might have been sex, or even something more innocent.[38] It is startling to think that Mary could ever truly have contemplated divorce – which would have made her a social pariah, would have given Hugo custody of her children and would have destroyed Arthur's political career. More likely, Mary simply chose not to think of the consequences at all. As Laura later said, it was a case in which 'they hurt other people because they liked themselves too much . . .'.[39] But, for whatever reason, Mary faltered. After Madeline had failed to acknowledge her daughter's easily decipherable code in the summer of 1885, Mary no longer attempted to confide in her. In fact, she seems almost to have stopped communicating at all.

Desperate and panicked, Madeline Wyndham increased the barrage, while still maintaining that nothing was wrong. In frenzied underlinings from Hyères, as Mary's birthday approached, she exhorted the Elchos to '*Cling* on to doing things together . . . *come nearer to each other* . . . you must *both* work together . . . don't get separated in *your lives*.'[40] On the Elchos' wedding anniversary, invoking the memory of the '*good Dear good* single-minded Child' Mary had been two years before, she demanded that 'Hugo . . . keep you from all *pitch* . . . I know he first loved you for *all that* & Married You to have a Wife different from all the world. I'm sick of some of the Wives I see . . . I love you. I believe in you. I worship you.'[41] Mary broke her silence with cheerful obfuscation and a generous approach to the truth. 'Hugo read . . . the birthday exhortation & wondered whether you thought I didn't care for him any more!' she said, 'but I told him yr words were as warnings not as remedies . . . I don't think two people could easily be more united than we are & will always strive to be . . . I would rather kill myself than make you miserable & disappointed in me.'[42]

Mary fell pregnant shortly afterwards (her second son, Guy

Lawrence, was born on 23 May 1886). Yet the fact of her pregnancy was not enough to calm a 'wretched' Annie Wemyss, who had also heard the rumours, and that autumn recruited Laura to keep Mary and Arthur apart. Laura enlisted Frances Balfour. The two conspired to prevent Arthur from going to Stanway in December, for the house party which was fast becoming an annual tradition, ditching it themselves in order to keep him away: 'v [sic] good of us I think!' said Laura, who used her own six-months' pregnancy as an excuse.[43] In the early months of the new year Laura trailed Mary like a shadow: almost every engagement with Arthur set down by Mary in her diary, whether visiting Sir John Millais' new gallery or drinking hot chocolate at Charbonnel et Walker in the West End, notes Laura gently, inexorably interposing herself between the two, trying with all her might to reduce their relationship to innocent friendship.

SIX

Clouds

As soon as the Stanway party ended, Mary left to join her family for their first Christmas at Clouds. The Wyndhams had finally moved in in September 1885. Throughout the autumn her excited younger sisters had bombarded her with letters giving her every detail of their 'scrumtious [sic]' new domain.[1] If Mary was disappointed by Arthur's previous absence, she showed no signs of this to her family. She arrived at Clouds, loaded down with 'millions of packages', Ego, his nurse Wilkes (known as 'Wilkie'), her poodle Stella and a cageful of canaries, and was rushed around the house by her sisters demanding to know if it was exactly as she had imagined. All Mary could manage was 'delightful'.[2]

The house was enormous. Built of green sandstone with a red-brick top floor, it looked like a storybook house that, like Alice, had found a cake saying 'eat me' and mushroomed to a hundred times its normal size. 'I . . . keep discovering new rooms inside and windows outside,' marvelled Georgie Burne-Jones on her first visit in November.[3] Half a century later, an estate agent's particulars listed five principal reception rooms, a billiard room, thirteen principal bedrooms and dressing rooms, a nursery suite of two bedrooms, twelve other bedrooms, a separate wing of domestic offices including thirteen staff bedrooms, stabling for twenty-three horses, garaging for four cars (presumably carved out of the stabling facilities) and a model laundry.[4]

The nerve centre of the house was a spacious sky-lit central hall, two storeys high. Opening off it at ground-floor level were Percy's suite of rooms – bedroom, bathroom, dressing room, study – and the reception rooms – billiard room, waiting room, smoking room, dining room, adjacent dining service room, and the long south-facing drawing room and music room, connected by double doors, where floor-to-ceiling French windows revealed a wide grass terrace melding gently into the misty Downs beyond. Magnolia trees clustered up against those walls, with a border of roses, myrtles and rosemary beneath. Spiralling stone staircases in the hall's corners led up to a vaulted, cloistered gallery overlooking the hall, off which were the family's bedrooms; and up again to the nurseries and housemaids' rooms on the top floor. The lower ground floor was the masculine domestic sphere. There the under-butler slept, guarding the gun room, wine cellars and butler's pantry where the family silver and other valuables were locked in the plate closet.[5] There too were the butler's sitting room, odd-man's room, lamp room, gun room and brushing room, dedicated entirely to brushing dirt off woollen clothes.

The servants' offices, where the majority of Clouds' thirty-odd indoor staff slept, were connected to the main house on the ground floor through the dining service room and on the lower ground floor by a web of subterranean passages. The offices were a long, low wing designed by Philip Webb to look like a series of cottages, with un-cottage-like proportions. The beamed servants' hall was nearly 40 feet long; the housekeeper Mrs Vine's bedroom and sitting room two-thirds as large. The housekeeper's ground-floor rooms led directly to the china closet, the table linen room, the still room, store rooms, larder, game larder and bakehouse: all her responsibility and domain. Forbes the butler slept on the first floor, next to the footmen's rooms, where he could keep an eye on them. Footmen, chosen specifically for their height, good looks and turn of calf, were apt to be troublesome. Further rooms for visiting valets were beyond. At the far end of the offices was the gardener's cottage of Harry Brown, who had come with the Wyndhams from Wilbury; beyond that stood the stables with their controversial bricks.

The vast kitchen was modelled on a medieval abbot's kitchen at Glastonbury. Huge joints of meat roasted on a spit over the fire kept turning by a hot-air engine. The dripping, caught in a vat beneath, was sold to East Knoyle's villagers for a penny per portion. Next door the scullery maids scrubbed stacks of dishes and dirty pans. In a separate laundry building containing washing house, ironing room and drying room, four local girls washed and rinsed muslins, linens, cottons and woollens three days a week, mangling, starching and ironing for another two. A house like Clouds might go through on average 1,000 napkins a week; soap and soda were delivered annually by the ton and half-ton.[6]

The imaginative gardens, designed for tête-à-têtes, were a collaboration between Madeline Wyndham and Harry Brown. Madeline's bedroom on the main house's east side overlooked a series of gardens, walled on one side by the offices (which were covered in vines and fig trees). The gardens were 'a succession of lovely surprises', said Harry Brown, with rose gardens, yew hedges clipped to resemble peacocks' tails, a chalk-walled spring garden blooming annually with tulips, narcissus and cyclamens, and a pergola garden. The garden to the house's north-west, with its winding 'river walk' (so-called by the family), was wilder. Cedar trees towered in the distance. The walk itself was planted with bluebells, primroses, Japanese iris, azaleas, bamboos, magnolias and rhododendrons.[7]

When the Wyndhams moved in, the house was not quite complete. The hall's chandeliers had yet to arrive; the drawing room's intricate plasterwork was not finished until 1886. The plumbing was so full of glitches that Percy complained it required the assistance of the house carpenter and an engineer for 'a common warm bath'.[8] The house had to be unpacked, and decorated. 'Lately the floors have been strewn with scraps of carpet and we have stood with our heads on one side . . .,' said a perplexed Mananai.[9]

When finished, the house had a distinctive scent of cedar wood, beeswax and magnolias[10] and was decorated with near-monastic simplicity. Percy's bedroom was papered in Morris print. Otherwise all the ground-floor rooms were painted white, their woodwork unpolished oak. Against the hall's stone walls hung two large tapestries: 'Greenery' commissioned from Morris & Co., and a Flemish hunting scene. Over the vast fireplace was a large painting, believed to be by the Italian Renaissance painter Alesso Baldovinetti, of *The Virgin Adoring the Christ Child with the Infant St John the Baptist and Angels in a Forest*, bought by Percy at auction.[11] A Morris carpet, pale pink, green, blue and white, covered the floor. The hall had little furniture: a Broadwood piano, four black-lacquer cabinets, and chairs upholstered in Morris's 'Honeysuckle' design.

The light-flooded drawing room, filled with comfortable sofas and chairs, was piled high with periodicals and books rebound by Madeline Wyndham in her favoured vellum. There was no library, books were everywhere in the house, with a trolley for trundling them about.[12] At the drawing room's far end stood Madeline's 'scrattle table' – at which she sketched, and wrote, hands constantly moving even as 'her mind was free, moving among her guests'.[13] The furniture was eighteenth-century Hepplewhite or Chippendale. On the walls – finally displayed to perfection – was the Wyndhams' collection of many years: works by the Pre-Raphaelites; the Etruscan School; and Old Italian Masters. Over the main staircase hung Burne-Jones's cartoon of the Ascension, depicting in glowing raw umber and gilt 'the figure of Christ blessing those on Earth from above surrounded by the Arch-Angels'.[14] This might well have been the house depicted by Henry James in *The Spoils of Poynton*: 'the record of a life . . . written in great syllables of colour and form, the tongues of other countries and the hands of rare artists . . . all France and Italy, with their ages composed to rest. For England you looked out of old windows – it was England that was the wide embrace.'

In every room cushioned baskets awaited Madeline's pampered fleet of fox terriers; more than thirty peacocks and peahens strutted through the gardens. The South Terrace beyond the drawing room rang to the 'wild satanic laughter' of a pair of African jackasses;[15] fifty to sixty doves, which were fed in the Walnut Tree Court, flew freely about the rooms.[16] Three times a day, Madeline scattered birdfeed outside to attract wild birds. A packing box used originally for Mananai's possessions was turned into a squirrel house, still bearing the faded legend 'Miss Wyndham's bedroom'.[17] The house teemed with life.

The Wyndhams' arrival at Clouds coincided with George's return from the Sudan with tales of some 'hot' engagements and a souvenir in the form of a 3-foot-long Crusader sword liberated from a Sudanese prisoner of war.[18] Madeline was 'simply *brimming over* with thankfulness' at entering the house with her family safe and well.[19] From the very first Christmas the family showed themselves diligent and generous squires. Madeline provided each of East Knoyle's 190 or so schoolchildren with a new, warm jumper.[20] Semley station's employees were invited to toast and ale on Boxing Day. On New Year's Eve the family threw a staff ball with dancing from 10 p.m. to 3 a.m.; an orchestra was bussed in from Salisbury, chairs laid out along the passages for sitting out and rooms provisioned with card tables for those who preferred gin rummy to waltzing. A music show was held in which footmen and kitchen maids displayed their talents.[21] George reinforced his hero status by rescuing a village child who had fallen through the bathing pond's ice – although, due to ongoing plumbing problems, he could not have a hot bath afterwards. 'There is something refreshing in the idea of patrician and plebean [sic] after their common danger being relegated to the humble copper kettle of daily use but that is not what I am paying for,' wrote Percy to his architect Philip Webb, unable to resist a good-natured dig.[22]

Percy, like all his family, was delighted with their new house. Clouds was the embodiment of their exceptionalism. And though the Wyndhams' friend Godfrey Webb thought, privately, the house 'the largest and ugliest in England', for the most part the Wyndhams were flooded in praise. 'Influential people (or donkeys as you would call them) are putting it about that this is the house of the age. I believe they are right,' Percy wrote to his architect, as he surveyed his new domain.[23]

The villagers of East Knoyle and Milton greeted the rising up of a great house in their midst with feudal-like enthusiasm. They twice turned out to cheer the family's arrival, East Knoyle's church bells pealing in celebration, when Percy, Guy, Mananai, Pamela and Fräulein arrived on the afternoon of 23 September 1885, and when George and Madeline, delayed by George's regimental inspection, followed the next day.[24] The handsome, eccentric family was a source of fascination: village children whispered that drawling, impeccably dressed Percy had his valet wash the coins jingling in his pocket, so bleached clean did he seem (in fact, such a practice was quite common and the rumour probably accurate). By contrast Madeline 'never seemed like an ordinary rich person . . . she . . . was the easiest and most sympathetic person to talk to that I have ever met,' remembered Violet Milford, one of the daughters of the Canon of East Knoyle church.[25]

The house and the village existed in symbiosis. The Wyndhams had brought some staff with them from Wilbury – Tommy the valet, Eassy and tall, tranquil Bertha Devon, a housemaid who joined the family in Cumberland and spent her entire service life in their employ. Others were recruited from the locality. When a bad spate of influenza struck East Knoyle, Madeline Wyndham took Mananai and Pamela with her to visit the sick 'nearly everyday',[26] and shortly afterwards employed a London-trained nurse permanently to attend the parish's sick. Each day lunch's leftovers were delivered by the little girls and Fräulein to the cottages of the poor – piled up, as was customary, in one pungent mess.

The village's children remembered Punch & Judy shows in the hall at Christmas; charity bazaars where the female Wyndhams manned the stalls; vast feasts held to celebrate the marriages of each of the Wyndham children where all the toys in the nurseries were turned out on to the lawns – a very heaven.[27]

Clouds was to become famous as a 'palace of weekending', in the phrase of William Lethaby, the architectural historian and propagandist for the Society for the Protection of Ancient Buildings and for the Arts and Crafts Movement, whose writings disseminated the works of his friends Philip Webb and William Morris to the next generation.[28] The press would focus on the fact that, from the late 1880s, Clouds was where Arthur Balfour spent each Easter, passing his days playing golf on the private links built by Percy, and engaging in brilliant 'general conversation' at dinner, of which he was always the star. Mary recalled those Easters in later years: when she met the golfers for lunch in a 'small furze hut' on the links, and as the party drank Château-Yquem provided by Percy, discussions between Balfour, Percy, the physicist Sir Oliver Lodge and George Wyndham, among others, ranged across politics, philosophy, literature and science, while 'the gorse shed its fragrance and the larks sang'.[29]

Clouds, a place where politicians of all complexions, primarily Souls, convened, was a house of esoteric delights, overseen by a consummate hostess. Madeline Wyndham was impervious to obstacles when the opportunity of delighting people arose. On a September day in 1883, Mananai and Pamela's lessons had been interrupted by the sight, from the schoolroom window, of an elephant trundling a yellow cart down the drive. Madeline Wyndham, taking a morning constitutional on the Downs, had encountered a travelling menagerie and persuaded it to divert its course so as to amuse her daughters. 'We fed the "oily phant" with buns and bread and he . . . drank some beer, his ears were enormous just like umbrellas,' Mananai reported excitedly to Mary.[30] At Clouds, Madeline Wyndham's munificence was given full force.

Regular guests arrived to find hand-bound copies of their favourite books at their bedside (a favourite family anecdote concerned a tiny bound copy of the Lord's Prayer, which contained a slip bearing 'the Author's Compliments').[31] In the evenings, Madeline plied them with blankets while listening to recitals in the hall. Masseuses were on hand to give 'Swedish rubbing'; in front of a blackboard, Lodge (later President of Birmingham University), who played a key role in the development of wireless telegraphy, gave lectures on 'electrons' and 'cyclones'; gymnastics classes were conducted in the garden; and invariably in a darkened room somewhere in the house a spiritualist was conducting a bout of table-turning for the Wyndhams' guests.[32] Madeline had been a convert to spiritualism since inviting her first medium to Wilbury in 1884,[33] and at Clouds the Wyndhams hosted the most prominent theorists of the day – Edward Maitland, Gerald Massey, Edmund Gurney, Frederic Myers and Lord and Lady Mount Temple.[34] Walburga, Lady Paget, an eccentric vegetarian, thought Clouds perfection in all its entertainments, except for the adders that slithered through the Downs preventing her from walking barefoot through the morning dew.[35]

In microcosm, Clouds reflected 'the oncoming of a great new tide of human life over the Western World', in the words of the sage Edward Carpenter – a post-Darwinian, post-Industrial Revolution experimentalism, seeking to find meaning in and improve the new age.[36] The spiritualist craze exemplifies the way, in this age, optimism and anxiety combined. Balfour, Ruskin, Tennyson, Watts, Leighton, Oliver Lodge, Sigmund Freud, Gladstone and William James, psychologist brother of Henry, were all members of the Society for Psychical Research (the SPR), founded by a group of Cambridge scientists in 1882 'for the purpose of inquiring into a mass of obscure phenomena which lie at present on the outskirts of our organized knowledge'.[37] Their number included two of Balfour's brothers-in-law: John, Lord Rayleigh, husband of Evelyn Balfour; and Henry Sidgwick, husband of Eleanor Balfour. In an age of extraordinary exploration, it seemed quite possible that science might be able to communicate with a world beyond the earthly plane. One of the SPR's founders, Frederic Myers, was a reluctant atheist and spoke for many when admitting that his spiritualism was driven by the desire to 're-enter . . . by the scullery . . . the heavenly mansion out of which I had been kicked through the front door'.[38]

Madeline Wyndham, who designed beautiful prie-dieus for her children, and illustrated biblical tracts to hang above their beds, had no difficulty in reconciling her powerful religious faith with a belief in a 'sproits and spiris [sic]'.[39] Pamela, who adopted her mother's creed more enthusiastically than her siblings, in later life explained her teachings: 'I learned that death is an incident in life . . . that communication with those we call the dead, under certain conditions is possible . . . never was I led for a moment to think that [spiritualism] should stand in the place of religion . . . Spiritualism supports rather than conflicts with [the] narratives of the life of Christ.'[40]

Percy was more sceptical. But he was certainly a little superstitious. In the spring of 1885, as builders were putting the finishing touches to Clouds, a tall woman dressed in black appeared, asking to see the house. She was shown inside – such requests were not uncommon. She stood in the dusty hall, the walls rearing up around her. 'This house will be burnt down and in less than three years,' she announced, before disappearing as mysteriously as she had arrived.[41] When later that year Percy arranged with Webb for the insurance of the house and its outbuildings, he expressed particular concern about the provision for loss by fire.

Clouds' magical luxury depended on a silent army of staff. Its occupants woke to fires crackling in the grate, laid soundlessly by a housemaid who had risen long before dawn and had then scurried downstairs to clear away the previous evening's detritus: wine-stained glasses, full ashtrays in the smoking room; pieces of paper from a game, torn up and carelessly thrown aside. While the family and guests breakfasted, staff flung open windows to air bedrooms, whipped off still-warm sheets to remake beds perfectly and emptied chamberpots. Then they dusted, swept, polished and mended linen before preparing the bedrooms again for their occupants to dress for dinner (men attended by their valets, women by their ladies' maids); and again while the house dined, they were drawing curtains, lighting candles, turning down beds. Rarely did they throw their exhausted bodies on to their own mattresses before eleven or twelve at night.

Sarah, 'the pretty 2nd housemaid' at Clouds, was probably glad to leave service when she married Pearson the coachman and set up in his rooms above the coachhouse. She was fortunate in being able to live with her husband. Married footmen, valets or butlers lived separately from their wives, setting them up in a nearby cottage, and visiting them on their days off. The wife of William Icke, Clouds' butler from 1892, was housekeeper to two spinster ladies in East Knoyle. Her loyalty was rewarded when they left her their house in their will.[42] Housekeepers and cooks, who bore the courtesy title of 'Mrs', could actually be married – the Wyndham children's nanny of Cumberland days, Horsenail, had in fact married Forbes, graduating to housekeeper in the days before Mrs Vine. Otherwise, a female servant who married would immediately leave her employ.

In 1891 there were over one and a half million domestic servants in the United Kingdom – almost 16 per cent of the workforce.[43] Service was an honourable profession with loyalty and affection on both sides. Eassy and Bertha Devon both stayed with the Wyndhams until retirement, the former then moving to a cottage in East Knoyle. Nonetheless, in 1898 the average length of stay by a servant in a household was less than eighteen months.[44] The turnover at Clouds, from the names on the ten-yearly censuses, was not notably different. The reasons were numerous: marriage; a promotion elsewhere; or abandonment of domestic service entirely. Periodicals like the *Lady* complained of young men and women with 'ideas above their station', thinking themselves too good for service. As the century wore on, many did, rejecting the snobbish hierarchy of the servants' hall for the greater freedom and excitement available in other jobs. All Madeline's daughters bemoaned the impossibility of finding good staff.

In 1884, domestic calm was rocked by a young woman's distress: 'poor Lucy the housemaid in London I'm afraid she has gone mad – she went for a holiday & came back *quite off her head*'. The situation, relayed by Mrs Vine to Madeline, and thence to her daughters, was grave, if comical. Lucy, whose head Madeline thought had been 'turned' by the marriage of her fellow housemaid Mary Brown, veered between lucidity and moments of 'wild' behaviour. Following a composed conversation with Dr Gibbons, the doctor summoned to examine her, Lucy 'came down and said to Bertha "if I take *any one* I think *I'll take Dr Gibbons!*"'

While amused by Mrs Vine's decorous alarm, Madeline nonetheless took the matter seriously. She reported to Mary:

> it is quite too awfully sad . . . she is *full of* delusions thinks people are coming to take her *away* & that something dreadful will happen because Mary Brown had to sign some cheques for her that they will f[i]nd out she could not wright [sic] and a lot more I told her that she must not let her self give way . . . but . . . she is so miserable she would break her heart Bertha & Charlotte had to sit up with her & hold her down in bed. *Don't* talk about this with anyone but is it not horrid?[45]

History does not relate what happened to Lucy. She does not appear in the 1891 census either for Clouds or for Belgrave Square. Presumably she was dispatched back to her family: it is likely that Madeline took care to make sure someone would look after her.

Reportage of such untoward incidents was part of the traffic of communication between Madeline and her daughters: their own children picked up snippets and came to Clouds wide-eyed, alert to a servant to whom such gossip had lent an air of celebrity. Lizzie Beaver, the still-room maid (in charge of cakes, jam and preserves, so a good person for hungry children to befriend), nearly died when, returning from the village to Clouds early in the morning of 31 December 1886, she got lost in snow and fog, and was only found at midday on New Year's Day, frozen half to death. Howard 'the married stable-man' slipped over when carrying a heavy sack and injured his back badly enough to be confined to lying 'quite still' for a lengthy period of time. The daughter of Wareham the under-coachman suffered from paralysed legs, 'the awful result, it was thought, of sitting on a cold stone when she was very hot'. Eassy raised the alarm in 1888 with fears about her own heart, although Dr Collins pronounced her as suffering only from 'nervous shock' – most likely a panic attack, for reasons unknown. In 1892, Enfield, who had replaced Forbes as butler in 1888, was struck by a sudden 'chill' and 'rheumatic pains' one Friday night that left him 'unable to wait at dinner', followed swiftly by 'inflammation of the brain . . . he died in convulsions at 2.30 o'clock'.[46] Enfield's wife, who had gone to London 'to be confined', was left to give birth to a fatherless child.

In her youth Madeline Wyndham had compiled a photograph album of 'all the dear Servants at Petworth', with handwritten commentary beneath, explaining who each subject was.[47] Yet she, like most, thought nothing of loaning her daughters a spare footman when they had large house parties 'in the same way the poor borrow a frying pan, or a rub of soap', said an ex-butler, Eric Horne, scornfully in a bestselling memoir published in 1923.[48] Percy rewarded his favourite, William Mallett, the clerk of works responsible for all maintenance on the house and estate, with a house that was two cottages knocked into one. It allowed Mallett – who had worked his way up from house carpenter – a comparatively palatial four bedrooms for his family of eleven. But Percy's attitude towards his staff was aristocratic, to say the least. Hyde, Clouds' head keeper, lost a finger when Percy swung round carelessly and pulled the trigger of his gun. That might have been sheer absent-mindedness. The occasion on which Percy shot a beater called Fletcher in the foot for picking up the wrong pheasant most certainly was not.[49]

SEVEN

The Birth of the Souls

As Percy became East Knoyle's squire, he abandoned national politics for local. To an extent, his hand was forced. Gladstone's 1884 Franchise Act extended household suffrage to the countryside, adding 1.7 million voters to the electorate.[1] Of far more radical effect was the associated 1885 Redistribution Act, which in Robin Hood fashion took seats from over-represented rural constituencies to give to the under-represented towns. Manchester's representatives were doubled from three to six, Wiltshire's reduced from fifteen to six. Percy's West Cumberland seat was one of over seventy abolished.

H. M. Hyndman's Democratic Federation, whose members included William Morris and Eleanor Marx, daughter of the revolutionary thinker Karl, did not think it went far enough. It showed its socialist colours by renaming itself the Social Democratic Federation and organizing a series of unruly street meetings of the unemployed demanding 'work or bread'.[2] At the opposite end of the political spectrum, Percy thought it the beginning of the end of aristocratic rule. Paradoxically he was saved, in his mind, by Gladstone himself.

In June 1885, Gladstone resigned, discredited by General Gordon's martyrdom and finally brought down after being defeated on an amendment to the Budget. Lord Salisbury formed a caretaker government. An election was held over three weeks in late November and early December. Almost on the day the election ended, Herbert Gladstone 'flew the Hawarden Kite', leaking to the press the spectacular news that his father, deep in thought over the summer, had converted to Home Rule and was prepared to take office to implement it. The election results showed how meaningful this was. Parnell's Irish Nationalists, now formally committed to Home Rule, held the balance of power.

That Liberalism should be allied to Home Rule was not inevitable in the shadowy boxing and coxing that took place over Christmas and in the early new year. Herbert Gladstone's bombshell, partly a ham-fisted attempt to drum up support for Home Rule across the fractured Liberal party, alienated significant Whig and Radical tranches of the party. Gladstone appears to have wanted the Conservatives to put the measure forward themselves. But it became clear that Salisbury's conception of empire demanded unity, not the pluralistic view Gladstone proposed.[3] In January 1886, Parliament reconvened under Salisbury's minority government. Gladstone moved an amendment to the Address (that is, to the Queen's Speech). Supported by the Irish, he brought the government down, and himself to power for a third time.

The news was greeted with gloom at Clouds. 'What *do* you think of the Govt being out?!!!! Worst fears realized, says Papa,' Mary told Hugo.[4] The next day, still enraged, she wrote Hugo an impassioned letter sitting in bed after breakfast: 'the irish [sic] party can turn *any* Government out or in, me thinks!. . . besides which its [sic] infamous that the old scoundrel should have had the joy of getting in again . . . I'm sure he is singing in his tub lustily of mornings & Mrs. G must be much elated & foreign politics will go to the devil again . . .'[5] Mary adhered to the Salisburian view and thought Home Rule must lead to imperial disintegration. But neither Mary nor Percy had fully read the runes of the vote. Twenty Whigs, led by Lord Hartington, had voted with the Conservatives, against the amendment. The Liberal party's disintegration had begun.

A week later, Mary, now some six months pregnant, visited London to buy furniture for the Elchos' new house in Chelsea, 62 Cadogan Square.[6] The Elchos had left North Audley Street after a little more than a year for another rented house in Hans Place in Chelsea of which they proved no more fond.[7] Mary's political fervour had been superseded by thoughts of interior design, as she plotted how to achieve Morris-inspired style on the Elchos' comparatively limited budget. She was staying with her parents-in-law in Mayfair, and had left Ego with her parents at Clouds; after a series of visits to friends throughout January, she felt as though she had barely seen her son for weeks, and she told her mother she felt 'quite shy' of seeing him again.[8]

It was an exceptionally cold winter. The freezing temperatures amplified distress caused by prolonged economic depression. In early February serious riots broke out – literally on Mary's doorstep – after sparks flew when socialist marchers, up to 10,000 of them, were provoked by servants of the gentlemen's clubs along Pall Mall. Windows throughout the length of Clubland were smashed, shops on Piccadilly looted, 'nobs' pulled from their carriages and stripped of their valuables. For several days London looked like 'a city under siege'. As a thick black fog blanketed the city, wild rumours spread of a further march of 50,000 unemployed.[9] Mary was strangely oblivious; 'there was a demonstration of the unemployed today & they broke all the windows in St. James's',[10] she told her mother in an offhand postscript to a letter about beds. Thereafter, her letters resumed their exclusivity of subject: furniture. 'I think about *nothing* else.'[11]

This was not quite true. A week after the riots, around St Valentine's Day, Mary went privately to visit Arthur Balfour at 4 Carlton Gardens, which had been at the heart of the affray. Twenty years later, she wrote to him preparing to recreate the incident: 'I must settle to pay my first visit to yr house . . . and be received by you alone and step over the threshold and I shall remember a certain day exactly 20 yrs ago. f-rst k-ss.'[12] Shortly afterwards, Mary wrote to Hugo from St James's Place in a particularly affectionate manner. 'Me feels xceeding [sic] full of tremendous love for Wash,' she told him.[13] It would set a pattern.

At Easter, Mary and Hugo went to Stanway. They had not been alone in the country 'for a "minit" hardly since we married', said Mary, explaining to her mother why they would not spend the holiday with the Wyndhams at Clouds.[14] Their days at 'Stangewange' were a success. 'You can't imagine how delicious it is here & we're having the nicest Time, I think since we married,' Mary told Laura Lyttelton. Laura immediately passed the news to Arthur verbatim, adding, with masterful tact: 'Knowing you a little I think [this] will please you . . . I am v. happy about this . . . and you must be too, dear old friend.'[15] Was wily Laura double-bluffing: did she really know what had taken place at Carlton Gardens just a few weeks before? Possibly – for Margot Tennant, to whom Laura was close as a twin, allowed to Wilfrid Blunt, years later, that Arthur might once have kissed Mary, although she adamantly denied the possibility of anything more.[16]

A few weeks later, in London, Laura gave birth to a healthy boy. At Stanway, Mary, now entertaining a party including the Brodricks and Godfrey Webb, rejoiced. But Laura's apparent good health began to fade. On 24 April 1886, with an ashen Alfred and Margot by her bedside, she died, her last words: 'I think God has forgotten me.' She was twenty-three. Tommy Ribblesdale telegraphed Stanway with the news: 'all over between 9 & 10 this morning'. 'She was not able to struggle through after all, poor thing,' Mary wrote in her diary that night as thunderstorms raged outside and light flooded through the oriel window into the hall. 'It makes one utterly miserable.'[17]

When Laura had written to Arthur, she had added a postscript. She had a premonition that she might not survive childbirth and wanted to say goodbye – just in case. 'Probably I shan't – die I mean but if I do don't say "She might have been etc . . ." cause I can't be,' she told him.[18] In fact, Margot's statement that 'Laura made & left a deeper impression on the world in her short life than anyone I have ever known' was, for once, without embellishment.[19] The number of grandees who flocked to Laura in her final days was astonishing for a young woman who had only recently broken into Society – Spencer Lyttelton cattily commented on the Bart's ill-concealed pleasure – notwithstanding his grave anxiety – 'at being surrounded by so many Lords and Honourables and receiving such an amazing quantity of inquiries'.[20] Burne-Jones created a memorial, choosing a peacock to symbolize the brief splendour of her life. Laura's death left Mary bereft. She wrote bleakly to her mother:

> We had so counted on living . . . our lives together . . . at least I feel how much I had counted on it . . . & bringing up our babies & helping one another . . . all the future was mixed up with her; for she twined into everyone's joys & sorrows . . . it seems beastly being allowed to live when other people . . . the best & most needed people are not.[21]

In her will Laura left Mary a Chippendale cradle, and a crescent necklace that was a wedding present from Arthur to Laura. 'She must wear it because 2 of her dear friends are in it, as it were,' Laura directed. It was presumably a public benediction intended to scour out any remaining hint of scandal.[22] In fact, Laura's death – or perhaps her final letter to Arthur – temporarily drove a wedge between the two. The day after Laura's funeral Arthur visited Mary at the Elchos' new house. Alone in the half-finished drawing room he attacked her for being 'hard' and failing to give him the 'comfort' he sought. He did not explain what that 'comfort' was. Probably Balfour, unmoored by Laura's death, did not know himself. Mary, as so often in moments of extreme emotional turmoil, was tongue-tied. After Arthur had left, she spent a sleepless night poring over her feelings. The next day she wrote to apologize for her inability to lessen the 'awful blank' left by Laura's death. 'If you could really know my thoughts "hard" would be the very very last word you could apply . . . I would do anything for you . . . you must forgive me.'[23]

In mourning, Laura's friends and family withdrew from Society for the remainder of the Season. The Gang all later believed their particular closeness had been fostered by this intense period in the sombre late spring of 1886. In the summer, Margot and the Ribblesdales joined the Elchos quietly at Felixstowe, and later visited Stanway with George Curzon, Evan Charteris and Arthur.[24] Mary's engagements throughout the autumn were predominantly with the Gang. In October, the Elchos were at the Tennants' Glen with Arthur, the Ribblesdales, Godfrey Webb and George Curzon. In November, they entertained at Stanway those same people, minus Webb, but plus Violet Manners, wife of John Manners, the future Duke of Rutland, Lucy Graham Smith (another Tennant sister), Doll Liddell and Earl and Countess de Grey. Ten days later they were at Ashridge in Hertfordshire, home of Lord and Lady Brownlow, with the Brownlows' nephew and heir Harry Cust, the Brodricks, the Pembrokes and Arthur. In December, they were at Clouds, with George Wyndham, the Ribblesdales, Arthur, the Pembrokes and Margot; in January, at Wilton with Sir Jack and Lady Horner (the latter, Frances Graham, was Mary's childhood friend) and Harry Cust.[25] Returning to Society's 'dreary ocean', the Gang had found how much they preferred their company to that of anyone else.[26]

Society frowned upon cliquishness. It was considered somehow improper. More unusual in the autumn of 1886 was that a group containing Liberals and Conservatives was meeting at all. Gladstone's determination to press on with Home Rule had torn his party, and Society, apart. In June, his Home Rule Bill was defeated by the Conservatives, allied with ninety erstwhile Liberals, an uneasy combination of Radicals led by Joseph Chamberlain, the

charismatic, opportunistic ex-Mayor of Birmingham, and Lord
Hartington's Whig grandees. The defectors became known, in Lord
Randolph Churchill's phrase, as Liberal Unionists, the allied forces
as Unionists. As Wilde had Lady Bracknell explain, Liberal Unionists
now 'count as Tories. They dine with us. Or come in the evening,
at any rate.'

The schism over Home Rule paved the way for almost twenty
years of Conservative hegemony. The Whig defection rendered the
Unionists almost impeccably the party of the aristocracy, with an
unassailable majority in the Lords. It allowed the Radical element
of the Liberal party (those that remained) formerly at the fringes,
tempered by the Whigs, to move to the mainstream.[27] It was to give
grist to the Lords' argument that their role was to prevent 'hasty
and foolish' legislation by a hotheaded Commons. In the short
term, it split Society. At Grosvenor Square, home of the devoutly
Liberal Tennants, Margot was sent from the table in disgrace for
declaring at dinner that she thought Gladstone had erred in his
judgement (the unrepentant Margot was unruffled: when the Bart
came to bring her back to the table, he found his youngest daughter
swinging her legs on the billiard table enjoying one of his cigars).[28]
By the autumn Unionists and Liberals no longer met.

Only the Gang refused 'to sacrifice private friendship to public
politics'.[29] In Margot's grand recollections, 'at our house . . . and
those of the Souls, everyone met. Randolph Churchill, Gladstone,
Asquith, Morley, Chamberlain, Balfour, Rosebery, Salisbury,
Hartington, Harcourt and, I might add, jockeys, actors, the Prince
of Wales and every ambassador in London'. Margot thought it 'made
London the centre of the most interesting society in the world and
gave men of different tempers and opposite beliefs an opportunity
of discussing them without heat and without reporters'.[30]

In later years the Souls looked back proudly on their influence
as a cross-party group containing some of the country's brightest
political hopes. They were buoyantly confident of the abilities of
their men: Margot recounted an afternoon spent by Souls women

discussing which of George Curzon, George Wyndham or Harry Cust would become Prime Minister.[31] Politics was the warp and weft of the Souls' daily lives. But they were more than that: a 'fascinating, aristocratic, intellectual coterie',[32] a group with a 'special charm'.[33] 'I think they sent us all back to reading more than we otherwise would have done, and this was an excellent thing for us,' said Daisy, Countess of Warwick, one of the Prince of Wales's Marlborough House Set.[34] Others mocked them for being self-absorbed, cliquey and pretentious. Those who did not spend all their time on the hunting field found them intellectually insubstantial. 'They read the Bible & they read the Morte d'Arthur in the same spirit,' said Wilfrid Blunt.[35]

In November 1886, Mary sat for a chalk and crayon portrait by Edward Poynter. Hugo, for unknown reasons, had resisted the idea, and Mary found the sittings a 'nuisance'.[36] In the portrait, Mary, wistfully pensive, leans back on a chaise, gazing into the distance. She is surrounded by aestheticism's accoutrements: a japonaiserie screen; blue and white ceramic vases. Her hair is fashionably shirred; her waist, in her plain mustard-yellow gown, tiny (the envy of her friends, she said proudly). One hand loosely holds a sketchbook, another book lies unopened before her. She looks deep in thought: a beauty with greater things on her mind. The features of a child are still there in her face, but her languid ease suggests someone increasingly comfortable with her place in the world.

Poynter captured many elements of a typical Souls woman in this portrait. He reflected her style of clothing – Souls women did not, by and large, indulge in feathers and furs but dressed 'with a kind of aesthetic smartness all their own', said Lady Tweedsmuir, wife of the author John Buchan.[37] Arthur was quite alarmed when Mary proposed having a gown made by Worth, the grand Parisian couturier of the day, commenting that he did not expect to recognize her in such finery.[38] Poynter also alluded to her intellectual, artistic bent (as a corollary, the tables of Souls hostesses were comparatively frugal by the standards of their time and class.

Conversation, rather than rich food, sustained their guests,[39] and Souls women were, in general, notably slim).

Yet Poynter, himself not renowned for his sense of humour,[40] had failed to capture the essence of Mary, and the group to which she was integral. Her family thought the portrait far too solemn, capturing none of the 'dancing gaiety' of her eyes, or the swallow-like quickness of her movement.[41] In the flesh all the Souls – charismatic, mostly young and unusually good-looking – seemed simply to be having fun. Daisy Warwick considered them 'more pagan than soulful'.[42] Lady Tweedsmuir described them as 'a little suspect as not conforming to the rules of the social game'.[43] They were impossibly flirtatious with one another, while publicly advocating chastity. They were irreverent, renaming the group's elder statesmen, the Cowpers, Brownlows and Pembrokes, 'the Aunts'. Balfour, their lodestar, was 'the adored Gazelle'. They loved games: 'Clumps', requiring participants to guess by questions abstractions like 'the last straw', 'the eleventh hour' or even 'the last ball Mr Balfour drove into the [golf] bunker before lunch'; 'Styles', parodying well-known authors in prose or verse; 'Epigrams', inventing new ones; 'Character Sketches', describing someone present in terms of something else, such as a vegetable, building or colour.[44] Their patter was based on quick, inconsequential wit and a ready turn of phrase. Mary commented later of Harry Cust that 'Before his fair neighbour had finished her soup she would find herself plunged into dissertations on eternity', but normally this was accompanied by peals of laughter because, in the words of Lord Vansittart, Cust, a notable wit, was 'as happy to stand on his head as on his dignity'.[45]

Society was fascinated by them, ridiculed them and envied them in equal measure. 'There is a "set" in this hotel who hate & abuse our "set" they call us "the Souls" . . . & say we are always laughing & that we read Herodotus & those sorts of crimes,' reported D. D. (Edith) Lyttelton, Alfred Lyttelton's second wife, while on a trip to Cairo.[46] This was inherent in the name bestowed upon them during the 1888 Season, although no one could recall exactly how it happened. In the spring, Mary attended a dinner party at Lord and Lady Brownlow's house. The Gang engaged in their usual heated debate. 'You all sit and talk about each other's souls. I shall call you "the Souls"; said Lord Charles Beresford, an outsider, a courtier. Mary was sure that the quip – which no one thought very funny – was a well-rehearsed line, trundled out several times that season.[47] But it stuck, with all its undertones of mockery. The Souls always professed to hate it, and further denied being a clique at all.

Those denials convinced no one. In London, they were constantly in and out of one another's houses. Outsiders finding themselves in the country at a house party of Souls often made their excuses and left: 'either . . . they were bored with us or . . . they saw that we were bored with them', Arthur said to Mary of Field Marshal Wolseley and his family, who left Wilton fully two days earlier than planned.[48] Conversely, at a house party held by the non-soul Baron Ferdinand de Rothschild at his magnificent Buckinghamshire château Waddesdon Manor, it was Mary and Charty Ribblesdale who retreated, to Mary's room, 'exhausted' by the talk of their (non-Souls) fellow guests. They were soon joined by Hugo and his sister Hilda Brodrick, whereupon the intention that Charty should read Shelley aloud was abandoned in favour of an afternoon of vivacious chat and much 'chaffing' of Hugo.[49] Three weeks later, Mary, Daisy White, George Curzon and Hugo whiled away the train journey from London to the Pembrokes' Wilton House in Wiltshire by learning poetry by heart; the following Sunday at the Cowpers' Panshanger in Hertfordshire, a large number of the party, Mary included, decided to forgo church in favour of a morning in which 'we sat out on the grass talking [about] . . . Dickens etc . . .'[50] – for the Souls, notwithstanding their name, did not share the previous generation's religious fervour.

Given such proximity it is unsurprising that the Souls developed their own 'ganglanguage', incomprehensible to the outsider: 'dentist', a private meeting; 'floater', an embarrassing situation; 'stodge', the company of women; 'flash' or 'sparkle', the company of men.[51] The vocabulary is revealing, for a Souls gathering was quite different from the traditional, gender-stratified house party where men shot, women read, sewed and talked, and the two sexes united only briefly to eat: at damp outdoor lunches where the women joined the 'guns'; in the drawing room at tea-time; and in the dining room at dinner, after which the women once more left the men, now to their port, smoking and billiards. The young niece of Lord Wenlock, whose wife Constance was a Soul, was startled when, attending a house party at the Wenlocks' Escrick Park in Yorkshire that mixed Souls and their more conventional counterparts, she found that certain men including 'Harry Cust, Evan Charteris, Doll Liddell . . . seemed to prefer the society of ladies and stayed at home on stormy or doubtful days, reading aloud to my aunt and her friends while they painted or modelled – or sometimes just talking, whimsically, wittily (as I know now, if I didn't then) all day long'.[52]

Women were the driving force behind the Souls, yet still they measured their social success by their impact upon the men of the group. If a rising political star (his own talents daily on show in the Commons to the press and strangers in the galleries above) talked to them for hours, it was a reflection of their own intellectual capacity, as well as their physical charm, for of course this talk was always amusing and flirtatious as well.

When writing of themselves in old age even the Souls struggled to recapture their evanescent charm, which was of the bon mot; behaviour that startled, but amused; a delightful but fundamentally unthreatening disregard for convention. Lady Violet Bonham Carter, daughter of Henry Asquith, and a child of the next generation, thought the Souls had a 'liberating and civilising' impact on Society, and she appreciated that 'much of our fun and freedom was a direct heritage from them'.[53] The Souls' benign rebellion pushed the boundaries. It did not breach them. The best illustration comes from one who was not a Soul. Intellectual, acerbic Lady Frances Balfour thought the Souls morally wanting, and far too frivolous. Her daughter Blanche Dugdale recorded her fury on returning from church at Whittingehame (Arthur's East Lothian home) to find nine-year-old Blanche playing backgammon for half-crown stakes with Hugo.[54] Frances had visited Mells, Somerset home of the Horners. She described the scene at dinner to her sister-in-law Lady Betty, the wife of Gerald Balfour, another of Arthur's brothers:

> Lady Ribblesdale talking of a Peacock said it was a voluptuous bird, at which old Mrs Graham [Frances Horner's mother] took exception and said 'that word beginning with a "V" ought not to be mentioned' I stood up for it and said it was what we all would be if we knew how, on which the old lady nearly fainted, and Lady Ribblesdale screamed with laughing, and asked the dear old soul if she would like to be if she knew how, and then there was a rapid proposal that a class should be formed and a Professor found (Lady Ribblesdale proposing Swinburne) to teach us the way wherein to walk. Wild nonsense but so refreshing I felt inclined to walk all round the room on my head.

Notwithstanding her fundamental disapproval, Frances recognized the group's merit: 'There is no doubt that with a hostess who understands how to manage them and with a real personality there is something very interesting in the "gang" . . . All these people have lived together through some of the great experiences and feelings of life, they know each other to the very core, and the absolute freedom and ease are delightful . . .'[55]

At heart, this was a group of very good friends, competing fiercely in romance, politics, friendship. Only the Souls would read out 'Collinses', the effusive letters of thanks sent after each house party, from guests recently departed to 'roars of mirth & groans of contempt' from those remaining, as Mary, Ettie, Harry Cust and Harry White did one November day at Stanway in 1890. 'We acted like traitors that afternoon!' said Mary to Ettie, with a 'crushing sense' that her own letter was even at that moment being read out 'as a sample of idiocy!'[56] Tiny, fascinating Ettie Fane, the Cowpers' niece, drawn into the circle after her marriage to Willie Grenfell in 1887, was one of Mary's and Arthur's closest friends. 'I feel really that *you* & *I* (& Laura [Lyttelton] who left so swiftly so long ago) stand very much for the souls [sic] – for we *were* really – the *soul*! & centre in a way of the elusive set,' Mary wrote to Ettie in old age.[57] Privately, to Arthur, Mary called Ettie 'Delilah', crowing when Ettie, the least intellectually able (or interested) of the group, failed to grasp some point of debate.[58] Margot once challenged Balfour with not minding if Mary, Ettie and she all died. 'I should mind if you all died on the same day' was Balfour's laconic response.[59]

At twenty-three, George Wyndham, who had moved into the Gang's orbit through Mary, scored a palpable hit when he secured the hand of the widowed, exceptionally beautiful Sibell, Countess Grosvenor, over a reported eighty rivals, including George Curzon. Sibell was nearly a decade older than George, a mother of three, and renowned for her indiscriminate warmth and sweetness.[60] When she clasped someone's hand in her own soft one, said the Anglo-Irish hostess Elizabeth Fingall, it was never quite clear whether she knew whose hand it was.[61] Sibell had been charmed by George's exuberant volubility and intense romanticism – the poet 'riding to hounds across his prose, looking with wonder upon the world as upon a fairyland', as T. S. Eliot described him[62] – and his dark, 'French' looks:[63] those of a troubadour according to Elizabeth Fingall, who added that George lived 'every minute of his life at high pitch'.[64] In maturity, George earned the tired sobriquet of 'the handsomest man in England'.[65] But it was possibly Madeline Wyndham's old friendship with Sibell's father-in-law, the Duke of Westminster, that made the Duke finally, reluctantly, agree to Sibell's marrying the bumptious young man. He stipulated that Sibell maintain her title after marriage. It was unthinkable that the mother of his heir, Bend'Or, should be plain Mrs George Wyndham.[66]

George's unmistakably oedipal choice was regarded with misgivings by many who knew him. Alfred Lyttelton expressed concern about the effect on a 'smart youth . . . very keen about his profession and about intellectual things . . . from a family where there is throughout an air of Bohemian quasi-culture' of being 'plunged into deadalike decorous ducal circles coldly hostile to him and all that produced his unstupid but ill-ballasted personality'.[67] George survived – but Sibell was no match intellectually for him. Soon enough he took up with Gay, Lady Plymouth, and conducted a contented lifelong affair.

EIGHT

The Summer of 1887

In January 1887, while staying at Clouds, Mary realized to her horror that she was pregnant again. She chided '*Naughty* Wash' for 'pinting [sic] too soon after Betsey at Panshanger',[1] breaking the news in a carrot-and-stick manner: 'if ou comes veggy early! Migs will receive ou in cot & no more precautions needed, for Migs is quite certainly in the family way,' she told him.[2] Hugo had been expected back several days before. Mary suspected, with good reason, that he had been delayed by another woman's charms. She used the promise of sex to entice him back.

Mary was furious about being pregnant. Her younger son Guy was barely six months old. Mananai was due to be presented that spring. Mary had been looking forward to showing her younger sister the ropes in her first Season. Pregnancy required her to scale down her social activities. It made her feel fat, dull, unable to compete socially among her friends. The mid-Victorian days of ten or twelve children were past. Souls women, appreciating their figures, their health and their consuming social lives, did not have many children.[3] There were ways of achieving this. Carefully coded advertisements in women's periodicals recommended purges of pennyroyal and compounds of aloe and iron that would restore an ailing young lady to her former good 'health'. It seems that at least some of Mary's friends employed these, but Mary decided that she 'daren't send for Zach's stuff its too naughty', and resigned herself to the inevitable:[4] 'Me looks forward to it [the pregnancy] with disgust & loathing . . . my season with Mad knocked on the head. Migs propose Pints *dis*pose,' she mourned.[5]

Mary was still in her first trimester when she attended George and Sibell's quiet marriage in the private chapel of the Westminsters' Cheshire house, Eaton Hall. The service was conducted by the Archbishop of Canterbury. Only immediate family on both sides attended. In what must have been a significant blow to George's ego, *The Times* reported that the Countess Grosvenor had married *Guy* Wyndham of 16th (Queen's) Lancers, with George acting as best man.[6] The Wyndhams celebrated the occasion more lavishly on their return to Clouds with a vast tea for Milton's and East Knoyle's inhabitants, with a band playing from the terrace, a cricket match for the adults and a bag of sweets and a bun for each child.[7] When George and Sibell made their first visit as newlyweds, the villagers followed the still fairly widespread tradition of intercepting their carriage and replacing their horses with eighty men who pulled them up the driveway to Clouds themselves.[8]

While on honeymoon in the Italian Lakes, George received a telegram from Arthur Balfour. In March 1887, Sir Michael Hicks Beach, Ireland's Chief Secretary, had resigned, citing cataracts that had left him nearly blind. The grounds for resignation evoked those of Sir George Trevelyan, Cavendish's successor, whose hair turned completely white within twelve months of taking the job, and who resigned a year after that, pleading to be released from a post that was, in his words, 'not a human life at all'.[9] In a shock appointment, Salisbury now chose his favourite nephew to fill the vacancy. Balfour's appointment provoked incomprehension at Westminster and jubilation in Dublin: 'We have killed Cavendish, blinded Beach and smashed up Trevelyan. What shall we do with this weakling?'

taunted the Irish crowds.[10] So startling was Robert Salisbury's decision that it has prompted the suggestion (probably incorrect) that it gave rise to the popular phrase that suggests when 'Bob's your uncle' anything is possible.[11] Now Arthur asked George to join him as his private secretary. Citing the Wyndham tradition of public service, George cut short his honeymoon and hotfooted it back to 'throw my lot in the political boat'.[12]

George's new post was a triumph for the Wyndhams, establishing, in the Souls' fiercely competitive world, how close the family was to the 'adored Gazelle'. But both offices were dangerous. Cavendish's and Burke's murders were still fresh in people's minds. Arthur, the tenth Chief Secretary in as many years,[13] pointed out with typical detachment that Ireland was a place where people tended to lose their reputations, their lives or possibly both.[14] Shortly before Arthur's departure, Mary visited him at Carlton Gardens. It was a Wednesday afternoon, fast becoming their ritual meeting time when in London, for on Wednesdays the House rose early. Perhaps it was the urgency lent by anxiety that provoked what Mary described as a 'small very private and personal incident (gear changing!)' in the same downstairs sitting room where they had first kissed a year before. Mary gave no further clues to what the incident might have been, beyond teasing Arthur that it would not appear in his memoirs.[15]

Some years later, Mary explained to Wilfrid Blunt the exact nature of sexual relations among the Souls. 'Nearly all the group were married women with husbands whom they loved & by whom they had children, but each had her friend who was a friend only.'[16] Those friends' relationship was 'a little more than friendship, a little less than love'. So far as Wilfrid could understand, this meant everything but 'the conjugal act'; or, from the male perspective, 'Every woman shall have her man, but no man shall have his woman.'[17] Later correspondence indicates that Mary and Arthur developed a sexual relationship involving role-play and mild sado-masochism (Arthur's fondness for vigorous spankings lends disappointing force to the accusations frequently levelled at public-school-educated Englishmen). Quite possibly this 'incident' was the first time that Mary – then almost three months' pregnant – and Arthur engaged in such activities.

Arthur left a few days later, leaving with Frances Balfour a pouch to be opened only in the event of his death. 'Accidents have occurred to a Chief Secretary for Ireland and (although I think it improbable) they may occur again. If the worst (as people euphemistically say!) should happen,' said Balfour, Frances was to cut open the pouch with her penknife and 'read the scrawl inside. It relates to a matter with which only you can deal.'

Arthur did not need to elaborate on these instructions, or on his request that in such an event Frances check through his papers for any incriminating correspondence (Arthur's preparations for his departure included burning a multitude of letters, many, presumably, from Mary). Fifty years later, an elderly Frances and Mary sat down together to open the pouch. 'My dear Frances,' wrote Balfour:

> I write this in a great hurry, but as you will only have to read it in the event of my death you will forgive my handwriting. I think you and all whom I love will be sorry that I am not any longer with you. But you will be able to talk it freely over with each other and all whom such an event may concern. There is however one who will not be in this position. I want you to give her as from yourself this little brooch which you will find herewith: and to tell her that, at the end, if I was able to think at all, I thought of her. If I was the means of introducing any unhappiness into her life I hope God will forgive me. I know she will.[18]

The year 1887 marked Queen Victoria's Golden Jubilee. The Queen was reluctantly persuaded out of purdah for a Season glittering with magnificent balls, processions and banquets. Mary spent it more quietly in intellectual self-improvement. She was a keen attendee of weekly ethics classes organized by her sister-in-law Hilda Brodrick, who hired a Girton graduate as tutor. The day chosen was Wednesday, so male Souls could join. The small group that gathered each week included Mary, Betty Balfour, Charty Ribblesdale, Lady Pembroke and Ettie Grenfell. The sessions, on themes including 'Conscience self love etc' and 'Kant', were a qualified success. 'Miss Anderson gave us a lecture which as none of us (except Betty) knew anything about the subject or had read anything was rather above our heads,' Mary told her diary, noting that week's essay: 'Is it necessary for ethical reasoning, to assume or establish an ultimate end to rational action?' Attendance diminished as the Season wore on. Mary was just one of three participants at the final class in early July, although their numbers had been boosted when Willie Grenfell and Tommy Ribblesdale joined after the House rose. The triumphant ethicists went out for a 'farewell ethical luncheon' that continued into the early hours of the morning: 'we argued about the word implied & implicit till 1 o'clock & then couldn't sleep from excitement', Mary recorded.[19]

A brief respite followed, as Mary, Hugo, the Ribblesdales and their eldest son Thomas went for a few days to Lyndhurst in the New Forest, staying in the Crown Hotel. The weather was baking, and the Forest even more lovely than Mary had expected. 'We have been out all today laying [sic] on our backs looking up at the trees [while] Charty read aloud,' Mary told her mother. Later in the day Hugo, Tommy and little Tommy raced around, hot, flustered and excited, trying to catch butterflies in nets. That night both couples dined with Sir William Harcourt, who had served in Gladstone's most recent Cabinet as Chancellor, and Harcourt's wife Elizabeth, and then took a moonlit drive back to their hotel. The trip was a 'great success' for the two flirtatious couples.[20]

Shortly afterwards, Mary went to Clouds. Hugo quickly absented himself, busying himself in London for the Season's final weeks. Madeline Wyndham proposed that Mary should stay at Clouds for the rest of the summer rather than return to Stanway. With some misgivings, Mary broached the idea with Percy. After 'incubating' the issue for a few days, Percy expressed himself in favour. 'Pupsie is like Migs & likes to make up his mind & face a thing *slowly* but then definitely for ever! (not like weathercock Wash),' Mary told Hugo. To her amusement, Percy had seized on the plan as a means of protection 'against Mumsie's indiscriminating hospitality': using Mary to keep 'away people he don't like!' 'I hope the poor mad sister won't be forbidden as being bad for Migs i.e. disagreeable for Pup,' added Mary.[21] The 'poor mad sister' was Madeline's sister Mary Carleton. Widowed early, with two small children, Dorothy and Guy, and little money, she was one of Madeline's many lame ducks. Percy found her intensely annoying.

Throughout the summer Mary had misgivings about Hugo. She knew his inclination for flirting with other women – 'pairing off with a conk & having long tête-à-tête & purely (or impurely) personal conversations'[22] – and feared he was neglecting his Commons' duties. 'You see too much of Violet [Manners] & [I] am getting uneasy,' she told him in early August,[23] for Violet, the most artistic of all the Souls women, did not subscribe to the group's morality in the way Mary's other friends did. A few weeks later, under pretext of recounting a heated lunchtime debate with Hilda Brodrick and Betty Balfour on J. S. Mill's *Utilitarianism*, Mary wrote Hugo a lengthy letter about 'systematic selfishness' and the necessity of quelling one's hedonistic will.[24] The subtext was not hard to see.

Mary's magpie-like, irreverent approach to Mill, twisting his theories to serve her own ends, reflected a frequently criticized trait of the Souls: their alleged want of intellectual depth. When Margot Tennant devised a plan for a Souls' journal entitled 'To-morrow: a Women's journal for men' (the proposed contents of the first issue included 'Persons and Politics' by Margot; the 'Rise and Fall of Professional Beauties' by Lady de Grey; 'Foreign and Colonial Gossip' by Harry Cust; a short story by Oscar Wilde; a book review by John Addington Symonds and 'Letters to Men' by George

Wyndham),[25] the press pounced on the idea, the *News of the World* revealing with glee that Webber's suggested title had been 'Petticoats'.[26] Sir William Harcourt gently mocked the plan: 'Ah, it is their bodies that I like; and now that they are going to show us their souls all naked in print I shall not care for them.'[27] In fact, the journal never came to pass.

By late August, Mary, Hilda and Betty had finished Mill and were planning two days of Butler's sermons and dissertations before taking the 'plunge into Sorley's Ethics of Naturalism, which I *hope* & *trust* to have finished before practical Physics in the shape of giving birth to an infant puts a temporary stop to my Ethics – I shall study Physiology first and as intelligence dawns, & the babe looks & smiles at the light, I shall study Psychology combined with jurisprudence & so I shall get back to Ethics again,' Mary said.[28] The other goings-on of the house impinged little upon her. 'Mr. Adeane's here (Marie's brother) rather a muff I think,' she told Hugo.[29]

Charles Adeane, whose sister Marie was a maid of honour to the Queen,[30] was a twenty-three-year-old Cambridgeshire landowner. He had been courting Mananai since her debut that spring. Of all the sisters, Mananai came closest to replicating their mother's 'sweetness and social charm', without the underlying steel.[31] Few were likely to exclaim, as Mananai did, how 'lovely' February was as a month, and mean it.[32] Her solemn interest in clothes and titles prompted Percy to nickname her 'Madeline the Mondaine'.[33] As a child she had had a tendency to 'twitch! & wink! Terribly',[34] and despite being older by two years, her development had always noticeably lagged behind the precocious Pamela's. Like Guy Wyndham, she was a lesser star in the family constellation, but she was passionately supportive of her siblings, championing their achievements and mourning their defeats with utter sincerity, and beloved by them for it.

Mananai found the Souls' intellectual jousting daunting. Harry Cust earned her lasting affection by confessing to her that he was just as bashful as she: a lie, but a comforting one.[35] She felt far more at ease with Charlie Adeane, good-hearted, rather ponderous, apt to pontificate about the problems besetting agriculture, and from a more stolid family of courtiers (although not entirely without spark: Charlie's jovial uncle Alick, a groom in waiting, had provoked one of the Queen's most famous comments when he recounted a risqué joke at a state dinner. 'We are not amused,'[36] she replied).

Portrait of Miss Madeline Wyndham, aged sixteen: Mananai on the brink of adulthood, by Edward Burne-Jones.

None of the Wyndhams was particularly impressed by Charlie. Mary and Pamela found the 'longueurs' in his conversation a little trying.[37] With glee Mary told Hugo that the hapless suitor had tried sounding out Fräulein in confidence about his prospects – a confidence not kept.[38] After leaving Clouds, Charlie tried to send Mananai a bracelet as a gift. Madeline Wyndham refused to allow her daughter to accept it. In a friendly but reserved letter, she explained that the Wyndhams thought Mananai too young to marry and did not approve of the five-year age gap between the lovers. Her response was without a shadow of the affection shown to Hugo when he was courting Mary – and he also was five years older than his intended bride.[39] Displaying the tolerant good humour that he almost always managed to employ with the Wyndhams, Charlie agreed to make no declaration to Mananai just yet. He asked whether he might send the bracelet to Madeline Wyndham, who could then give it to her daughter; 'may I say, with my love?. . . Certainly being in love is not cheerful,' he added, assuring Madeline that he had read over her letter 'about fifty times'.[40]

Madeline Wyndham's excuses were a pretext. As Souls, it did not matter that Charlie was a Liberal. What mattered was that Charlie's income, from the Cambridgeshire estate he had inherited upon his alcoholic father's death, was just £3,000 to £4,000 a year. He could not hope for any more. Given the parlous state of eastern England's arable estates, he might end up receiving markedly less. As Percy commented, Charlie and any wife of his would not be '*poor*' but they would not be 'at all rich' either.[41] Madeline Wyndham thought her charming daughter could do better.

The last weekend of August found the Wyndhams at Clouds with Sibyl Queensberry and her two youngest children, Arthur and Edith Douglas, known respectively as 'Bosie' and 'Wommy' (the nicknames themselves abbreviations of 'Boysie' and 'Little Woman'), and with Wilfrid Blunt and his teenage daughter Judith. Sibyl and her children frequently visited Clouds, all the more since Sibyl's acrimonious divorce from the abusive Marquess of Queensberry that year. On Saturday, Arthur Balfour, George Wyndham and Henry James were due to arrive.

In the months since his arrival in Ireland Balfour had shown the Irish – and Westminster – that they had underestimated him. The Unionist policy was to kill Home Rule with kindness, but conciliation went hand in hand with coercion. Balfour made good on his promise to 'be as relentless as Cromwell in enforcing obedience to the law'.[42] Anyone inciting tenants in the rent strike, known as the Plan of Campaign, was immediately imprisoned. Prisoners' complaints about the putrid conditions in their cells were met with short shrift: the connection between diseased lungs and Irish patriotism was interesting, said Balfour drily.[43] By late August, the political world was alight with the news that the Government was putting the Irish MP John Dillon on trial for his part in the Plan of Campaign.

George, erstwhile 'Fenian', proud descendant of the Patriot Lord Edward, was now an instrument of one of the most brutally effective periods of repression since the British had crushed the 1798 Rebellion. Yet the Wyndhams managed to reconcile the two. George wanted to save 'darling Ireland', as Mary called it,[44] and to gain 'high office'. Quelling agitators could, just about, be interpreted as helping the country reclaim calm. And the Wyndhams were ambitious. They ignored any contradiction, including Madeline Wyndham who while visiting George in Ireland trawled through antique shops, collecting commemorative buttons of the heroes of '98 to distribute to her children and grandchildren, and requested all family members making the trip to do the same.[45] Wilfrid Blunt was resolutely of the opposing view. Ireland was his latest anti-imperialist hobby horse. In 1886, he had visited Ireland and subsequently published in the *Pall Mall Gazette*, which was under the editorship of the sensationalist journalist W. T. Stead, a devastating exposé of the barbarity of the evictions he found there.[46] He now intended to return to Ireland in October to join the fray. He was keenly looking forward to confronting Balfour at Clouds, but by the time Balfour arrived Blunt was already on the back foot, because he had decided that he was in love with Mary: 'the cleverest best & most beautiful woman in the world with just that touch of human sympathy which brings her to the level of our sins', he wrote in his diary.[47]

The family's reverence for Balfour cast Blunt into a deep gloom. 'Balfour is here under particularly favourable [circumstances] as he is in love with Mary Elcho, to whom he makes himself of course charming, but, possibly for the same reason, I do not like him much . . . He has a grand passion for Mary – that is quite clear – and it is equally clear that she has a tendresse for him,' said Wilfrid as he watched the two, heads bent in conversation, drift off on long walks. 'But what their exact relations may be I cannot determine. Perhaps it is better not to be too wise, and as all the house accepts the position as the most natural in the world, there let us leave it.'[48]

It nonetheless made Blunt bad-tempered. No one – except Mary – escaped criticism in his diary. James, 'always a little behindhand' in conversation, was disappointing – 'For a man who writes so lightly and well it is amazing how dull-witted he is.'[49] Judith was unacceptably mute at dinner while Pamela and Bosie played boisterous rhyming games. Blunt's pen was most acidic about Balfour: 'As a young man he must have been charming and still has some of the ways of a tame cat.'[50]

On the tennis court, a red-faced and ferocious Blunt, partnering George Wyndham, triumphed over a nonchalant Arthur and Guy Wyndham. That night at dinner, Balfour admitted, to Blunt's astonishment, that Home Rule was inevitable: that his party's coercion was merely stalling. 'When it comes I shall not be sorry,' Arthur told the assembled party. 'Only let us have separation as well as Home Rule; England cannot afford to go on with Irishmen in her Parliament. She must govern herself too.'[51]

The next day Arthur and George left Clouds for Ireland. Mary, always feeling a little guilty after spending time with Arthur, wrote a particularly affectionate letter to Hugo, professing herself to have been 'mad with *low* spirits' in his absence. '[Y]ou are such a deeer [sic] companion to Migs,' she added, looking forward to a honeymoon planned by the Elchos after the birth of the child 'as a caged bird to freedom'.[52] Two weeks later Blunt mounted the hustings at a public meeting. 'Men of Galway,' he declared, and was promptly pulled down by English troops and arrested. 'We are trying to put yr cousin in gaol. I have not heard whether we have succeeded,' Balfour wrote to Mary as Blunt awaited trial, imagining that Blunt would be 'horribly disappointed' if he were set free.[53] On 27 September, at Clouds, Mary gave birth to her third child, a girl named Cynthia ('Cincie') after the goddess of the moon, in tribute to Clouds. A month later, Mary Carleton died and Clouds received two new inhabitants, her orphaned children, Dorothy and Guy, who came to live with the Wyndhams as their wards.[54] Madeline Wyndham went into mourning for her sister, leaving Percy to chaperone Mananai on the round of country-house visits that autumn. Percy was 'splendid', Mananai loyally reported, but he had no experience in the art of marrying off a daughter and no inclination to develop the requisite skills now.[55]

All that autumn, Home Rulers massed in Trafalgar Square, their numbers swelled by socialist agitators and members of the unemployed. In Ireland, police shot down rioters at Mitchelstown, and Balfour stood by them. In London, in November, a non-violent protest organized by the Metropolitan Radical Federation demanding the release of William O'Brien – imprisoned again for his part in the Plan of Campaign – turned into 'Bloody Sunday', when police set upon the marchers, whose numbers included William Morris, Annie Besant and George Bernard Shaw. In the resultant fighting, which spilled along the Strand, Parliament Street and all the way to Shaftesbury Avenue, two policemen were stabbed to death, a young clerk called Alfred Linnell killed and a further 200 injured. It was to prove the last great outing of the London crowd.[56] In the Commons Irish MPs compared Balfour to Heliogabalus, a Roman emperor who revived himself by bathing in children's blood.[57] At Christmas, Arthur wrote to Mary in red ink: 'Greetings from Bl[oo] dy B[a]lf[ou]r, I write to you in the hue appropriate to my sanguinary character,' using the name by which he was now most commonly known in Ireland and to the world at large.[58] Six months later, when buying a copy of *Funny Folk* to while away a train journey from Stanway to Clouds, Pamela was diverted by a cartoon she found therein depicting Balfour as Dr Jekyll and Mr Hyde in reference to R. L. Stevenson's recent smash-hit novel. Better still, Pamela told Mary, 'the "ill-starred advisors were you & Mamma!!!"'[59]

The Wyndhams had, very publicly, made it clear where their allegiances lay. In January 1888, Blunt was sentenced to two months' hard labour in Kilmainham Jail. He secured maximum publicity, first refusing to swap his greatcoat for the standard prison-issue one that barely covered his knees; and then bringing a case against Balfour for assault.[60] The more liberal minded of the Wyndhams' friends – the Morrises and the Burne-Joneses – staunchly supported Blunt. Janey Morris thought it a 'splendid commotion'.[61] The Wyndhams believed, as George said, that 'Wilfrid is . . . temporarily out of his senses.'[62] They left him to his latest hobby horse. On the very day that Wilfrid was returned to his cell after his failed appeal, Percy, Madeline Wyndham and Mary arrived at the Chief Secretary's Lodge to hold 'high revel', in Wilfrid's own phrase. He passed a sleepless night in his cell composing anagrams of his rival's name on a slate. The Right Honourable Arthur James Balfour of Whittingehame became 'How! Am I not Arthur B. a huge thief, the brutal gaoler of Irishmen?'[63]

NINE

Mananai

That spring, the Wyndhams broke with their fast-establishing tradition of Easters at Clouds. On Good Friday, Pamela wrote to Mary from Madeline Wyndham's darkened bedroom at Belgrave Square. Their mother had been given 'a fresh brain tonic' by Dr Cumberbatch and 'is going on capitally'. She was 'quite quiet', and either Pamela, Mananai or Percy was constantly at her bedside. 'Darling Mary it is such a relief that she is better isn't it?'[1]

From the tone of Pamela's letter it is clear that this was not the first such episode, although it may have been more serious than most. Certainly it was closely concealed. Visiting the Poynters around this time, Percy was horrified when Agnes Poynter said something to suggest that 'she knew *how* Mamma had been unwell. I hope it was my fancy but I fear not,' Percy reported to Mary, questioning her closely as to whether she had 'by any chance' told Georgie Burne-Jones (Agnes's sister) 'that Mamma was muddled, or had a temporary loss of consciousness, or in short anything of that kind?'[2] Whatever reply Mary sent is missing from the letter-books Madeline Wyndham compiled when in better health.

The catalyst, most likely, was the combined pressure of Mary

Carleton's death, the responsibility of her new charges and no doubt
Charlie Adeane's inexorable progress – for he and Mananai became
engaged in May. 'Thank goodness there has been no "scratching up
of dirt"! but everything has been as "serene as oil!"' Mananai
exclaimed to Mary.[3] The Wyndhams invited Charlie's mother, Lady
Elizabeth, and her second husband Michael Biddulph, a Liberal
Unionist banker, to a slightly stolid engagement dinner at Belgrave
Square which wanted, Percy said, for 'our two brightest stars' – Mary
and George – to liven it up.[4] A recovered Madeline Wyndham swallowed her misgivings and embraced Charlie with the warmth that
she had Hugo. Charlie began addressing her as 'M.M.', short for
'Mother Madeline', and soon proved an infinitely better son-in-law
in every way. 'I like what I know of Charlie, I like him very much,
the more I see of him the more I like him,' Percy told Mary stoutly.[5]

Six weeks later on a Monday afternoon in late July, Mananai and
Charlie were married, as Mary had been, at St Peter's Church in
Eaton Square. The nineteen-year-old bride, reported *Modern
Society*, wore a white satin dress embroidered with silver, ruched
with crêpe lisse on to which was pinned orange blossom, as was
traditional. A diamond-encrusted sun (an Adeane family heirloom)
pinned her tulle veil to her hair. Mary's toddler sons Ego and Guy
were pageboys in blue satin and rather alarming-sounding 'fanciful
hats and feathers'; the bridesmaids, among them Pamela and
Dorothy Carleton, wore white crêpe dresses and bolero jackets,
white tulle hats, pink stockings and heart-shaped enamel brooches
with a double heart picked out in pearls and diamonds – a gift
from the triumphant, not entirely indigent bridegroom.[6]

The newlyweds spent the first part of their honeymoon at
Panshanger. It poured with rain every day, but, holed up reading
aloud to each other in Lady Cowper's boudoir, Madeline and Charlie
were 'much too happy to care for the elements'. '*Tout va bien*,'
Charlie assured his 'beloved M.M.' in a letter marked 'private', so
not to be read out at the breakfast table or handed around to family
members as such letters often were. 'Madeline is *quite well* . . . &

perfectly comfortable.'[7] Charlie's coded message was scarcely needed. Madeline Adeane's ecstatic letters expressed delight at every aspect of 'this delicious new life'. 'I . . . wonder if you felt and thought the same as I do,' she asked Mary, longing for a 'confidential chat'.[8] She could hardly wait to show her family 'how truly, and *blissfully* happy I am – letters are very nice but not quite satisfactory. I don't think that I shall have to tell you because I think that when you see us you will *see* how happy we are,' she enthused to her mother.[9] 'She is so beloved your & my Madeline,' Charlie told his mother-in-law, '& *so good*. No words of mine can express my love & adoration for her – she is *a perfect woman* – & that article which is rare is certainly the most wonderful & most beautiful of all God's works – much love to you my dearest – to whom she owes her existence, to whom I owe my love.'[10]

The Adeanes snatched a brief visit to Stanway where the Wyndhams were staying with Mary. As a married woman, Madeline Adeane could now chaperone her sister, and so she and Pamela experienced the novelty of walking alone outside for the first time in their lives. The Adeanes then headed for Victoria Station and the boat train that would carry them (Madeline Adeane dressed in her new 'most comfortable' travelling clothes: a grey suit with hat and veil to match), Charlie's valet, Madeline's lady's maid Alice and a vast amount of luggage to the Continent.[11]

'Fancy me in Paris!' said Mananai the next day as she lay on her bed in the Hôtel Meurice, gazing out of the window at the Tuileries baking in the August heat, revelling in the sounds of bells ringing, horses' hooves clattering and whips cracking outside. 'Charlie knows Paris very well,' she informed her mother, recounting drives up the Champs-Elysées and through the Bois de Boulogne; an 'excellent' band in the Jardins d'Acclimation; and visits to the Invalides and the Louvre. Shortly afterwards, defeated by the heat, they retreated to Chantilly to stay with 'dear Baronne de St Didier', one of Lady Elizabeth's large network of friends eager to fête the newlyweds. Everything was a source of wonderment to Mananai from the tremendous amount that French grandees seemed to eat and drink to the turquoise-studded gold butterfly that awaited her on her dressing table at Chantilly: so clever, it could be either a brooch or a hairpin.

'Fancy me in *Switzerland*!!!' exclaimed an incredulous Mananai two weeks later, snatching a moment before 'déjeuner' to write to George from the Hôtel National on Lake Geneva, while Charlie peered out of the window, examining through opera glasses the boats on the lake. They had attended a breakfast 'for 16!!!' held by the Baronesse de Rothschild ('quite the ugliest lady I think I have ever seen but most kind'), at which guests entered as if to dinner, in pairs, and were quite outnumbered by footmen.[12] From Switzerland they headed onwards to Italy. 'Florence is the most perfect Paradise of the sightseer,' George advised Mananai: 'you have everything packed in the space of Belgrave Square, and can walk in and out of scores of historical Treasure-houses of Beauty with all the ease of a turn in the East garden and round by the green river at Clouds . . .'[13] The Adeanes read diligently in anticipation. 'We have just read *The Makers of Florence*, Charlie is now finishing *The Makers of Venice* & I am going to begin *Lives of Italian Painters* by Jameson,' Mananai reported to George.[14] They kept a joint diary, and Mananai filled a 'birthday book' (that is, an autograph album) with the signatures of all the people they met along the way.

Travel worn, weary and still blissfully happy the Adeanes returned to England in September. They went directly to Clouds, where they were crowned with wreaths made by Fräulein and slept in a bed decorated by Madeline Wyndham with handmade angel wings. From there they went to Babraham to open the house, shut up since the death of Charlie's father nineteen years before. Charlie's old nurse accompanied them. She was so overwhelmed by the occasion that she broke down and wept when they arrived.[15]

Babraham Hall near Cambridge was a rambling red-brick Victorian-Jacobean mishmash possessing, thanks to Charlie's profligate father, a disproportionately large ballroom and a somewhat incongruous Italianate colonnade. Mananai was undaunted. An exploratory drive around the estate revealed 'belts of trees and banks of firs' that she thought somewhat reminiscent of the Wiltshire Downs. She took out a subscription to her mother's favourite periodical the *Garden* and began devising plans for wild flower beds like those of Clouds – perhaps even a small golf course like the one that Percy had recently built.[16] Cautious Charlie may have cavilled at the cost of the latter, but he gave his new wife free rein inside the house. She painted the upstairs rooms white and papered the downstairs reception rooms with Morris patterns. She poked about in the attics hoping to find treasures as Mary had done (there were sadly few), covered bulky, old-fashioned cabinets with curtains and swathed tables in lengths of silk sent to her by Madeline Wyndham for that purpose. 'All I do is a feeble imitation of you,' she told her mother cheerfully.[17]

Mananai threw herself with relish into the life of a county squire's wife. She made friends with the local gentry, visited the poor of the estate and the nearby villages, entertained the tenant farmers and their families to tea. 'Our life is that of an ordinary English house,' Charlie said, by which he meant ordinary for the landed gentry, since most English households did not portion their time between '1 day's partridge shooting to 2 days' croquet (new) tennis – walking, talking, reading'.[18] Perhaps the only hint of the bohemian roots of young Mrs Adeane was the pet fawn that followed her, like a puppy, everywhere she went.[19]

TEN

Conflagration

Madeline Adeane's precipitate departure from schoolroom to matronhood grieved Pamela intensely. She bickered with Fräulein and snapped at Dorothy,[1] itching to enter the adult world. The Wyndhams had a tradition of taking each daughter to Ireland for their first 'grown-up' visit.[2] In September 1888 it was Pamela's turn. She was bewitched by this first visit to the country of her ancestors: 'it is like an enchanted land', she rhapsodized to Mary from Killarney, looking out from her bedroom window on to lush green fields, a lake 'twinkling and sparkling in the sunlight like beautiful Lohengrin's armour' and shadowy mountains in the distance, shifting colour from smoky grey to 'hearts ease purple'.[3] She and her parents visited George and Sibell, the de Vescis at Abbey Leix and, briefly, the Vice Regal Lodge. 'It is *great* fun visiting and it . . . doesn't feel like me; I feel very "grown-up" going down to dinner in long reach-elbow gloves,' she told Mary, drawing for her sister 'word pictures' of her fellow guests.[4]

Pamela returned to a Clouds echoing with Mananai's absence, counting down the months until her own debut. The sisters were briefly reunited when the Adeanes spent Christmas at Clouds. But by the new year the party was just Percy, Madeline Wyndham, Pamela, Dorothy Carleton, Fräulein, Mary, now pregnant for a fourth time, and her three children. George and Sibell were in Ireland, Guy in India with his regiment, Hugo off shooting. Mary was planning to leave for Stanway the following day. The Charteris trunks stood packed and ready. That night, Mary sat up score-keeping for her mother and Fräulein in an animated game of piquet, going to bed rather later than planned.[5]

When the clanging of a bell woke her from a deep sleep Mary presumed it to be the bell that rang around the house at 8 o'clock every morning to rouse its inhabitants for breakfast. She 'got out of bed, put on dressing gown, picked up a few things almost leisurely', when her bedroom door was flung open by Bertha Devon, now head housemaid, with five-year-old Ego in her arms crying, 'Oh Miss Mary, you must leave the house the house is on fire.' Mary rushed on to the landing, 'saw the ruddy glare & heard the low sharp snapping'. At that moment, Percy dashed past. He told her that Guy and Cincie had been carried to safety by their nurse-maid Mrs Fry. 'I was wild to see the children at once & rushed down to find them.'[6]

The passages down which she raced were already filling with dense, scorching smoke. Once safely outside in the freezing January night she found most of her family, a night-gown-clad Madeline Wyndham desperately bruised from hoisting the Baldovinetto off the hall's wall and toppling off the chair on which she stood under its weight (the bruises were so deep that they did not fade for weeks),[7] but only one of her children: a small scared Ego in his red dressing gown still being held in Bertha Devon's arms. 'Mama and I were in despair,' said Mary, 'helpless distracted anguish . . . we could see Guy & Cynthia *nowhere* & . . . the roaring crackling flames & the showering sparks & smoke spreading everywhere made one wild with fear . . .'

'Don't Mamma, don't,' screamed Pamela as Madeline Wyndham and Mary tried to force their way back into the burning building.

'Where's Fraulein, has anyone awakened Fraulein?' Percy shouted above the din, having forgotten in his panic that he had awakened her himself. 'Then', said Mary, 'through the panic and the terror came the cry of "they're here, they're safe"': Fräulein and Mrs Fry carrying Cincie and Guy. In the time it had taken to wrap the small children in blankets to protect them, the smoke had made the passage down which Bertha carrying Ego had fled impassable. Only Clouds' warren of entrances, exits and passageways had allowed them to find another route.

The horse-drawn fire engines sent from Mere, Wilton and Salisbury were horribly delayed by the perilous conditions. Wilton's horses fell down three times on the icy roads in the 18 miles between the two houses, and were ultimately too injured to continue, requiring fresh horses to be borrowed from nearby farms. Villagers, who had rushed up the hill in wagons from East Knoyle and Milton, helped the house carpenters form a human chain that saved most of the Wyndhams' treasures from the ground floor: books were piled high in dog baskets on the lawn; paintings, furniture and even the huge Morris carpet from the drawing room were saved. Someone (presumably a plucky housemaid) flung out of the window the contents of Mary's trunks (not the trunks themselves, Mary hastened to add), which were caught by Mary and Fräulein standing underneath. The firemen reached Clouds too late to do more than contain the fire and save the offices from becoming part of the conflagration.[8] As the great chandelier in the hall crashed down in a shower of glass and sparks they aimed their hoses at the flames now dancing from the roof of Clouds, but 'the flames seemed rather to like the water', and fuelled by the draught provided by the hall roared more fiercely still. It was so bitterly cold that the captain of Wilton's fire brigade froze solid to the side of his ladder. The villagers retreated to their wagonettes, munching on egg sand-wiches and 'hugely enjoying themselves', said Mary, likening them, without rancour, to the crowd at the races in William Powell Frith's *Derby Day*.

On the slippery terrace, with the trees laced with hoar frost silhouetted behind them, the family stood '& . . . watched the dear house burn'.[9] Unknown hands covered them in a scarecrow assortment of warmer garb: over Mary's orange dressing gown she sported several shawls and an ulster, and on her head a bowler hat. 'Oh, my Bible, and oh, my canaries!' cried Pamela, wringing her hands beside her. Madeline Wyndham, standing a little apart with a rapt look on her face, was silent. She wore 'a rough homespun coat' over her nightgown, remembered one neighbour, 'and the lace frills escaped beneath the tweed sleeves and fell over her hands which were flung out in an unconscious gesture of wonder at the sight. She was entranced by its beauty and terror.'[10]

The cause of the fire, it was later discovered, was a lighted candle left by a sleepy housemaid in a linen cupboard. A moment of carelessness – born, doubtless, of exhaustion – resulted in a conflagration that gutted the house, leaving only its shell standing. It took three days for the smouldering ashes to cool enough for it to be safe to approach the ruins; the cellar was still hot for a week after the fire. Burne-Jones's cartoon of the Ascension was lost, many items on the first floor and everything on the second floor. 'All the childrens [sic] lovely wardrobe toys silver cups birds etc & all the nurses clothes & money *gone*,' mourned Mary. The contents of her trunks served to dress all the females in the household. 'Mrs Fry looks very nice in my red lawn tennis jersey & skirt,' she told Frances Balfour.

Two weeks later, back at Stanway, Mary was hosting Doll Liddell, Gladys de Grey, Emmie and Eddy Bourke, the Pembrokes, Harry and Daisy White, George Curzon, Alan Charteris and D. D. Balfour. D.D., who later married Alfred Lyttelton, was no relation to Arthur Balfour. A London businessman's daughter, she was drawn into the Souls by merit of her brilliant talk and engaging intellect. Curzon, meeting her for the first time, was drawn by her considerable personal charms and tried to grope her when they were momentarily alone in the dining room at breakfast.[11] The Whites, the only non-British Souls, were Americans who had been in England since 1884 by reason of diplomat Harry White's position as First Secretary to the US Legation. Daisy White, a close friend of Edith Wharton's since childhood, was well admired, pretty, ambitious, and a key player among the rivalrous female Souls.[12] That evening, the party dressed as Cavaliers and Puritans, and sat on the stairs, moonlight streaming over them as D.D. and Emmie sang. 'Most of us looked quite picturesque and we all felt very sentimental. I wish you had been there and then it might have been perfect for me; or as perfect as anything can be,' Mary told Arthur.[13]

In fact, and unusually for Mary, she had counted the days until the party ended.[14] The fire had left her 'physically abattu . . . as if everything had been wiped out of my brain with a clean sponge or *burnt* away'.[15] Each morning was devoted to writing 'Fire letters', replying to the scores of condolences she received – many asking if it was true that Clouds really had been razed to the ground. 'I've done 25 today & yest & spent whole mornings in bed, writing and blotting self & sheets,' she recounted to Arthur some two weeks after the fire itself.[16]

In the fire's aftermath, the family 'knew nothing except how much we all loved each other & how close together we were drawn'.[17] '[H]ow tightly we are bound . . . how we all stand and fall together,' George Wyndham said to his mother.[18] Volatile Pamela was 'very brave and behaved splendidly' despite the loss of everything she owned, but she had nightmares about the fire for years.[19] To doubt-less intense relief Madeline Wyndham's nerves held up under the strain: perhaps the destruction of her jewel-like house confirmed her belief that the forces of light and darkness walked hand in hand. At least, she often said, death had never entered into the house.[20] Yet the utter destruction of Clouds – what Georgie Burne-Jones called 'that beautiful monument of loving and successful labour'[21] – was, said Betty Balfour, a 'heart-breaking event'.[22] Philip Burne-Jones cited the calamity to Gerald Balfour as philosophical proof of the existence of evil.[23] The most romantic of the Wyndhams' children echoed this view. 'Who the gods love die young,' said Pamela, describing Clouds as 'too ideal to live'.[24] From Ireland, George vowed to 'begin at once defeating evil Fortune and making it lovely again'.[25] Both he and Pamela regarded the fire, the first calamity they had faced, as an indication that the world must have been corrupted. Their self-conscious bravery is a reminder of how distinct Disraeli's 'two nations' of rich and poor remained: it displayed the arrogance of the Wyndhams' 'Plantagenet' strain. Of all the Wyndhams' children only Mary put the loss in perspective, not railing against fate, only pitying her parents. 'I've aches and aches for them and I have not suffered half enough it's too hard; all their love and labour lost, when one *did* so want them to enjoy the well-earned fruits of all their pains,' she wrote to Arthur.[26]

The conflagration in *Poynton* destroys, for ever, the work of a lifetime. The Wyndhams defied this. Webb's estimate for rebuilding was £26,741 17s. To Percy's relief, the insurers of the house and its contents paid in full, £28,345 12s from the Sun Insurance Company and £27,000 from the Royal Insurance Company, enabling him to rebuild Clouds identically – except with fire-proof flooring, additional tin-lined water pipes to avoid further troublesome plumbing and a new boot cupboard for Percy in his dressing room – and to refurnish it, replacing treasures lost in the fire. Percy calculated that he was only £3,000 out of pocket.[27] The Wyndhams moved into the offices for the duration of the rebuilding, operating a reduced staff and having only close friends to stay. 'It is a good thing that our architect was a socialist because we find ourselves just as comfortable in the servants' quarters as we were in our own,' commented Madeline Wyndham cheerfully.[28] They re-entered the 'Beautiful Phoenix', as they termed it, two and a half years later on 29 August 1891.[29]

ELEVEN

The Season of 1889

In Society's collective memory, the 1889 Season was a good one, enlivened by the Shah of Persia's visit, and the bursting into the public consciousness of the Souls after a dinner held by George Curzon for his thirty or so closest friends at the Bachelors' Club in Piccadilly. It was also the Season in which George Wyndham entered Parliament as the Conservative Member for Dover after a by-election in July 1889 ('Isn't it *delightful* George being an M.P.? & for Dover too such a nice place,' said Mananai);[1] and the eighteen-year-old Pamela Wyndham finally made her debut.

'The Babe', as Pamela was known to her family and their friends, appeared to have been granted all the blessings that accrue, fairytale-like, to the youngest child. With her delicate features and refined air,[2] she was considered the most beautiful of the sisters, second only to George in terms of Wyndham looks and, like him, 'literary and clever', as Mary remarked admiringly.[3] Pamela's contemporary, Edith Olivier, whose father was canon of nearby Wilton, said that Pamela 'seemed to pour ideas into one's mind like an empty glass'.[4] Like George, galloping across the Downs at sunrise and quoting Ronsard, Pamela rejected crude reality in favour of an idealized past. From a young age she collected folk ballads, and noted picturesque examples of village dialect. She read avidly, and kept a tally: seventy books for 1889. She adored the Brontës' tales of wild moors and love against the odds ('I can always read anything by them,' she told Mary),[5] the romances of Scott and the diaries of her FitzGerald ancestors. George addressed Pamela as 'Pamela III' in homage to Lady Edward (their grandmother, Lady Campbell, being 'Pamela II'); and there was certainly something regal in the way she comported herself. She disparaged 'the tyranny of the red blotting pad' over Mary, which meant that her sister spent her time writing letters rather than reading books: Mary's never diminishing 'nest egg' of unanswered letters 'is too much of a time-sucker with you!' said Pamela.[6]

Pamela in her late teens, by Violet Manners.

On seeing Pamela at this age Wilfrid Blunt was struck by her similarity to Mary, but Mary disclaimed the resemblance:

'Imagination I may have but wit *never*! & I was so silent.'[7] In fact they were very little alike. Pamela was born demanding attention: she was passionately jealous of those she loved. From little more than toddlerhood she sobbed if a sibling received a letter or present from their parents and she did not. At Clouds, she was queen. Villagers and guests alike were well accustomed to recitals from Pamela, singing folk ballads while accompanying herself on her ribbon-bedecked guitar, a Lacôte – the Stradivarius of guitar makers – which she received for her eighteenth birthday.[8]

Pamela had a constant sense of expectation, of greatness imminent; a sharp tongue; a facility for damning with faint praise; and her mother's love of birds: 'they would fly to her finger when she called, which she thought was marvellous', remembered Sir Stephen Runciman, a neighbour and contemporary of Pamela's children.[9] The comment might be a metaphor for Pamela's relationship with people, and when she entered Society, people flocked to her, attracted, no doubt, by her air of lofty unconcern. She did 'not allow her partners much time for talking or nonsense but kept them going', said Percy approvingly of her tendency to whisk young men efficiently around the dance floor.[10]

At almost a decade younger than most of the Souls, Pamela was still too newly arrived in Society to be a guest at Curzon's farewell dinner on 10 July 1889. Curzon had been diagnosed with lung trouble. He intended to summer in the healthful Alps, then travel across Central Asia to Persia, the buffer between India and Russia and fulcrum of Anglo-Russian rivalry. Renowned even at twenty-eight for his imperious manner and a self-confidence so fervent that people thought it must be hubristic, he was doggedly pursuing his long-held ambition to be India's Viceroy.

Persia's Shah was in fact being honoured that very same night at a dinner given by Lord Rothschild at Waddesdon Manor – meaning that some of those Curzon had invited could not attend the Bachelors' Club. The guests arrived to find a long, well-dressed table lit by candles, covered in blue glass and silver, and decorated with crystal bowls of flowers. Behind each chair, instead of footmen, stood club servants. On each chair was a lengthy piece of doggerel by Curzon listing and eulogizing each member of the Gang, both present and absent. Margot Tennant, always mindful of posterity, swiped her copy and recorded the work fifty years later in her memoirs. The verse on Mary and Hugo, with its sly reference to Hugo's infidelity, exemplified Curzon's tone:

From kindred essay
LADY MARY today
Should have beamed on a world that adores her.
Of her spouse debonair
No woman has e'er
Been able to say that he bores her . . .

Curzon's recital of his poem raised his already ebullient guests to exuberant spirits. Raucous singing and dancing followed. Even the normally reserved Balfour was capering as if possessed amid fun 'so loud it was impossible to hear anyone speak'. Eventually the party adjourned to the Tennants' house in Grosvenor Square where they danced until the early hours. The survivors, including Lady Brownlow, made their way home via the old flower market in Covent Garden, weaving through sleepy streets hazy with the morning sun, their arms full of flowers.

By lunchtime reports of the Souls' wild evening were already being exchanged third hand. Frances Balfour had bumped into a fresh-faced Lady Brownlow before eleven o'clock in the morning and been brought back to the Brownlows' for breakfast. The house was 'cool as an icebox' and 'a bower of roses' as usual, Frances told Betty Balfour that afternoon, passing on the gossip as soon as she received it. As Lady Brownlow furnished Frances with the details of the night before, her nephew Harry Cust stumbled in, still bleary-eyed, startled to see visitors already present. Lady Brownlow repaired to her bedroom with Frances in tow. She settled Frances into a comfortable chair, and grilled her guest on her views concerning the immortality of the soul.[11] It is understandable that Arthur, fond of her though he was, described Adelaide Brownlow as 'occasionally quite terrible'.[12]

The dinner made the Souls famous. By 1890 the *World* was devoting articles to 'this highest and most aristocratic cult . . . as liberal in its views as it is exclusive in its composition . . . Certain intellectual qualities are prominent among the Souls and a limited acquaintance with Greek philosophy is a *sine qua non*.'[13] Three years later Henry Labouchere's radical *Truth* got its hands on an 'Expression Exam paper': a quiz set by female Souls to while away a rainy afternoon and printed it in full:

1. Explain the following: The dull box. A greenhouse. A gorge riser. Gilletmongering. Atrophasia. Stinche. A Lou-good. Jephson. Whippingham. A felbrig. A float-face. Barloon.
2. Describe accurately the Block including the duties of the Mopper and the chief blockites, and explain in a few lines: a Stodgite, a groffality, blue face and horns, a John Stone, a Molly Corker, poivre aux pieds, manchettes, Eternity soup, six cloisters, type drawers.
3. Analyze the following phrases: This is distinctly Sir Giles. She almost pecked him. He has got a touch of egg. I have got three dentists today. Je suis mariée, vous n'êtes pas. He's got a cruet.[14]

The Souls professed themselves appalled by the disclosure, presuming that an enterprising servant must have filched the crumpled-up paper from a wastepaper basket.[15]

'Lady Mary' was one of those unable to attend the dinner, but her absence was nothing to do with the Shah. Instead she was in bed at Cadogan Square, frustrated and bored. Six weeks previously, she had given birth to her fourth child, a boy, christened Colin. The story went about among Mary's friends that when asked the sex of the child, Hugo said he did not know: 'the usual hardy annual', he presumed.[16] Mary was not hardy. More or less annual childbirth had weakened her to the extent that, a month after Colin's birth, and despite for the first time following to the letter her lying-in's requirements, her condition was so far from improved that she was returned to bed.[17] Dr Collins warned her that she would risk her life if she had any further children. By Mary's own account it appears to be at this point that sexual relations between the Elchos ceased entirely for a period of some six years.

The rude health of Mary's childhood had long since abandoned her. Her family and friends attributed it to her frenetic socializing. She rushed around, forgot to eat, slept little, never sat still and worried constantly. A light schedule consisted of 'only one, or perhaps two! Operas a week'.[18] Mananai thought Mary should be forced to stay in bed one day in seven simply to regain the energy she expended.[19] Instead Mary, who was prone to illness and on occasion thought herself the victim of septic pneumonia, arsenic poisoning and diphtheria, relied upon purported 'miracle cures'.[20] In the spring of 1891 after a particularly fierce bout of influenza, she took the 'Salisbury system: lots of hot water, which really does suit me & meat, no farinaceous food & very little vegetable'. 'Sounds odd, doesn't it? but its [sic] really easier to digest & for the pains gives more nutriment & doesn't create fermentation acidity etc,' she explained to her sister-in-law Evelyn de Vesci, adding that her mother 'told me I looked 5 years younger!'[21] She became dependent on her annual spa trips to the Continent, taken at each Season's end, to recoup the reserves of health and energy she had plundered during the rest of the year.

As transport to the Continent became cheaper and faster, spa tourism became a feature of the English social calendar. Each mineral spring – Kissingen, Baden-Baden, Ems, Schwalbach and Carlsbad to name just a few – had different medicinal properties. A multitude of guidebooks (most in convenient pocket editions) explained to the eager health tourist which resort would best suit their ailment: which of the alkaline, saline, sulphurous and ferrug-inous waters were aperient and which suited those prone to diar-rhoea; which were best for gout, for skin diseases, for anaemia, for

chlorosis and for 'female diseases' (these covered everything from
hysteria to failure to conceive). Many also listed the notables who
favoured each spa, allowing the socially ambitious, and snobbish,
to factor in the calibre of fellow cure-takers when choosing their
destination. Kissingen, the first spa Mary visited, in August 1890,
was her favourite. By the turn of the century she rarely ventured
anywhere else, making the journey each August, third class by rail,
after several weeks' worried consultation of Bradshaw's railway
timetable. She detailed with relish in her letters home all the
elements of her 'kur' and her body's response, dutifully swallowing
the three revolting glasses of water required daily that were mixed
with whey to mitigate their horrible taste. At the giant *Kurhaus*
that lay in the centre of each town she was subjected to inhalations,
to lengthy baths and to 'douches' in which the bloomer-clad patient
stood inside a cage and was pummelled by jets of water from all
angles. The only respite came when she was menstruating, for then
the treatment temporarily ceased: '[I] am rather longing for Bets[ey]
so's to give me a Kleine Pause,' Mary informed Hugo wearily from
Kissingen in 1900.[22]

Throughout the Season, Mary had received reports of Pamela's
excellent progress through the social scene. Pamela nonetheless
maintained an amused distance from 'worldly' Society's preoccupa-
tions. She thought a Saturday-to-Monday at the Brownlows'
Ashridge quite the nicest of the summer – principally, so she told
Mary, for an 'Elysian conversation' about books and poetry with a
fellow guest, Frank Myer, which proved so different from the
commonplace small talk dwelling on dance partners and grandees:
'he talked so agreeably, & after the ordinary "partner shah twaddle"
it was doubly delightful'.[23] Her dancecard was perpetually full, but
Pamela always expressed her preference for intellectual engagements.
While dinners with the Burne-Joneses and Henry James were 'really
delightful',[24] she described balls and parties in a wry, self-mocking
tone, amused at her own frivolity, clear that, unlike most, she could
see the Emperor's new clothes for exactly what they were.

At a ball held by the Rothschilds towards the end of July, Pamela was inundated with compliments on her gown: a simple white tulle dress, its bodice trimmed with 'a tiny wreath of forget-me-nots'. It was a 'dream-dress', she told her admirers. The inspiration had appeared to her in sleep the night before. On waking she had headed straight to Woollands' department store and trimmed the dress herself. 'It was *such* fun & really it looked very pretty & *every* one admired it!!!' she boasted to Mary, proving by her own effort the prophetic power of dreams – a concept in which she wholeheartedly believed.[25]

Pamela's Season ended in a flurry. She danced until 4 a.m. on consecutive nights (at Mrs Hope's and at the Dudley House Ball). The next day she lunched with her parents at White's to watch the Royal Procession. The gentlemen's club had been opened to women specifically for that occasion. 'It was like another Jubilee all the poor women kept fainting all round in the crowd, they kept handing glasses of water and salts to them from where we were.' In the evening, they attended the opera, *Otello* at the Lyceum, where only the fact that Desdemona was 'very ugly & rather fat' made the harrowing last scene bearable. The next day Pamela wrote to Mary as London emptied and the Wyndhams prepared to visit the Leconfields at Petworth. 'It seems incredible that *my* first Season should be over . . . I am not at all sorry it is over but filled with a sort of placid triumph at having managed to have had such a *delightful* time on this to most people unsatisfactory Earth!'[26]

Mary was delighted to receive Pamela's 'capital' letter.[27] She had packed off children and servants to Stanway, and on doctor's orders was spending a blissful fortnight at Felixstowe's Bath Hotel, doing nothing but lying on a wicker chair, basking in the sunshine, reading intermittently and looking out to sea. Much as Mary missed her children 'it really *is* a great rest being *without* them for a time', she admitted to Evelyn de Vesci. She received regular updates from Mrs Fry, and by return of post sent to her children paper 'jumping donkeys & cats & clowns' that she made to amuse them.[28] 'I shall hardly know [Colin] when I see him,' she added. 'Babies alter *so much* at first.'[29]

In September 1889, the Wyndhams gained another grandchild when Mananai gave birth to a girl at the Adeanes' London house, 65 Cadogan Place, a new-build just doors down from the Elchos. The Adeanes had been hoping for a son, and Mananai had decorated Babraham's nurseries accordingly: the day nursery papered with a Morris trellis of birds and roses, the two night nurseries painted pale yellow and pale blue.[30] They bore the disappointment of the sex bravely. 'Having a little baby does make me love you more . . . if that is possible,' Mananai told her mother, who came up to London with Percy and Pamela after the birth.[31] Mary 'loaned' her the use of Wilkes as a nurse. Charlie, who spent most of his wife's lying-in at her bedside eating muffins, gave her a small enamelled locket studded with diamonds intended to hold the baby's first 'fluff'.[32] Pamela was godmother, but she felt nonetheless 'left behind & wretched' with 'Mamma, you & worst of all Madeline . . . all three away from me on a shelf of experience I knew nothing about', she later recollected to Mary.[33]

Because the child was a girl she was christened with little fuss, a month later, after Mananai had been churched. The Wyndhams and Pamela were again in Ireland so Georgie Burne-Jones was Pamela's proxy at the font. Mananai wore a white 'nun's veiling dress' that had been part of her trousseau and a white felt hat with a large bow. The infant, who made 'just enough cry to be lucky',[34] was named Pamela Marie after her maternal and paternal aunts who stood as godmothers – and 'Of course because of Lady Edward FitzGerald,' said Queen Victoria knowledgeably when she enquired of her maid of honour the child's name; she recalled meeting the famous beauty when she was a small child and Lady Edward's looks had long gone. 'Is it not wonderful she should have such a memory and take such an interest in all one's belongings? It sounds trivial but these are the little things that make one love the Queen,' said Marie Adeane.[35]

TWELVE

The Mad and their Keepers

In 1891, after two years of travelling, George Curzon returned to England. The Souls celebrated with another Bachelors' Club dinner. Yet snobbish Curzon was appalled by developments in his absence. As the Souls gained in prominence, they had invited into their midst the talented and amusing, regardless of social background. For Curzon, the 'degradation' wrought upon 'our circle' was epitomized by 'the Cosquiths', a shorthand he used to describe Herbert Henry Asquith, the middle-class barrister shortly to leapfrog directly from Liberal backbencher to Home Secretary under Gladstone; and Oscar Wilde, lecture-giving aesthete, whose notoriety had taken a darker turn with the publication of his first novel, *The Picture of Dorian Grey*, in instalments in *Lippincott's Monthly Magazine* (it was deemed so scandalous that the newsagent W. H. Smith refused to sell those editions of *Lippincott's* at its stalls).[1]

'Gone forever is the old Gang and a few magnificent souls [sic] like you and Harry [Cust], [Doll] Liddell, Mary Elcho and myself remain. The rest are whirling after new Gods and baring their heads in the temple of twopenny Rimmons,'[2] Curzon told Harry White, sadly and grandly, upon hearing that Ettie Grenfell had invited Oscar and Constance Wilde, Henry Asquith and his wife Helen,[3] and the actor-manager Herbert Beerbohm Tree and his wife (also called Helen) to Taplow Court, the Grenfells' house in Berkshire. Curzon urged White to capsize the interlopers' punt while on the river.[4] In fact, Mary had turned traitor too. In the previous six months alone, she had gone to the theatre '*à quatre*' with Wilde, Arthur and Ettie, and had had Wilde to dine at Cadogan Square where he kept his end of the table 'alive with paradox', and her guests, including Arthur, George and Sibell, and Edward Burne-Jones, stayed until well after midnight: 'so I suppose they weren't bored', she said with relief.[5] With her consuming interest in people, and her expansive warmth, Mary was to become renowned for introducing new people into the Souls.

That same summer, Curzon forced an uncomfortable confrontation between himself and Wilde at the meeting of the Crabbet Club, an all-male club that met annually at Wilfrid Blunt's Sussex estate. The Crabbet's stated purpose was 'to discourage serious views of life'. Its annual meeting consisted of a poetry competition and a night of Bacchanalian excess. Its membership, recruited by Wilfrid and George Wyndham in collaboration, was primarily male Souls. By convention each new member was subjected to 'jibes' – a grilling on his life and work.[6] The two new members that summer were Curzon and Wilde. Curzon demanded that he be the one to grill Wilde.

As recorded by Blunt in his diary, Curzon was ruthless: attacking Wilde for his treatment of sodomy in *Dorian Gray* and suggesting that Wilde engaged in such practices himself. The fleshy Wilde at first smiled helplessly, but eventually gave 'an amusing and excellent speech'. The debate continued until dawn when some of the Club, including Curzon and George Wyndham, went to swim in the river, followed by a game of lawn tennis – 'just as they were, stark naked, the future rulers of England', said Wilde.[7] Shortly afterwards, Wilde met the Wyndhams' cousin Bosie Douglas, and their destructive mutual infatuation began. Bosie later joined the Crabbet, but Wilde never attended another meeting – an indication, probably, of his distaste for it.

The following year, the poetry competition's theme was 'Marriage'. Harry Cust's offering brimmed with ironic self-knowledge:

Various vigorous virgins may have panted
Wailing widows wilted in the dust
To no female has the great God granted
Grace sufficient to be Mrs. Cust

Harry Cust, by his lover, Violet Manners.

Contemporary paeans to Harry's heavenly blond appearance must be measured against the adolescent Judith Blunt's cool estimation: 'fat podgy and coarse, his hair and eyes too light for his red complexion'.[8] Indisputably, 'Cust bulged with sex.'[9] His quicksilver charm could, and did – quite literally – lay all before him. His 'harem'[10] included his long-term mistress, Violet Granby (as Violet Manners had become when her husband succeeded as Marquess), and Lucy Graham Smith. Harry did not adhere to the Souls' morality. He conceived sexual improvidence as an aristocratic right; moral restraint was mealy-mouthed and middle class. 'What if all had been forbidden *but* the apple? Imagine polygamy advanced by God and man, and at this moment all the upper classes would have been dwelling in the joys of illicit constancy and despising the cowardly unenterprising middle classes who were forced to content themselves with profligacy,' he mused to Mary in 1887.[11] Violet had little truck with Souls morality either. By 1892, she was pregnant with Harry's child.

By the summer of 1892, Pamela was the only one of the Wyndhams' children yet to be settled. In May, Guy had married Edwina Brooke (nicknamed 'Minnie'), a widow with two children who was five years older than he. Both Madeline Wyndham's sons had sought out maternal figures, but this marriage was to prove very happy. Shortly afterwards Harry Cust joined the Wyndhams for a performance of Wagner's *Tannhäuser* at Covent Garden, part of a sell-out season of German opera conducted by Richard Mahler. In retrospect, the choice was ominous. *Tannhäuser* skated on the edge of respectability, examining the choice between sacred and profane love. Wilde used it in *Dorian Gray* to reflect the darkness of his hero's own soul.

Seven years before, Laura Tennant had pitied women, who were expected to fight with 'unarmed breast . . . as strongly as the cap and pied man', and warned Mary about the capacity of the world 'to see things in embryo'.[12] As Mary sat in the Wyndhams' box and saw Harry's exaggerated flirting with Pamela, leaning low over her to point out some detail in the programme, whispering in her ear, she was filled with foreboding. Harry was a close friend, but he was a dangerous proposition. His behaviour had the capacity to damage Pamela's reputation severely. Yet it was possible that Harry was serious. To test if it was so, Mary invited him to Stanway when Pamela was there. By unspoken rule, if he accepted, it would mean that he planned to court her in earnest. Harry turned down the invitation. Mary and Madeline Wyndham decided to nip things in the bud before any further harm was done. They forbade both parties from seeing each other. A month passed in this way, causing Pamela intense anxiety as she scanned crowded ballrooms for his tall blond figure, playing out in her mind what would happen if he 'accidentally' appeared.

Harry's eventual appearance was every bit as dramatic as Pamela might have hoped. On 15 August 1892, a fortnight before Violet Granby gave birth to his daughter, Harry pitched up unannounced in Belgrave Square's drawing room before a startled Madeline and a delighted Pamela. The incident, as recounted by Pamela to Mary, had aspects of a drawing-room farce. Barely had Harry managed to explain that he had turned down the Stanway invitation because 'He does not want to make love to me (only less crudely expressed by him!)'[13] than the butler Icke precipitated into the drawing room a young 'Mr. Allhuisen' who was intending, most likely, to pay court to Pamela. Harry was hustled off into the front drawing room by Madeline Wyndham, Pamela left to sit and drink tea with the hapless 'Mr. A' while trying to eavesdrop on the muffled conversation behind the double doors.

Behind those doors, Madeline Wyndham laid down the law in somewhat unsatisfactory fashion. She told Harry he could see Pamela only if he promised to stop his 'coarse flirting'. If and when he was willing to seek her hand in earnest, then he could. Harry promised. Pamela was delighted, although she protested that Harry had never been flirting. 'His manner which has grown upon him misleads people . . . he says "How do you do" as if it was "you are the Soul of my Life" but he is unaware of this, I really believe like people who clear their throats continually,' she explained to Mary.[14]

Osbert Sitwell, meeting Pamela in middle age, recognized the discordance between her image and her reality. 'She was – though she in no way realized it – far from being a rather remote, reasonable woman, under which guise she saw herself, presented herself, and was accepted, but, to the contrary . . . violently and enchantingly prejudiced in a thousand directions.' Her sitting room was filled with photographs 'of the most astonishing rakes and rips' whom Pamela would 'unflaggingly, and with the greatest display of ingenuity defend' or, where defence was impossible, 'ignore'.[15] Pamela declared that she would not be 'deceived by outside views!!!',[16] but she was more than capable of deceiving herself by her own tortuous logic.

Pamela maintained to Mary that the best way for her to get over Harry was 'by *knowing* him not by not seeing him', since separation only allowed her to gild him in her imagination. 'If I in any way let my friendship with him spoil my life it would be voluntary foolishness on my part . . .' she added.[17] Mary worried that Pamela was motivated merely by pique. When she found out that Pamela – who as Madeline Wyndham's 'Benjamina', a biblical allusion to Jacob's beloved youngest son, could twist her mother around her little finger – had persuaded Madeline to invite Harry to Clouds she was horrified. She immediately wrote to Madeline warning against this course of action. It was too late.

Harry joined the tail end of a house party to find Pamela distracted by the company of a young man called Arthur Paget.[18] It was idyllic late-summer weather. The party had spent a 'delicious' week making excursions to Stonehenge, and taking long walks across the Downs. Pamela confessed to Mary privately that she thought more 'highly of [Paget than] any man before . . . delightfully clever, original & nice – good & kind & honest (what a funny lot of adjectives strung together!)'.[19] Harry sulked, moped and glowered until finally (as no doubt he designed) Pamela confronted him on the Sunday afternoon in the empty hall, whereupon he told her 'all that he meant *not* to say (so he says) but *I* think, it was all that he *did not expect to feel*'.

Pamela wrote the conversation out in full for Mary. The exchange is worthy of a cheap melodrama, with Harry the moustache-twirling villain. Harry declared his love, explained (without explaining why) that he was not free, and asked Pamela – supposing that, in two years or so, he could make himself free – whether she would agree to be his wife. To Pamela's surprise, as she stood incredulously by the fireplace with hands like ice, she found herself saying that she was not sure:

'In the Summer I was afraid I let you think more than I was prepared actually to *do* – I think that I have changed.'

And he put his head against the mantelpiece, & looked very miserable, & said: 'Perhaps you are right'

'But I cannot believe it – it seems so odd if you could, would you ask me to be your wife?'

'I would'

'And if in this next year I was to marry somebody would you mind?'

'I would mind *awfully*'

& then we were quiet for a long time.

Harry then broke out into a rage of self-recrimination, berating himself for having broken his word to Madeline Wyndham, blaming his intolerable, uncontrollable jealousy, his feeling that to lose Pamela would be to miss 'a most perfect good':

& again & again, I kept saying 'I do not think you mean it – are you serious – do you really love me or do you think you do?'

'I love you, & you only, & you always'

Mary, would even the most self-blinded flirt say that? Surely he would have kept to the suggested vaguenesses that he has hitherto spoken in – not compromised himself unless he meant it?

Harry's final words were a masterpiece of manipulation: 'I want to try & get as right as I can – and in the mean time no words of mine are to tie you in the very *least* – think of nothing I have said – when you are tired of me . . . you are to throw me away like a sucked orange, & marry the best man you can – though I shall be *furious* if you do – but that will be nothing to you.'[20]
On hearing of this 'episode', Mary was furious: 'just like him I feel inclined to say & think he has shown great want of self-control *his great vice*. Why not now if he really means it?' she asked her baffled mother.[21] Mary's fingers were crossed for the 'nice-sounding' Arthur Paget, but she knew the 'horribly clever' Harry and her own sister too well for that. Mary was right. By Christmas Arthur Paget and another young suitor had been dispatched, the Wyndhams' friends were beginning to gossip that the unorthodox parenting methods practised at Clouds were coming home to roost, and Percy was concerned enough to write to Mary about the matter at what was, for him, some length.
As a rule Percy concerned himself little with his children's marriages. His personal experience made him sympathetic to the pull of 'magnetisme, attraction'. He thought parents pushing their children into loveless, wealthy marriages were simply 'wrong'. But he believed that relying upon mere attraction was far worse and he baulked at the 'apparently insane' justification of 'love conquers all' woven by his youngest daughter and Harry Cust.[22] When he tried to enumerate the risks of marrying a man like Cust, he had

to put his pen down, overwhelmed by the multitude that presented themselves. Eventually, he adopted a light-hearted tone, dividing the world into two camps: the 'mad' and the sane, who were their 'keepers'. 'Myself, Mamma and Pamela are undoubtedly mad, Mananai I am *sure* is a keeper.' Mary seemed to veer between the two. Percy was clear where Harry stood. 'N.B. He, Cust, is sane,' he wrote in a tiny postscript that revealed the root of his misgivings: for, spiderlike, Cust seemed to be playing with Pamela, trapped like a fly in his web.[23]

THIRTEEN

Crisis

As Christmas approached, the atmosphere at Clouds was tense. Percy's doubts about Cust were growing, as were his fears for his wife's state of mind. His irascibility was enhanced by the presence of all four of Mary's children in the nurseries. Mary, considered by her contemporaries to be a devoted mother, was frequently absent from her children for extended periods of time: she spent almost six months of both 1890 and 1891, whether at a house-party, on a cure, ill, or in London, apart from them.[1] During such absences, Mary frequently left her children at Clouds. It saved the Elchos the expense of running Stanway in their absence; and Mary disliked taking her children to Gosford, believing the journey too long. Cynthia Charteris visited Gosford for the first time that she could remember when she was six years old.[2]

Three and a half years of no physical relations had shown what a binding force sex had been for the Elchos. They bickered like children. In January 1891, Mary sent Evelyn de Vesci a long apology for their recent confused departure from Abbey Leix. The morning they were due to leave, Hugo refused: 'said he had a boil on his nose & sat on his bed & would not dress'. Mary stormed off to the railway station, servants and luggage in tow before her rage quelled. She returned and played the 'ma[r]tyr'. Eventually they took the later train that Hugo had wanted. In the process, Mary accidentally made off with John de Vesci's latest copy of the periodical *Nineteenth Century*. She told Evelyn that she had left it with the railway porter. 'I hope he will get [it].'[3] Evelyn was wearily familiar with contre-temps like these.

Mary's letters to Hugo, which had once mixed admonitions with caresses in 'Spression', were now primarily couched in plain English: asking her husband where he was, when he was coming back, and why he did not reply. Any compliment seemed more an attempt to provoke him into good behaviour than a response to it. Hugo's incessant infidelity was so poorly concealed that at one point Ettie Grenfell (herself the recipient of his attentions) intervened to urge him, at the very least, to exercise a little discretion.[4] At the turn of the decade Hugo began a relationship with the renowned beauty Hermione, Duchess of Leinster, a distant kinswoman by marriage of Mary's.[5] By the early 1890s he was more frequently at Carton, Hermione's house in Ireland, than at Stanway. If, as he sat at dinner underneath Lord and Lady Edward FitzGerald's portraits, joking with Hermione's friends, he felt any pangs of guilt he did not show it.[6] Mary reproached him for his inconsiderate behaviour, chal-lenged him on his gambling, asked him questions about children and arrangements: in short, engaged him in the minutiae of married life. Hermione told Hugo that his love for her was 'the one happi-ness of her unhappy life'. In her eyes, the errant son and disap-pointing husband was the perfect lover.[7]

Mary was widely regarded as a saint for putting up with Hugo, and her perceived forbearance regarding Arthur Balfour was consid-ered, even by the most morally exacting of her contemporaries, to be 'wonderful'. In 1891, Arthur had returned from Ireland to take up the post of Leader of the House of Commons, and First Lord of the Treasury. The 1892 election delivered Gladstone to power for a fourth time, and put Arthur in opposition. The greater free time this afforded him meant that he and Mary were ever more in proximity. Yet, remarked Ettie Grenfell, 'I *cannot* make it out – 'she [Mary] seems never to see him [Arthur] alone, positively to avoid it.' Ettie put this down to Mary's 'prudence . . . I do admire her courage intensely.'[8] 'Lady Elcho is an angel: of all the women I know, an angel,' said Lady Lyttelton, wife of the soldier Sir Neville.[9]

Privately there remained, in Mary's phrase, an 'unstable equilibrium!'[10] As she drily pointed out to Arthur, on the increasingly rare occasions when Hugo was with only his family 'he has more time for observation'. On a summer's evening in 1890 when all three were visiting the Adeanes at Babraham. Hugo materialized in Mary's room before dinner and tormented her with questions. Had Arthur ever openly expressed his fondness for her? What exactly had he said? Such questions 'screw up my entrails! And make me feel quite quivering,' Mary told Arthur the next day, apologizing for her silence all evening. '[C]hilld to the bone' and feeling 'particularly helpless and nervous', she had been unable to talk to him normally. Sitting after dinner in the Italian Colonnade, she had only been able to hope, impotently, that Arthur would ask her to watch the moon rise on the other side of the house, allowing her to escape Hugo's sardonic gaze. Arthur didn't.[11] Mary was anguished. She perpetually feared that Arthur would abandon her for a younger, prettier woman who could offer him more by way of sex than she.[12] Arthur, capable of cattishness, did not always dispel those fears. In a particularly low blow he even once eulogized Hermione and her artistic skill.[13] 'No woman, wife or mother is ever quite her own master,' said Mary.[14] Hugo's and Arthur's behaviour often forcibly reminded her of that.

By the time Mary arrived at Clouds on 21 December 1892, she had not seen her children for over a month. Her primary concern was for Ego, still overly nervy after a bout of scarlet fever he had contracted in the autumn, but she put it down to Christmas excitement. A shoot planned for 28 December had kept the Adeanes and their girls at Babraham; George and Sibell were at Eaton in Cheshire with the Westminsters; Guy and Minnie were in India. It being a high day and holiday, Hugo was present too.

On Christmas morning the children's stockings were crammed with toys. As the family walked to East Knoyle church, three-year-old Colin delighted every passer-by with a prattling 'Merry Christmas'. Just a few hours later he was struck by scarlet fever; Hugo and the other children fell sick the next day. Five-year-old Cynthia remembered 'a timeless blur of bewildered suffering. Burning heat, raging thirst, tossing and turning in sheets that seemed on fire'.[15] In a journal that recorded her children's infancies and early youths, Mary recalled that she had been ordered by the doctor not to go to her children in case she caught the fever herself. But she had already had scarlet fever in her late teens, and would have been immune. In fact, as Mary recorded to George in a letter just a few days later, Mary had stayed by Colin's side until Hugo 'begged me to go with tears in his eyes' for 'the others' [children's] sake'. Half an hour after Mary left him, Colin died. Heartbreakingly, Mary was told that Colin had been conscious and had asked for her.[16]

'I think there must be *no* heartache like that of losing a child,' said Pamela as she watched over Mary, lying 'very still' in her quiet darkened room.[17] 'I am sure she is brave & *wonderful*,' wrote Mananai impotently to her mother as the news reached the Adeanes at Babraham; 'kiss her from me.'[18] Colin was buried on a sunny bank under a laburnum tree in the East Knoyle churchyard. By convention Mary did not attend to see the small white coffin decked with flowers go into the earth. A notice in the *Evening Times* alerted the world. Letters of condolence flooded in, offering varying degrees of comfort. Almost all spoke of how close Mary had been to her son, how much she had loved him, how happy his life had been.

Around 14 per cent of infants born in England and Wales between 1860 and 1900 never reached their first birthday. Disease was the most common cause of death, and scarlet fever, gastro-enteritis, dysentery, measles, smallpox and tuberculosis among the most prevalent diseases. Upper-class children had a better rate of survival: approximately 8 per cent of infants died in their first year, and 5 per cent between the ages of one and five. The old assumption that parents of this era were somehow immune to infant death has been discredited. Parents cared deeply, particularly when, like Mary, they had no strong religious faith to console them.[19]

Outwardly and for the sake of her children she put on a 'resolute, almost jaunty brightness'. Cincie, who tiptoed out of the nursery to find her mother sitting on the stairs 'weeping as if her heart must break', knew differently.[20] Mary was plagued by the fear that Colin had died in pain, alone, thinking his mother had abandoned him. She asked Arthur whether life could be checked without great suffering. Arthur employed all his philosophical detachment to help her, but his reductionist argument – 'It was right that you should be absent . . . it would have been most wrong because most useless that you should be present' – can have helped little. But he had a stronger argument: it was 'not the last farewell, the last look, the last word that *ever* matters', but the life preceding it, 'the endless trifles of which everything really important consists'. Between Mary and Colin 'there never was anything in your relations . . . which now you need desire to be unsaid or undone. How rarely can a mother say this of any child?'[21]

Mary and her children, accompanied by a nurse and Cincie's governess Miss Jourdain, did not leave Clouds until March: Guy Charteris had developed complications from the fever and was too ill to be moved until then. They were to convalesce in Hyères, joining Madeline and Percy who had developed the habit of wintering there. Hugo was to make sporadic visits from London.

The departure was bleak. Guy was sewn up in an eiderdown to protect him from the cold; Cincie wept all the way. Mary had been set on cramming her entire family into one sleeping car, and only with great difficulty was dissuaded from sleeping top-to-toe in a bunk with Cincie, an instinct that seems driven by vulnerability rather than frugality. A party of friends and relatives saw them on to the boat train in London; another met them at Hyères where they settled into a tiny doll's-house of a place called the Villa Marguerite.

Anyone who has grieved will be drearily familiar with the path that Mary trod that 'long and un-ending' spring, as the exaltation of grief gives way to the dull realization that what seems an experiment in loss is actually a new reality. Without a strong faith – throughout her life, her letters spoke little of God – or her mother's spiritualist beliefs, Mary found little to console her. 'I do *not* feel as if he were near!. . . but then I should hate & could not bear to feel that he was hanging about, missing the spring and wanting to live,' she said to her mother. Not knowing what to think, she had only unanswerable questions and a deep sense of guilt. Watching her children grow stronger and play among the same olive groves she had run through as a child, she felt some relief, but 'Spring intensifies everything.' She was 'horrid', she told her mother, and nothing could help her.[22]

Mary and her children left Hyères in mid-May and went straight to Felixstowe. In deep mourning, Mary eschewed the Season entirely, only stopping briefly in London to see Madeline Adeane, who had given birth to a third girl, called Madeline after herself. She then left to summer in Sweden where a Dr Widegren had promised to restore her to health. With a distracted mother, the Charteris children ran wild and unruly. They did not return to Stanway until October 1893, almost a year since they had first left it.[23] Colin's death drove his parents still further apart. Hugo's absence is notable in the records of this period. Reading Mary's bald account of her son's death in *Family Record* it is hard not to escape the conclusion that she blamed Hugo for her absence from Colin at his death – even, perhaps, for his death. That, even as Mary mourned, in Hermione Leinster's nurseries was a six-month-old son, a child that was undoubtedly Hugo's, cannot have failed to intensify Mary's deep-seated grief and rage.[24]

In mid-August Arthur attended a Saturday-to-Monday at Ashridge. Harry Cust, the Brownlows' heir, Violet Granby and their mutual young cousin Nina Welby were among the party. A drawing of Nina by Violet shows a dark, slim, pretty girl with a distinctly doleful air. Nina was utterly in Violet's thrall, and well known to be besotted with Harry. Arthur described to Mary an uneventful weekend. He had unsuccessfully tried to evade the clutches of Adelaide Brownlow and been 'carried off' by her for a long walk before dinner: 'she nearly makes me cry with boredom'. He had written a little more of *Foundations of Belief*, which he had begun in 1892 (it was his second book following on from *A Defence of Philosophic Doubt* published in 1879),[25] played some lawn tennis and had a nice talk on art with a young female guest. 'H.C. seemed to me rather to neglect his harem – those who were there – but was pleasant enough to the outside world.'[26]

Shortly afterwards, Harry went to Clouds. His behaviour seemed promising. 'He does not flirt in the coarse way he did but is deferential & attentive & vy. pleasant to evry [sic] one. He & George have endless arguments on Poetry,' Madeline Wyndham told Mary.[27] Percy thought Pamela looked prettier, happier and more hopeful every day, though he maintained some misgivings. 'I *hope* it may all turn out well,' he told Mary. 'I wish I had better grounds for *thinking* it would.'[28] It seems likely that at this point Harry and Pamela became secretly engaged. George Wyndham subsequently told Wilfrid Blunt that only the thought that Lucy Graham Smith might 'make trouble in the matter' had prevented an announcement before Lucy had been duly mollified.[29]

As Harry left Clouds, the state of affairs was 'like an extremely delicate weather glass', said Pamela.[30] She knew the dangers of marriage to Harry, but it offered the chance to do more than 'just live and be passive'. 'I feel I could without any hesitation jump into a chasm for someone . . . or cut off a finger – or anything *real*,' she told Mary. Her letters were filled with rhetorical flourishes: she was a lone warrior going out to meet an army; a sailor refusing to turn back at the sight of stormy seas. She discussed the conflict between her 'hill self' – the self of thoughts, ideas and inspiration, found in church and at Bayreuth – and her 'earth self' – 'the one who talks, sleeps and comes down to breakfast'[31] – in a convoluted discourse that would have done justice to George pirouetting in the House of Commons. She explained to Mary:

> One thing I have learnt in my life & I am glad I have learnt it so young, is that to look for peace & happiness in perfect *entirety* is a wild goose chase in this world . . . in the end the *chances* of happiness are more equally balanced than one thinks, what may seem 'wreckage' viewed in one way – may not be more 'wreckage' than lives outwardly perfectly matched.[32]

It was doubtful logic.

In September, Madeline Wyndham took to her bed. Her guests were told she was suffering from rheumatism and a bad cold. It is likely that her nerves were succumbing under the strain. Pamela and Mananai, who was visiting, were left to hold the fort. Pamela took pleasure in the ill-concealed surprise of their eminent guests – mostly male Souls – at finding her and Mananai hosting with not one of the Souls hostesses, like Mary, Ettie or Margot, in attendance. She took equal pleasure in defeating their attempts to make her change her mind about Harry. On a sunset walk Richard Haldane, a Scottish Liberal Imperialist barrister who was gradually being drawn within the Souls' ambit (and whom Walburga, Lady Paget, a fellow guest that week, thought conversed 'in epigrams and aphorisms'),[33] told Pamela that Harry was a man she could better help as friend than as wife, and that he 'should not regret it' if she 'postponed a decision'. The following week Asquith, now Home Secretary, and courting Margot Tennant, talked urgently of silk purses and sows' ears. Later that day it was Arthur's turn. From Sweden Mary had begged him to make Pamela see sense, but Arthur was 'on a pedestal of perfection as always' and could not bring himself to come down off his plinth to talk about Cust, 'so we reached home again having discussed civilization!'[34] said Pamela mischievously, particularly delighted to have outwitted Arthur, whose understated intelligence always made her own pretensions seem florid, and whose loyalty to Mary made her feel scorned. Pamela liked having primacy in people's affections.

For almost a decade, the Souls had prided themselves upon their moral precepts, on behaving in a more high-minded fashion than the Marlborough House Set, who were perpetually plagued by scandal. They were the intellectual, spiritual, thoughtful face of the aristocracy, with men and women in the group existing on an equal plane. This was blown out of the water by what ensued. Unbeknown to everyone except the participants, Harry and Nina Welby had been conducting an affair for the previous year, aided and abetted by Violet, who pushed forward Nina, her acolyte, as her candidate for Harry's wife, knowing that that way she could maintain her hold over her lover. At Ashridge, as a 'leave-taking' Harry and Nina spent 'some nights together . . . with the result that she had become or thought herself with child', wrote a fascinated Wilfrid Blunt in his diary some months later, agog at the scandal that threatened to undo the Souls.[35]

In the aftermath of the affair, the Souls shunned Violet, the Machiavellian Circe who had sacrificed the virginal Nina to her own sexual ends. Such outrage over premarital sex was to a degree dissimulation. It happened among the elite. It is suggested that Lord and Lady Randolph Churchill had used Lady Randolph's unwed pregnancy to secure their families' approval of their match.[36] Even among the Souls, Margot Tennant used Wilfrid Blunt to relieve her of her virginity – if his diary can be believed.[37] But it was not common, and a scandal like this was unthinkable. In September, Nina wrote to Harry to tell him that she was pregnant. Harry either did not reply, or replied 'with great brutality'.[38] In desperation, Nina sought Violet's help. Violet, in Nina's words, took 'the matter out of my hands' and bruited the affair about the Souls, imploring the Brownlows, Balfour, Asquith, Curzon to help save Harry from 'worldly disgrace' and make him marry Nina.

The resultant chaos is reflected in the tangle of papers in the Whittingehame archives, with the instruction 'Mr Balfour says burn eventually' scribbled across the front. By unspoken agreement, Arthur, as 'High Priest' of the Souls, was to resolve the crisis. His inclination to destroy this evidence is unsurprising. 'I am coming to you on a matter of life and death' reads an undated scrap of paper from Nina; 'Oh! I feel more fiendish than anyone can ever have felt before' reads a letter from Violet. A letter from Lady Welby-Gregory, imploring Arthur to use his influence to make Harry marry her daughter is followed by outraged missives from Adelaide Brownlow deploring her nephew's behaviour; and telegrams from George Wyndham and George Curzon, Balfour's lieutenants, 'tearing about the country on one sad errand after another' trying to settle the matter and keep it hidden from the outside world.[39]

The matter was so heavily hushed up at the time that even those within the Souls were not sure of exactly what was happening. To this day, accounts differ.[40] 'Believe nothing that you hear,' George told Ettie Grenfell. 'No one whom you will meet knows the whole truth & those who know a part spend their time in perverting it.'[41] 'I am so anxious so anxious,' said Pamela, bombarding Sibell with questions and God with her prayers.[42] By this time, George had broken the news of Nina's pregnancy to his family, and Madeline Wyndham, collapsing along with the whole house of cards, had been hustled off to Bournemouth in an invalid's carriage (that is, a railway carriage fitted out with a brass bed and sprung mattress so that she could lie flat all the way).[43]

There was only one way this matter could be resolved. Harry must marry Nina, although Balfour had to threaten Cust with social ostracism and political exile before he complied.[44] On 3 October 1893 Harry stood once again before Pamela by the hearthstone in Clouds' hall. With George lurking quietly in the background he revealed to Pamela the full extent of events and his impending forced marriage. 'Whatever I did, sad, mad and bad I always said to myself, "I have got Pamela, *like a star in a cupboard* to come

back to,' said Harry.[45] Pamela did not castigate Harry then, or ever.
She had already cast him as a Christlike figure and reserved her
anger for the world that had sacrificed him on the altar of conventional morality. Harry described Pamela as 'a little heroine thro'out
& a little saint as well'.[46] He immortalized their mutual sacrifice in
the poem 'Non Nobis', which presented Pamela as that saint and
himself as a flawed mortal purged by suffering.

It was inevitable, perhaps, that the Wyndhams should send Pamela
abroad to escape the scandal. The Adeanes had been planning a trip
to India. Percy paid for them to take Pamela with them: no expense
spared. A passage was booked on the *Ganges* in November[47] (fortunately not on the same ship as Lucy Graham Smith, who was also
dispatched to India by her family to recover from Cust). In the
intervening weeks, Pamela was sent to Saighton Grange, one of the
Westminsters' houses in Cheshire, where George and Sibell lived, to
stay with them.

Many years later Osbert Sitwell commented to Pamela on her
apparently unlimited reserves of social grace. In response Pamela
showed him her scarred palms: to maintain composure when
enraged she clenched her fists so tightly that her fingernails cut
into the skin.[48] She remembered this time as a blur of pain and
suffering: shaking and sobbing in Saighton's chapel while clasped
in Sibell's arms. But in front of the other guests she tried to maintain her composure. She sang old sea ballads and read Blunt some
of her poetry. He thought her 'delightful, with wit and sense and
feeling'; her poetry 'really excellent, original and good, far beyond
what is usual with young ladies', and was so taken with his young
cousin that he was moved to compose one of his acrostics, a
favoured seductive tool, using her name – Pamela Genevieve
Adelaide Wyndham – to praise her to the skies,[49] as a woman
capable of inspiring a knight to valorous battle, 'empires [to] bend
and break' and 'kingdoms [to] crumble down'.[50]

Such was Society's understanding of a common code that when,
on his return to Crabbet a few days later Wilfrid read the bald

announcement in *The Times* 'that Harry Cust has been "recently married" to Miss Welby',[51] and that the newlyweds had departed England for the Continent[52] – without the customary engagement announcement – he immediately knew something was up. As George Curzon made his way to the Carlton Club in Pall Mall, he was 'inundated with enquiries' from intrigued acquaintances who had also seen the suspicious notice. London was pricking up its ears for a scandal. The Souls closed ranks. 'Since H.C. has, though tardily done the right thing I am sure you will agree that we should now try to save both of them from the consequences of this foolish delay,' Curzon proposed in a note dashed off to Arthur as soon as he was safely inside. He suggested they cobble together a story that 'will impose upon none of the innermost circle: but if industriously circulated may shut the mouths of the public'.[53] The approved version, neatly typed and sent *inter alia* to the Tennants at the Souls stronghold of the Glen and to the intractable Brownlows, explains a long attachment, familial opposition on both sides (due to Harry's 'entanglements with married women': a positively safe vice now in light of recent events), a decision to marry 'at all hazards nonetheless'. The story contained enough truth to be almost plausible, although as Nina's elder brother Charles said ruefully, 'it's a thin veil at best'.[54]

'Flirtation practice' had brought the Souls to the edge of public scandal and they recoiled. 'To a good many pretty tough and experienced men and women of the world this has been a positively startling revelation of the things that can happen amongst people presumably refined and well-meaning,' said Lord Pembroke.[55] Eight months later, Wilfrid Blunt lunched with Margaret Talbot, not herself a Soul, to find she had given up all vanity, in part 'thanks to the hideous scandals connected with Harry Cust, they have frightened her, as they have many others'.[56] Violet was shunned. Harry's own status within the group never quite recovered. By the spring of 1894 he was out of politics, his editorship of the *Pall Mall Gazette* his sole occupation, and to the next generation a tired, somewhat seedy figure with only the faint glow of someone of whom greatness had once been predicted. The Cust affair showed how determinedly the Souls, despite steps towards gender parity, were of their time. Violet was deemed the ultimately culpable sorceress; Harry, albeit deceitful, the mortal man unable to control his impulses. When it became apparent shortly after the marriage that Nina was no longer pregnant – the inescapable conclusion being that Nina, forced by Harry, had had an abortion[57] – D. D. Lyttelton thought that Nina should die of shame. 'I don't want her to, though I generally feel it to be the only solution,' she added charitably.[58]

FOURTEEN

India

Several weeks later, on a grey November's day, Pamela stared out of the window of the boat-train taking her from Victoria Station to Southhampton, sick with misery. The most prosaic details of ordinary life that flashed past – 'even the milk-cans & the papers at the station' – were 'each a separate little agony' reminding her of a world that she was leaving behind.[1]

The weeks between Harry's marriage and Pamela's departure for India had not been easy for any of the Wyndhams. Madeline Wyndham remained in the throes of a breakdown at Bournemouth, under the care of a nurse until early December. Percy stayed at his wife's side. Pamela was kept at Saighton, out of Percy's way. Their relations, already at breaking point, deteriorated still further when Percy found out in late October that a stream of letters and keepsakes were still passing between Harry at Fontainebleau and Pamela at Saighton. '*How long is the writing to continue*,' he demanded of Mary as he realized Sibell's limitations as a chaperone: 'In my judgment the things [sic] seems *very far from over* with the chains, rings and copies of Browning poems!. . . I feel that they are all so sunk in fatuity that no words can save them.'[2] Enraged by his daughter's 'freaks' and tears, furious about the affair that had caused his wife's breakdown, Percy was astonished that Pamela did not have the sense to realize that 'Letters from [Harry] after his marriage that would have been harmless under ordinary circumstances cease . . . to be so after what has passed between them.'[3] Percy decided to ban all communication between Pamela and Harry henceforth, but the edict – delivered at Mary's suggestion more softly by herself – did not end matters completely. The lovers continued to communicate through Sibell. 'Except by English law I am not one bit married, save to Pamela only,' Harry told Sibell in a rather belated conversion to chastity, while also declaring Pamela 'the one pure perfect love of my life'. Pamela received each message with joy. She seems to have thought of Nina not at all.[4]

As Pamela prepared to depart for India she saw nothing but pain ahead 'for the next 10 years'.[5] Her gloom did not lift once on board the *Ganges*. Minna, Pamela's and Mananai's shared maid, began unpacking their travel trunks. Mananai and Charlie set off to explore the ship and peruse the Captain's list of their fellow travellers. Pamela sat in her cabin 'very mis[erable] very alone', clutching a bundle of Harry's letters and a prayer book that he had sent her, waiting for the clock's hands to reach midnight, the hour appointed for the *Ganges* to steam out. 'It hardly seems real,' she wrote in the first of many lengthy letters to her confessor Sibell. Desperate for the smallest details about Harry, Pamela implored Sibell to write the moment she saw him with 'long minute descriptions: colour of clothes etc or even if his dog was with him'.[6]

The passage, and passengers, to India were familiar to an imperial nation. Ships carrying brave soldiers (returning from leave to garrison the Jewel in the Crown) and 'the Fishing Fleet' (unfortunate young ladies who had failed to secure a husband in England now trying their luck abroad) passed Gibraltar, made their way through the Suez Canal and across the Gulf of Aden to Bombay. Pamela was surprised to find how accurate the caricatures were: 'the people on the steamer are beyond *words* – typical – & more like the young ladies in "shirts" & skirts in the *D[aily] Graphic* than I ever expected', she told Sibell.[7]

Mananai was more optimistic about the calibre of passengers. 'There are very many nice people on board, especially men,' she told her mother, scrolling off a list of names as proof. She was particularly taken by one Lieutenant Baker-Carr of the Rifle Brigade, a 'delightful & very good looking man' who reminded her of her brother Guy. Robert Baker-Carr was a seasoned veteran of India, about to take up a post as the Viceroy Lord Elgin's aide-de-camp. To Mananai's delight, he was the son of an acquaintance of Madeline Wyndham from her Irish youth. 'I am trying to describe the people to amuse Papa,' said Mananai, but she was doing her best to sell the dashing infantry officer to her parents, and to Pamela as well.[8]

Pamela was not openly dismissive of Mananai's plans, but she did not leap to embrace new prospects either. Shipboard life was busy: games of deck quoits and shipboard croquet by day; and nightly concerts. Pamela had brought her guitar with her, but she sang her folk ballads rarely and socialized less. She preferred to be out on deck watching the blue horizon flash unchangeably past: marvelling at the 'wonderful Opal days . . . such sunsets . . . *such* Waves & Sea'. At dinner she escaped from the chatter of the Captain's table as soon as was polite and stood in the darkness on the ship's prow, watching it plough 'a great white *path* up the Waters', with 'the flying fish, & the funny porpoises, & the lovely phosphor' lighting up its way. The greatness of the ocean, its space and darkness, gave Pamela a momentary sense of perspective and escape. Surrounded by 'something Unimaginable . . . it was all perfect, & beautiful, & *great*, – & wiped away the dreadfulness of those 3 months'.[9]

The *Ganges* docked in Bombay, and the party, accompanied by Baker-Carr, headed north for game-hunting near Peshawar, the town that lay at the mouth of the Khyber Pass on the Afghan border. All their Kipling, all the tales of India they had heard and their distillation in exhibitions visited had not prepared Pamela and the Adeanes for the country's assault on their senses. The dusty windows of the rackety train revealed 'a new world – new Birds, new grasses, new animals, *everything* new'. The rushing air was hot and filled with alien smells and sounds. They stretched their legs at stations 'swarming with natives in *brilliant* clothes', and as the train puffed and hissed at the siding drank soup quickly boiled up for them in the waiting room. Once they had reached their destination they travelled in 'touges', little dog-carts pulled by small sturdy ponies – 'too delightful', said Mananai – while bullock carts bearing their piles of luggage brought up the rear. They jolted past Buddhist rock temples and past Muslims at prayer in the mosque: '[they] touch the ground again & again with their foreheads . . . some pray out loud – calling on Allah in high mettalic [sic] tones', Mananai reported.[10]

The north-west border, from where the Khyber Pass – Kipling's 'narrow swordcut in the hills' – led to Afghanistan, was tribal land, bandit country. Through the Pass wound the 'kafilas' of traders heading for Peshawar. The cries of the tribesmen, the clattering of iron pots over hazy campfires, the musty exotic smells of camels, carpets and musk: Kipling had imprinted all these images into the minds of the British public. They were accustomed to press reports touting imperial derring-do in the frequent skirmishes between the British and the guerrilla forces of the bandits. The slash-and-burn tactics employed by imperial forces to stabilize the region were quietly overlooked. Soldiers who burnt down villages, slaughtered livestock and destroyed food stores sat at odds with the propaganda of a noble, civilizing Empire.[11]

At Peshawar the party camped out in the wild and trekked over rocky terrain. By day vultures and eagles swooped overhead through sparkling blue skies; on nighttime drives through the arid country they heard the terrifying howl of jackals in the dark. 'This *is* the land of the Bible,' said Pamela; 'it is *very* enchanted . . . & sometimes I am living in an Arabian Nights Tale – & sometimes in the old Scriptures & often – very often – in Fairytales. For there are Blue-birds here – the real Fairybird . . . and Night shuts down like a great Curtain on the day – & the stars quiver instead of shine.'[12]

They parted ways with Baker-Carr, promising to meet him again in Calcutta, and travelled on to princely Rajasthan, where on a swaying howdah they made their way through the forest to the sixteenth-century fort of Chittor. As they passed through the monumental entrance gate, 'the Native Guard played God Save the Queen ... it is wonderful the way the Natives Salaam & bow down to white people', said Mananai. They made their return at dusk, and as their elephants waded across a river the howdah began to pitch and slide. The mahout barked instructions at his passengers to shift their weight: 'we all clung on to each other ... there was *really* no fear & we were roaring with laughter all the time but it was anything but comfortable', Mananai told her mother.[13]

They visited acquaintances made on the *Ganges*, dined with them at Mess and reviewed the soldiers on parade, dazzled by the contrast between the dark skin of the Sikh soldiers and their vibrant red tunics and turbans. At Udaipur they toured the white stone palaces of maharajas. Mananai was appalled to find that they were furnished with pieces 'all from Birmingham cut glass beds & chairs & tables ... too dreadful'.[14] She thrived on the rough and ready nature of travelling – 'one goes to bed *regularly* & can wash & dress quite well' on trains – and was dazed by the sheer amount she saw: 'to me it['s] extraordinary to think that your little "Em-Wem" [Pamela] & "Jessie Rat" [Mananai] are seeing & doing all this – we can never be glad enough', she wrote, before remembering the reason that had brought them there and hastily amending the line to read: 'shall have *such* things to look back on & remember & tell you about shan't we'.

Mananai reported proudly to her parents every conquest her little sister made, from elderly misty-eyed Englishmen on ferries, made nostalgic for 'Home' by Pamela's singing, to those rather younger, attracted by her vibrancy.[15] Baker-Carr met up with the party again when they reached Calcutta. There too they found Eddy Tennant, the eldest son of the Tennant clan. Quiet, responsible, good-natured Eddy had been sent out to India to check on the progress of his sister Lucy Graham Smith. On paper he was immensely eligible: vastly wealthy, tall and good-looking. His fundamental shortcoming was summed up in one pithy sentence by his younger sister. 'Eddy lacks *drive*,' said Margot of her favourite brother.[16] More brutally one of Eddy's children, who had inherited his aunt's acidic streak, later declared that his father was so boring that he couldn't even remember what he looked like.[17] That Pamela and Lucy were in India for the same reason did not appear to disconcert anyone. Diffidently, Eddy made his interest in Pamela plain. There was an uncomfortable afternoon when both he and Baker-Carr accompanied Mananai and Pamela to the Eden Gardens cricket ground. The group got caught in a thunderstorm and retreated to the Adeanes' rooms to sit it out, where a drenched Eddy and Baker-Carr cast dark looks across the sitting room at one another.[18]

Pamela did not mention these suitors in letters home, but told her friends that she was 'much happier – happy even'. '"Miss Pam" . . . seems in tearing spirits and possessed of a mind that responds at once to every pleasurable stimulus,' said Arthur to Mary, having been shown Pamela's latest letter by George. 'I put her at the head of all the letter writers I know at least for certain qualities . . . the vividness of the presentation and the life and colour . . . glowing in every line were extraordinary.'[19] But Pamela was not so perennially buoyant as Arthur either supposed or hoped. To Mary and to Sibell, she confided that misery still frequently leapt upon her: upon receipt of a postbag empty of letters from Harry; upon glimpsing others in love, as when the party met up with Guy and Minnie Wyndham at Lucknow, who seemed to exist in 'a *nimbus* of pure happiness'.[20]

Pamela was no enemy of misery. She once proposed, in some seriousness, the instigation of a national holiday of grief: an annual two-day 'regular out of door . . . celebration of being really, thoroughly, impossibly, cruelly unhappy' in which people would only wear black and croon and rave in the streets.[21] Later in life she sank frequently into deep depression, sobbing in a darkened room for days, and recounting the experience at length to a select group of friends when she felt better. '"Life" is one damned thing after another . . . hardly has one pulled one's bleeding roots from under one severing blow, than one has to trail them before another hatchet,

& have yet another length hacked away . . . I wonder why – then – we are all sent into the world with such a longing for joy: for happiness as one's birthright,' she wrote to Mary later in life.[22]

The seeds of her emotional self-indulgence are plain to see in her letters written at this time, but the unhappiness of a heartbroken twenty-two-year-old is very real, her isolation in chattering, stifling rooms, bemused and angry at the hordes around her who seemed to have happiness so easily in their grasp. At those times 'all the strength & philosophy' that she tried to practise 'goes for very little . . . one flattens ones nose against the glass window, at the hot sausages inside', she told Sibell. In Lucknow's steamy heat, with green parakeets chattering about her, Pamela's heart and mind were back in rainy England with Harry.[23]

Those writing to her from England were evasive on the subject of Harry. '. . . I feel so far away & wonder sometimes if anybody but myself remembers anything about that time,' she said to Sibell.[24] Pamela felt as though a curtain had been drawn across her past as soon as she stepped on board the *Ganges*. She did not know that the story was far from forgotten and that Arthur was once more engaged in damage limitation – this time on her behalf – as the scandal threatened to rear its ugly head once more.

Of all the Souls, Lord and Lady Brownlow had felt the greatest rage, as they railed at their nephew's 'deception'. Lady Brownlow openly denounced Nina; Lord Brownlow refused to countenance Harry's continued representation of Stamford, the Lincolnshire parliamentary seat that was in the peer's control.[25] In fury, Cust announced his intention to stand as the Unionist candidate for North Manchester in a by-election planned for the spring of 1894. Most of the Souls were alarmed by his impetuous decision, drawing attention to himself when he would do better to lie low. But Balfour, conscious that the previous autumn he had promised to help Harry escape social opprobrium and political ostracism if Harry would marry Nina, agreed to support him.

Millicent Fawcett, a radical Liberal Unionist and President of the National Union of Women's Suffrage Societies (the NUWSS), caught wind of the 'most ghastly story' of Harry, Nina and Pamela. Appalled that Cust should represent the honest burghers of Manchester,[26] she began to circulate the story around local political associations. She tried to recruit Lady Frances Balfour, a fellow suffragist, to her cause. Harry promptly sought the help of Arthur, who confronted Mrs Fawcett, fearing rightly that to leave the belligerent Harry to deal with the situation was a recipe for disaster.

The clash between Mrs Fawcett and Harry Cust posited radicalism and suffragism against historic patriarchy. 'Up to our generation the whole of the social punishment in these cases has fallen on the woman and none or next to none on the man,' Mrs Fawcett told Balfour. 'But now, whether we like it or not, a movement is making itself felt towards equality . . . if for the last four or five generations the H Custs of the world had been disciplined by a healthy "coercion" of law and public opinion, the whole of this pitiable business might have been prevented and two lives at least saved from going to shipwreck . . .'[27]

The idea of opening out patrician Harry Cust's behaviour to the common man's judgement was anathema to the Souls. Balfour, suppressing his own misgivings about Cust's candidacy, icily told Mrs Fawcett that he could not see how episodes in Cust's private life made him unfit for public duty. He reproved her for making 'the unhappy story of a most unhappy woman [that is, Nina] . . . the common topic of political gossip' through 'the length & breadth of Manchester'. He threatened her with legal action if she continued to mention 'Miss Wyndham's' name.[28] Lady Frances explained that while she personally abhorred Cust's behaviour, 'all that need be known in Manchester was the seduction of his wife before marriage . . . and that would not tell against him in a working class constituency'.[29] Cust, adopting an ill-considered and heavy-handed approach that displayed his contempt for women and for anyone he did not consider his social equal, threatened Mrs Fawcett with a libel suit for defaming himself by repeating the story.

Then, as now, justification was a total defence against defamation. One cannot defame a person by saying something about them that is true. Accordingly, and in return, Mrs Fawcett threatened to subpoena everyone who knew anything of the matter, including Balfour: all of whom she intended to call as witnesses to Harry's actions. Prominent local politicians, many of them with Radical roots, began to weigh in, expressing their disgust at the idea that Cust might be imposed upon them by a decadent aristocratic 'clique in London'. In June, Balfour finally told Cust, in terms courteous and unequivocal, that, for the sake of the party and the Souls, he could not stand.[30] The existing Unionist candidate for North Manchester stood again, and Cust did not stand for re-election at Stamford in 1895, remaining in political exile until 1900, when he re-entered Parliament as member for Bermondsey, another working-class constituency, where presumably his past did not tell against him.

Of all this, Pamela was almost ignorant. Their party set sail from Bombay on 20 March 1894, on the *Peninsular* – 'one of the *best* ships & we have the best cabins on board', reported Mananai to her parents.[31] There were a few disappointments: Charlie had not bagged himself a tiger, and time constraints had forced them to drop items from their itinerary: 'one can't do everything'.[32] Most importantly, Pamela finally seemed better. Mananai had been as encouraging as she could to Baker-Carr, on Pamela's behalf. They left with the Lieutenant promising to write, and to visit when next in England. As Pamela and the Adeanes lay out on deck at night, looking up at the moon and stars and tousled by warm night winds, their previous crossing's misery seemed a world away.

The travellers docked at a misty Southampton in April, with Pamela's guitar intact, and a parrot that Mananai had brought back home for a pet. In the summer that followed, Pamela's family spoke with relief of her buoyant spirit; how pretty and well she was looking; and enthused about her hordes of admirers, and innumerable engagements. 'How much *better* she is again,' said Mananai, hoping that finally her sister's fortunes would improve.[33]

FIFTEEN

Rumour

The travellers returned to a political landscape irrevocably altered by Gladstone's retirement from politics little over a month before their return. Few had thought that the octogenarian's fourth ministry, which began in 1892, would be anything but short-lived, although the young Welsh Radical David Lloyd George was one of many in the Commons who marvelled at how, in moments, the shrunken figure huddled on the front bench could become 'an erect athletic gladiator, fit for the contest of any arena'.[1] But Gladstone was broken when his second Home Rule Bill, after battling its way through the Commons – in a sense literally, for a fistfight broke out on the benches between Unionists and Home Rulers at its final reading – was rejected by the House of Lords. In an incandescent final speech in the Commons, Gladstone asked his fellow Members how long 'a deliberative assembly, elected by the votes of more than six million people', could continue to be defied by the inherited wealth and privilege of the Lords.[2] As he left the House for the final time that evening, making his way to Windsor to offer the Queen his resignation, he was applauded to the rafters by MPs, all aware, even then, that an era was at an end.

Since 1886, Unionists had dominated the Lords. They now presented themselves as a bulwark against demotic liberalism, protecting the nation from a Liberal party apparently moving ever further leftwards. Lord Salisbury's 'referendum theory', in a nutshell, stated that if a government elected by the people put forward controversial legislation, the people ought to be given a chance to decide specifically on that legislation. The Lords were exercising their veto on behalf of the country. At heart, they claimed that they knew better the vacillating public's wishes than their directly elected representatives. It was an intellectually hollow argument, and constitutionally dangerous – but it appeared to be vindicated when the Unionists triumphed at the polls in 1895.

Gladstone's successor was Constance Leconfield's brother Lord Rosebery, his former Foreign Secretary. The choice was not Gladstone's: the Queen, who could not bring herself to thank in person the 'most disagreeable' of all her ministers,[3] further breached convention by deciding on his successor without seeking Gladstone's advice. She deliberately overlooked Gladstone's Chancellor, Sir William Harcourt, who, despite being of landed birth, had introduced in his most recent Budget the devastating salvo against the landed classes of death duties of 8 per cent on all estates worth over £1 million. Lord Rosebery, a blue-blooded imperialist, was as close to a Tory as the Liberals could offer.

The choice was a bad one. Rosebery, acutely shy, prone to deep depression since being widowed in 1890, was not up to the increasingly difficult task of leading a government from the House of Lords. In the Commons, Harcourt, thwarted and overlooked, was as unsupportive as possible,[4] and his devoted son Lewis (known, not always entirely fondly, as 'Loulou', and renowned for his capacity for manipulative intrigue),[5] who acted as his father's private secretary, spread rumours already doing the rounds that Rosebery was having a homosexual affair with his own secretary. The secretary was the 'excellent, amiable' and 'instantly loveable' Francis, Viscount Drumlanrig ('Drummy'), eldest son of Sibyl Queensberry, and the

Wyndhams' cousin.[6] Whether or not the rumours were true (and Drummy's extraordinary elevation to the peerage after just one year of service as Baron Kelhead of Dumfries, and his appointment as lord in waiting to the Queen, did little to dispel them), Drummy's father had believed them enough to pursue Rosebery to Bad Homburg in August 1893, threatening to thrash him to the bone. Only the intervention of several other spa-goers, including the Prince of Wales, the Chief Commissioner of Police and the Society lawyer Sir George Lewis, drove Queensberry out of town.[7]

When Drummy began to court Pamela on her return to England in 1894, the Wyndhams did not put a stop to it, but they were uneasy. Their reserve was in marked contrast to the enthusiasm of Drummy's immediate family, in particular his doting grandfather, Alfred Montgomery. From later elliptical references to concerns about the 'opinion of the world', it is clear that Pamela had heard the rumours too, and that she knew her family were unenthusiastic about the match.[8] At the end of the summer, Pamela told Drummy she could not marry him, being unable to love him as she had Harry Cust, 'simply & honestly – & without knowing why'.[9] A few weeks later, Drummy became engaged to someone else.

Throughout the summer and autumn of 1894, Pamela's misery had been growing. The anniversary of the break with Harry loomed. The past year, she said, 'makes one afraid of living. The waking every morning – the needle of pain coming through sleep.'[10] She was suffocated by her feelings, unable to 'make Mamma the receptacle' but terrified of 'getting shramped [sic] up instead of opening out'. She scribbled out her 'bursting feelings' to Sibell in lengthy letters,[11] but felt keenly that she should keep them from her immediate family. In October, she and her parents visited Mary at Gosford. Pamela let slip some of her misery to her sister, and, despite a sympathetic response, was immediately mortified at 'even letting you [Mary] think I had anything but the easiest surroundings . . . [or that] I'm always like that'. As soon as she left, she wrote to Mary to apologize, blaming 'Betsey' for making her overemotional: 'there is nothing about me that isn't really to make life easier & happier for me . . . I was a coward to let you say there was! It is entirely in my own hands – and is my own fault if I'm unhappy, or ill.'[12]

But by then Pamela had been provided with an opportunity to express her feelings. The Wyndhams' stay at Gosford had been cut short by devastating news. Drummy, attending a shooting party in Somerset given by his fiancée's family, had been found dead in a hedge, his collar and head 'very much sprinkled' with blood from a gunshot wound through the mouth.[13] The coroner, hearing evidence of Drummy telling a beater that he was going back to look for a partridge he had winged, and of the single strangely deadened shot that rang out moments later, made a finding of accidental death: another sad example of a loaded gun going off as its owner climbed a stile. The fact that Drummy's body had been found nowhere near a stile and that the post-mortem suggested that his mouth had been wide open when the shot was fired was carefully overlooked.[14]

The Wyndhams immediately returned south, meeting Drummy's shattered family in London, before taking them to Clouds. 'Cousin Sib' seemed shrunken inside her mourning garb, Bosie was thoughtful and gentle. During their brief stay in London, Pamela accompanied Wommy to a dreadful interview with Alfred Montgomery, who seemed more interested in talking to Pamela than to his own granddaughter. She described it to Mary: 'He kept saying "he was so fond of you – he loved you so – how fond he was of you – let me look at you – ah my dear" – & then breaking down – and all the time I felt like *swords* inside me the "one-moment-too-lateness" of Life.'[15] Now, at Clouds, Wommy seemed simply dazed, 'but I am afraid she [Wommy] feels it terribly at night when she is alone', Pamela told Mary, kept awake by the sound of sobbing echoing down the corridors.[16]

Pamela plunged into a frenzy of self-recrimination, castigating herself as 'blind and afraid', unworthy of Drummy's love. It is clear she knew that Drummy had killed himself, suspected that it was related to the rumours about Drummy and Lord Rosebery, and thought she could have saved him by marrying him. She crucified herself accordingly, enduring the limpet-like affections of Wommy who, having always hero-worshipped her cousin, now refused to leave her side, insisting on sharing her bed and watching her as she slept. Bosie did not stay long at Clouds before disappearing to be comforted by Oscar Wilde.

Pamela plummeted from a rhapsody of grief into a deep depression. Plans had been made for the Wyndhams, Sibyl Queensberry and Wommy to travel abroad in the new year, escaping scandal once again with a flight to the Continent. In the meantime Pamela was sent to Babraham to recuperate, although with limited opportunities to do so, since Wommy came too. A worried Mananai plotted ways to restore her younger sister to health and spirits. Still hopeful for Baker-Carr,[17] she wrote to her mother proposing to effect a meeting between the two when Baker-Carr returned on leave. Madeline Wyndham's reply does not survive, but it is evident from Mananai's reluctantly parroting response that her mother poured cold water on the plan: 'I *quite* agree if she [Pamela] is not *very* much in love not to *help* her marry a man not rich enough for the comfort of Life . . . let her *wait* now that she can . . . & help her to meet [a] nice man with money enough.'[18] Pamela barely noticed, consumed by the feeling that she had let down her family and herself. 'Ever since I was grown-up I wanted to be worthy of all the rest of you. Of Mamma, & you, & all,' she told Mary. With Harry gone, Drummy dead, scandal in the air and her mother on tenterhooks, Pamela felt only that she had failed. 'I don't mind the mills of God grinding small if only they wouldn't grind *so* slowly: – I think I have had an *eternity* in the last 3 years.'[19]

SIXTEEN

Egypt

In 1894 a new play was put upon the London stage. *The Case of Rebellious Susan* by Henry Arthur Jones considered the plight of Lady Susan, who wanted revenge on her philandering husband. Lady Susan leaves her husband and travels to Cairo where she has a brief romance and falls in love. But, mindful of convention and of her place in Society, she returns to England and her cheating husband and they are reconciled. In a final display of rebellion she refuses to reveal the details of the affair to him unless he will do the same regarding his.[1]

At the insistence of the actor-manager Sir Charles Wyndham (no relation to the Wyndhams) and his leading lady Mary Moore, the version that made it on to the stage at Wyndham's Theatre on Charing Cross Road was deliberately ambiguous about whether Lady Susan had actually been unfaithful. Chastity was 'that one indispensable quality in respect for womanhood', Sir Charles told Jones, asking how he could expect 'married men to bring their wives to a theatre to learn the lesson that their wives can descend to such nastiness, as giving themselves up for one evening of adulterous pleasure and then return safely to their husband's arms, provided they are clever enough, low enough and dishonest enough to avoid being found out'? Reluctantly Jones agreed, but his published preface to the play maintained what he believed to be the moral of the piece: 'That as women cannot retaliate openly, they may retaliate secretly – and *lie!*'[2]

The revised play, a roaring success, was part of a wave of productions considering 'the marriage question', which began in 1889 with the first English performance of Ibsen's *A Doll's House*, but is better exemplified by Wilde's smash hits in the early 1890s. In *An Ideal Husband*, *Lady Windermere's Fan* and *A Woman of No Importance* the pure unyielding wife is pitted against the 'fallen woman', while an ostensibly upright husband has a dark past. Love, secrecy, scandal and convention all play off against one another. The overwhelming impression is that in Society the truth is something to be dispensed carefully and in very small doses.

In 1892, Wilde had suggested Mary take a walk-on part in *Lady Windermere's Fan*. Mary asked Wilfrid Blunt's advice, but he dismissed the idea out of hand.[3] By 1894, Mary was fair placed to play the wronged wife in any of those dramas. That summer, the Elchos' marriage had reached a critical point. Hermione Leinster, suffering from incurable tuberculosis, had gone to France to live out her final months in a more temperate climate.[4] She packed off her sons to relations and left with her mother and sister for the south of France. Over the course of the summer the Elchos came to an agreement. Hugo would go to Hermione until the end came. When it did, Hugo and Mary would reconcile and have another child to seal their marriage. In the intervening period Hugo's sister Evelyn de Vesci was to act as go-between for the Elchos. It seems that even the long-suffering Mary baulked at maintaining anything more than cursory contact with her husband during this time.

In August 1894 Wilfrid Blunt and Bosie Douglas made a pilgrimage to Shakespeare's birthplace of Stratford-upon-Avon, stopping at Stanway en route. They arrived unannounced to find the Adeanes, George Wyndham, Arthur Balfour and Mary playing cricket while a band of brightly dressed Neapolitan musicians serenaded them from the sidelines. Hugo was in the Engadine in Switzerland on a cure, Mary about to depart for her own spa treatment at Ems. The following days were filled with Stanway's standard amusements: croquet in the rain, a golfing trip to Cleve Hill, evening games of battledore (an early form of badminton) played across a string rigged up in the hall. Normally Hugo's absence gave Mary a chance to spend time with Arthur without challenge. But this time, while Arthur played golf, Mary was not on the links but sitting with Wilfrid in an inn garden nearby while he read poetry to her.

In the years since Blunt had first discovered his fascination for Mary a friendly, cousinly relationship had sprung up. In 1887, he had been allowed back into Egypt, and his small family were now accustomed to spend half their year at Sheykh Obeyd. Over a decade after the British occupation had started, Egypt was the fashionable holiday location of choice for upper-class Englishmen and women. Large elegant hotels sprang up in Cairo and Alexandria catering for linen-clad panama-hatted tourists eager to visit the Pyramids and cruise down the Nile. 'Someday I must take my children there!' Mary had told Blunt on receipt of his latest tales of desert life in 1893.[5] Blunt insisted to himself that he had built El Kheysheh, the little pink guest house in Sheykh Obeyd's grounds, expressly with Mary in mind.[6]

On Blunt's last night at Stanway he found himself momentarily alone with Mary and 'by a sudden inspiration kissed her'. 'She turned pale, said nothing, and went away to Arthur,' Blunt told his diary, but the seed had been planted.[7] The next morning Blunt and Bosie left to continue their journey. Mary got up early to say goodbye and went for a short walk with Blunt in the churchyard that lay adjacent to the house. In the churchyard, in the rain, Mary agreed to go to Sheykh Obeyd that winter.[8] A few weeks later, lest Mary should waver, Wilfrid sent the keen horsewoman one of his finest Arab horses from the Crabbet stud – 'the most delicious hack I have ever been on – it's like riding a swallow', said Mary blissfully.[9]

In October 1894, Hugo left for France and Hermione. Mary was quite alone at Gosford. The news of Drummy's death had just broken, and her family had hastened back to Clouds. The Wemysses were spending October in the spa town of Maldon, oblivious to any developments in the south of France since, fearing their reaction, Hugo had decided not to tell his parents anything at all.

When, through a helpful busybody, Annie Wemyss discovered the whereabouts of her son she was, she told Mary in the reproachful letter that followed, too upset for several days even to put pen to paper. Having found her tongue she did not spare her daughter-in-law: 'I do not lose sight of your goodness . . . you must have reached heights of charity and self-effacement of which I should have been incapable of even dreaming.' But the fact that Mary had given her 'sanction' to Hugo was in Annie Wemyss's mind the most terrible thing of all.[10] 'Many seemingly crooked things get straight,' Mary said evasively. She did not reveal the pact's full details, knowing that it would send her mother-in-law into an even greater frenzy of righteous indignation.[11]

Mary's own family were incapable of bringing up the subject. Pamela made glancing allusions to Mary's 'trials', but there were no more encouragements from Madeline Wyndham to 'cleave together'. Matters between the Elchos had now reached such a pass that the Wyndhams could only remain silent, and hope that in time things would improve.

Hugo's departure was the provocation for Mary's own trip to Egypt and the bargaining tool that enabled her to go. Ignoring the warnings of her friends, she booked her passage on the *Bengal* at exactly the time that Hugo left. In late December, in the middle of the worst winter that anyone could remember Mary, ten-year-old Ego, eight-year-old Guy and seven-year-old Cincie, Cincie's governess Miss Jourdain and Mary's latest maid crossed to Cairo in terrible seas (Mary, teased Arthur, seemed always to attract the stormiest of crossings). They arrived at Sheykh Obeyd, dusty and footsore, in the freezing early hours of 5 January 1895.[12] Mary woke later that morning to sparkling blue skies and 'paradise'. She embraced everything about her new surroundings, the Bedouin clothes that Wilfrid had left out for her, the heat, the silence and flickering shade in the garden as the leaves of the gemeyseh tree rustled in the wind and sunlight sharpened off the white stone dome of Sheykh Obeyd's tomb. The children were terribly happy 'grubbing in a little Bedouin tent a few yards from this house', she reported to Evelyn in the first of many anodyne letters;[13] their party had made a trip into the desert, with Mary, Wilfrid and Anne Blunt on Arab horses and the children and Miss J on donkeys. Photographs of this excursion show Mary still in a western riding coat and top boots, white blanket draped over her head to protect her from the dust, a green and white umbrella in her hand. Behind her a black-clad Miss J looks hot and uneasy on her donkey; the children are so small one can scarcely make out their faces.

All Mary's friends had warned her before she left that Wilfrid would try to seduce her. They reiterated these warnings in every letter they sent. She kept her letters home cheerful and bland, proffering sanitized tales of picnics of dates and fresh camel milk in Bedouin tents. 'The little bits we get of *real* Eastern life are very interesting,' she told Evelyn in a letter headed 'Desert, Cairo'. 'We might be living in the time of Joseph (this is just about where Potiphar's garden might have been).' Staying with the Blunts was delightful: 'so *much* nicer than being in an hotel'.[14] The true story of what happened lies in Wilfrid's own account, and in Mary's later correspondence with him: for of all her diaries that remain, the volume for 1895 is missing. The inference that it was destroyed, possibly by a diligent descendant, is inescapable.

Four days after Mary arrived she appeared at the main house alone, dressed in Bedouin clothes and asking Wilfrid to show her Sheykh Obeyd's tomb. When they were by the tomb Wilfrid kissed her once again and in the flickering shade of the gemeyseh tree the cousins sat and talked. Mary confessed her childhood crush on Blunt, and on gentle pressing revealed something of her relationship with Arthur on which others had speculated for so long. 'To him she is pledged far more than to Hugo,' Wilfrid duly noted in his diary. 'She loves and honours and respects him, and he is constant to her, and she has always been constant to him, and she is bound to him by a thousand promises never to give herself to another. On this understanding he has been content that their love should be within certain limits – a little more than friendship a little less than love.'[15]

Mary's explanation to Wilfrid is the clearest indication we have that her relationship with Balfour had not been consummated. That night she wrote to Arthur confessing that Wilfrid had 'made a little love': confessing and needling simultaneously. Arthur replied almost immediately from a fog-ridden London where he was battling 'the important trifling of politics' and influenza: 'All the things I really want to say are unsayable so that if you wish to know them you must imagine them for yourself. Think of what you would like best to hear and have faith that that is what I should like to speak. I do not think you will be far wrong.'[16]

It is as close as Arthur would ever come to a declaration, but hardly a satisfactory one. It was also too late. A few days before that letter arrived, Mary had sent the children and Miss J into Cairo, to see the museum, while she stayed in bed, recovering from a bad cold. In the late morning, as she dozed in her cool darkened room, she was woken by a soft knock on the door. It was Wilfrid who found, as he had hoped, Mary alone. One thing led to another. 'My extremest hopes were achieved,' Wilfrid wrote in his diary that evening, jubilant at having seduced the cousin he had been pursuing for so long.[17] It was almost certainly the first time that Mary had had sex with anyone other than Hugo. Wilfrid did not think that she had 'intended quite all that happened',[18] and Mary later agreed. 'We might have been lifelong friends but *you* excluded it with yr eyes open,' she said, explaining that she before 'had only had to do with *different* men' – the men of the Souls who flirted, cajoled and kissed, but never (at least not in Mary's experience) crossed over into 'the conjugal act'. Later still, when nostalgia had cast a rosy glow upon everything to do with her time in Egypt she would tease the 'unscrupulous' Wilfrid for having taken advantage of her.[19]

In early February, the party set out on what Blunt called their 'desert honeymoon'. As intended, Anne and Judith accompanied them only on their first day, after which they turned back, leaving Blunt and Mary, albeit 'chaperoned' by the children and Miss Jourdain and numerous servants, on their own. Each night, in the wadis where they pitched their camp, Mary secretly left the tents set up for the women and children and went to Blunt, under the canopy of his travelling carpet a little way away. The clandestine visits did not go unnoticed by all the members of the party. 'I think the Arabs with us knew that we were lovers,' confided Wilfrid to his diary: 'indeed they must have known it, for there were Mary's naked tell-tale footsteps each morning in the sand . . . Mary is now my true Bedouin wife.'[20]

Far from being intimidated by the desolate, unforgiving land-scape, Mary felt free for the first time since her Cumberland child-hood. 'I was made for the desert,' she told Wilfrid proudly. 'I *knew* how to live in a tent (have "blackened cooking pots!") & to rise high on a camel with streamers flying in the . . . wind! It all came to me by instinct.'[21] Years later, even a kettle's singing in an Edinburgh convalescent home recalled to her the sound of Wilfrid's servant, Mubarak, playing to the company on his flute, as they reclined under tents made of rugs set among the sandhills, and conjured up the memory of 'lying in a tent in the hot clean sand & making foot prints in it': the telltale signs left of the lovers' nighttime wanderings.[22]

On their return from the desert, the affair continued. Judith, who was in her early twenties, dropped by El Kheysheh one evening, to find 'H.F. ['Head of the Family', Judith's nickname for her father] sitting on Mary's bed . . . They looked horribly confused but I suppose it means nothing,' she recorded in her diary.[23] Cynthia's biographer believes that both the little girl and her governess had some idea of what was going on.[24] It would seem impossible that Anne Blunt had not noticed as well. But Mary buried thoughts of Anne, of Arthur, of the fact that she had taken her mother's lover as her own. 'I am & *always* shall be sorry for wounding the feelings of anyone I care for but otherwise its difficult to wholly regret days of beauty & romance,' she assured Wilfrid later.[25] 'I am quite happy living in the present,' she told Evelyn innocently in early February, just after her return to Sheykh Obeyd.[26]

The ramifications of the past and thoughts of the future could not be held at bay for ever. The next day – Valentine's Day – Mary broke the news to Blunt that 'it being the 36th day . . . she is certainly with child'. Blunt received the news with sheer delight – 'For me it is a pure gift from heaven.'[27] Throughout the affair, Mary had alluded with concern to possible 'consequences'. Her period came like clockwork, and a rough and ready calculation with the dates suggests she fell pregnant almost the first time she slept with Wilfrid. Perhaps this knowledge informed her recklessness: since she was damned she might as well embrace it. Yet from Blunt's bald report now that Mary was 'a little troubled and anxious' one can sense a world of apprehension and confusion for her. 'She will not, if she can help it, give up her husband, or her children, or her friend,' he told his diary.[28] Nor can Mary have forgotten that six years before her doctor had warned her that another pregnancy would risk her life – the reason why she and Hugo had not had sex in all that time, and why she could not now hope to pass off the child as Hugo's, even if she wanted to. Almost magically, a solution to the latter problem appeared to present itself: the next day, they received a letter from Hugo announcing his imminent arrival – and, hot on its heels, the author himself appeared, bowler hat plonked firmly on his head and Cymru, Hermione's fluffy chow, on a chain.

Hugo had made the decision to go to Egypt long before he notified his wife. Settled in Menton, the quieter town down the coast to which he and Hermione had moved from Monte Carlo, he had become uneasy. Insidious rumours about the state of the Elchos' marriage had already begun to trickle back to London: the *World* had reported mischievously that it was *Lady Elcho* nursing the Duchess of Leinster in the south of France, and he was equally worried by rumours of Mary's activities. 'She is leading an odd sort of life & I fear people may be talking [about] them,' he explained to Evelyn.[29] 'I think I ought to go . . . to let it be known I have been in Egypt. I know that she [Mary] is wildly happy . . . & not really wanting me. But this does not make any difference.'[30] Hermione became agitated at the very thought of Hugo leaving her, and several times she had made pitiful attempts at suicide with an overdose of chloral pills, a crude sleeping aid. Now, despite her state, Hugo deemed it necessary for him to make a brief visit to Egypt, informing Mary of his imminent arrival only when he was already on his way.

On Hugo's arrival Wilfrid seethed silently at the sight of his rival enjoying himself in the Egyptian sunshine, with apparently no inkling of what was going on. He was anguished at the sight of Mary dressed once again in Western clothes, as the party, which now included Frederick Harrison, a hearty diplomatic acquaintance of Blunt's, visited the Cairo museum. He cheered darkly when Hugo went out in a boat on the lake to shoot duck and capsized. But he was enraged when he found Hugo's 'Christian hat' left in the Bedouin tent in the grounds: evidence that 'she who was my Bedouin wife' had brought a stranger into his tent. 'When I get her once more into the desert I shall cut off her head,' he vowed.[31]

Wilfrid's revenge was more subtle than that. An overnight expedition to Goshen was planned, to give Hugo and Harrison a brief taste of the desert, camping on the supposed site of the house of Potiphar, to whom Joseph of the fabled many-coloured coat was sold as a slave. The party were not all so accustomed to such expeditions: 'd'you remember how *funny* F Harrison looked in his grey dittoes [sic] & white puggery [sic] & miss J *on donkey* with a Margate Sands straw hat!' Mary reminded Wilfrid.[32] Later, Harrison published in his memoirs letters to his family describing this desert expedition: the women of the party in 'long flowing white burnouses [hooded capes] and Oriental head-dresses worn over embroidered satin, looking like Roxana and Fatima', Blunt biblical in his white robes, his hawk-like face craggy and sunburnt. He wrote of being woken by a 'thin moon like a scimitar' shining through a cranny in his canvas tent, of watching, in the cool early morning, the sun 'rise out of Mount Sinai', and dawn feasts of tea, coffee, fruit, dates, chicken, lamb and tongue. Only when Harrison, a keen mountaineer, begins to liken the sand on the dunes down which they slid to Alpine snow is one brought back to earth with a bump.[33]

If the desert could inspire even the plump, prosaic Harrison to lyricism, then the expedition should have been an ideal time for a reconciliation that would enable Mary to pass off the child as Hugo's. Blunt put paid to that. 'I would not allow Mary to share her tent with Hugo as that would not have been proper. Suleyman and all the Arabs know that she is my Bedouin wife,' Wilfrid told his diary primly. And so Mary and Judith slept in one tent, Hugo and Harrison in the other, with Blunt rolled up in his blue and white carpet set up under a bush 'a little apart' so that Mary could come to him 'as in the night of our honeymoon'.[34]

It seems unlikely that Mary was quite so reckless, but nor did she go to Hugo that night or any other. A few days later Hugo left. From the Grand Hotel Abbat in Alexandria, waiting for his passage back to France, he wrote Mary an awkward letter in which he could only sidle up to intimacy in the third person. He hoped that his 'Wigs' understood that he had not been able to say all he wanted. 'Perhaps I made her feel how I loved her . . . have loved her all the time more than she knew & more than even perhaps I knew – perhaps it is not too late to shew her even now – though I don't deserve that she should care for me . . . please take care of yourself little Wigs & let us be together again soon & stay together . . .'[35]

Hugo was frozen, and Mary unable to make a move herself, too guilty to deceive him, or preferring, almost literally, to bury her head in the sand. With foolhardiness doubtless partly provoked by fear, she plunged back into the desert one final time. This time the expedition planned was lengthy and dangerous: just Mary, Wilfrid and Anne on a camelback pilgrimage to St Anthony's monastery, lying in the heart of the Eastern Desert between the Kalala mountains and the Gulf of Suez, a place that no European woman had visited for 1,500 years.

'I am wretchedly, I suppose stupidly anxious about Mary,' Hugo confessed to Evelyn, having tried without success to dissuade Mary from going.[36] The journey, as recorded by Wilfrid in his diary, is a jumble of images: of Mary carrying apples and biscuits in her pocket like a schoolboy; Mary in a white robe up to her waist in water in the Red Sea 'like Andromeda clinging to the rocks'; Mary collecting shells near their camp, an oasis of palms a few yards from the sea hemmed in by high precipices of brown stone; Mary's black hair tangled in the canvas after a fierce hot wind had blown down her tent in the night, a tent where Wilfrid had been only shortly before – for every night, despite the presence of Anne so close by, the footsteps in the sand made their way from Wilfrid to Mary.

And then over time danger crept in, as Mary grew tired and provisions grew short; vultures ringed their camp at night, watching and waiting in the dark. When finally at the monastery, Blunt lit three candles to Sheykh Obeyd and left them burning as they made the long journey back. They returned exhausted, travel-weary but still high on the excitement of the desert. 'There is no doubt now of her pregnancy, & she suffered not a little from the lack of substantial food,' Wilfrid wrote in his diary upon their return. 'Still no harm has been done & her courage has carried her through – only we are glad that she can rest. It has been a delicious time for it is not often given to lovers to lead thus a wholly married life for 15 days.'[37] Mary herself never regretted a moment. 'I was made for the desert & so I do not forget those few days of life spent there – the night by the sea & the dome palaces & many other things . . . we were sons & daughters of the desert & the desert loved us & we it,' she wrote to Wilfrid a few years later.[38] They returned to find 'much changed'. The old Khedive had died and been buried in Egypt; George Curzon was engaged to the American heiress Mary Leiter. And it was not long before Mary received a telegram from Hugo that finally spelt an end to her time in Egypt.

Hugo returned from Egypt to find Hermione with 'death written on her face'. On an early-spring afternoon in March, in her bedroom at the Hôtel des Îles Britanniques, she slowly but inexorably slipped from life. When it was over, Hugo sat by her still, throughout the long afternoon, 'and it seemed just as it often has when she has been tired & sleepy, only she smiled all the time,' he told Evelyn. That night he dined, as always, in the adjacent sitting room with the connecting door ajar 'as she liked to have it . . . & I have gone backwards & forwards – & it has been the same as other nights excepting that she has not coughed – nor sent for me when she woke up'.[39] That night he telegraphed Mary. 'Am unhappy. Shall go Grand Hotel Rome', where Mary was to meet him.[40] Hugo left Menton the next morning with Cymru the chow, too miserable to write or even speak.[41]

Understanding immediately the meaning of this cryptic telegram, Mary went to bed early and wept – or so she said. 'I cannot bear to think of it – I did *love* her . . . and if I feel it what must you feel?' she asked Hugo in a lengthy letter she wrote a few days later. When Mary was truly overcome by emotion, she lost her tongue. Here, the words positively dripped off her pen: the letter is suffused with praise for Hugo's loyalty, almost gushing as she writes of her own 'love' for Hermione. She promises to be a 'help and comfort' to Hugo, prays 'that you will love me & that we may help each other to live our life as we ought to live it'. Doubtless Hermione's sad death did touch Mary's heart. But her overblown tone – more characteristic of Ettie than of herself – spoke only one thing. As Mary prepared to tell Hugo of her pregnancy she was doing everything in her power to remind him of their bond, to stress her generosity so that he might exercise his.[42]

Mary and her party sailed from Alexandria on Tuesday 26 March.

They met Hugo in Rome on Friday, took a train via Milan to Basle, then another overnight train to Calais, and crossed the Channel on Sunday. They were at Cadogan Square by 5 p.m. Arthur Balfour 'turned up' shortly afterwards to see Mary; Mary, tired out, went to bed before dinner.[43] The next morning she rose early to see her lawyer Mr Jamieson, had tea with Evelyn de Vesci, dined with George and Sibell, and just two days later was at Stanway, where, she informed her mother, for the foreseeable future she intended to stay.

Mary's precipitate and uncharacteristic haste to leave London and the prying eyes of her friends was for a good reason. She was 'bent on keeping . . . dark' the 'beautiful secret' of her pregnancy[44] for as long as she possibly could; '*nobody* need ever suspect anything', she told Wilfrid, assuming that no one but a few curious Souls would ever trouble to compare dates.[45] 'All that society resents is a scandal and so long as Hugo is mute & shields her with his marital countenance, Mary's woman friends will only think she has been quite right to enjoy herself, and that they wd have done precisely the same if they had had the opportunity,' said Wilfrid.[46]

SEVENTEEN

The Florentine Drama

On 14 February 1895, the day that Mary told Wilfrid Blunt of her pregnancy in Egypt, Oscar Wilde's *The Importance of Being Earnest* premiered at the St James's Theatre in London. Critics hailed it as an almost perfect comedy, audiences loved it. But the opening-night atmosphere was uneasy for insiders. After Drummy's death, his father had focused his vitriolic attentions upon the relationship of his youngest son, and Queensberry had made known his intention of throwing a bouquet of rotting vegetables on to the stage at *Earnest*'s opening night. Forced by police presence to abandon this plan, he left a note for Wilde at his club instead. Later much would turn upon whether the near-illegible scrawl, handed unsealed to a club servant, was addressed to 'Oscar Wilde, ponce and somdomite [sic]' or 'Oscar Wilde, posing as a somdomite [sic]'. In any event the message, discreetly placed in an envelope by the embarrassed club porter, was a terrible insult. Urged on by Bosie, disregarding the warnings of the more worldly-wise, Wilde sued for libel. The trial opened on 3 April 1895.

'How dreadful this libel suit is . . . poor darling Cousin Sib there seems no end to all she has to bear,' Mananai wrote from Dresden where the Adeanes were enjoying a season of German opera, and marvelling at the disproportionate pomp of the Saxon state's miniature court.[1] Cousin Sib was with Wommy and the Wyndhams in Florence waiting for the spring, which even there seemed slow to arrive after the worst winter that anyone could recall.

The reports were dreadful. Queensberry's ruthless counsel Edward Carson QC stopped at nothing to prove the truth of Queensberry's statement: Wilde was either a sodomite or he had posed as one. He put rent boys on the stand. He all but destroyed Wilde under cross-examination. The flippancy that served the playwright so well in the theatre scandalized when uttered in the forbidding Royal Courts of Justice. As Wilde denied kissing a youth on the grounds that he was too ugly, and as detail after sordid detail was revealed, it became daily more apparent that Wilde could not hope to escape criminal prosecution for what were, after all, illegal acts.

Wilde refused the advice of his friends to flee to the Continent. He lost his libel case. On 26 April he appeared in the dock charged with offences under section 11 of the Criminal Law Amendment Act. The Wyndhams, like most of Society, thought that Wilde had brought this upon himself. Their concern was for Bosie. With Percy abroad, George took on the responsibility of paterfamilias. A truculent, defiant Bosie told him that nothing on earth would induce him to leave London or Wilde until the trial was over. 'You may be sure that nothing will . . . he is quite insane on the subject,' George told Percy. 'Were "W." to be released . . . Bosie would do anything he asked, & no entreaty from you or his mother could weigh with him.' But Arthur Balfour, who had been 'told the case' and its most sensitive details by the prosecution, had reported to George in confidence that 'W. is certain to be condemned.' The evidence of the 'systematic ruin of a number of young men' that was to be put before the court was too serious not to require a scapegoat; the strength of 'public feeling' against Wilde was 'fiercely hostile . . . among all classes'. George now secured from Bosie the promise that, if 'W.' were imprisoned, 'he will do what I ask'.[2]

George further gave Bosie advice, although 'when I call it advice I should call it an offer'. If Bosie agreed to leave the country George would see to it that he received an allowance, and that 'we [meaning the Establishment] would all fight his battle'. The Wyndhams' cousin Algy Bourke had even offered to ensure that Bosie was not expelled from their club, White's. Sibyl's hopeful suggestion that Bosie should join the party in Florence was nipped in the bud: 'for Bosie's own sake & ultimate chance of shaking off all this nonsensical view, he must break fresh ground', said George, proposing Ceylon, or Australia 'which would enable his friends to say that he was going to prove himself a man'.[3] The unreliable Trelawney Backhouse claimed that Wilde's prosecution was the tit for tat offered by the Establishment to prevent Queensberry going after Rosebery once more. These conspiracy theories seem likely to remain unproven.

Thanks to the Wilde affair, Percy and George were toing and froing from London. In late March Arthur passed on to Mary in Egypt gossip delivered to him by Margot at a London dinner party, 'telling me that Eddy Tennant is going out to Florence with the Hon'ble P and that she and Charty want him to propose to Pamela!' 'He is an excellent fellow,' added Arthur, wishing him 'every luck', but obviously amused, for placid, affable Eddy was no match for his inexorable sisters.[4]

The putative Florentine romance was a slow-moving affair. Eddy seemed 'very much in earnest', but the matter was 'too long and important to go into in letters', Percy insisted to Mananai when she asked for an update.[5] In the end the Wyndhams' friend Walburga, Lady Paget, brought matters to a head. Lady Paget (whose daughter Gay, artistic and a devoted vegetarian like her mother, would soon begin a long-running affair with George Wyndham) was an inveterate matchmaker. Thirty years before, she had helped bring about the engagement of the Prince and Princess of Wales. In early May she invited Pamela to stay for a few days at her villa in the hills above Florence. While Pamela was there, she asked Eddy to dinner, and after dinner suggested they both walk with her on the moonlit terrace looking out over the distant city lights. At this point, Lady Paget told her diary, she gave an elaborate shiver and withdrew, leaving the tentative lovers alone. On taking his leave that evening Eddy bowed low and kissed his hostess's hand. 'I knew then that the balance had dropped on his side,' Lady Paget wrote.[6]

Legend has it that while they were in Florence Pamela told Eddy that she could never forget Harry Cust. The conversation probably took place that night.[7] In any event, Eddy had proposed, but Pamela had not accepted. By agreement Eddy returned to Glen, leaving Pamela to mull things over with her family – including George, who arrived shortly afterwards, feeling that with Wilde now a fortnight into his prison sentence and Bosie safely abroad he had earned his holiday.

Despite his sisters' conquering of Society, there remained residual suspicion of the Tennant men. '[L]ots of people love *Laura* and me and Lucy or Charty,' Margot had explained to George Curzon in 1890, but Society looked down on 'boys parents place hills', as being 'not common':[8] by which she meant 'unusual', but which might be read more straightforwardly as nouveau riche, more vulgar and less charming. As much is evident in E. F. Benson's novel *Dodo – A Detail of the Day*, published in 1893. The eponymous heroine, child of an industrial tycoon who slays all before her as she becomes the hit of London Society, was widely rumoured to be based on Margot. Dodo's family, the Vanes, have not the same success: 'somehow none of Dodo's glory got reflected onto them'.[9] A decade later, St John Brodrick complained of a visit by the Tennant brothers to Gosford where they had been 'distressingly familiar . . . you cannot make gentlemen'.[10] Eddy's looks, wealth and kindness could not dispel the feeling that something in him did not quite 'fit'.

Were Pamela not twenty-four, had the Harry Cust debacle not occurred, it is quite possible that the Wyndhams – certainly Madeline Wyndham – would have resisted Pamela's marriage into the Tennant clan. In the end, Eddy clinched it with a letter. He was an excellent letter writer, of quiet humour and with an air of comforting gravitas. Whatever he said, it worked. Pamela wrote an acceptance in reply and walked with George through the sun-baked streets of Florence to the post office, where she also telegraphed Mananai the news: 'Engaged E.T. still private.'[11] Eddy, who swiftly returned to Florence, was more fulsome when breaking the news to Charty: 'A little letter to tell you great things, if my hand will not shake. The uncertainty is at an end and Pamela accompanies me through the world to the end . . .'[12]

'You can imagine my surprise! I think they have all been in such a whirl . . . they have forgotten about everything! & kept us all in the dark!' Mananai exclaimed to Mary. She swallowed her disappointment for Baker-Carr – '*poor* man . . . he has known now for some time it was practically impossible' – and embraced this new prospect. 'To think that such a nice person should . . . come forward – and at last no obstacles . . . one can only be deeply thankful.'[13] 'Waiting and waiting would never have done for Darling Pamela,' Mary agreed, now back at Stanway from Egypt, amused, if a little irritated, that she had to wait several more days before her '*extraordinary* sister' sent her a telegram of her own.[14]

Eddy arrived in Florence to jubilation: '. . . I seem to be holding some one in my arms all day long in congratulations and even the old concierge woman looks disappointed that I have no embrace for her.'[15] Yet none of Pamela's family pretended that Eddy would be other than a 'very nice husband', and provide Pamela with the means to make a happy home. Wilfrid Blunt thought privately it was 'no great marriage' for Pamela, thinking of 'the somewhat coarse fibre in [Eddy]',[16] but George spoke to outsiders with generous condescension of a 'nice simple letter' he had received from Eddy.[17] Mary, reminding her parents of the 'many "fan breaking" times & sick monkey faces we have passed thro',[18] thought the calm prospect offered by marriage to Eddy, 'so sensible, so reposeful, so himself', was enough. Pamela would appreciate 'the change, the peace of mind, the . . . clearing . . . away of doubts &

emptiness & vain regrets'.[19] Implicit in all the family's comments was that Pamela would have to provide any spark in the marriage with her 'splendid natural spirits . . . & capacity for enjoyment'.[20] As for the power balance in the match – that was evident even to six-year-old Cincie Charteris, for 'When I announced Pam's marriage to Cincie, she merely said "Did Auntie Pansie arx him to marry her, or did the man arx her?' Mary reported to Arthur.[21]

The Wyndhams returned to England, but not before one final upheaval. On their last night in Florence Percy was in the palazzo's drawing room when his peace was interrupted by a bone-shaking roar. His manservant Giovanni knew the sound's significance. 'Saying "il est mieux de s'asseoir" he sank into the largest armchair in the room,' Percy told Guy. 'Oh god god god,' shrieked Madeline Wyndham, who was with Pamela, Eddy, Dorothy and Fräulein in the ballroom as the force of the earthquake cracked walls around them and tumbled bricks down the chimney. The earthquake destroyed treasures in Florence's Duomo and caused a stampede at the Opera House in which several were killed. The palazzo's inhabitants were thankfully unscathed. Dorothy displayed 'her usual calm' and slept like a top until morning; to Percy's relief the more highly strung members of his party appeared no more unnerved.[22] 'Pamela has a faculty for sensational catastrophes which is really out of place, unless in a novel,' said George upon hearing the latest instalment of the 'Florentine Drama'.[23]

Mary's greatest concern about Pamela's engagement was that the wedding and attendant festivities required her to see everyone she knew. All spring she had kept a low profile at Stanway. Even once in London, two days before Pamela's wedding she reproved her mother for letting slip the news to Lucy Graham Smith: 'telling a female Tennant is like telling the Town-Crier, why did you tell her? Wicked Mum!' she wrote, despite admitting that Lucy would have guessed when seeing her at the wedding anyway.[24]

Mary had let herself 'slide & glide' and now had to face the consequences. Yet she is at her most cipher-like this summer. Her diary is missing, although this would probably not have revealed thoughts, only whereabouts and actions. To gauge her interior self we can only judge from that which she presented to others. Her letters to her family and friends that summer are masterfully normal. In August she even mentioned to Arthur 'baddish nights' caused by pregnancy-related pains, moments of being 'frightened and miserable in the watches of the night'[25] – for Mary must have been afraid that she might not survive the pregnancy that was against her doctor's orders.

Mary had confessed to Hugo about her pregnancy on returning to Stanway that spring. Hugo's reaction is reported second hand – Wilfrid's report of a conversation he had with Mary later that summer. On that account, Hugo was silent for three days. Then he said, 'If it had been Arthur I could have understood it, but I cannot understand it now . . . I shall forgive you, but I shall be nasty to you . . .' Mary also told Wilfrid, rather irritably, that Hugo's primary concern was that Hermione's family would think the Elchos had reconciled sexually while Hermione was dying.[26]

The next occurrence, again recorded by Wilfrid, is his receipt of a furious letter from Hugo, blasting him for having 'wrecked the life and destroyed the happiness of a woman whom a spark of chivalry would have made you protect'. In Hugo's letter, Mary 'was a happy woman when she went to Egypt, and her misery now would touch a heart of stone'. Then came a letter from Mary, breaking off all contact: 'You did try and wreck my life and the only thing that prevents my being utterly angry with you is that I believe you *did* care for me in a way,' she wrote.[27]

The letters' linguistic similarity, dwelling on the word 'wreck', suggests that Hugo stood over Mary as she wrote it. This would seem to be the case, since shortly afterwards Mary wrote to Wilfrid again. Again it is a transcription, but recognizably Mary's voice. She was sorry that he was upset – 'I know you are suffering' – but she was matter-of-fact. She discussed how she thought things could

be managed. Wilfrid was to behave towards her mother and George
– neither of whom knew anything yet – 'just as usual'. In time, she
thought things would blow over. 'These things must be done gradually,' she told Wilfrid:

> I can only be deeply grateful to [Hugo] for not making my life
> unbearable . . . It is a cruel thing to destroy a person's *ideal*, when
> they have a love & admiration for one person & make them feel
> one is something quite different from what they imagined – all
> one can do is to labour painfully to build up a new image & to
> deserve it, to earn it . . .[28]

Wilfrid told George the following month on his return from Italy.
George, the 'largest-minded' of all men in such matters, seemed to
understand: '[he] neither blames me nor finds it strange', Wilfrid
noted in his diary.[29] From Mary's reproof to Madeline Wyndham
in July, it seems that she had still not told her mother the truth of
the child's paternity by then.

Wilfrid found Mary's sangfroid baffling. In the days before the
wedding he enlisted Judith, to whom he had intimated some and
possibly all of the truth,[30] as a makeshift spy and sent her to storm
the fortress of Cadogan Square. She reported:

> [T]he door opened cautiously and revealed the end of Mary's nose
> and one eye through the crack . . . I was immediately let in and
> taken to the dining room where Miss Jourdain and Mrs Guy
> Wyndham still sat at lunch. Mary is looking well and was extremely
> cheerful. She asked where you were . . . when lunch was over Mary
> took me upstairs and we talked about things in general and nothing
> in particular . . .

After that, Judith and Anne Blunt went to view Pamela and Eddy's
wedding presents, laid out on display at George and Sibell's house,
35 Park Lane, since Belgrave Square was still let. 'Old Madeline was

most affectionate to us both, Percy was amiable, Pamela kissed me if I remember right four times in the course of 30 seconds . . . Sibell was most caressing and sat in a corner holding mother's hand when she was not holding someone else's . . . There is evidently not a shadow of anything between us and the Wyndhams,' concluded Judith.[31]

On 11 July 1895, Pamela and Eddy were married at Holy Trinity Church on Sloane Street, in London.[32] Pamela's hopes for a wedding at Salisbury Cathedral had been dashed by the Tennants citing logistical difficulties. But there were nods to her fondness for rustic life. Her ten bridesmaids (including Wommy, Dorothy and little Cincie Charteris) resembled shepherdesses in white chiffon and large white straw hats trimmed with white roses – albeit wearing diamond-and-pearl lockets that were the bridegroom's gift. Pamela's low-cut satin bodice and full court train were embroidered with silver thread, the skirt trimmed with handmade Brussels lace and her fashionably large sleeves chiffon like her veil. She wore sprays of orange blossom in her hair; a 'circle of brilliants' pinned her veil in place. As she and Eddy made their way back down the aisle Pamela, her veil thrown back, diamonds glinting in the light and a 'seraphic' expression on her face, seemed 'like a thing inspired . . . I have never seen a bride so lovely,' thought Lucy Graham Smith, erstwhile rival and now one of Pamela's many new sisters-in-law.[33]

After much agonizing, Wilfrid, fearing that Hugo might cause a scene, decided not to attend the ceremony, or the reception, held by George and Sibell at Park Lane. He claimed he had missed his train. To his chagrin, he suspected that the Wyndhams did not much care about the veracity of his excuse. Nor did a dance held by George and Sibell the following week provide any further intrigue. George was on 'fine form', ebullient at hosting his first dance, and waxing large on epicurean delights. Wilfrid sat by Madeline Wyndham to watch the dancing. They talked of Mary and of Pamela 'in a way of affection there has not been these twenty years'. Once again Wilfrid was confounded. It seemed 'clear that Mary has not taken things at all as tragically as I have . . . Why should I repine?'[34]

Wilfrid and Mary finally met in late August, clandestinely on the London-to-Brighton slow train, at Mary's direction. Wilfrid recorded their conversation almost verbatim in his diary. Heavily pregnant, dressed in a black dress with a white scarf and a pearl necklace, Mary was looking 'well and strong and pretty' and cheerful. She gave every appearance of being happy to see him. Wilfrid had brought her a basket of peaches to remind her of the apples she carried in the desert, and as she munched her way through them she recounted how she had dealt with Hugo's interrogations and weathered the storm of the last few months. She had refused to be drawn on the 'seduction' beyond the bare fact of its occurrence. 'He asked me "whether I intended to bring it up with his own children" and I said I supposed so and that was all . . . he will not take any notice of it [the baby], but nobody will remark that.' Now, she said, the Elchos never talked of the matter: 'perhaps he [Hugo] does not think of it'. She said that Arthur, though a little jealous of Wilfrid, suspected nothing either.

There is nothing to suggest, beyond Wilfrid's tendency to embroider, that this is not an accurate account of the conversation. As discussed on that journey, George was indeed made a godfather of the child, and Wilfrid did provide through him. Nonetheless certain statements leap out oddly. It cannot be, for example, that Mary was genuinely considering calling the child 'Zobeyde' if it were a girl, as Wilfrid insists.[35] And while it is probable that she was hoping the child would be a girl, so as to avoid 'the dynastic question of the Wemyss inheritance', she cannot truly have meant it when she said, 'I know my own children will die as a punishment to me,'[36] particularly since she had lost a beloved child only three years before. Hugo required Mary to play the victim in order to forgive her; Blunt could only accept Mary, pregnant with his child yet seamlessly maintaining her life as Lady Elcho, if she was racked with secret remorse. Wilfrid departed the train, as agreed, at Preston Park, leaving Mary, still eating peaches, to travel on to the final stop alone, where she was to be greeted by a Campbell cousin, Edward Stanford.

Mary Pamela Madeline Sibell Charteris was born on 24 October 1895 ('a most delicious little baby girl, exactly what I wanted', Mary told Blunt disingenuously of the 'family baby' who was named after one side of the family only).[37] To the great relief of her family and friends Mary was unharmed by the birth, and recovered well.[38] She was delighted with the child, from the first the most beautiful of all her children, and rapturous in the description she gave to Blunt: 'She is absolutely round plump healthy and beautifully made, very dark with long soft brown hair – huge glittering eyes with long drooping lids and pencilled eyebrows, *lovely* hands bewitching mouth and *arched* feet . . . when she opens her eyes she looks you thro' and thro' – and she might be gazing fearlessly across the desert.'[39] Wilfrid met the child for the first time in a rendezvous at an inn near Cheltenham the following year,[40] an engagement that was deliberately planned in Hugo's absence for Mary was acutely aware that 'a meeting might be very terrible'.[41] Four years later, Blunt still sent letters to Mary via Belgrave Square, lest Hugo catch sight of his handwriting. 'There's a letter to you from Wilfrid, Mary, extraordinary fellow that he is! Why doesn't he write to you at your own house?' Percy's bemused response demonstrates just how successfully the secret was kept.[42]

In the years to come Mary would often be vexed by Wilfrid's reproachful urgings to see her and their daughter. But when she felt like it she was quite willing to remind him of her time as 'yr Bedouin wife'; to speak meaningfully of 'footsteps in the sand!!'; even to revisit the romance. 'I *am* lost – in a tent,' she told him blissfully in 1901 after 'stumbling' across him and his blue and white carpet while on a solitary early-morning walk through the grounds of Clouds.[43] Some five years after that she gloated over a nighttime visit to a convalescent Wilfrid in London when her 'somewhat unorthodox treatment' had managed 'in a few seconds, [to] turn an invalide [sic] into a distinctly rampageous young man'.[44]

After each sexual encounter, Mary assured Wilfrid that it was the last, threatening with relish to become the model of 'professional cousinly' rectitude, 'quiet and undisturbing'. 'I shall have on a quaker or salvation Army bonnet . . . or a nun's veil . . . or rather my soul will be draped in suchlike garments . . . I shall be as dull as anything,' she announced after her nighttime visit in 1906.[45] Perhaps one of the strangest twists of this tale was that by this point Dorothy Carleton was living with Wilfrid, ostensibly acting as his nurse but actually having an affair with him. When Wilfrid recovered, he 'adopted' Dorothy so that she could continue to live with him, as she did, until his death in 1922. It caused the final breach between Wilfrid and Anne, and occasioned much bitterness from Judith Blunt and Dorothy's brother Guy. The Wyndhams accepted it without a bat of the eyelid, and continued to be as close to Dorothy as they had ever been.[46]

The real distress for Mary came when she revealed to Arthur the truth of her child's paternity, and genuinely did have to destroy an ideal. A cryptic letter from her in the spring of 1896 speaks of an unhappy afternoon spent at Arthur's house at 4 Carlton Gardens. 'I hated having to distress you,' she says.[47] Mary was already five months pregnant with Yvo, the Elchos' true 'reconciliation baby' born in 1896, who was the apple of Hugo's eye, so the revelation cannot have been her pregnancy. But she did not lose Arthur. In fact, it reminded him – as it had Hugo – that Mary could be desirable to other men. And as one thinks of pregnant Mary, elegant in her black dress and pearls, dismounting at Brighton to be met by her cousin, with her hold on her husband, her 'friend', her children and her social life intact, it is very hard to resist giving her a silent, heartfelt cheer.

EIGHTEEN

Glen

The Souls thought the marriage of the youngest Wyndham to the eldest Tennant would provide a new nexus of power. 'I am so glad they have got anyone so delicious as Pamela to take over Glen!' Frances Horner enthused to D. D. Lyttelton.[1] It did not take Pamela long to rectify these misapprehensions nor much time before a civil war had developed between her and her redoubtable sisters-in-law.

After a brief honeymoon, Eddy and Pamela made their way to Glen, where the entire Tennant clan had decamped for the summer. Wilfrid Blunt, on seeing Pamela briefly in London just before, thought her looking 'very slight, and rather pale, and perfectly lovely', and also happy: 'not rapturously . . . but perhaps sufficiently'.[2] Pamela assured her family that she was indeed happy, and thankful, she declared to George, for the decision she had made in Florence.[3]

But Pamela's tone was muted, and there are clues which indicate that her honeymoon, such as it was, had been a shock to her. In 1918, Marie Stopes's bestselling *Married Love* confronted its fascinated readers with the necessity of the female orgasm, attributing many of the neuroses of modern women to unsatisfying marital relations. Pamela, when she was nearly fifty, told Marie Stopes that 'meeting with your book has given me a sense of fellow-feeling & comfort'. She referred to a conversation in which 'I have never spoken to anyone as I did to you'.[4] It is hard to escape the conclusion: sexually, Pamela and Eddy were a mismatch.

For both Pamela's sisters, the novel delight of sex had eased their transition into married life. Pamela was precipitated into a new world without that comfort. Glen compounded her loneliness. A mock-baronial monstrosity, windswept and cold, the house was 'so *different* to what I have always lived among', she complained to George, shrinking into herself and longing for the light and air of Clouds – 'it is as if Morris were not – nor had been'.[5] Meanwhile the fundamental differences between the Tennant and the Wyndham ways of life were daily becoming more apparent.

'I find Sir Charles very difficult to get on with,' said Pamela, 'a curious grown-up child – with whims & tantrums' and a line in selective deafness that drove her to distraction. She found the Bart overbearing, dictatorial and ridiculously sentimental: 'Eddy says he can't read Prayers without wobbling,' she told George exasperatedly, and at dinner, she explained, 'the conversation trails like a winged bird, lower and lower till it gradually settles down among stocks and shares, or the indifferent among the poems of Burns.' 'It's true . . . there is an awful leg to the table corner which takes all my thoughts; – it's the kind of leg to the table you can't forget, but still I think it's his fault rather'.[6]

Pamela had been dominant in her own social circle. By marriage to Eddy she was 'grafted' on to the Souls, 'a world of friends already so formed & complete' a good decade older than her.[7] She had no inclination to assume a junior role, and was constantly enervated by her sisters-in-law's reminders of how much better they knew 'dear Eddy' than she; and, in Margot's case, how, until her own marriage to Asquith in 1894, she had been Glen's chatelaine in all but name. Mary advised Pamela to remember that the Tennants were akin to the vultures in the Bible verse: wherever there was death and destruction, there they would be, teasing out pain and worrying away at weak spots.[8]

The Tennant women were caustic, unsentimental and matter-of-fact. Their frank approach pierced Pamela's pretensions; their claims on Eddy provoked uncontrollable jealousy in her. She professed horror when, rhapsodizing about the Scottish hills on a carriage ride with Charty, she saw that her companion, head down, was knitting furiously, heedless of the beauty all around. She deplored their habit of facing conflicts head on. In retaliation, she became ever more vague and ethereal. 'The more I see of them,' she wrote to Mary of her sisters-in-law two years into her marriage, 'the more I realize what *very* remarkable women they are [and] I don't mean it in a wholly complimentary sense . . . they have so many qualities that *equip* them almost unfairly for the fray of Life compared to most other women.'[9]

Pamela seized upon the opportunity provided by her first pregnancy to escape. Eddy had promised to take a house in Wiltshire, and paid over the odds to secure the rental of Stockton House, just a few miles from Clouds. While waiting for it to be made ready, Pamela retreated to her childhood home. Barely six months after her marriage, she was back at Clouds, embroidering hats with Wommy and knitting the intricate patterns at which she excelled for the baby due in July 1896. She wrote Eddy long letters about the minutiae of her days, her quick pen sketching out a scene in its quintessence: the obsequious waiter who had served her and Wommy with tea at Mere; the children round the maypole at Clouds; Charlie Adeane lecturing the assembled company at Clouds with his views on matters ranging from educational reform to poultry breeding.[10]

Eddy visited Pamela when he could in between conducting family business in London and shooting and fishing at Glen. He diligently corresponded with her when he could not. Adoring and fearful of his beautiful wife, Eddy canvassed opinions among his sisters and sisters-in-law as to the best possible nursemaids and governesses;

trailed around Glen's nurseries with Pamela's latest letter in hand checking that everything from skirting-board length to the new Morris wallpaper accorded with her instructions. He dealt with all Stockton's furnishing and staffing – by convention, Pamela's domain – even down to buying the glasses, linen and crockery for the servants' hall, sourcing and interviewing staff.[11] Notoriously parsimonious, Eddy had long been casting a critical eye over the extravagance of the Bart's practices at Glen, but, to Margot's rage, he encouraged his wife to buy whatever took her fancy for the new house. He gave each of Pamela's points his full attention, whether considering 'Wommy's [newly trimmed] Hat' ('sounds fascinating')[12] or the news that Pamela had dreamt on three successive occasions of flowers ('it is curious').[13] He scoured Glen from top to toe for a book of Scottish songs she was missing; he was enraptured when she wrote to him of a drawing she had done, and was 'longing' to have it framed and hung up.[14] He was thrilled when she told him that she was beginning to read about politics in the newspapers.[15] And as Pamela's complaints about her first pregnancy steadily increased – a litany of aches and pains, neuralgia, indigestion, excessive 'wriggling' from the baby and haunting dreams – Eddy provided all the sympathy for which Pamela could have hoped. By the end he was swearing never to leave her again.[16]

'He is A.1.,' said Madeline Wyndham delightedly, likening Eddy's stoicism to the way that they had tested the chandeliers in Clouds' hall, hanging on them many hundredweight more than they would ever bear: 'I feel [that he] is like a Chain *tested* to bear so much weight that the *small* weight of every day life must hang light on it.'[17] Her remark was provoked by an incident in which Pamela, departing from Clouds with the mountains of luggage that accompanied her class's perambulations, had failed to see that boxes meant for London were marked accordingly. Half their things had disappeared, presumably Stockton-bound. Mary concurred with her mother's views: Eddy was 'a very kind good unostentatiously upright & useful man . . . so wonderfully sweet & gentle & nice'.[18]

At Stockton Eddy and Pamela replaced footmen with housemaids (Margot thought it an affectation). Pamela declared herself Eddy's 'loving Wyf [sic]', and him her 'dearest husband', but her descendants believe that by the late 1890s she was already involved in several affairs – one with the ambitious young architect Detmar Blow, a romantic figure with dark curls and dashing manner; another with Ivor Guest, heir to a steel fortune.[19] Nor, true to her words in Florence, did Pamela forget Harry Cust. They continued to see one another, although, as a scribbled note from Harry to Pamela at the turn of the century attests, they preferred such visits to be made when her husband and children were not around.[20]

Pamela's main focus was her children. Clarissa Madeline Genevieve Adelaide, known as Clare, was born on 13 July 1896, Edward Wyndham Tennant, or 'Bim', on 1 July 1897, 'Kit', Christopher Grey Tennant, on 14 June 1899, David on 22 May 1902 and Stephen on 21 April 1906. Pamela was enchanted by them – more accurately by her boys. She quickly earned a reputation as a devoted mother. But motherhood did not dispel her lurking unhappiness. All the Wyndham children found it hard to leave the cradle of their family. 'I feel I have . . . transplanted *very* badly and am always lean & hungry for want of the soil I am accustomed to – *everywhere* except at home, I feel like a mangy fir tree with a bald top,' Mary remarked to her mother, on leaving Clouds after a visit, some three years after her own marriage.[21] Yet in those early years of her own marriage Pamela wept inconsolably every time she left Clouds.[22] In later years, she recalled vividly a visit by Wilfrid Blunt to Stockton. 'I was still so unhappy, and so strangely situated in my new life that I remember answering you almost in a dream when you said how you hoped everything was well with me.'[23]

In her enforced summers at Glen Pamela locked herself away in the library with a pile of books, emerging only to play with her children. At dinners, she sat aloof and silent. Charty taxed her with this. Pamela recounted their conversation to Mary, triumphantly scornful of Charty's 'pathetic' attempts to appeal to her vanity: 'she said she wished I would take more *trouble* to make people *like* me! and . . . know how clever I *could* be . . . "*perhaps* . . . you may meet a man at dinner & *never* see him again – and he may *never* know what a wonderful memory you have! How you can say pages by heart, how quick you are at understanding & what a lot of funny little stories & things *you know*"'. Pamela added, 'I said I did not think anyone could recite at dinner & that if one was going to get to know a person I could not shell out *all* I had before fish.'²⁴

With Pamela's most recent tearful departure from Clouds fresh in her mind, a worried Madeline Wyndham advised her daughter to 'get [Philip] Webb or [Detmar] Blow to build you your large Family Cottage for your own that you may live in it & love it & the Babes also'.²⁵ George came up with another plan. He was fast earning a reputation as one of the most promising young back-benchers of Salisbury's ministry. His trenchant support of 'Uitlander' rights in one of the Boer republics, Paul Kruger's Transvaal – the Uitlanders were the disenfranchised foreigners exploiting the Transvaal's gold rush – had earned him the nickname of 'the Member for South Africa'. George was part of a new breed of imperialists seeking a more aggressive foreign and colonial policy. Their figurehead was Joe Chamberlain, the Colonial Secretary, who compared the position of Uitlanders to helots, and had secretly colluded in the botched coup of 1895 that attempted to overthrow Kruger's Government, the Jameson Raid. In 1897, Chamberlain pushed the appointment of Sir Alfred Milner as High Commissioner overseeing Britain's Southern African republics. Behind a judicious façade, Milner was a fanatical imperialist, determined to render British supremacy in South Africa complete.

The imperialist faction was buoyed by the glorious spectacle of the Queen's 1897 Diamond Jubilee. Almost half a million imperial troops and a panoply of native royalties processed through a London garlanded in bunting, past billboards advertising the very best imperial products, to pledge allegiance to their Empress at a service of thanksgiving at St Paul's Cathedral. Gladstone dismissed it as 'the spirit of Jingoism under the name of Imperialism', while Salisbury privately deprecated its vulgarity, but the public was intoxicated by this visual reminder of the sheer reach of Britain's power. Gloomy political naysayers began almost immediately to look for the nadir that must follow this imperial zenith, referencing Gibbon's *Decline and Fall of the Roman Empire*.[26]

Polymath George had been dabbling in journalism for a number of years, earning his reputation with a promising introduction to North's *Plutarch* and translations of Ronsard's poems. In the winter of 1897/8 he was in the process of launching *Outlook*, a periodical intended to combine in a weekly paper his favourite interests, politics and literature, with a strongly imperialist slant.

George thought Pamela would be the perfect contributor. Shortly after her engagement, Percy had teased her and Mananai with a newspaper cutting, claiming that they, with their Liberal husbands, were nonetheless 'Tory by birth & conviction'.[27] Furthermore, both Charlie and Eddy fell to the far right of their party's spectrum, Liberal Imperialists, or 'Liberal Imps', who privately harboured doubts about Home Rule and were reluctant to advocate disestablishment. One might call them Liberal by birth rather than by conviction. Pamela's early attempts to educate herself politically had quickly failed for lack of interest, but instinctively such views as she had corresponded with George's: romantic, nostalgic and imperialist. George thought her writing skill might even be better than his. 'How I wish you would write something, anything!' he told her early in the new year of 1898. Urged on by her brother and her family, Pamela began.

For the first time in her life when faced with a blank sheet of paper, she baulked. Since childhood she had shown an interest in letter-writing unmatched by her sisters: crossing words out and replacing them with others more apposite, dwelling on form as well as substance. But now her mind, she admitted to George, felt like the five fingers of the hand, all spread out in different directions. She agonized that she couldn't possibly know enough to start;

or that she had more to say than she could ever put down. 'My dear when you have seen more, felt more and thought more than others, you have *always* too much to say,' replied George. Whatever she wrote was sure to be interesting, 'the point is to make it intelligible'.[28] Words were something to be wrestled with, stripped down to sinews and bones: 'a *faculty* for writing is a pearl of contentment', George proclaimed, writing lyrically of days in his own turret writing room at Saighton, with its whitewashed, book-lined walls, oak writing desk and two armchairs in cosy conversation before the fire.[29]

Once Pamela took 'the plunge!' she scarcely looked back.[30] Sheaves of letters whisked between brother and sister as they discussed everything from subject matter to Pamela's proposed pen-name. Pamela agonized over editing; George discursed on the art of prose-writing and the importance of style, counselling brevity as he lectured at length. Pamela's Glen days were now full as she scribbled and crossed out, read, read more, and rewrote. At George's suggestion she began with a series of sketches, 'painting in words' the world around her. He suggested that she look at an essay by a young Irish writer in the periodical *Nineteenth Century*. William Butler Yeats was doing 'for Irish Faery lore just what you could do for Wiltshire . . . invent new names for your people and places and then reproduce their words exactly . . . giving the sensation which they aroused in you'.[31]

Pamela's resulting essays were serialized in *Outlook* under the pen-name of 'Clarissa'. While comparisons with Yeats were fallacious, her keen ear for dialect and her ability to skewer an apposite and unexpected turn of phrase gave them a certain charm. 'I love your imagination,' said George; 'sometimes I think of it as a horse turned out to grass: so happy and irresponsible and quaint.'[32]

For the same reasons that Pamela's writing so appealed to *Outlook*'s readership, it has not stood the test of time. Pamela depicted a sun-lit, semi-feudal world in which peasants tugged their forelocks and uttered naive wisdom; children were tow-headed and rosy-cheeked, the aristocracy wise, benevolent and handsome. As imperial propaganda, it was magnificent. It was not a realistic portrait of the nation. When Heinemann published 'Clarissa's' essays as *Village Notes* under Pamela's own name in 1900 braver critics hinted as much. It was marketed as studies of life in 'a typical country village', illustrated by fourteen photogravure illustrations that 'Mrs. Tennant . . . an amateur photographer' had taken herself. 'The modern cottager is a very wide-awake person, who reads penny novelettes and likes her clothes made "in the fashion"', pointed out the *World*. The *Glasgow Herald* took exception to Pamela's rendition of the Scottish dialect ('"Parn" is not the Scotch for pan, nor "coof" for cough'). But by and large the reviews were soft and deferential. They praised Pamela's fresh and sympathetic approach, and the restraint and sparseness of her style. It was 'eminently soothing', said the *Pall Mall Gazette* (still under Harry Cust's editorship), just the kind of thing to read in a hammock; she had written it *con amore*, reported the *Globe*, in a typically breathless phrase.[33] Pamela was not so foolish as to take these condescensions as compliments. 'The harshest blow was "pretty booklet"', she commented wryly to Mary.[34]

Yet Pamela did not wish to engage in the actuality that might take her work beyond 'pretty' and 'soothing'. Like many great ladies, Pamela visited London's slums, Bim trailing behind her, clutching a tin of sweets for the 'poor children'. She did a considerable amount of charity work, later in life, becoming involved in a home for working mothers in Westminster, offering those mothers an annual fortnight's holiday in her Wiltshire village.[35] But that was not her reality. She stopped Bim's visits to the slums when he grew too disturbed by the squalor,[36] physically removing him from the cause of distress. She similarly excised from her interior world unpalatable facts that might cause her that same distress, or even bring her to face mundane reality. Pamela's literary world was no mere fiction. It expressed how she willed her existence to be.

NINETEEN

The Portrait, War and Death

In December 1898 Percy received a letter from an American expatriate who had inherited Watts's mantle as the finest portrait painter of the day. 'I am looking forward with the greatest of interest to painting your three daughters,' Sargent told Percy.[1] A price of £2,000 was agreed, and a preliminary meeting between painter and subjects at 44 Belgrave Square arranged to take place early in the new year. Percy had begun thinking of commissioning a portrait of his daughters in 1895, as soon as Pamela became engaged. His pencil sketch of stick figures from that time is fortunately made intelligible by a written explanation: 'Mary at tea table with pot in right hand. Pamela guitar by her side (dog in lap?). Mananai first finger of right hand within leaves of a book, background of trees; tennis racquets and balls in foreground – all three looking out of the picture'.[2]

Three years later Percy made good on his plan. The Wyndhams were flourishing and finally seemed to be attaining the fame that Madeline Wyndham had always thought they deserved. Guy Wyndham had been stationed in South Africa, although his wife Minnie (now mother of his three small children), Mananai and Madeline Wyndham mourned that he was not being promoted as quickly as he ought. George as always was achieving the lion's share of glory. On 10 October 1898 he took a long stride towards his goal of being 'a Minister of Victoria' when he was appointed Under-Secretary at the War Office: the youngest MP to sit in that office since Lord Hartington in 1865. George was jubilant at his promotion, largely 'because it will please you & Papa', he told his mother. In strictest confidence he sent his parents Salisbury's letter offering him the post: 'it belongs to us three for the present and to the archives at Clouds when we are all gone'.[3]

Just a few weeks before, George had been passed over as Curzon's replacement as Under-Secretary at the Foreign Office in favour of Mary's brother-in-law, St John Brodrick (the thirty-nine-year-old Curzon had been spectacularly promoted to Viceroy). Madeline Wyndham had gone into a furious decline, wildly speculating about conspiracies to keep her family down (indeed, Salisbury had opposed George's promotion on both occasions, disliking George's exuberance, verve and florid romanticism).[4] Now George was being given Brodrick's old post. It did not sour the family's delight.

George's promotion signified the strengthening of the jingoist faction of Salisbury's ministry. That September, Sir Herbert Kitchener's troops in the Sudan had finally avenged General Gordon's death, defeating the Mahdi at the battle of Omdurman, The Wyndhams and East Knoyle's parishioners had been among the first to hear the news. The Wyndhams were hosting a party that included the general Lord Roberts and Brodrick, at the time still in his old post. On Sunday morning, as the party made their way to church, Brodrick received a telegram. He handed it to the rector to read out. As the news of victory at Omdurman boomed forth from the pulpit, as if by magic the guns of the camps on Salisbury Plain echoed out their confirmation of the news.[5]

The triumph at Omdurman raised Anglo-French tensions to boiling point. Within George's first few weeks of office, the Fashoda incident in which both countries laid claim to the strategically key Southern Sudanese town brought them to the brink of war, although they both climbed down. 'George is in high spirits . . . he and the ultra-Jingo section of the party are all for war,' Wilfrid Blunt commented in his diary.⁶ Charlie Adeane's sister Marie (now married to the civil servant Bernard Mallet) thought that George had forced the Government's hand over Fashoda: she had heard from a source at court that 'he is almost the best hated man in the House of Commons . . .'.⁷

George's sisters were meanwhile most anxious that their portrait grouping should not appear contrived. Mary's suggestions for a 'reposeful' setting with all three studying a book or staged as 'if the *Evening Post* had just come & one was reading a letter to the others' were resoundingly rejected. Their discussions grew more tense. Pamela announced her intention to dress in blue and Mananai was wearing pink chiffon. Mary, who had her own plans to wear 'cream or white, with perhaps some fur', was concerned. 'Don't you think Pink white & blue will look rather like a Neapolitan ice?' she asked her mother, appealing for her help to steer the obdurate Pamela from her choice.⁸

Few managed ever to change Pamela's mind, and neither Madeline Wyndham nor Mary appears to have given it a serious try. Mary abandoned her plan to wear a dress she already owned and ordered a new white chiffon gown to match Mananai's pink: 'same sort of *shape* will look well I think'.⁹ The sisters and their parents had a preliminary dinner with Sargent at Belgrave Square in February 1899. Even arranging a date which they could all attend proved almost impossible. Mary had spent the first weeks of the new year in an Edinburgh nursing home, recovering from an operation to correct a prolapsed uterus, the result, it is to be presumed, of her two recent pregnancies in quick succession. She reported the details of her 'curating' to her mother in minute detail: morphia suppositories, chloroform-induced bilious attacks and 'a pessary (*round*) . . . which I am told is a *perfect fit!*'¹⁰ Mary took her 'Spring-Cleaning' and '*Furnishing*' in good humour. She revelled in the peace and quiet of the nursing home, free from the demands of servants and friends. A bored Hugo was being unexpectedly uxorious and visiting her daily, and she had managed to persuade the nurses to allow her to keep Cymru by her side. The chow inherited from Hermione had become Mary's most beloved pet. Mary delighted in the way Cymru, whom the denizens of Kissingen had once mistaken for a wolf, guarded her and frightened visitors, doctors and fellow patients; only recently, she informed her mother, he had nearly floored 'an invalid lady bobbing round the corner from the bath room in the red dressing gown & curl papers'.[11] Nonetheless, four weeks of bed-rest had left her 'thin and pinched', and she looked, she told her mother, 'exactly like Miss Havisham!'[12]

The final composition was suggested by Sargent after that dinner – a brilliant choice that reveals their characters and nervous energy more clearly. None of the sisters seems to have felt there was anything pointed in Sargent choosing a pose of indolence. Once his initial sketching had outlined the group, each sister sat separately as the artist began work in earnest.

The experience of sitting to awkward, gruff Sargent was not reflective of Madeline Wyndham's enjoyable time with Watts. Additionally, London in February was inhospitable. On several occasions the sittings had to be curtailed when 'smelly thick yellow fog' made it too dark to work.[13] No number of fires seemed capable of truly warming Belgrave Square's vast drawing room. Pamela, pregnant with Kit, caught influenza and refused to leave her house; Mary, in the throes of 'Betsey' and fearing that her face was still insufficiently plump to be painted, directed all her energies to getting Pamela to Belgrave Square without swallowing a mouthful of fog (her favoured method involved a Shetland rug covering head and face). Mananai diligently made the lengthy journey from Babraham for each sitting without tardiness or absence and finally succumbed to the 'demoniacal Influenza' while at Belgrave Square.[14] The doctor ordered a period of total bed-rest for several weeks, forbidding her to travel back to Babraham. 'Sargeant [sic] must be fairly puzzled at the intricate health problems presented to him,' said Mary.[15]

At Easter, while the rest of the Wyndhams went to Clouds, Mananai was still tucked up in bed at Belgrave Square. She was in good spirits, snug in her room, a fire blazing in the grate, an amenable 'little nurse' on hand, reading her mother's copies of Ruskin on the Pre-Raphaelites and delighting in Madeline Wyndham's annotations to the text: '*What* wonderful people and *dear* B.J.'s name just mentioned with promise of *great* fame & the start of *Morris & Co*! I long to ask you *all* about it for you know it all – how *curious* Miss Siddal was.'[16]

Charlie Adeane was less content. His four daughters were well cared for in Babraham's nursery, but he was unaccustomed to being without his wife, and was worried about her health. 'It seems that when once you have fallen a victim a victim you remain . . .' he told his mother-in-law sternly. He had begged Mananai to stay at home, 'to no avail . . . her sense of duty with regard to that blessed picture overcame all caution', and he expressed the hope that no further sittings were planned until the whole family decamped to London for the Season in May: 'it is almost too much of a nuisance & I do not appreciate a solitary life at this time of year'. Charlie insisted that he, not his parents-in-law, would pay for the nurse currently tending Mananai, and declared his intention at Babraham 'to lay on hot water pipes all over the house cost what it may!'[17] 'It was a very unfortunate time of year to choose for a picture to be painted. But I suppose these painters are tyrants. This one is a real drill-sergeant,' Charlie added in a postscript, employing a rather good but almost certainly unintentional pun.[18]

The picture was the final straw for Charlie, tired of playing second fiddle to his wife's family. For months Mananai, who fell pregnant again that summer, had been fretting over the welfare of Minnie Wyndham and her children while Guy was away. The political temperature was rising. A conference between Milner and Kruger at Bloemfontein in June 1899 over Uitlander rights ended in deadlock. 'It is our country you want!' Kruger told Milner with tears in his eyes. In August, Guy Wyndham received a longed-for promotion: Deputy Assistant Adjutant General under Sir George White, the commander of the British forces in Natal. 'I suppose it is a great honour but I do trust there won't be war,' said Mananai.[19] From the War Office, George assured his family that there would not. Mananai began to relax. She was past her first trimester, she felt preternaturally well and active. The baby was kicking strongly and, as she told her mother, 'I always like it so much when they begin to be lively it is quite company! & a little "individual" is'nt [sic] it.'[20]

Neither George nor the War Office thought Kruger's and Milner's elaborate schemes of bluff and double-bluff would come to a head. But the daily reports grew darker. On 4 October George wrote to his mother to tell her that 'between you me and the gatepost we mobilize on Monday'.[21] A week later Kruger delivered an ultimatum to Milner. The British were to withdraw their troops from the border of the Transvaal and send back all the troops currently on their way out to South Africa or face war. Such a concession was unthinkable for the British. The ultimatum expired at 3 p.m. GMT on Wednesday 11 October. 'Well it has come,' said George.[22] Britain was at war.

Salisbury's Government greeted the news with a kind of relief, for Kruger's aggression saved them from having to justify war to the public. In fact, the British public greeted the news with a great outpouring of truculent jingoism. Still drunk on the glory of the Diamond Jubilee, most people thought that it would be mere days – weeks at most – before Britain put a handful of backward Boer farmers firmly in their place. Bunting was strung up in Trafalgar Square; Kipling and Swinburne composed verses for the occasion published in *The Times*.[23] Theatres hastily revised their programmes, putting on suitably imperialist productions: Wilfrid Blunt reluctantly accompanied George to Sir Herbert Beerbohm Tree's production of *King John* at Her Majesty's Theatre – full of 'jingo tags and no popery talk', said George.[24] Blunt was hoping the fracas would prove the Empire's downfall, but he did not really think that it would. The cream of the British army was at that very moment being shipped out to Africa. And George heartily denied rumours that the War Office was ill prepared. 'Don't pay the slightest attention to alarmist rumours, we are well enough ahead with our work,' he assured his mother.[25]

It soon became painfully apparent that this was not true. Poor communications and inadequate preparations paved the way for a series of disasters on the veldt hollered out by paperboys on every street corner at home. On 31 October 1899, when the war was almost three weeks old, Mananai was at Babraham. 'We are all very well here,' she reported to her mother, enjoying the crisp late-autumn day, 'only almost sick with anxiety [about Guy Wyndham] . . . still the days are going by and each day brings the end of the War nearer.'[26] But the evening's headlines reported the disastrous battle of Ladysmith: 12,000 British casualties and Sir George White's forces driven back to the besieged town by a torrent of Boers who now blockaded them in. Among those soldiers was Sir George White's Deputy Assistant Adjutant General.

Mananai slept fitfully that night with battle images storming around her head. At 3 o'clock in the morning she woke up 'to find quite a "*show*" of . . . "Betsy" . . . a bad threathening [sic] of a "miscarriage" I who had *never* had any symptom of such thing before', she told her mother. Charlie roused the coachman and head housemaid and sent for the doctor. For twenty-four hours Mananai lay 'like a log', clinging on to the hope promised by each passing hour. 'The little thing is *splendidly* lively,' she assured her mother from her bed. '[Doctor] Wherry and Nurse consider me *out of the wood* & so do I now . . . Don't you worry about this Darling, I feel quite sure we have warded it off.'[27]

This collective optimism proved sadly unfounded. At 9 o'clock on the evening of 2 November 1899 Mananai gave birth to a twenty-four-week-old child. 'The premature baby was unfortunately a boy & lived 12 hours this has been a great aggravation of the blow . . . Madeline however is going on well and with her fund of sound sense is well & that is the only thing we care about you & I!' Charlie wrote to Madeline Wyndham, who on receipt of the letter left Clouds immediately for Babraham.²⁸ Mananai's family were devastated by the tragedy, which they all believed had been brought upon her by reading of the horrific news of Ladysmith. Mary worried over might-have-beens: wishing that an incubator had been handy; dwelling on the peculiar fact that the child had managed to live so long, yet no longer. Madeline Wyndham tried to console herself with the fact that the child 'might not have been realy [sic] *sufficiently developed* to be perfect or *strong* and might only have been a weakling'. On receiving her mother's long, sad account of the scene at Babraham, of Charlie's '*gentleness & brightness*', of Mananai's '*quietness & wonderful* resignation', Pamela was simply distraught.²⁹

'You must not grieve for Madeline,' Madeline Wyndham told her youngest daughter sternly, 'as those who have no hope & make *yourself* ill & thereby make *her* & all of us more unhappy & give us *more to bear* than we have already! Your duty now is to . . . write Madeline a cheerful letter for *outside things do interest her* & they take her mind off the sorrow . . .'³⁰ Madeline Wyndham took comfort in the fact that, like herself, both Mary and Pamela had had '2 boys running . . . so let us *hope & pray for that for her* . . . don't think of anything emotional but pray pray pray because sometimes . . . dwelling on the horrors of the war . . . does *overmaster* one [and] makes one feel as if one must *die* of it & it would be *dreadful* if we all died of fright & Guy were to escape & come home & find us dead . . .'³¹

In December 1899 came Black Week, a trinity of defeats that stupefied an already bewildered British public: 'The bloody waste of Magersfontein, the shattering retreat from Stormberg . . . Colenso that blundering battle . . .', in the words of H. G. Wells.³² At Colenso, the cruel climax, Louis Botha's 5,000-strong Boer force, concealed behind the Tugela River's steep banks, mowed down Sir Redvers Bullers's army of 18,000 men. In a few short hours, and assailed by an enfilade of bullets that came 'in solid streaks like telegraph wires',

Britain's strongest force in the field since the Crimea was decimated. 'It is a weird and soul-shaking experience to advance over a sunlit and apparently a lonely countryside, with no slightest movement upon its broad face, while the path which you take is marked behind you by sobbing, gasping, writhing men, who can only guess by the position of their wounds whence the shots came which struck them down,' wrote Arthur Conan Doyle, whose rose-tinted account of the conflict, *The Great Boer War*, falters when it comes to Black Week.[33] 'I never saw a Boer all day till the battle was over,' said a dazed General Lyttelton, Alfred's brother.[34]

Christmas at Clouds was bleak. A pale and anxious Minnie Wyndham could think of nothing but Guy, trapped at Ladysmith in an apparently never-ending siege. George arrived and went straight to bed, worn down by the flu and on the brink of nervous exhaustion. Madeline Wyndham prayed constantly in front of her prie-dieu, and urged her daughters to do the same. Percy was left to sit by the fire in his favourite armchair, fulminating impotently at the shortcomings of generals who had not even thought to send a reconnaissance force before them. 'I wish the ferret [Pamela] had been at Colenzo [sic],' he told Mary. 'I think she would have asked questions about the banks of the river.'[35]

TWENTY

Plucking Triumph from Disaster

Black Week shook Britain's confidence and forced a complete over-haul in the Government's conduct of the war. With the eyes of the world upon it, Britain was faltering. Its army had showed itself 'mortal and human', its officers simply 'the pleasant, rather incom-petent men they had always been', the troops 'neither splendid nor disgraceful . . . just ill-trained and fairly plucky and wonderfully good-tempered men – paying for it', said Wells.[1] 'The history of the future will have to summarize the causes of the decline and fall of the British Empire in three pregnant words – "suicide from imbe-cility"', declared a trenchant commentator in the *Review of Reviews*, urging root-and-branch military reform.[2]

Lord Roberts – 'Bobs', as he was known – was brought out of retirement to replace Sir Redvers Bullers, and told, in the meeting in which he was appointed, that his only son was one of the Colenso dead. The change in command was not enough to protect the War Office from allegations of ineptitude from either Radical anti-war Liberals, led by Henry Labouchere ('Labby'), or Alfred Harmsworth's *Daily Mail*, just three years old. George was anticipating an attack when Parliament reconvened in February 1900. But 'I think I have a pretty good case,' he said. 'Anyway I am keeping low like a Boer and shall not fire until they come into the open.'[3]

The Opposition came into the open at the Queen's Address, which declared, 'we are not interested in the possibility of defeat: it does not exist'. The Opposition moved for an amendment deploring 'the want of knowledge, foresight and judgment of Her Majesty's Ministers in preparation for the war now proceeding'. 'Arthur was *most* foolish to speak at all,' said Margot of Balfour's pitiful response. 'Some want of passion in his nature' made him unable to give the 'grand uplifted bugle . . . sort of speech' the situation required. Balfour's intellectual, measured oratory was completely out of step with a country thrown from jingoistic euphoria to the pit of despair in barely three months.[4]

The role of standard bearer fell to George. Fuelled by incandescent patriotism his speech was, by agreement of all who heard it, the making of his career. He spoke for an hour and thirty-four minutes, leaving out 'about a quarter of the stuff' he had prepared. He admitted that blunders and miscalculations had been made. But soon there would be 150,000 British troops in South Africa. The question now was one of faith and courage. Long live the British Empire! said George. All Hail Her Majesty! When he sat down, 'I thought they would never stop cheering,' he told his mother.[5]

'George has *covered* himself with glory . . . I have *never* heard anything better in my long experience of the House . . . is it not splendid! *all* the best and severest judges would agree my praise is not exaggerated,' Arthur wrote to Mary, in tones more characteristic of his excitable protégé.[6] Margot acknowledged that George 'defended a very attacked office in a very critical moment & did it quite xtraordinarily [sic] well'.[7] 'The speech has given him Cabinet rank,' Percy claimed exultantly.[8] Arthur agreed. George's rise seemed now 'beyond the reach of fate'.[9]

The press hailed George as one of the 'men who will lead Britain into the twentieth century'. His very person seemed proof that

Britain could still breed heroes. '[F]rom man of fashion to soldier, from politician to statesman, from speaker to orator, from dilettante to critic, he has never yet shown himself contented with the beginning or with the outside,' commented one article that Pamela liked enough to cut out and keep. The 'completely thoroughbred' George with his 'aspiring and adventurous' temperament, 'vivacious and lofty expression' and 'richly sonorous voice' reassured the public that Britain could reach greatness once again.[10]

As if by magic, or rather thanks to Bobs, British fortunes began to turn, with the relief of Cecil Rhodes at Kimberley and victory at Paardeburg. On 28 February Ladysmith was finally relieved. The Wyndhams rejoiced at the news that Guy Wyndham was safe and well, but '[h]ow *could* they have survived. . .?' asked an appalled Mananai,[11] reading press reports that the troops had subsisted on a daily diet of just 1½ biscuits, 30 ounces of meal and a Bovril-like soup called Chevril. The relief forces immediately sought out Guy, eager to tell him how George's speech had made them feel finally as though the country were behind them.[12] The British public held their heads higher. Labby's determinedly 'pro-Boer' stance in *Truth* made him, in the estimation of the *New York Times*, 'the best-hated man in Britain'.[13] On St Patrick's Day Mananai attended a concert at London's Albert Hall where a new patriotic song to the tune of 'The Wearing of the Green' raised the roof with uninterrupted cheering for over ten minutes.[14]

Mananai followed each day's triumphs and reverses in the press with near-obsessive avidity. Her anxiety for the nation provided an outlet for, and distraction from, her personal grief. Pamela had sent her a copy of her latest work, a religious, mystical compilation of poetry and prose entitled *The Book of Peace*. 'It is a good book, full and sharp, with the sweet-bitterness of Birth and Death,' George told Pamela after first 'incontinently' reading the work: 'You have washed the Gates of life . . . from the insolent and vapid scribblings with which they have been defaced.'[15] In the first weeks after the baby's death the book barely left Mananai's side. Once she had convalesced she sought out those neighbours who had been bereaved in the war, and devoted herself to charity work, volunteering at the Soldiers and Sailors Yeomanry Hospital, and collecting clothes for the troops abroad.[16] Even the most minor of reverses could cast her into a deep gloom. 'I sometimes despair of the end,' she told her mother. Mananai herself would never make the link, but the analogy with her own grief is clear to see.[17]

That grief is plainly evident in Sargent's portrait. Sittings began again in the spring of 1900. Of all the sisters, Sargent had been most keen to work on Mananai. Pamela had to beg her parents to exert all their influence on Charlie to make him allow Mananai to return for more sittings. The Wyndhams prevailed, and Charlie and Mananai made their way to London for a week of sittings at Sargent's studio (as Madeline Wyndham pointed out, much warmer than Belgrave Square at that time of year). The air of patient sadness that Mananai gives off is palpable and at odds with the frippery of her white gown as she gazes off into the distance, apparently lost in thought.

Detained at Clouds by a host of responsibilities, Madeline Wyndham was unable to make more than one brief visit to Babraham around Easter time. Instead she deluged her daughter with gifts. During that spring hardly a week went by without some kind of package arriving at Babraham, whether it was a toy kitchen and modelling clay for the little girls, hundreds of flower bulbs for the garden, or Battersea enamel boxes of the kind that Mananai collected (Madeline Wyndham had begun to practise enamelling under Alexander Fisher. With her own stove set up at Clouds, she was rapidly becoming a proficient amateur. However, on this occasion she was so keen to send Mananai a present that in her haste she melted it). In May an 'overwhelmed' Mananai opened a parcel containing a belt – 'so "out of the way" . . . & will give such "cachet" when I wear it' – and a spangled black net dress – 'so beautiful & yet so French & smart (such a horrid word but the only one to express one's meaning)'. That same day came the 'blessed' news that 'Mafeking is well!'[18]

At the news of Mafeking's relief after a 217-day siege, punctuated by plucky 'Kaffirgrams' of Colonel Baden-Powell ('All well. Four Hours bombardment. One dog killed' was a typical example),[19] flag-waving hordes poured on to Britain's streets in such jubilation that 'mafficking' was added to the *Oxford English Dictionary*, to denote indulgence in extravagant demonstrations of exultation.[20] A fortnight or so later Bobs's troops entered Pretoria. In London, Sargent's portrait of the sisters was the hit of the Royal Academy's Summer Exhibition. '[T]he greatest picture which has appeared for many years on the walls of the Royal Academy,' said *The Times*. The Prince of Wales dubbed the sisters 'The Three Graces'. Pamela received particular attention for her spectacular looks.[21] The portrait hung in the billiard room at Clouds as intended (a room now painted dark blue to complement the portrait)[22] but was frequently sent off for public viewing. 'What it has seen and heard if it could only speak!' said Madeline Wyndham in 1908 as the picture returned from the Franco-British Exhibition and the Exhibition of Fair Women at London's New Gallery; the Watts of Madeline also appeared at the latter.[23]

That the subjects of the portrait were George Wyndham's sisters enhanced their celebrity. Six months after his Commons speech, George remained the hero of the hour. In August, Mary was delighted to find that every English paper she read in Kissingen spoke of George in glowing terms, and everyone she met was eager to congratulate her on her brilliant sibling. 'He is no longer Lady E.'s brother but I am Wyndham's sister that's as it *should be*,' she told Hugo proudly.[24] On 1 September the British public's delight knew no bounds when their troops annexed the Transvaal. 'The country is war-mad . . . blatantly and truculently out of their minds,' George told Madeline Wyndham. He knew there would be a back-lash eventually, 'but while it lasts I make hay'.[25]

TWENTY-ONE

The 1900 Election

On receipt of Mary's proud missive about George, Hugo must have felt a little sour. In recent months his own fortunes had followed rather too closely those of the British in South Africa, without the corresponding upturn. Since Hermione's death and his fortieth birthday in 1897 his outlook had become ever gloomier. 'Time is advancing and we two with it,' he told Mary dolefully on her thirty-eighth birthday in 1900. 'Its rot to talk about *old age*,' replied Mary staunchly, but her assurances that Hugo had never been so youthful 'in being & in seeming' fell on deaf ears.[1] The fundamental problem, as Mary said, was that 'it's dreadful for you having nothing to do'.[2]

Hugo, whom Balfour once summed up as 'too self-indulgent to succeed and too clever to be content with failure',[3] was a casualty of politics' modernization. He was bright but lazy, reluctant to attend the Commons as often as he ought. In 1892 Balfour described Hugo's speech on the subject of payment to MPs as 'one of the most brilliantly amusing speeches I have ever heard in the House', but Hugo's time as a Member of Parliament was mostly notable for his annual, impassioned speech recommending that the House should rise before Derby Day.[4] Politics was still predominantly the preserve of the elite, but whereas a generation or two before Hugo might have held a Commons seat without much effort until he was raised to the Lords, now there was more competition. Seats which once had been in aristocrats' gift were now determined by the electorate, and the choice of candidates who stood for them now subject to the deliberations of the Conservative Union. Against the odds, Hugo had taken Ipswich in 1885, but he was 'chucked!', in Mary's phrase, in 1895.[5] At the time, Blunt thought this a misfortune for Mary as Hugo 'will have nothing to do being shut out of public affairs'.[6] Instead, he hung about with brittle, hard-living members of the Marlborough House Set, habitués of the popular press's 'best-dressed' lists, who frittered away time and money on the Continent yachting, gaming at Le Touquet, and watching bullfighting in Spain. Mary berated him for 'The "Common" folk you herd with!!!' and the 'bad ways & foolish tricks' they encouraged. 'I wish you were a fox hunter & would live 6 months in one place or that you had a passion for agriculture!' she said, but she knew that Hugo was 'not really keen about things & never [had] been'.[7]

In 1900, it was briefly mooted that Hugo might stand as Unionist candidate for Bristol in the general election to be held that autumn. All summer long, Mary bombarded him with excited letters making plans for the campaign trail, 'quite ready to be a thorn in yr side & to help in every way I can'.[8] The candidacy went to Sir Walter Long, a Unionist who had made himself a name on the Local Government Board and the Board of Agriculture. Mary was crushed, particularly since she only found out this news from Arthur: 'you must have known it was most cruel not to tell me, you said you had been asked – I wired to you . . . I talk to you about it in every letter & you say nothing, so I quite believed it,' she wrote to Hugo in a frenzy from Paris. 'I suppose he [Arthur] couldn't squash Long,' she added, unintentionally rubbing salt in the wound.[9]

The decision was a further emasculation at Balfour's hands. In 1899, Hugo had gambled his way to his most spectacular loss on the stock market yet: around £80,000, roughly £7.4 million today.[10]

'At last the crash . . . has come and Hugo is undone!' Mary told Arthur from the Palace Hotel in St Moritz, where she had met Hugo, post-cure, and been told the news.[10] Furious and anguished, Lord Wemyss bailed Hugo out, but made good on his oft-repeated threat to tie up Hugo's inheritance. He set up a trust of £100,000 for the Elchos during their lifetime. Arthur was one of the trustees.[12] It is hard not to see a punitive element therein.

Arthur was often as baffled by Mary and Hugo's push-me-pull-you relationship as everyone else, and in particular, the way she tolerated his continuing, flagrant infidelity. 'I cannot conceive why you permitted yourself to be saddled with her,' Arthur wrote, on hearing that Hugo had dumped his latest paramour, the actress Mrs Patrick Campbell, on Mary at Stanway for three weeks in 1896, while 'Mrs. P.C.' recovered from a theatrical flop and conducted an affair with Hugo under Mary's nose: 'Had you been in robust health, with no worries . . . of your own, I should still have thought that England might have been searched through before a less suitable recipient of three weeks' hospitality could have been found.'[13] An answer is found in a letter from Mary to Percy in 1899. Percy had written lamenting that Mary would not be able to enliven a sticky dinner with her presence. Delighted, Mary replied, claiming to have inherited from Percy her consuming interest in people from all walks of life: 'If I thought about it at all I should probably find that I prided myself on being a sort of Nasesmith [sic] Hammer! Able to crack iron hazelnuts to cut thick or thin – and to sing (or talk) both high & low!'[14] James Nasmyth's steam hammer, one of the Industrial Revolution's greatest inventions, could vary the force of its blow. In a famous demonstration the hammer was used to break an egg in a wineglass while the glass remained intact. Hugo, difficult, childish, stubbornly impervious to improvement, was the iron hazelnut Mary could not crack. He gambled;[15] he rowed with tenants on the Stanway estate so that she and Smith, Stanway's agent, had to step in; as a 'landlord and financier' and a 'husband' Hugo was hopeless. 'I wish Hugo would do himself justice,' she told Arthur. 'I wonder if it's my fault and if I could manage him differently and better. He makes one always hope and yet he so often disappoints hope, one can neither count on him nor give him up!'[16]

As Mary made her way to Gosford that autumn, flustered and despondent at the prospect of a perpetually aimless Hugo, her sisters were preparing for their own stint on the campaign trail. Eddy Tennant and Charlie Adeane had been approved as the Liberal candidates for Peebles and Huntingdonshire respectively. Margot had her doubts about both men's conviction. The Boer War had provoked yet another rift in the fragmented Liberals between anti-war Radicals and pro-war Imperialists. Over a period of months Margot delivered Eddy several lengthy lectures on corporate political loyalty: 'What no man who thinks for himself like you & Adeane can grasp (tho I know you do) [is that] they don't come off these big things H Rule Disestablishment etc . . . they *don't* happen . . . Compromise & stick to yr regiment even if they are going to do a stupid thing.'[17] Margot was still more mistrustful of Pamela. As she revealed to Eddy tidbits of the party leadership struggles between Asquith, Henry Campbell-Bannerman and Lewis 'Loulou' Harcourt she hoped, pointedly, that 'Pamela will keep our party dirty linen to herself.'[18]

Pamela was not interested enough to be a double agent. Mary was astonished to find that she was even '*really* canvassing'. 'I am *indeed*,' Pamela triumphantly replied from the rented Peebles villa from which the Tennants were conducting their campaign, although 'I don't know enough about politics to "canvass" in the ordinary sense of the word . . . I just tell them how keen I am my husband should win – how long we've been here & how many children I have!'[19] Pamela did not quite express Lord Salisbury's visceral loathing for the 'nauseous mire of a general election', requiring 'weeks of screwed-up smiles and . . . mock geniality . . . the chuckling reply . . . to the coarse joke . . . the wholesale deglutition of hypocritical pledges',[20] but she intensely disliked the campaigning process: 'long drives, of 18 miles home in pelting rain & wind after a whole days visiting & canvassing & putting up at little evil smelling whisky-drenched Inns and attending hot long meetings!' Unruffled by public singing, she hated public speaking.

She gave a talk to the 150 members of the Women's Liberal Association of Innerleithen, learnt by heart in advance, with 'a dreadful stomach-ache from nervous excitement & terror'.[21] Her sisters-in-law were horrified by what they considered an insufficiently committed approach, particularly since the Bart was bankrolling Eddy's candidacy. When the Tennants visited Glen halfway through the campaign, Charty cornered Pamela at breakfast for a 'tremendous talking to'. Politics were 'the *life* of the country, the history that is being formed around one', she said hectoringly over the marmalade, imploring Pamela to exercise 'a mind that merited being *bent* upon wider issues', and praising 'powers of *observation*' that warranted being turned to '*larger* matters'. As always, Pamela gave Charty short shrift. 'It was really all very good advice but I am perfectly certain [if] I read all Joe [Chamberlain]'s speeches I shouldn't be much the wiser for it! [and] if in going into cottages, I tried to speak about what I don't understand, I should make lamentable mistakes & failures.'[22]

Canvassing was more than ever a requirement of an expanded franchise. From the turn of the century there was a marked expectation that women would take a more involved political role.[23] Charty and Pamela both accepted that, although Pamela dragged her heels. For Kate Courtney, Liberal Unionist sister of the Fabian Beatrice Webb, political involvement led her to suffragism: 'I cannot understand the state of mind of a man who encourages women to canvass electors . . . organize meetings, speak at them, and even coax and bother electors to go to the poll by every art they possess, but draws the line at the simple act of voting themselves. It is nothing but stupendous egotism,' she said in 1913.[24] None of the Wyndham sisters expressed any particular position on female suffrage. In this they resembled most women of their class, feeling that the social and political influence they wielded was far in excess of that granted by a vote, and with corporate loyalty to class outweighing that to gender.[25] The person in the family who felt most strongly was Eddy, a strident opponent, who later became President of the Scottish Anti-Suffrage League.[26] (It is cheap but irresistible to suggest that Eddy had suffered enough from strong women in his life.)

Mananai was the only one of the three sisters truly to enjoy campaigning. The Adeanes were funding Charlie's campaign themselves, and they had thrown themselves into the contest with vigour. They had set up camp in a 'snug pretty little house' lent to them by Lord Sandwich on his Hinchingbrooke Park estate and were planning, said Mananai, 'to work as hard as we can & be on the spot for all the meetings'.[27] Mananai thrived on the excitement. Each day she met up with a band of local Liberal women: the wives of the local chemist; the Hinchingbrooke estate's land agent; and the leading local non-conformist – and canvassed from 10.30 in the morning until 6 or 7 each night, ticking off lists provided to them of 'doubtfuls' and 'Tories', snatching quick lunches, once in the carriage and once, to Mananai's rather doubtful delight, in a 'pub'. On one day in 'a poor sort of street in Huntingdon' she visited seventy houses before lunch. Indefatigable in her charity work, she immediately saw an opportunity to do some good: 'Some make me very sad . . . they are so ill & poor – as soon as the Election is over I shall be able perhaps to help them a little.'[28]

A year later Benjamin Rowntree's landmark study of poverty in York shocked Britain into acknowledging the relentless urban destitution that meant for a family to survive on an unskilled labourer's wages they:

> must never spend a penny on railway fare or omnibus . . . never go into the country unless they walk . . . never purchase a halfpenny newspaper or spend a penny to buy a ticket for a popular concert . . . should a child fall ill, it must be attended by the Parish doctor; should it die, it must be buried by the Parish. Finally, the wage earner must never be absent from his work for a single day.[29]

A similar survey by Charles Booth in London rammed the point home. Scientific evidence showing the parlous state of the nation fed into anxiety about Britain's Boer War performance and gave heft to calls for social reform. Army recruiters had been appalled to find that the majority of volunteers were so malnourished that they did not reach the required minimum height of 5 foot 3 inches. 'The building up of the nervous and muscular vitality of our race [is] the principal plank of any Imperial programme of reform,' said the Fabian Sidney Webb, husband of Beatrice.[30] In the decade that followed, imperial interests were used to justify ostensibly 'socialistic' reforms of New Liberalism such as the provision of child welfare measures and free school meals.

Imperial concerns had placed themselves firmly at the forefront of British political life, but Bobs's victories still cast a glow over the 'khaki election', which returned 402 Unionists, 183 Liberals, 83 Irish Nationalists and two members of the Labour Representation Committee. 'Things have touched the button now & I think we shall see very interesting Times in the next few years,' Margot told Eddy[31] – but Eddy, like Charlie, had been defeated. 'Khaki was well worked by them . . . the tide is going too strong against us owing to that wretch Labby we are all branded as traitors and pro-Boers!' mourned Mananai.[32] At Glen, Pamela bit her tongue as Margot provided tips for the next campaign.[33]

George was returned at Dover with a huge majority. In November, he was appointed Ireland's Chief Secretary. 'I think it will be a very fine appointment . . . It will give George a great opportunity of xcercising [sic] his judgment & tho a very hard place I think his charm will attract them,' said Margot.[34] After a meteoric rise (although still without the Cabinet rank he yearned for) George had returned to his ancestral land. Katharine Tynan, an ardent nationalist, saw in him Ireland's hopes of salvation. But George's position was more ambiguous than that. For he appointed as his Under-Secretary Antony MacDonnell, the outstandingly able 'Bengal Tiger' who had made his name as an administrator in the Indian Civil Service and was widely rumoured to be a Home Ruler. George avowed to Balfour that the Irish Catholic MacDonnell was 'non-partisan'. Yet he agreed to MacDonnell's condition – set out in a letter from MacDonnell reminding George that he was a Liberal, Irish Catholic – that he would accept the office only if he could offer more than 'mere secretarial criticism' and be 'given adequate opportunities of influencing the action and policy of the Irish Government'.[35]

TWENTY-TWO

Growing Families

Sargent's portrait had caught the sisters like flies in amber, frozen for ever in trinity. In reality, their worlds were moving ever further apart. Of all the siblings, Mary and Pamela saw each other the least. They were 'widely unlike', and while Cincie Charteris diplomatically tried to attribute their prolonged absences from each other to 'their very different ways of life' – Mary 'was at everyone's beck and call' while Pamela 'exercised a certain thrift in the spending of her time'[1] – the fact was that Mary often found Pamela difficult and remote. Mary was 'devoted' to Mananai ('as well she might be' said Cincie[2]) but with the perspective given by an age difference of a decade, she recognized her youngest sister's flaws better than the rest of her family, and was capable, on occasion, of a 'heated . . . skirmish!' with her, something that faithful Mananai would never do.[3] Publicly, Mary maintained her support of her difficult sister: 'I know you'll forget any little hardnesses of speech about your Pamela. I could not bear you to think me stupid enough not to see her extra out-of-the-way cleverness,' Margot wrote to Mary in 1900 – a rare enough apology from Margot, suggesting that Mary must have defended Pamela quite forcefully.[4] 'It is the fashion to abuse Pamela,'

Mary remarked almost twenty years later to Lady Desborough (as Ettie Grenfell became after Willie's elevation to the peerage), thanking her for understanding her sister as she did.[5]

In 1902, however, Mary and Pamela were united by the common bond of pregnancy, giving birth just weeks apart in May. The children were born into a new era of peace – the Treaty of Vereeniging that marked the end to the Boer War was signed on 31 May, the day that Mary's third daughter was born. They were Edwardians, not Victorians: Bertie, the Prince of Wales, who succeeded his mother upon her death on 22 January 1901, was crowned Edward VII in August 1902, after appendicitis had forced cancellation of the original ceremony in June.

Bertie's designation inspired a host of nicknames – '"Edward the Caresser" & (only I think this is too prophane [sic]) "King of the Jews" . . . Mrs K[eppel, Bertie's mistress] has been called "Mistress without Robes" . . . very wrong only rather funny,' reported a shocked but amused Mananai to Percy.[6] Mananai had been in London for the Queen's death, when a 'pall of unknown sadness' fell over 'a mourning City'. As bells tolled and paperboys' sandwich boards shrieked of war, Mananai had mourned 'poor England', a country beset by misfortune and change.[7] The coronation and the peace promised the fresh and new. Pamela longed to call her son, born on 22 May, 'David Pax! It sounds so short and manly,' she told Mary. At Pamela's suggestion, Mary named her own child Irene Corona after the peace and the coronation, although she was known always as 'Bibs'. Pamela and Mary were both delighted with their new arrivals. 'David Pax is such a squawler . . . you never heard such a voice – peppery & imperative,' said Pamela.[8] Mary thought Bibs was like spun wire, with a combination of fragility and toughness 'that makes me *ache* for the little creature . . . her eyes shine like stars'.[9]

Both sisters knew how anxiously Mananai awaited the birth of her own child due that autumn. After the terrible loss of 1899, Mananai began to visit Schwalbach, a German spa providing the 'iron cures' recommended for 'women's problems'.[10] She also subscribed to the popular theory that a baby's sex might depend on the month in which it was 'started': 'I had a feeling I *must* begin the *same* day of the *same* month as last time (May) . . . I don't feel to trust any other month,' she told Madeline Wyndham, herself enthusiastic about the scheme.[11] Her sisters felt a twinge of guilt at having so effortlessly succeeded where Mananai had failed. 'You, at least, can feel you have not mopped up a possible son from darling Madeline!' Pamela told Mary when Bibs was born.[12] To quiet disappointment, in October 1902, Mananai gave birth to a fifth girl, named Helena.

Helena Adeane was the only one of the newborn cousins whose paternity was not questioned. The Adeanes were devoted to one another, moving together between London and Babraham, where at the turn of the century Charlie built a large hall in the grounds, named the Madeline Hall after his wife.[13] In January 1901, Charlie went to Egypt, while Mananai, run down after the election's excitement and her exertions during the 'benevolent season', made a longed-for trip to Ireland to see George and Sibell, followed by several weeks' convalescence in the gentle sunshine of Hyères. 'It will be so strange being a "grass widow",' she said of this rare separation.[14]

It is unlikely that the angelically blonde Bibs was, as some rumoured, actually Arthur Balfour's child. Bibs looked like her undoubtedly legitimate brother Yvo, and Hugo doted upon her – in marked contrast to his coldness towards Mary Charteris. More plausible is the suggestion that David Tennant was the son of Edward Grey,[15] a close friend of the Tennants', godfather to their second son Christopher, a reluctantly prominent Liberal Imperialist and an obsessive birdwatcher and fly-fisherman, pursuits of which he wrote lyrically in a series of essays published under the title *Recreation*.[16]

Fishing was the foundation of the two Edwards' friendship, forged in the mid-1890s. Their decades-long, quietly affectionate correspondence is mostly blow-by-blow accounts of days thigh-deep in a rushing river, with only occasional intrusions of finance or politics.[17] Both quiet, unostentatious and honourable men,[18] they were politically as well as temperamentally aligned. Both became senior members (Grey was a Vice-President, Eddy a member of the Executive Committee) of Lord Rosebery's Liberal League, a vehicle for imperialist views founded in 1902 when Rosebery, who had supported the Boer War and advocated 'cleaning the slate' of 'obsolete policies' like Home Rule, moved to the cross-benches.[19]

The reluctant politician: a beaky Edward Grey at the despatch box.

Pamela's instinctive jealousy of Grey as a rival to her husband's attentions was quickly mollified by admiration of his character. By the turn of the century, she numbered Grey and his wife Dorothy among her closest friends: 'two of the elect', she said, 'each of them nearly the nicest person in the world'.[20] The Greys divided their time between Fallodon, Grey's Northumberland family seat, and a small tin-roofed cottage in Itchen Abbas, a village in the New Forest within cycling distance of the Tennants in Wiltshire. Beneath the reclusive Dorothy's forbiddingly reserved façade, she was, in Pamela's estimation, 'a woman in a thousand . . . gracious, sympathetic, eagerly appreciative of all distinction in thought, action and character . . . No one who ever knew her well was not the better for her influence . . .'[21] The connection between Pamela and Grey was particularly intense. They had 'nearly every taste and interest in common'. The 'peculiar sympathy' between their minds 'eludes words, because it is so intimate!' said Grey.[22]

It was common knowledge within political circles that the Greys' marriage was, at Dorothy's request, *un mariage blanc* – a sexless marriage. Most thought the courteous Grey was celibate. But Lloyd George, the unabashedly philandering 'Welsh Goat', maintained that Grey was a man of 'sham honesty' in both public and private life.[23] Certainly Grey's reputation as the most reluctant of politicians sits oddly with his part in the 'Relugas Compact' of 1905 in which he, Asquith and Haldane tried to weaken their leader, Campbell-Bannerman, in the Commons by forcing him upstairs to the House of Lords. As for his private dishonesty, Marie Belloc Lowndes – Pamela's close but indiscreet friend – recalled in her memoirs that after many years of marriage Dorothy Grey had suggested to her husband that they resume a physical relationship, but Grey refused. The implication was that Pamela had forbidden it, but the anecdote is inconclusive. Pamela would most likely have issued this edict even if she was not having sex with Grey.[24] Pamela was very demanding with those she loved.

This approach extended to her children. Charlie Adeane spoke to Mary with 'the greatest admiration' of the way in which Mananai 'has obtained *complete* control over all her children by *love & influence*. Punishment & Reward can never obtain this. I think you all inherit this wonderful power – a very rare one – from your mother.'[25] This was certainly true of the docile, loving and obedient Adeane girls. But Pamela's was a hothouse love. She loved her children 'in a French and not an English way' said Osbert Sitwell, commenting on Pamela's wish to be constantly with her children – 'the last thing, as a rule, that an English parent of her kind would desire' – and to 'regulate absolutely' their lives.[26]

'O, I almost wish I didn't love the children so dreadfully,' Pamela said, recounting her anxiety when Stephen suffered scarlet fever.[27] She immortalized her children in two of her most successful books: *The Children and the Pictures*, in which the subjects of the Bart's Old Masters came alive and joined the Tennant children in midnight adventures; and *The Sayings of the Children*, which recorded their childish wisdom. She kept them close to her, yearning for the days when they went no further from her than Glen's village school each morning on their ponies,[28] sobbing when delivering seven-year-old Bim to the train that was to take him to boarding school for the first time,[29] and making every excuse to keep her younger sons at home. Only Clare, whom she thought 'spiritually short-sighted',[30] did she willingly send to school. She was fiercely jealous of the children's nanny, Rebecca Trussler, a stout, middle-aged Cockney who joined the family in 1906.[31] When Stephen – whom she dressed, long after his infancy had passed, as the girl she wished he had been – was eight years old, she appeared on stage with him in a charity tableau at the Royal Albert Hall, cradling him in her arms as though he were an infant.[32] Her children were her acolytes. 'What a child we could have,' she once told her son David with reference to their striking good looks.[33] Such looks were on constant display. Visitors arriving at Glen were startled to find the family seated in greeting, in the hall, 'in a sort of photographic pose': a tableau of perfection, with Clare pouting gently, Stephen perched on her knee,

and Pamela, the beautiful, youthful mother, at the centre of it all.[34]
As a young man, Stephen wrote a scrap of thinly veiled autobiography in which Pamela appears as the remote Lady Brandon, 'whose charm and beauty had greeted her in the glass every morning for more years than she cared to remember [and] was greedily exacting as to the admiring allegiance of her family and immediate circle'.[35]

Pamela's approach to childrearing was considered strange. 'I never care for a woman draped in her children – let them go,' said Margot.[36] 'I do NOT cart my children about like Pamela,' Mary retorted hotly to Hugo when he charged her with having taken Bibs to Clouds to amuse herself, rather than leaving her at Stanway with her nanny, Cliffe: implicitly the latter was better parenting as providing stability and routine.[37] Cliffe herself complained, as politely as she could, of the Liberty Hall atmosphere among the Tennants when visiting with Mary Charteris and Bibs in 1906, shocked that nine-year-old Clare, attending school in Salisbury each day, 'as a rule dines with her mother, at 8, I feel that is much too late for *Mary* . . . they do not rest at all in the *day*.'[38]

Cliffe sometimes struggled to impose a routine on her own rambunctious charges. In *A Family Record* Mary recorded a plea she received at Gosford from Cliffe, with Yvo, Mary and Bibs at Stanway, asking '. . . Our Dear Ladyship . . . to write certain things down for them *what they are not to do* . . . the chief things are, if I may name them, getting out on the roof, *or between* the *ceiling* and plaster, *climbing the garden wall* . . . after the fruit, or going down to the cellars where the furnaces are, or in the place where Mr. Fletcher keeps the chimney sweep brushes . . .'. '[B]etween the ceiling and the plaster!' marvelled Mary, equally delighted and appalled by her children's ingenuity.[39]

Mary's love for her children was laissez-faire. They were 'lapped in love', given 'deeply-imbued confidence' and 'cherished',[40] but she combined 'with the maximum of fondness the minimum of possessiveness'.[41] She longed for her children's confidences, but never demanded them.[42] The greatest crime her children could commit was to display a lack of enthusiasm. Cincie recalled that when she was well into middle age Mary would still exclaim, '"Ices! Cincie, *Strawberry* Ices!" . . . in the exact tone of voice in which one says "Din Din" or "Walkies!" to a dog'.[43] Mary's children, like her friends, had to compete for her attention with a host of daily trivialities. ('Mary is generally a day behind the fair and will only hear of my death from the man behind the counter who is struggling to clinch her over a collar for her chow,' said Margot.)[44] They took advantage of this to run wild. But from an early age they were brought into the orbit of their mother's guests, an ever more eclectic mix.

In 1902 Mary met the Fabians Beatrice and Sidney Webb at a dinner hosted by George Bernard Shaw. The Fabian Society, the epicentre of Edwardian intellectualism, was explicitly not a political party, but advocated a practice of 'gradualism' by which the ruling classes would be subtly indoctrinated with ideas of 'practical Democracy and Socialism'. The Webbs' Coefficients Dining Society included among its members the poet Henry Newbolt, Edward Grey, Richard Haldane and Lord Milner. Mary returned to Cadogan Square, shining-eyed, full of talk about how her new friends had promised to save her from being first against the wall when the revolution came. 'I suppose you are going to ask the creatures to Stanway,' Hugo remarked.[45] By September, Beatrice was recording in her diary time spent with 'Lady Elcho, a fascinating and kindly woman married to a card playing aristocrat, living in the most delightful old house'.[46] Through the Webbs, Mary met H. G. Wells. By 1903, C. R. Ashbee, who set up Arts and Crafts workshops in Chipping Campden, near Stanway, was writing in his diary of visits from 'Lady Elcho the wonderful the nonchalant the strangely fascinating', whirling over, often with Mrs Patrick Campbell in tow, extravagant in crackling black glacé opera coat. 'Tigrina', as Mary called her, had become a frequent visitor at Stanway, as had Harold Large, a charlatan psychic whom Mary nonetheless found amusing. She had become renowned for having 'these outré people around her'.[47]

Her children called the more eccentric of these her 'Freaks and Funnies'. Stories that sound apocryphal were in fact true – for example, Mary's telegraphing Hugo from Taplow with instructions to provide beds at Cadogan Square for three 'spiritual' disciples of a Persian sage invited to London by Sir Arthur and Lady Blomfield: 'It's just a sort of neighbourly thing that does help people . . . they'll dash round to [the Blomfields'] flat before breakfast & return after dinner just to sleep . . .' she told him.[48] She found that her guests provided her with all the friction needed to spark a house party into life. Beatrice Webb divided the world into two sorts: the 'A's ('Aristocrats, Anarchists and Artists') and the 'B's ('Bourgeois, Bureaucrats, and Benevolents'). Mary challenged her to define where she (Mary) stood. Beatrice characterized her as 'the purveyor of the Bs to the As! A very rare thing requiring great sympathy and one [must] be able and willing to intellectually subordinate oneself, to be able to carry a hostile force to another'. Notwithstanding the barb therein, Mary was thrilled: 'what she said is really what I mean . . .'.[49] 'Don't you agree with me, Mr. Balfour, that the only excuse for a dinner party is that it should end in a committee?' Mrs Webb challenged the Prime Minister across the dinner table at Stanway.[50] In 1907 Mary triumphantly reported to Balfour that 'le beau Norts' – the staunchly Tory Robert Norton – 'has fallen head and crop over and become a collectivist', while Beatrice Webb had succumbed to two glasses of champagne on Saturday night and the following morning 'actually gone to church. . .!'[51]

In the first decade of the twentieth century, Stanway was a house where an ambitious young man could make his mark over the 'general conversation' that was rallied across the dinner table like a game of tennis. In Cynthia's memory, Mary was the delighted spectator, turning her head from side to side with each parry. Yet all knew Mary was largely responsible for generating this conversation: her gift was to throw in 'bones' on which experts could seize and opine. 'If for an instant [the conversation] flagged over an entrée or a plover's egg she lifted it again and withdrew herself to listen. The result of course was that we all felt we were at our best and came away radiant with satisfaction,' recalled C. R. Ashbee.[52] Mary and Balfour were a well-practised double act. Cincie Charteris drew a picture of long afternoons spent in the 'boudoir', Mary's personal sitting room: curtains drawn across the two great mullioned windows to keep out the icy cold and the fire lit, vigorous debate among some guests, while others nodded off gently in the corner, the reading aloud of treatises and poetry, chows underfoot and sleeping on cushions, books and pictures piled up around:

> Arthur Balfour, Walter Raleigh, George Wyndham, Harry Cust, Charles Whibley, H. G. Wells, Evan Charteris, Hugh Cecil, Maurice Baring, Lady Desborough . . . whose voices and laughter I can hear again; while now with tempered heat they earnestly discuss some burning question of that day; now, like verbal ballet-dancers, glide, twist and pirouette in airiest fancies; now rollick in fantastic exuberant nonsense. I remember how the hours flew, and how much I used to dread the dispersing sound of 'that tocsin of the soul – the dinner bell'.[53]

In 1905, the thirty-six-year-old Mananai fell pregnant for the seventh time. This pregnancy felt quite different to the others. 'I have never felt so "unjumpy" I think before,' she reported to her mother. In October, the Adeanes went to London, sending their five daughters to Clouds. The wet-nurse had been booked, Mananai's bedroom newly painted and papered, and the expectant mother was upbeat and enthusiastic: 'whenever "Twinkie-Twankie" (this one's name!) chooses to appear . . . we shall all be prepared!'[54] On 3 November, after seventeen years of marriage and, curiously, six years to the day after their first son (the 'dear little Boy Baby') had died, Madeline and Charlie became the jubilant parents to a healthy son, Robert. 'This wonderful gift is a mighty relief and a load off our backs . . . The anxiety has weighed on us for many years and just in a moment it was gone!' said Charlie.[55]

The whole family was 'wild with delight'.[56] Mananai's always affectionate letters reached new heights of effusion. 'I couldn't half thank you or at all thank you Angel for fresh proof in this Joy of the Worlds & Worlds or rather Heavens & Heavens of never failing LOVE you shower upon me & mine . . . Bless you,'[57] she wrote to her mother, when Madeline Wyndham sent little Robert a present. Mananai greeted each new ounce with wonder: 'this week [he] has put on 14 . . . & nice firm flesh! Isn't it a mercy?. . .' she exclaimed to Mary, as she completed her lying-in.[58] Her great fortune made her 'long . . . to give large pieces' of happiness 'to the many who have none or so little[.] the feeling of Thankfulness is overwhelming . . . Baby is a splendid little fellow & we are so grateful for him.'[59]

Mary and George were godparents. As part of her duties, Mary warned her brother-in-law against indulging the child. Charlie acknowledged 'The inclination . . . to spoil a Benvenuto' but assured Mary of his 'implicit confidence in Madeline's sagacity . . . she is a very remarkable woman – I can say that to you – & her character is so strong that it must influence any children under her care'.[60] In contrast to the quiet christenings of his sisters, Robert's was celebrated with pomp, at Babraham. The estate's labourers were given the day off. With characteristic diffidence the Adeanes had only let it be known that the service was not private. They were astonished and touched to find the church packed full. A large tea followed; plans were made for enhanced Christmas festivities in due course.[61] With little Robert laughing and crowing in his cradle, everything for Mananai seemed more than perfect: 'LOVE . . . seems to radiate around,' she told her father.[62]

TWENTY-THREE

The Souls in Power

Little over a week after the hollow peace of Vereeniging marked the end of a gruelling guerrilla war, another political titan departed the public arena. In early June 1902, the elderly Lord Salisbury finally relinquished his post as Prime Minister. Arthur Balfour made his way to Windsor for a secretive meeting with the King. Two days later, his name was put forward for approval at the Unionist party conference. It was a nominal gesture. No one was likely to oppose the man groomed for decades as Salisbury's successor.

As the news of Arthur's succession became public Mary was at Wilton in perfect weather, hugging to herself news that she had known since he was summoned to Windsor. 'My dear P.M. & F.L.T., L.P.S., & L.H.C.', she wrote jubilantly to him, savouring the flock of titles that were now his: Prime Minister, First Lord of the Treasury, Lord Privy Seal and Leader of the House of Commons.[1] Her old friend and rival Daisy White had already begun quizzing her about when exactly she had known of Salisbury's intention to resign; and when Daisy tried to show off her own inside knowledge by alluding to the still-secret resignations of various Cabinet ministers (part of the inevitable shuffle that accompanied the handover of power) 'of course I took it as news', said Mary magnanimously.[2]

Mary had given birth to Bibs less than a fortnight before, but she had no intention of recuperating quietly. She was the confidante of the most powerful man in the country, and she revelled in her role. Balfour's ascendancy marked Mary's heyday. They were 'the great days of Mary Elcho at Stanway', in H. G. Wells's words.[3] To say that Mary came to power when Arthur did is no exaggeration. She had the ear of the Prime Minister, controlling access by guest list and seating plans. Her invitations soared accordingly: she was asked to great houses of influence she had not visited for years, and made the guest of honour at London dinners, where the most influential and ambitious men in the country hung on her every word. She reported such triumphs to Balfour: the compliments on 'gown, figure, face, prettiness' paid her by Lord Revelstoke, senior partner of Barings Bank – and an old admirer of Pamela's – until she hardly knew where to look; a confidence from Sir John ('Jackie') Fisher 'that he had finished the Army thing' (Fisher was a member of the Esher Committee which had been set up in 1903 to recommend reforms in the organization of the War Office in the wake of the Boer War) while waxing large on Balfour's fine treatment of Britain's naval force.[4] Ten months later Jackie Fisher was First Sea Lord, implementing a radical restructuring and modernization of the navy, and hurling Britain into a naval race with Germany.

'I appear to be having one of those odd and apparently causeless "booms" of appreciation which some people have at intervals, they go in cycles regardless of any change of circs [sic],' Mary told Arthur in 1904, after a successful visit to Chatsworth, the home of the social and political grandees the Duke and Duchess of Devonshire. On Hugo's account the assembled company had been fulsome in their praise of Lady Elcho after her departure, talking 'of how nice I was! Isn't that odd? And absurd – I *have* to tell you!' Disingenuous and delighted, Mary continued: 'Of course I do think the discovery that I am a *well-informed* woman must greatly add to my assets – prestige! I really must try and live up to the part.'[5] The following month, she visited Dresden, where sixteen-year-old Cincie, was being 'finished'. On the promise of a meeting with the Kaiser, she hastened on to Berlin, with only the oldest of gowns and without a maid. The meeting turned into a two-hour tête-à-tête. 'You'd have laughed to see us,' she remarked to Balfour. 'Me on sofa, as if we were a play, and Fursts, Grafs and Admirals in the next room gazing and muttering! The only people in the same room were Lady E[dward] C[avendish] and Chancellor Bülow and Sir Frank [Lascelles, the British Ambassador in Berlin], who came up every 20 minutes with cigarettes . . . [I] had quite a "succès fou".'[6] At a time when Anglo-German rivalry was increasing Mary, fearlessly, had 'got' the Kaiser 'onto our army and his army and of course as his soul is in that subject we got beyond making conversation and had a very interesting evening', discussing the recently published Esher Committee's reports. The autocratic Kaiser, unsurprisingly, was fiercely opposed to the proposals which recommended 'divided responsibility' between an Army Council and the General Staff, and the abolition of the office of Commander-in-Chief.[7]

Mary's social confidence gave her new confidence with Arthur. She had been badly shaken by a visit paid to England by Mary Curzon in the summer of 1901 that was part convalescence from the harsh Indian climate, and part reconnaissance, gauging for Curzon the political climate at home. Arthur did not trouble to conceal his obvious attraction towards the Viceroy's beautiful American wife. At a house party at Wilton, according to the Vicereine's report to her husband, Mary took Mary Curzon to her room for a 'dentist', that was in fact a grilling as she tried to ascertain just how close Mary Curzon and Arthur were. She refused to accept her rival's protestations that she was 'only in the galère with [Arthur's] other friends' and that Mary Elcho was 'the only one that matters with AJB in the least. "No" says she, "I know when he is interested and he loves being with you".'

An incident the following day did nothing to assuage Mary's fears. On leaving Wilton it had been arranged that all three – Arthur,

Mary and Mary Curzon – would lunch at Willis's Rooms in London later that day. Mary Curzon and Arthur arrived at the appointed time, but Mary did not turn up. The two lunched alone; afterwards, expressing anxiety, Mary Curzon suggested that they go to Cadogan Square to find Mary. She wrote to her husband to describe what happened next:

> we asked for her, and the footman went off to fetch her, while we waited in the library. Suddenly Mary appeared, wild-haired in a filthy dressing gown, and for two seconds we all stood quite still. Then Arthur said, 'Well, why didn't you come?' 'Come where?' said Mary. 'To lunch' said A. 'You never asked me', cried Mary and hurled herself on a sofa. Arthur said, 'You must be mad.' Then Mary said, 'Don't you think I would have come if I had thought you wanted me? Would I miss an hour when I could be with you? I have suffered agonies to think you didn't want me, and you had promised to lunch alone with me.'

The encounter ended badly. Mary Curzon made her excuses and left, but not before Balfour, in front of a near-hysterical Mary, made Mary Curzon promise to dine with him alone at the Commons that night.

Was Mary Curzon exaggerating the anecdote to provide her husband with gossip? Perhaps – but the nugget of truth is there, and Balfour's 'stern and cold' treatment of 'his poor trembling wild Mary' is easy to believe.[8] Mary Curzon herself returned to India wary of Balfour. 'When the sun shines and women smile, he is a picturesque, rare, enchanting creature . . . In times of stress he is, I think, harsh, and just a little selfish.'[9]

Mary when confident was a very different creature from the distraught figure in the filthy dressing gown. As she flourished as a hostess, the sexual element to her relationship with Arthur appears to have become more pronounced. Their correspondence opened with the same lack of ceremony as always: Mary's abruptly, with no heading, and signed off as 'Melcho'; Arthur's addressed as always to

'A tall strong woman': Madeline Wyndham, in her early thirties, by G. F. Watts.

'The Hon. P': Percy Wyndham as a young man, by Frederic Leighton.

Playing at romance: Guy, Mary and George Wyndham at Cockermouth Castle, 1867.

The adoring father: Percy Wyndham with George.

Madeline Wyndham with the toddler Pamela on her lap at Hyères, 1873. On the reverse Madeline has scribbled a clandestine note to Wilfrid Blunt.

Mary, as a wide-
eyed eight-year-old
in Cumberland, by
Valentine Prinsep.

Mary in her early twenties, by Sir Edward Poynter. Mary found the sittings a 'bore'. Her children thought Poynter failed to capture her vitality.

A young Wilfrid Blunt, smouldering into the camera.

'Pretty Fanny': Arthur James Balfour in less obviously seductive mode.

George Wyndham, hard at work, and already showing the signs of age.

A rhapsody in white: the Adeanes at Babraham in 1897. From left, Mananai, Madeline, Sibell, Pamela and Charlie.

The next generation at Clouds. From left, Mananai's daughters Madeline and Lettice Adeane prepare to sally forth with Pearson the coachman. Madeline Wyndham, holding one of her beloved dachshunds, looks on from the steps.

The men in their lives, as seen by the cartoonists of *Vanity Fair*.
Clockwise from top left: Harry Cust, Percy Wyndham, Hugo Elcho and Eddy Tennant.

Mary and Balfour in
old age, with one of
Mary's beloved chows.

Pamela in her fifties,
communing with the birds.

'My dear Lady Elcho'. But Mary's letters were newly coquettish, and far more explicit, with coy references to 'punitive expeditions', and teases about long hours in bed in the morning, playing with a 'beastly little "Beast" of yr [Arthur's] own making'.[10] '2 hrs is what I like: one for boring things and one for putting you in yr place . . . on yr knees at my feet,' Mary told Arthur in 1904, after managing to snatch two hours on a Sunday afternoon alone in his room at a house party in Oxfordshire.[11] Three years later on Valentine's Day she sent him a sketch of 'somewhat obscure objects . . . a birch rod . . . a brush and a tin bottle of squirting grease (smells of peppermint!)',[12] taking childish glee in the nursery-punishment element of their relationship that appealed to her love of secrets and private jokes.

The 'boring things' were 'talking business' – the business of politics.[13] When in public, Mary preferred to generate debate among others rather than hold forth on her views. In their private confabulations Balfour was one of the few to receive the benefit of Mary's 'moral, social and intellectual opinions' that Margot Asquith claimed to be 'more interested in . . . than [those of] most of my friends' – high praise from the waspish Margot.[14] Mary's children teased her that Balfour piled her letters unopened into his desk drawers, but in fact he seems to have sought, and greatly valued, the benefit of her wisdom and instinct. As Arthur's confidante, Mary operated in the manner of most political wives at the time: listener rather than adviser, a sounding board to be trusted implicitly where colleagues could not.[15] Most political wives did not aspire to more, and Mary was no different. Her own political foray on to the parish council was short lived: depressed by a committee's inability to get anything done, and feeling as though she were 'skinned alive', she abandoned her seat as soon as she could.[16] Throughout Arthur's forty-one months as Prime Minister, the two discussed posts, policy and crises. Mary's advice on appointments focused on personality as much as policy: the alchemy that could make a successfully balanced Cabinet work was not far off that required to make a successful house party 'sing'. 'There must be some heaven-born Chancellor somewhere outside . . . Cromer or Dawkins, or *Hugo*!!' she told Arthur, as he began devising his new Cabinet in 1902, a mischievous reference to Hugo's unremitting gambling. She was more serious about her brother's prospects: 'I suppose you know you won't have a happy or peaceful life – with me – until brother George is in the Cabinet!'[17] Despite Balfour at first insisting that he could 'see *no* chance of George having anything', George, while retaining his position as Irish Secretary, ultimately, and no doubt thanks in part to Mary's tenacity, was brought into the Cabinet.[18]

Arthur peopled his Cabinet with Souls. Civil servants were astonished to hear the Cabinet addressing each other by their first names, as the old friends they were.[19] But their golden age was beset by problems. The new century had brought a new dawn, and, as the fog of jingoism cleared, a number of developments allowed the electorate to see the Unionists in a clearer light. It was a party that did not seek to remedy the legal position resulting from the notorious Taff Vale judgment of 1901 (which, by allowing employers to sue trade unions for damages arising from strike action, had a chilling effect on the ability of the labouring classes to protest), a party that, having compared Uitlanders to helots, was willing to import cheap indentured labour from China to work on the Rand. The 'Chinese Slavery' scandal was a gift for the Liberal Opposition. St John Brodrick's conduct as Minister for War during the Boer War began to be vilified and the Government's justifications for war looked shabby.

In January 1903, at George Curzon's suggestion, a Coronation Durbar was held in India. A deserted plain outside Delhi was transformed into a tented city with its own post office, shops, telephone and telegraphic facilities, police force (with specially designed uniform), hospital, magistrates' court, up-to-the-minute systems of sanitation, drainage and electric light, and a small light railway carrying spectators from Delhi to the site. It was another example of the Viceroy's extraordinary energy, zeal and vision. He had devoted his rule to scouring out the corruption that mired

India, hauling the sub-continent into the modern age by reforms, commissions and sheer determination. That, and his self importance, more grandiose than ever, earned him many enemies. Wits dubbed the event the 'Curzonization'.

To Curzon's chagrin, Edward VII did not attend, sending as his representative his brother the Duke of Connaught. But Society flocked to the social event of the year – even Pamela. 'I thought she would not bring herself to leave the children,' said Percy mildly, but she and Eddy were on board a ship nicknamed the 'Roll Britannia' that carried them out to India.[20] A mortified Mary was not among them. At the eleventh hour Cincie had fallen ill and Hugo went to India alone. Mary was so disappointed she refused even 'so much as to look at a newspaper – I was much too angry at not being there'.[21]

Each day of the Durbar was crammed with entertainments: games of polo, military reviews, bands, exhibitions of local handicrafts, dinners, balls and firework displays. Pamela enjoyed the 'comédie humaine' and the house-party atmosphere among the luxurious tents of the elite, where the Duke of Hesse was nicknamed 'The Tower of Babel' (presumably for his facility for languages or his volubility). On the final day over a million people lined the tented city's streets to watch the concluding procession: one which '. . . I suppose', said Curzon to Arthur with typical modesty, 'the papers will describe as the most wonderful procession of the century'.[22] Surprisingly clear black and white footage survives: a parade of elephants, each more gorgeously arrayed than the last, topped by maharajahs glittering with gold and jewels, the Duke and Duchess of Connaught and finally Lord and Lady Curzon. That night the sky was lit up by fireworks, as the Indian and European elite rubbed shoulders at the grand Coronation Ball. Mary Curzon was looking lovely, Pamela told Mary, 'but very colourless and worn'. Pamela wondered too whether Hugo had 'altogether enjoyed his stay in India?' He had seemed rather 'homeless & wandering sometimes . . . I was awfully pleased when he came once or twice & sat in my tent.'[23]

Mary did not know. Hugo had been characteristically uncom-
municative. After Cincie had recovered, Mary had taken her children
to Madeira, to escape England's foul weather. From there, she
berated her husband for 'the howling desert of loneliness & igno-
rance of all yr plans in which I have been living'.[24] Yet only in
curiously oblique terms could she try to persuade him to refrain
from behaviour still more hurtful. A tiny 'hinge' at the bottom of
her letter reads: 'I hope you have got a little offering for each child
– it makes nurse cruel to Yvo if you have nothing for Mary she,
nurse, cries all night about it. It's cruel & does such injustice to
yrself.'[25] Only by invoking Yvo could Mary hope to make Hugo be
kind to Mary Charteris. It is a small clue that, despite Mary's
predictions, Hugo did not treat Blunt's daughter as he did his other
children.

The Durbar was not an unmitigated success for the Viceroy. Some
six months before, Curzon had had a run-in with the 9th Royal
Lancers, denying the whole of the notoriously exclusive regiment
leave for six months when it refused to reveal which of its members
had clubbed an Indian cook to death. Racially provoked murders
were far from uncommon in colonial India: during the previous two
decades eighty-seven Indian batmen, menials or cooks had been
killed by British troops. The British public did not share Curzon's
concerns. The Lancers became a cause célèbre in the papers; Edward
VII protested on their behalf. In a calculated snub the Duke of
Connaught chose the Lancers as his escort at the Durbar. As the 9th
passed by, the watching elite rose to their feet with deafening cheers.
'As I sat alone and unmoved on my horse . . . I felt a certain gloomy
pride in having dared to do right,' Curzon recalled in his memoirs.[26]

Pamela arrived back in England, relieved beyond measure, to a
house decorated in celebration by her children. She hated life on
ship: 'the smallness of one's cabin, the constant noises, the loath-
some smells . . . I think I was a tree in a former existence. This is
my first incarnation I am sure & certainly my timbers cd never
have been planted in a *ship*,' she grumbled to Mary.[27] Like all who

had been in India, she agreed that they had never seen such an outrageous spectacle, nor ever heard of such an unpopular Viceroy. 'Whether this is because his reforms are too good or his manners too bad seems doubtful,' said Balfour.[28] But he too was tiring of a Viceroy who treated anything less than absolute acquiescence to his proposals as a personal affront.

That month, the Liberals moved a vote of censure against the War Secretary St John Brodrick over his conduct of the war recently concluded. '*Never* wish for anything overmuch,' Balfour remarked drily to Mary, thinking back to three years before, when Hilda Brodrick had spent sleepless nights praying for her husband's promotion.[29] Brodrick was saved only by George Wyndham's Land Purchase Bill making its way through the Commons. The Irish Nationalists knew that if the vote against Brodrick succeeded, the Bill would fall with the Government. So they refused to vote with the Liberals against Brodrick. Brodrick remained in his post, but his reputation was beyond salvage. Wyndham's Land Act was passed. It instigated a workable land-purchase scheme that allowed tenants to buy the land they farmed from their landlords – unquestionably George's finest legacy, and one of the high legislative points of an otherwise unexceptional ministry.

Less than a decade before, the Souls had promised so much. Yet, in power, Arthur Balfour already seemed out of date. His detached, intellectual approach did not suit a country anxious about imperial decadence; he was not able – or willing – to control the fire-and-brimstone elements of his Cabinet, chiefly Joe Chamberlain, his Colonial Secretary. Arthur, capable always of seeing all sides of an argument, was unwilling to come down off the fence. This was conclusively demonstrated by his approach to tariff reform, a policy proposed by Chamberlain in 1903 that bedevilled the Unionists for the next decade. Tariff reform, or 'Imperial Preference', was Chamberlain's answer to imperial crisis: imposing a system of protective tariffs on trade from outside the Empire to forge imperial ties and provide the funds for much-needed root-and-branch social reform. The United States had grown great on protectionism. But the British believed they had grown great on free trade. Tariff reform provoked an emotional response – in particular among Liberal Unionist Whigs like the Duke of Devonshire and the Chancellor, Charles Ritchie – that no amount of intellectualizing could alter.

Balfour would never express himself openly for or against the policy. Possibly this was wise, for only in that way could he hope to hold together two mutually repelling forces: Chamberlain's reformers and the free-trade Whigs. His own musings on the subject, *Economic Notes on Insular Free Trade*, published in pamphlet form in September 1903, advocated cautious protectionism; he sent them to Mary before publication, and she showed them privately to Hugo and to Percy, who both favoured the policy. Mary thought the *Notes* would appeal to protectionists – the question was whether they could persuade 'youngish and intelligent people', not so wedded to ancient 'moral imperatives', to consider abandoning such a fundamental tenet as free trade.[30] Politics was changing in many ways: Mary told Balfour that, if he did publish, 'you ought certainly to tell the important Press, they will surely review it'. Hugo, of a more old-fashioned cast of mind, believed all policy should be expounded by speech, in Parliament. He was appalled by the idea of employing the press in a publicity exercise: 'thinks sending these notes to the Press, a shocking idea! Odd, incorrect, altogether wrong. I thought I'd tell you that,' added Mary.[31]

Matters reached a head in September. In the late summer of 1903, Balfour and Chamberlain had privately agreed that, if the Cabinet would not accept Imperial Preference, Chamberlain would resign and campaign outside the Cabinet to test the waters of public opinion, and his son (and proxy) Austen would become Chancellor. By skilful manoeuvring, Balfour used the bluff of Chamberlain's resignation to rid himself of the most burdensome free-traders of his Cabinet, the Chancellor Ritchie and Lord Balfour of Burleigh. Momentarily, Balfour even seemed to have achieved his intended aim of keeping the Whig figurehead of the Duke of Devonshire in his Cabinet, but, bullied by his free-trade companions, the unhappy Duke resigned in October.

Balfour and Mary squeezed in a hurried meeting in London in the middle of the negotiations, before Mary left for Ireland to visit George. Arthur told Mary of all the latest developments – still secret to everyone else: his interview with Edward VII about Cabinet changes; St John Brodrick's impending demotion to Indian Chief Secretary; Ritchie's departure. He gave Mary permission to tell Hugo 'various items of the dramatic situation', which Mary duly did: 'he was much thrilled and very grateful for being told . . .', she reported back.[32] At Phoenix Park, Mary once again had the upper hand. Placing a marker for the future, George confided in her his hopes for the Chancellorship – 'the heart's desire of his life' – although Mary told him that Austen Chamberlain was lined up for it. She had yet not told George about Brodrick, and 'told him (for fun) without my saying anything to tell me his views. He hopes that St. John will stay at the War Office . . . I do wonder who will take his place? . . . It would be an amusing experiment to put in Arnold Forster but perhaps too much of an experiment.' Whether at Mary's suggestion or otherwise, Hugh Arnold-Forster, erstwhile Parliamentary and Financial Secretary to the Admiralty, was Arthur's choice as War Secretary, a significant promotion. He immediately rose to the task by setting up the Esher Committee that considered War Office reforms.

Notwithstanding Arthur's manoeuvrings, by the summer of 1904 it was obvious 'to anyone with Parliamentary experience that with the Conservative party torn with dissension and tottering to its fall, the coming Session would be its last', said George's private secretary Murray Hornibrook.[33] The more immediate crisis was to be George's. His Land Act had been a triumph. His intellect had risen to the challenge of the job. His nerves, fed by his mania for work, had not. He began to drink and smoke ever more heavily, slept little and forgot to eat.

'I am undergoing a phase of nausea at politics, nostalgia for poetry,' he told Pamela, declaring, as he did to Wilfrid Blunt, that he was sick of office. His mental state in these months was described, with admirable honesty, by Guy Wyndham in George's *Life and Letters*:

> Between the engrossing demands of other political problems, the toil of constant effort towards keeping the shattered and mutinous party together, and the sickness at politics which continued during the summer months . . . he was losing his grasp over the machine . . . a machine so erratic in its working that it needed daily and almost hourly vigilance . . . He had always been over-engined for his hull; and he allowed himself to be distracted by a multiplicity of interests . . . Artificial stimulants and bursts of physical exercise only ran up the overdraft. He was, in the vivid phrase of a friend, 'whirling rather than walking through his days'; and he could not stop.[34]

George was more or less in the throes of a nervous breakdown, one so profound that even Sibell could not help but notice it.

As soon as the summer session of 1904 ended, George and Sibell went to the Continent for an 'extended holiday' of six weeks. His secretaries were told not to contact him nor to forward any papers which could await his return. In George's absence MacDonnell drafted, on Dublin Castle writing paper, a devolution scheme that was published by Lord Dunraven's Irish Reform Association on 26 September 1904. It proposed an Irish Financial Council to govern purely Irish expenditure (albeit headed by the Chief Secretary and Lord Lieutenant) and the creation of a new statutory body to legislate on Irish business with which a Westminster Parliament 'was unable or unsuited to deal'.[35] In the words of John Redmond, the leader of the Irish Parliamentary Party, it was 'simply a declaration for Home Rule'.[36]

The result was political uproar. Ulster was enraged. The Unionist press, in the words of Murray Hornibrook, 'went for it'. On the opposite side of the political spectrum, the radical nationalist Michael Davitt considered it a 'wooden-horse stratagem' that attempted by half-hearted reform to subvert and demoralize the nationalist cause.[37] George wrote a letter to *The Times* the next day, claiming to be dumbfounded. He was ignorant of MacDonnell's scheme, and rejected it outright on behalf of the Government.[38]

WESTMINSTER CARTOON SERIES No. I. "They don't call it Home Rule, but the path is the same."

'They don't call it Home Rule, but the path is the same': Gladstone's ghost looks on approvingly as George Wyndham examines MacDonnell's Devolution Scheme.

There are two letters from MacDonnell that suggest that George had been told of the scheme, even if he had not listened – one found in a box of letters after his resignation, the other, trapped between the pages of a Congested Districts Report that George had taken with him to the Continent. The latter made specific reference to the manifesto, in which manifesto MacDonnell hoped George 'recognized the trace of conversations we have had'.[39] This incriminating letter suggests that, contrary to his claims in *The Times*, George knew and possibly even approved of the scheme.

Seeking to explain it away, Guy Wyndham could only proffer the weak explanation that his brother had not read beyond the first few sentences.[40]

George's true position is more difficult to tell. A decade later, Mary commented to Wilfrid Blunt that 'It is *curious* how each person wants to prove George to be the thing they love themselves or to twist him into their narrow horizon if they like *pink*! They say he *is* pink that he was a nationalist, that he was an R.C. this that & the other . . .'[41] In 1911, George would inveigh against constitutional reform of the House of Lords and the removal of its absolute veto, claiming *inter alia* that it would pave the way for Home Rule. Yet this lay in his more extremist future. What brought him down when Parliament reconvened in February 1905, and an amendment to the King's Address was moved concerning his own conduct, was that he could not be pinned down at all on what he had meant, what he had known, what he supported and what he believed.

Five years before, George had made his name in response to an amendment to the monarch's Address on opening Parliament. Now, he 'had to fight with his back to the wall under a hail of furious charges and envenomed insinuations, knowing that even on the benches alongside of him and behind him there was an atmosphere of sullen suspicion'.[42] He was accused of concealing 'ugly facts', of using MacDonnell as a scapegoat or a Trojan horse. 'Cannot the right hon. Gentleman give a plain answer to a plain question?' he was asked. George's family did not pretend that his conduct during those weeks in the Commons when he was under attack was anything other than a shambles. They had simply to wait for the horror to end. At the end of January, a leader in *The Times* declared that 'the Chief Secretary, owing it is understood to enfeebled health, has seen little or nothing of the country for the administration of which he remains responsible'.[43] Of all the attacks, this, for the 'Patriot' George, was one of the most bitter blows.

On 20 February 1905 he made his final speech as Irish Secretary in the Commons. He was shambolic, rambling and confused. On 6 March, Balfour announced to the Commons 'with the deepest regret' that he had accepted the minister's resignation, on grounds not of ill health – 'though I frankly admit that I do not believe that he would be at present able to support all the labours and all the anxieties of a great administrative office' – but because George 'is of the opinion that the controversy which has recently taken place both within and outside these walls has greatly impaired, if not wholly destroyed, the value of the work which he could do in the office which he has so long held'. Balfour refused to pronounce on 'the merits of that controversy',[44] or on the merits of George's decision. He made his support for him as plain as he could, while adhering to instructions given by George the night before 'not . . . from a colleague but from one of your closest friends. I beg of you not to praise me to-morrow. It will do you harm. Perhaps that argument will not weigh with you. So let me add, it will do me harm.'[45]

It was the norm for a minister to announce his resignation in person. George was too ill for that. By the time Arthur addressed the Commons, George was at Clouds, knocked out on sedatives. Pamela came over from Stockton, bringing Bim and David to lighten the atmosphere in the house, and was appalled by the heavy, bowed figure she found masquerading in her brother's body. 'I never saw such a strong vigorous life so brought to a standstill,' she reported to Mary, likening it to seeing a horse fresh from hunting pulled to a halt, heaving, with sweating flanks 'only the horse was George'. Pamela spent several days there. Madeline Wyndham was on 'iron hooks' of anxiety, Percy silent. It was clear to Pamela that Percy was using every ounce of his self-control not to break out in recriminations against his son and the world for having disappointed him so. Sibell was 'all she could be', Pamela told Mary, but they both knew that that was little more than the provider of a soft hand to clasp another's while she prayed.

Pamela treated George gently, taking him for long walks and talking over the old times. They played games of 'do you remember' from their childhood, reminiscing over 'old trivial happenings' at Wilbury and Isel. Every detail George remembered was greeted with silent relief by Madeline Wyndham that his crash had not permanently damaged his mind. Pamela and George spoke of Percy's unselfishness and 'self-control'; of poetry. Prompted by George, Pamela recited to him lines by heart. 'And there were only two long spells when he walked on as if he forgot things around him,' Pamela told Mary. At dinner the family feigned normality, maintaining chatter as George sat silently. His scattered interjections – 'Now go on, Pam, tell me some more stories' – were greeted with relief, 'and once', said Pamela, 'he had a real good laugh & said now that is excellent, in his tremendous emphatic manner, you know, and then, with a great sigh "I've not been amused for so long, just go on"'.

'Never should the outside world know, willingly, from me that he had been knocked out of step, even for a day or two, by all this,' declared Pamela, urging Mary to keep this letter private. Externally calm, Pamela was burning internally with 'spleen and rancour', a white-hot rage at those who had brought down this beloved Icarus who had flown too close to the sun.[46] And perhaps it was the Wyndham-religion that prompted Mary's oddly pragmatic analysis of the matter in her letter to Arthur, sweeping under the carpet the destruction, public and private, of her brother. 'George has profited by experience before . . . if he takes this right it may be a lesson to him . . . its [sic] very serious its *breaking* him so . . . but I think he will rebound all right,' she said, anticipating that George's 'nervous disposition' would act as a 'safety valve'.[47]

The Wyndhams all maintained, then and thereafter, that Balfour had been heroic in his support of George, approving Winston Churchill's account of the episode which makes the same claim. Publicly, they steadfastly refused to blame anyone for the incident. Katharine Tynan pressed Pamela and Mary on the issue several years later. 'My brother is nothing if not magnanimous,' said Pamela. Mary offered the same smooth façade: 'she . . . had no condemnation for any of those who had hounded him out of his beneficent public life . . .'; her only comment was: 'He was so full of all he was going to do for Ireland . . . that he could not help talking about it.'[48] But privately Mary thought that George had got into his secretary's 'clutches somehow morally', and his lifestyle had not helped: 'alcohol and nicotine are more insidious that [sic] microbes!. . . You have never been influenced that way. Bless you! I wish you didn't Atlas all the world,' she said to Arthur.[49]

On 4 December 1905, torn between free-trading backbenchers and Chamberlain, who, despite increasing ill health, refused to abandon his vigorous tariff campaign, Balfour resigned. He was replaced by Britain's first Radical Prime Minister – the Glaswegian Henry Campbell-Bannerman, known as 'CB', who formed an interim Cabinet. In the election campaign of January 1906 the Liberals, united in their support of free trade, confidently on the moral highground, were spoilt for choice on which issue to attack the Conservatives with next. They won by a landslide – their last outright majority to date, gaining 200 seats to bring their number to 397, to the Unionists' 156. In an unprecedented show of defiance by his constituents, Balfour even lost the Manchester East seat that he had held for twenty years, and had to be rushed back into the Commons via the more pliant electors of the City of London. 'Dearest Chang here's a to-do,' Percy wrote to his eldest daughter in his neat, backwards-sloping handwriting 'Arthur out with an enormous majority. I wonder what you think of it.'[50]

The ministry of Souls had failed, remarkably, almost cataclysmically, to live up to the hopes promised by these men when young. Balfour could not harness the forces under his whip; and the experience of government had fractured the Souls themselves, exemplified by the return, the day before Balfour resigned, of Lord and Lady Curzon. Britain's youngest, most glamorous, most brilliant Viceroy had been driven out of his post, and Balfour had let him go.

The occasion was a clash of egos between Curzon and Lord Kitchener, India's Commander in Chief. Tension had been building between the two men ever since Kitchener had taken up the post in 1902. In 1905 Balfour backed Kitchener over questions of military reorganization. Employing a by-now habitual bluff, Curzon proffered his resignation, and was appalled when Balfour accepted it. Few thought that Balfour had behaved wrongly: the Viceroy's delusions of grandeur had reached near-megalomaniacal proportions. But Curzon never forgave Balfour for what he considered a stab in the back, and Balfour's failure to arrange a single representative of the Government or the monarch to meet the ex-Viceregal pair as they stepped off the train at Charing Cross on 3 December 1905 was pure cattiness. A gathering of Souls, including Balfour, was at Stanway. The party decided it was too far to travel to London for the occasion. 'We were trying all Sunday to concoct a telegram of greeting which all, including A.J.B., could sign. Nothing less jejeune seemed to evolve itself than "Glad you're back", Hugo Elcho said. 'If we don't look out, it'll turn into "Glad your back's worse", remembered Ettie Desborough, making reference to the corsets Curzon wore for his perpetually weak back.[51] In the end, they sent nothing at all.

TWENTY-FOUR

Pamela at Wilsford

Eddy Tennant was one of the many new Liberal backbenchers to take their places in the Commons that spring. He had taken Salisbury from the Unionists, benefiting from the landslide and from Pamela's charms: 'there was many a Tory turned Liberal when they saw her – she was the most beautiful woman I ever saw', remembered one elderly constituent.[1]

Although united on free trade, the Liberals remained split between Radicals and Imperialists, the Cabinet reflective of both. During the campaign a sardonic Percy had written to Mary discussing a speech by John Burns, the Radical President of the Local Government Board: 'he is against the King & all hereditary Authorities to go. In two or three years time we may see the moderate liberal voting with the Conservatives and out the Government will go.'[2]

With Edward Grey the new Foreign Secretary, and Asquith Chancellor of the Exchequer, Eddy and Pamela were in the inner circle of power. In fact, Eddy – the 'moderate liberal' – was ambiguous about the direction of his party, and Pamela had long since ceased to feign any interest in politics. The Tennants' visits to Grey

– a world-famous bird expert – at Fallodon were filled not with political talk but with walks along the sea-shore to watch for eider-duck, curlew, whimbrel and dotterel and listen to 'their plaintive attenuated cries'; evenings were spent listening to Edward Grey read aloud. Pamela's times at Fallodon revived her, as though she were filling her lungs with the fresh sea air. 'I came back with a new stock of patience to hear wrangling voices with, and to cope with seeing the cook, & paying the bills and all the "dreary inter-course of daily life" . . .' she told Charlie Tennant, a cousin of Eddy's, after one such visit in 1908.[3] Eddy, Pamela and Grey had grown even closer since Dorothy's death, in February 1906, in a freak carriage accident. Pamela seems to have been the anonymous author of Dorothy's obituary in *The Times*, paying tribute to 'a friendship which has been one of the high privileges of my life'.[4] Thereafter Grey spent Christmases with the Tennants at Glen.

The birth of the Tennants' fourth child, Stephen, in April 1906 occasioned rumours that he was an 'Aarons baby', the product of a Society doctor said to inseminate artificially women who could not conceive with their husbands either by a stud of footmen or by the insertion of a teaspoon filled with sperm.[5] None of this can be substan-tiated (although Jervois Aarons was Pamela's doctor), but it speaks volumes about the state of their marriage that it was capable of generating such gossip. People were always willing to talk about the Tennants, particularly after the Bart's death in June 1906, whereupon Eddy inherited a 'considerable proportion' of the Bart's £3,151,976 estate,[6] and of the family empire, now no longer just chemicals but comprising another fortune in shares and mining.[7] Eddy was now chairman of, *inter alia*, the Union Bank of Scotland, Charles Tennant, Sons & Co. Ltd, Tennant's Estates Ltd and Tharsis Sulphur and Copper Company Ltd, and a director of the Mysore Gold Mining Company Ltd and several other mining companies besides.[8]

Since 1901, Eddy and Pamela had lived, when in London, at 31 Lennox Gardens in Chelsea, which the Bart had paid for during the term of his life.[9] Now, Eddy sold the family house in Grosvenor

Square and bought 34 Queen Anne's Gate, mere steps from the Foreign Office where Edward Grey spent his days. The Tennants commissioned Blow to add on a wing to house the Bart's collection of principally English Old Masters previously housed at Glen. The Gallery, which had a separate entrance, was opened to the public in May 1910, between 2 p.m. and 6 p.m. on Wednesdays and Saturdays.[10] To Pamela's delight, it was a success from the first, with 150 people visiting in the first two hours alone.[11] This was just one of many philanthropic gestures by the Tennants; Eddy's charitable 'obligations' were considerable, and all willingly undertaken.

In the summer of 1906, the Tennants moved into their new home, Wilsford Manor in Wiltshire. It was featured in a seven-page spread in *Country Life* on 29 September. A series of handsome black and white photographs accompanying the article showed an elegant stone house in the Jacobean style, with mullioned windows and graceful proportions. The gardens are mature, lush and well tended. The Manor looks as though it had stood undisturbed in its idyllic location for centuries. In fact, explained *Country Life*, the house had only just been completed by the architect Detmar Blow, whose previous work in Wiltshire had included the underpinning of the East Knoyle church tower some years before.

Wilsford's foundation stone had been laid by Madeline Wyndham in 1904. Two years later, the house was complete. From birth, it bore the patina of age. It had been built using local labour, sand from a paddock two fields away, and all the stone of the small farmhouse that had originally stood on the spot. In the course of digging the foundations, the remnants of an Elizabethan stone and flint wall and fragments of old mullions had been discovered, suggesting that a grander house had preceded the farmhouse. Pamela had not been surprised. The beautiful garden, with its yew hedges and great ilex trees, had always seemed to belong to a larger house. The stone and glass fragments were incorporated into the new building. In the digging, the builders had also discovered boar tusks, a few 'trifling coins' and numerous fossils, called locally

'Shepherd's Crowns'. Pamela would take the name for the title of one of her books.

To the side of the 'Jacobean' main building was a long, low cottage-like nursery wing with thatched roof. It overlooked on one side a courtyard with a large old tree in its centre, and on the other side the bowling green and lawns. At its far end was the Stone Parlour, a room open on three sides to the elements, and furnished like a cottage kitchen with scrubbed pine table and dresser, where Pamela sat with her children to draw, play, paint and write, drinking in the sweeping views over the lawns down to the River Avon which ran through Wilsford's grounds.[12] As far as the eye could see, the land belonged to the Tennants.[13]

The gardens were Wilsford's true glory, and the same process of strenuous preservation had taken place there in order to fit the ancient hedges and trees to the new house in the best way. Pamela described the process vividly to Wilfrid Blunt:

> transplanting enormous bushes & moving trees – Napoleonic measures in horticulture . . . You see my great desire has been to avoid, in our new building, the sight of bare walls. So to ensure this I have had the great big creepers moved, last autumn, & arranged onto poles, or racks (if they were voluminous) to support them. Then up went the walls, & then in March (when roses may wander) they were cautiously laid against the walls again – & there they now stand – vines, reaching to above the first floor – & roses topping the string course! My Delight!. . . well, I had one rose wheeled slowly up in a barrow by a stout gardener, three men holding her [the rose's] hair up in its wake, & staggering so you can imagine it has been worth doing.[14]

Those Napoleonic efforts had paid off. The gardens photographed by *Country Life* are verdant. A plate illustrating 'The House and Bowling Green' shows mature yew hedges, and an ancient tree under which sit two small figures in wicker chairs: Pamela, and a schoolgirl, Clare, enjoying the peace of the garden so recently created – in Pamela's words, 'a rambling farmhouse garden that has never been spoiled, and some yew hedges of a noble size'.[15]

While browsing through a little bookshop in London, Pamela had discovered a sundial, lying on its side in two pieces almost hidden away under dust and cobwebs, obscuring the words 'come light visit me' inscribed on its dial. She restored it, and placed it in the garden: 'So, there now it stands: "where leaves spread out their budding fan to catch the balmy air" . . . I feel [it] is enjoying itself out in the open once more,' Pamela told Sidney Cockerell, erstwhile apprentice of Philip Webb, and now the Director of the Fitzwilliam Museum in Cambridge.[16]

It was a very large 'Family Cottage' indeed, but Wilsford reflected Pamela and Eddy's aversion to ostentation. 'I want to be heard if I shout for my boots,' said Eddy.[17] The Tennants employed surprisingly few staff – a collection of maids supplemented by help from the local village – although there were eighteen gardeners for the grounds. The house was furnished elegantly and comfortably, and was papered with Morris prints; its interior bore the marks of the Arts and Crafts movement, with finely turned wooden balustrades flanking wide staircases. Visiting Wilsford almost twenty years after it had been built, Cecil Beaton, a friend of Stephen Tennant, recorded 'a large long oak room, very comfortable and informal with enormous soft chairs, bowls of fat hyacinths, freesia & a lovely untidy litter of books'.[18] A profusion of bird cages was hung along the walls and the house, as always, was massed with the fresh flowers Pamela loved: she had named each bedroom after her favourites: Celandrine, Jessamine, Hyacinth. As at Clouds, guests often found, beside their beds, books specially ordered for them, but 'Life at Wilsford was not luxurious at all – it was comfortable, yes – but no luxury,' said Susan Lowndes, daughter of Pamela's friend the novelist Marie Belloc Lowndes and her journalist husband Frederick and a frequent visitor to the Tennants.[19]

Wilsford was not a political house *per se*, but most of its literary guests reflected a strongly imperialist view, including Arthur Conan Doyle, Henry Newbolt and Lord Northcliffe, as the *Daily Mail*'s Alfred Harmsworth had become. Another frequent visitor was Oliver Lodge, whom Pamela had known since her childhood at Clouds. Invasion scares were moving from fantasy literature to the front page. It was the age of the 'dreadnoughts' – as England and Germany raced to build the behemoths introduced by Jackie Fisher that rendered all other battleships obsolete[20] – and of a corresponding realignment of foreign policy by Edward Grey as Britain entered into ententes with France and Russia.

George – a frequent and honoured guest at Wilsford – was fast becoming a figurehead of the naval lobby, coining the belligerent demand in respect of dreadnoughts at the Wigan by-election in 1908: 'We want eight and we won't wait!'[21] His support for tariff reform, once tentative, was now ardent, even as Balfour refused to move beyond his cautious position. George had ostensibly recovered from his crisis of 1904, but something had cut loose. He returned to the backbenches in 1906 'an incorrigible Tory!', glad to have 'shed our Financiers and Brewers', eager to fight for 'The Church', 'the Realm' and 'the Empire of the English',[22] allying with Marie's writer brother Hilaire Belloc over a mutual hatred of the 'corrupting influences' of 'Levantine finance' and the plutocracy, and displaying an overt anti-Semitism hitherto no more pronounced than that casually expressed by the rest of his class. Balfour laughed off George's new stridency, comparing him to his Tory ancestor Sir William Wyndham, who had refused to kowtow to Walpole's Whig hegemony. Wilfrid Blunt found his cousin's alteration of political character repugnant.[23] Pamela thought nothing of it. In her eyes George was a poet, and a poet he remained.

Margot Asquith – a less welcome family member – made her first visit to Wilsford in July 1906. She had to admit that the house was 'perfectly lovely', although she took pleasure in pointing out the impracticality of the thatch on the nursery wing; while it was 'charming from the outside . . . I cd hardly sleep for thinking of the heat of Clare's bedroom over the kitchen,' she noted in her diary.[24] Relations between the sisters-in-law remained strained. In 1903, Pamela had scored a palpable hit with an allegorical short story, 'in which Margot figures as a princess in a glass house, herself as a beetle beloved by God, and my father [Asquith] as a Muscovy duck . . .', Margot's stepson Raymond wrote in his diary, anticipating with interest a visit by the Tennants to the Asquiths at The Wharf, their house in Sutton Courtenay, Berkshire.[25] Yet the two couples were tied closer than ever since the Bart's death, which left Eddy in the peculiar position of holding the Chancellor of the Exchequer's pursestrings. Margot's marriage settlement had provided that she would receive £3,000 per annum while her father was alive, £1,000 per annum after his death.[26] The loss of income hit the Asquiths hard, particularly as Asquith's political duties became more pressing, and Margot's bridge habit became more expensive. In 1919, Eddy estimated that he had given Margot, by way of loans and extensions, around £25,000 in excess of her allowance (well over three-quarters of a million pounds in today's money) since the Bart had died.[27]

Margot took the opportunity of her visit to draw a character sketch of Pamela in her diary: 'remarkably clever & very beautiful. Charming with other people's children & a wonderful mother herself but she lacks nature & humanness . . . she has not felt anything very deeply yet, she has always controlled her own destiny . . . She is not a citizen of the world . . . she lives in an adoring, uncritical milieu . . .' She thought that Pamela, 'self-scanned and self-secure', would get 'more heart when her own has been squeezed'.[28] Pamela often defended herself against accusations of remoteness, claiming that it was simply shyness. But her frostiness towards Margot stemmed from dislike, as Margot well knew.

Margot's sketch had much truth to it. Pamela surrounded herself with acolytes, whether family or minor literary figures, and her papers are crammed with their missives: breathless pages from Wommy declaring undying devotion; paeans from F. W. Bain, bestselling author of *The Digit of the Moon*, addressing her as 'Shri' the beautiful, sensuous princess heroine of one of his tales;[29] a declaration from Sidney Cockerell that to him and Bain Pamela was 'a Great Golden apple out of reach on the topmost bough'.[30] One of the more intriguing is a folded scrap of almost translucent paper covered in tiny pencilled handwriting. It was written by an admirer in the gods at Covent Garden's Opera House watching Pamela in a box below. The author tracks her every move: her anxious study-ing of the programme; fiddling with her glove and bracelet; her asides to the man beside her; the expressions fleeting across her face as the violinist played on. Pamela looked tired and lost in thought, thought her correspondent, who presumably having tightly folded up this love letter pressed it into her gloved palm as they met briefly in the buzzing, brightly lit foyer before going their separate ways. The signature on it is almost illegible, but appears to read 'Sholto' – possibly Sholto Johnstone Douglas, a Queensberry cousin to whom Pamela was close.[31]

To all these people, Pamela played the great lady, bestowing upon them the gift of her company. Most of them rhapsodized in turn about Wilsford's perfect simplicity. Pamela instructed her staff to give food and alms to vagrants so that in their underworld Wilsford would earn a reputation as a 'safe house'. She welcomed into the house Bim's troop of 'village boys', sending off to Hamleys for quantities of cardboard armour and toy pistols for their games. She took her children on overnight excursions across the Downs in a colourful Gypsy caravan, burning sausages and pigeons that her children had shot over a campfire and singing them to sleep with folk ballads on her guitar. She entertained parties of youths, sending them off, with the caravan carrying their bedding, to sleep at Stonehenge overnight.[32] She had a pet bullfinch, Chuffy, who sat on her dressing table whistling a tune she had taught him, and who tried to drink her diamond earrings, thinking them 'water-drops'.[31]

The flipside is the many contemporary anecdotes that show Pamela in the worst possible light. Marie Belloc Lowndes recounted in her memoirs a dinner party at Queen Anne's Gate at which Eddy remarked to the assembled company in 'quiet measured tones' that he could not conceive what jealousy might feel like. Pamela, perceiving the comment as a slur upon herself, fled into the garden, pacing up and down and sobbing in full view while her uncomfortable guests continued eating inside.[34] Marie's daughter Susan recounted as a child at Wilsford catching sight through an open doorway of Pamela lying on the floor, literally biting the carpet in fury.[35] In family legend, as recorded in memoirs written by her descendants, she has become little more than a narcissistic horror, spoilt, demanding, vain and destructive[36] – a woman who, if she felt she was receiving insufficient attention, would rise from the table and implacably face the wall;[37] who asked Eddy to remove the motto 'Charles Tennant & Co., Chemical Manufacturers' emblazoned on the brick of Tennant's Stalk, the family's Glasgow chemical factory, disliking this public reminder of the family's trade roots;[38] and who so frightened her husband that he never charged her directly with her extravagance, but asked the company secretary to drop a gentle hint about her overspending.[39]

Charlie Tennant, who became one of Pamela's protégés, was the recipient of the best of her nature. Her letters to him are honest, thoughtful and humorous. She fretted about his happiness while working for the family company (she feared he was 'the square peg in a round hole, in Glasgow!'),[40] and made efforts to matchmake him with 'pretty girls', inviting him to attend the Peebles Ball with her goddaughter 'Pammy' Adeane,[41] told him of the time that someone had asked her the date of Easter that year and she, lost in thought, had answered, 'Oh, about the 18th or 19th of *Wilsford* I believe!'[42] As with all her closest friends, it was a rare letter from Pamela that did not contain some discussion of her current reading, from Mrs Humphry Ward ('[she] has a suburban way of describing life that doesn't hold one') to Gibbon's *Decline and Fall*, which Edward Grey had read aloud at Fallodon (she found getting her mind around Gibbon's complex sentences like trying to span the girth of an enormous tree: 'you feel you can't quite get round it, or if you do, it is only *just* done').[43]

TWENTY-FIVE

Mr Balfour's Poodle

On a summer's morning at Stanway, in July 1907, Mary was bearded in her bedroom by a furious Hugo. Once again he charged her with excessive socializing, this time on behalf of their children, and expressed the hope 'that the result of our dinners etc. will not be a double marriage, Violet [Manners]–Ego, Cynthia–Beb [Asquith]', adding 'that Cynthia spends all her nights with Beb at balls, and that V. and B. both look very second rate and that he's going to tell Cynthia and Ego so – this is the really worrying thing', Mary reported to Arthur.[1] The Duchess of Rutland (as Violet Granby had become) had a trio of daughters, known as 'the Hothouse' for the highly strung fascination they exerted over men, and the second of the three, Violet 'Letty' Manners, married Ego in 1911. Cincie and Beb, Asquith's taciturn second son by his first marriage, were already secretly engaged.

The children of the Souls, all well known to one another, were approaching maturity. They gave themselves the name of 'the Coterie' – later renaming themselves 'the Corrupt Coterie' in an indication of defiance. Mary's children were all, by their birth, part of the Coterie, although some with more ambiguous attitude than others. Mary's three eldest were young adults. The twenty-two-year-old Ego, recently graduated from Oxford, was 'rather a darling',[2] quietly humorous and diffident,[3] and still politically naive enough to have been devastated at Arthur Balfour's apparent betrayal by his Manchester constituents in the elections of 1906. Mary wished he could spend more time talking to Arthur: 'I should like him trained to be a good Unionist Conservative.'[4] Guy had suffered from his position as second son, and from the poor health he had endured since childhood.[5] At Oxford he racked up large debts and barely scraped a third.[6] Mary worried that whenever he was in a position of tension or stress he might 'crack up' under the strain.[7]

Cincie had an alien beauty, with wide-set eyes, and a razor-sharp intelligence left entirely unhoned by her education. Mary, with much agonizing, had dispatched the intellectual Miss Jourdain in 1896. She feared that Miss J's intense High Anglicanism was making Cincie overly religious,[8] and was unnerved by the governess's own emotional attachment to Mary herself. She replaced her with Fräulein Moskowitz, a 'dear, bird-witted little Viennese', known as 'Squidge' for her resemblance to a squirrel.[9] The expectation for Cincie was that she would 'marry a country house', but while in Dresden, aged sixteen, she had met Beb Asquith, and in the two years since had appeared totally uninterested in any other man.[10]

Cynthia's determination to be with the silent Beb – inexplicable to everyone except herself – placed Mary in a quandary. She found chaperoning a challenge – 'even if one is at the balls oneself . . . one cannot see what is going on', she said – and felt 'low and rather helpless' in trying to determine what to do, 'over the most difficult part of life – how much to meddle? . . . Our system is confused and illogical. I dare say general results work out the same! whatever systems!!' she lamented to Arthur.[11] Lord Wemyss – who, as head of the family, would determine what marriage settlement Cynthia would receive – was fiercely opposed to Beb because he was a Liberal. Mary's concern, which seems also to have been Hugo's, was that Beb lacked the qualities needed to make a success of himself. Mary's duty as a mother was to see her daughter well provided for by marriage financially, as well as emotionally. Finding that balance was the alchemy.

Mary's visits to Gosford were normally spent trying to avoid lectures from her octogenarian father-in-law on the subject either of her children or of Arthur's leadership of the Unionist party, both of which Lord Wemyss felt were being seriously mishandled. Mary found the former particularly enervating given the conduct of Wemyss's own son. Neither Hugo's gambling nor his infidelities had improved. A recent visit to Chatsworth when Mary, Hugo and his latest mistress, twenty-five-year-old Peggy, Countess of Crewe (a daughter of Lord Rosebery), were all present, had been a disaster. For some time, Mary's response to Hugo's affairs had been to offer quasi-maternal advice as to how her husband and his mistresses might bring out the best in each other. 'You exaggerate each other's peculiarities,' she said, encouraging Hugo to 'steady' the spoilt, witty, headstrong Peggy. Her attempts at Chatsworth to befriend Peggy had horrified Hugo. He responded by freezing her out. 'I ask you a perfectly harmless question – you jump as if you were shot, I come near yr room & you look at me as if I were a poisonous snake,' wrote Mary afterwards in reproof. 'I had really far rather that you spent the whole of every night with P. & behaved in a decent friendly way to me all day . . . but you are so aloof, so strange, so suspicious, so on wires – that you really make me inclined to . . . tell you that I think you an ass!. . . why should being pro her make you anti me?'[12] By contrast, 'My children are *not* immaculate,' Mary told Arthur, 'but they have some conscientious feelings, they are warm-hearted, friendly, and essentially domestic. They love being at home, they do not remember always but they would be grieved at distressing one and would shut a door to please one and do tiresome things occasionally because they feel them to be right and they *want* to please one . . .'[13]

In the autumn of 1907 Mary took Ego and Cincie to Italy, hoping that with Beb 'out of sight, out of mind' Cincie's infatuation would cease. The trip was exhilarating. 'One . . . gets to know one's children more in 20 days in these circs than in many months at home,' Mary told Arthur, although '. . . I feel rather as if my brain were lined with frescoes upon frescoes . . . and my mind is a jumble of Tuscan, Romanesque Gothic style!'[14] On Mary's return she went to Birmingham to listen to Arthur address the annual conference of the National Union of Conservative Associations on party unity over tariff reform. She had not heard Arthur speak publicly for some time and thought it '*excellent*': touching his 'top level qua "platform speech"', but she knew that 'human nature is alas! silly and small', and that people would continue to think that Arthur, by not taking a firm position on the issue, was Chamberlain's puppet, trying to lay the ground for the party's adoption of the policy in due course.[15]

Party unity was to be found only through opposition. Shortly after his defeat in 1906, Balfour announced that the Unionists would 'continue to control the destinies of this great empire' whether in or out of office.[16] Reviving his uncle's referendum theory, he explained in a speech at Manchester a few months later that the purpose of the House of Lords was 'not to obstruct and still less to run counter to the will of the community as a whole, but to prevent hasty and foolish legislation'.[17]

Campbell-Bannerman's ministry promised 'New Liberalism', a scheme of social reform by which the state took unprecedented responsibility for the welfare of its people. But friction between the Imperialist and Radical wings of the Cabinet meant that the reforms put forward between 1906 and 1908 were prosaic, focusing on reversing Unionist legislation on issues on which the fractured Liberals could still cohere, principally licensing measures and education (the Liberals were united on the need for stricter liquor licensing and in their opposition to Tory attempts to provide state funding of church schools). Still Balfour's Lords filibustered every measure of any significance: killing them outright, or wrecking them with amendments so that the measures were 'stripped and wounded and left half dead' as Lloyd George, now President of the Board of Trade, said bitterly of the mangled 1906 Education Bill.[18] In 1906, Percy had gloomily asked, 'We are now just where we were in 1885 on the brink of Democracy, when Gladstone saved us for 20 years by jumping into

Home Rule. What will save us now?'[19] The answer, it seemed, was the House of Lords.

The Lords' highhanded behaviour provoked Campbell-Bannerman to put constitutional reform proposals before the Commons in March 1908: a suspensory veto for the House of Lords (so that the peers could delay but not veto legislation); and the reduction of parliamentary terms from seven years to five. The Unionists howled that the Upper House was the watchdog of the people. Lloyd George gave one of his memorable ripostes: 'A mastiff? It is the right hon. Gentleman's [Balfour's] poodle. It fetches and carries for him. It barks for him. It bites anybody that he sets it on to.'[20] The Commons voted in favour of the reform, but within a month Campbell-Bannerman had resigned. He died in April 1908, still in residence at 10 Downing Street, from where he had been too frail to be moved.

Asquith was finally in power, although he had to cross the Channel incognito by night-train and ferry to kiss hands when Edward VII refused to cut short his holiday with his mistress Mrs Keppel in Biarritz, the French resort on the Atlantic coast popular for its bracing air, golf courses and casino. To date Asquith remains the only Prime Minister to kiss hands on foreign soil. His father's advancement did not improve Bob's prospects so far as Hugo and Lord Wemyss were concerned. Lord Wemyss fulminated against Asquith's final Budget as Chancellor which introduced the 'social-istic' measure of pensions for the elderly but was passed since, as a fiscal measure, the Budget was by convention inviolable by the Lords' veto.[21] Otherwise, Balfour's Lords continued poodle-like, in 1908 alone rejecting or mutilating bills for licensing, education and town planning, and two Scottish measures concerning smallholders and land values.

Mary was still encouraging Cincie to meet 'fresh people'. In the spring of 1908, Cincie brought an Oxford undergraduate named Ridley to Stanway. They were the only guests not well into middle age, but the evening demonstrated that the Souls had lost none of their old zest. At around midnight on Sunday, after a long dinner and much talk, the party was seized by 'a frenzy of song, dance and improvisation'. Arthur Paget – 'the Stanway Minstrel' and Pamela's youthful suitor, now a close friend of both Mary and Pamela (Pamela was godmother to his daughter, Pamela Paget) – seized his guitar; the carpet was rolled back; George Wyndham spouted Virgil while somersaulting across the floor; the 'Professor' – Sir Walter Raleigh – crowned by a wreath of roses, did the cake-walk with Cincie. The party spilled out into the garden to serenade Arthur Balfour (who had gone to bed some three or four hours before) at his window.[22] 'Mary – I must tell you – asked me to come "and see her quiet home life": I have never heard, and rarely made, more noise before . . . A. Paget is a "Pied Piper of Hamelin" . . . and we were rats who danced in time to his music,' George told Percy as he made his way back to London.[23]

In the spring of 1909, Wilsford village was 'rocked & shaken' by the revelation that its new Canadian curate, 'so excellent it seemed in every way', was a bigamist with a 'very bad past'. With the curate in a state of 'breakdown' and his wife in 'misery', Pamela took in their 'poor little boy . . . to get him out of the poor mother's way . . . He is lying looking at picture books on the rug now,' she told Charlie Tennant.[24] Meanwhile, Mary and Cynthia were setting sail on the *Empress of Britain* for the curate's native land, Mary equipped with a new grey-squirrel fur coat bought in London on sale for £30 to insulate herself against the cold.[25] Ego, now serving as a diplomatic attaché in Washington DC, was to join them as guests of Canada's Governor General, Earl Grey (a distant cousin of Edward Grey), and his wife. Ostensibly, Mary was making the most of an opportunity to visit old friends. Privately, she made no bones about the real reason for the trip: 'for Cynthia: general indefinable hope that change may be beneficial physically, mentally, spiritually',[26] she told Arthur; or, as she put it more candidly to Hugo, to keep their daughter out of 'the arms of Beb!'[27] Uncharacteristically, they travelled in some style, securing a double-berthed suite with a private bath and parlour, at a cost of £50. An extra £14 allowed first-class servant accommodation for Mary's maid. '[I]f we are ill the whole time and never sit in our parlour I shall die of disappointment at the money wasted, unless I die of sickness,' said Mary.[28]

Mary found Canada exhilarating, admiring its pioneer spirit, relishing the wild open spaces that reminded her of Cumberland, and enjoying the fact that post, routed via New York, took several weeks to arrive. She could breakfast in peace without Squidge or Nanny appearing with tales of domestic disasters. Now that she was in her late forties, the freshness of Mary's youth was long behind her, but she had not yet earned the respect and dignity of '*extreme old age*'.[29] Yet local self-made eminences fell over themselves to praise her at Government House dinners (everyone, she told Hugo mockingly, appeared to be a baronet and she had never heard of any of them). The attention was invigorating and inspiring. With characteristic enthusiasm, she began devising unrealistic plans for the future: she wished she could send her sons to the Macdonald College, a new and innovative agricultural college;[30] she wanted to return in the summer and explore the Rockies; perhaps even to invest in land. '[I] f I were a man I'd settle there [in British Columbia] & buy a fruit farm – in fact if I'd any capital, I'd buy a small valley right away – *I wish you would*,'[31] she told Hugo, adding, in a dangerous tactic that appealed to his worst nature, 'the difference between what you have & *pay* & what you *get* is positively El-Doradoish'.[32]

The travellers planned to pass through New York on their way back to London. Mary was already looking forward to a dinner planned with William Astor, the property magnate and newspaper proprietor. But barely a fortnight into the trip she received a telegram. Percy had fallen badly in the early hours of the previous morning and suffered a 'seizure'. A doctor and nurses were treating him at Clouds, Pamela and George were making their way there now. There was talk of 'brain leakage': it is most likely that Percy had suffered a stroke.[33]

Just days before, Percy had written a long and chatty letter to his eldest daughter. The Wyndhams had paid an enjoyable visit to

Petworth, but were now both plagued by colds; an unexpectedly large snowfall had offered temporary employment to London poor as street sweepers; George Wyndham had given a Commons speech on tariff reform that people were saying was the best thing he had done in recent years. The *Evening Standard* reported that Balfour was giving the issue of protectionism serious consideration, and Percy thought that even Lloyd George and Winston Churchill seemed to be recognizing its benefits. However, Percy was not feeling at his best. 'I am coming to a theory as to the way in which man & woman grow old,' he told his daughter, illustrating with a sketch:

the common idea

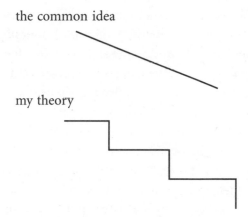

my theory

Percy never really recovered from this first stroke, which was partly attributed to his splenetic anger over the direction of the country. Henceforth he was perpetually in the care of two nurses. His doctor banned him from any further public speaking on politics.

His resolve was immediately tested. On 29 April 1909, in a rambling four-hour speech Lloyd George, now Chancellor, introduced his first Budget: a 'war budget' to 'wage implacable warfare against poverty and squalidness'.[34] It introduced direct taxation on spirits, estates and higher incomes (a 'supertax' of sixpence in the pound on incomes over £5,000 a year) and land taxes including a tax on the 'unearned increment' on the value of land enhanced by the effort of the community. The landed classes saw it as a war on themselves. 'This is not a Budget, but a revolution; a social and political revolution of the first magnitude' and 'obviously intended as one', declared Lord Rosebery both from the cross-benches and in *The Times*.[35]

In the months that followed, Lloyd George did not trouble to conceal his contempt for the parasitical leisured classes. But his Budget seems primarily to have been expedient. The pensions scheme had a £16 million shortfall; new social reforms required funding; local government was in financial crisis; naval expenditure was running out of control. If the Government could redistribute wealth at the same time as generating revenue, so be it. But Unionists thought it was dressing up a social measure in fiscal clothing: in Balfour's view, as one biographer has put it, this was 'unwise and dishonest'[36] and constitutionally dangerous. Mary thought the Government had disgraced itself by allowing its policy to be dictated by 'party enmity' while disregarding the country's wishes.[37] Both her Liberal brothers-in-law were seriously concerned by their Government's proposal.

Rosebery circulated around the Liberal League's executive a letter testing the waters to see who might wish 'to join a crusade against the Governments [sic] proposals if they knew that Lord Rosebery would lead the movement, and accept full official responsibility'. Eddy Tennant showed the letter to Edward Grey, and wrote privately to the League's Secretary discussing its implications. He did not go so far as to suggest that he might be among their number, but his sympathy for Rosebery's position is clear enough.[38] In an address delivered two days later at the National Liberal Club Edward Grey defended the Budget inasmuch as he suggested that it was not quite the revolution Rosebery had claimed – but he did not directly endorse it.[39]

All knew that if the Lords rejected the Budget, a constitutional crisis would ensue. Balfour's observation that the conventional prohibition of a veto related to an *alteration* of fiscal measures, not to outright rejection, was too subtle a distinction for most. The summer and autumn of 1909 were dominated by the issue. The undoubted star of the hustings was Lloyd George, addressing crowds of thousands.

At Limehouse in East London in July he addressed his audience on landlords: 'a gentleman . . . who does not earn his wealth. He has a host of agents and clerks that receive for him . . . He has a host of people around him to do the actual spending . . . His sole function, his chief pride, is the stately consumption of wealth produced by others.' At Newcastle's Palace Theatre in October he turned his guns on the dukes. "'A fully-equipped duke costs as much to keep up as a couple of Dreadnoughts," he said in the tone of one who is proposing a complimentary toast; "and they are just as great a terror and last longer," he added when the 4,000 had done laughing.'[40]

The genius of Lloyd George's rhetoric was the good humour with which he delivered his blows – but those blows were trenchant enough to prompt Edward VII to demand that Asquith control his excitable Chancellor; and for *The Times* to condemn the Chancellor for inciting class warfare – a demagogue, appealing only for 'men who have the crude taste for ginger', more suited to Speaker's Corner in Hyde Park or down the Mile End Road.[41] In fact, the tone of politics, gradually shifting since the Reform Acts of 1832 and 1867 and the legislation of 1884–5, had irrevocably changed. It was now impossible for a politician to make any kind of speech without 'the constant expectation of interruption' – whether heckling or more aggressive interruption since the Women's Social and Political Union (known as the WSPU) had begun to employ violent tactics in its campaign for votes for women, and had adopted a policy of harassing Cabinet ministers.

At almost every venue at which Liberal ministers spoke over the summer and autumn, a jostling, heckling crowd of suffragists was massed outside. At Limehouse, a man wearing the WSPU's purple, white and green, hauled down from a pillar by stewards, was roughed up so badly by the crowd that he was hospitalized.[42] The night before Lloyd George's Newcastle address, suffragists had smashed all the Liberal Club's windows after a fracas with local youths. The next day, *The Times* looked back wistfully to days when political meetings required no more than a couple of policemen on the door: 'The woman suffragists have changed all that. When a Cabinet Minister is announced to speak the local authorities close all the neighbouring streets to ordinary traffic, barricades are erected, and the county is scoured for extra police and quiet horses . . . no doubt, at a pretty cost to the ratepayers.'[43]

'I am very low about the future of this country and things generally. People are all on a wrong tack,' Percy wrote to Mary at the year's end, in spidery writing noticeably shakier than the neat script that preceded his stroke.[44] Mary was scarcely more cheerful. Her efforts to keep Cincie and Beb apart had failed. In October, Hugo got wind of the fact that the two had been seen together at a party organized by Letty Manners which Mary had chaperoned. Mary fought back:

> . . . Beb is very dogged & a hard worker . . . if money is to be confiscated from the 'leisure' classes – it will be better for Cynthia to marry, a man with grit who is hardworking & able to *make* money than a member of the aristocracy of the Charteris type (yr sons) – you say everyone has to make money nowadays – Beb is about the only man she knows who seems able and willing to do so.[45]

Mary timed her defence well. On 4 November 1909, after seventy days of parliamentary debate and 554 divisions, the Budget passed its last stages in the House of Commons by 379 votes to 149. Three weeks later the Lords rejected it by 350 votes to 75. The Radical *Daily News* fired red rockets into the London sky in anticipation of the battle to come. The first skirmish was just days later, on 2 December. By the early afternoon the House of Commons was packed, with not a single vacant seat on the floor, the Strangers Gallery full to overflowing and peers spilling over their reserved spaces into the side galleries. '[O]ne saw on every side rows upon rows of eager, attentive faces . . . mindful of the great issues at stake,' reported *The Times*. Asquith entered the Chamber just after 3 p.m., and shortly afterwards was followed by Balfour, to cheering from his backbenchers because he had been ill and it had been feared he might not attend.

The debate itself was short, barely two and a half hours. To lusty support from the Government side, Asquith declared that the Commons would be betraying its heritage and traditions were it to brook such interference and usurpation for another day. Balfour 'taunted the Government on having a perfect passion for these motions, which bound no one, hurt no one, probably encouraged no one, and certainly frightened no one'. By 349 to 134 the measure was carried that the peers' action was 'a breach of the constitution and an usurpation of the rights of the Commons'.[46] The House adjourned at twenty-five to six. Asquith went to the King who, at his Prime Minister's request, dissolved Parliament, and a general election was announced for January 1910.

TWENTY-SIX

1910

The entire Budget episode consisted of 'a series of risks – the government wagered that Lloyd George could make his radical plan work and breathe life into the flagging administration, and Balfour and his colleagues gambled that the electorate would endorse rejection by the Lords and reward the Unionists with an electoral victory', as R. J. Q. Adams has said.[1] In January and again in December 1910 the politicians went to the people, the elections bracketing a summer of secret talks between the party leaders as they tried to find a solution to the growing constitutional crisis.

The January electoral campaign was twenty-six days in total – the longest in political history. Hugo threw himself into it, passionately advocating tariff reform on hustings at Tewkesbury and Doncaster, and haring from Chelsea to Stanway then to Peebles over three days so as to cast his ballot in all his different constituencies. It seemed as though everyone had become politicized: Nanny Cliffe had manifested herself as 'a great politician – hates Mr. Asquith & longs for Mr. Balfour to come in again'. To Mary's distinct amusement, it appeared that her chauffeur, Turner, was a 'socialist': 'while Ego & I went up the hill [near Stanway] & were talking Tariff

Reform inside the farms – we came out & found that Turner was having an impromptu meeting on the road! & doubtless more than neutralizing any results we may have achieved!'[2]

Asquith had made it clear that, if re-elected, his party intended to address the Lords' veto with constitutional reform. As the election results came in, Mary was hopeful: 'things look healthier . . .', she told her father, 'if only we can keep on at this rate – both sides may end up even – they will then be dependent upon the nationalists who hate the budget and altogether their claws will be well cut & I think on the whole it's the best thing that can happen *just now* & Free Trade will be pretty well dead . . .'[3] The night before, she had been seated by the King at a dinner for the Duke of Connaught. The atmosphere was 'amusing . . . [for] of course the King has to affect a kind of neutrality . . . yet all the time one knew that feeling was running high & everyone was acutely excited'. Throughout dinner Edward VII received telegrams with the latest results from the constituencies. 'All the Peers' eldest sons are being returned,' he commented, which Mary took to 'express . . . his relief . . . [I] think he begins to feel that the Gov. miscalculated the real feeling of the *Country* (whatever *party* feelings may have been) when they made such a fuss about the Lords – & I think the King must feel relieved for he was very agitated at one time.'[4]

In the final tally the two parties were almost equal: Liberals 274, Unionists, 272. Eighty-odd Irish and forty Labour MPs held the balance of power. Eddy Tennant was one of over 100 Liberal MPs to lose their seats. When Pamela expressed disappointment, Mary gave her short shrift. Salisbury was 'a conservative town, if ever there was one', and besides, 'Eddy . . . hates practically everything that this Gov. has done & he ought to be on his proper side or none at all.'[5] The Budget had been mandated, but only just. The country was uncertain. For Percy this simply proved how ill suited the masses were to make decisions about the future of their country: 'Power has been taken from those who should hold power . . .' he said, blaming patrician and upper-middle-class 'vote hunting'. Once again, he predicted the death of his class. 'When the country has gone into the melting pot an aristocracy or governing Class call it what you will will arise, but it will arise from Trade and Commerce and our lineal successors are not likely to be among them. The grandsons of the Labour members more likely,' he told Mary.[6] George had a 'splendid majority' and returned to Parliament, guns blazing, ready for an Armageddon-like battle to the death. Edward VII made almost straight for Biarritz. The Budget was passed without division by the Lords at the end of April.

In March, fearful of approaching Hugo, Beb Asquith had taken the unusual step of discussing his financial prospects with Mary. He had earned £800 in the past year, and his father had promised him £600 a year more – a sum he knew was '*most* moderate' but hoped might be '*just* possible'.[7] Mary was still concerned. Violet Rutland had just written her a 'frantic private letter' revealing that her son John, now Marquess of Granby, 'admires C. much (great compliment for them to want a pauper!) and begging me to stem the Beb tide'.[8] Mary had long talks with George along 'the "Riviera"', Clouds' river walk, 'about Nyncie [sic] and Beb where they "argued all about it and about" . . .'.[9] But she was instinctively sympathetic to the determined young lovers: 'I do think that if poor old Squith [sic] can allow 600 it's awfully shabby if the Earl [of Wemyss] cannot give another 600. But his bitter politics will make him mad.'[10]

Weeks later, Asquith threw down the gauntlet with his Parliament Bill which proposed to replace the Lords' absolute veto with a suspensory one – and stipulated that the Lords had no veto at all on fiscal measures. In his Commons speech introducing the Bill, he set out two alternatives. The Lords could pass it, thereby castrating themselves, or they could veto it, in which case he would seek an immediate dissolution and recommend that the royal prerogative be used to create enough new peers to secure its passage – if that threat was not enough to make the Lords capitulate.

In fact, unbeknown to all but Edward VII's private secretary

Lord Knollys, the Archbishop of Canterbury and Balfour, there was one more option. At a secret meeting between the three at Lambeth Palace, Balfour had indicated that in certain circumstances he would be willing to form a government if necessary. Knollys told Edward VII of Balfour's offer in early May. The next day, history 'rattled over the traces' with the King's sudden death. His successor, the forty-four-year-old George V, was politically naive and totally ill equipped to deal with a crisis Asquith deemed 'without example in our constitutional history'.[11] On hearing the news of the King's death Asquith, on board an Admiralty yacht nearing the Bay of Biscay, was 'bewildered . . . indeed stunned' by this terrible turn.[12] He went up on deck to see Halley's Comet blazing in the night sky, a grave omen.

Edward VII's death flung the country into mourning – it was the summer of the famous 'Black Ascot' when Society turned out to the races in funereal dress – and provoked the two parties to seek a resolution to the brewing crisis. Over the course of the summer eight men – Balfour, Lord Lansdowne, Austen Chamberlain and Lord Cawdor; and Asquith, Lloyd George, Lord Crewe, Liberal Leader in the Lords, and the Irish Secretary Augustine Birrell – met more than twenty times in 'constitutional conference'. The fact of their meetings was public; everything else was secret, and the subject of frantic press speculation.

By the time of Cincie and Beb's wedding – held at Holy Trinity Church in Sloane Street on 28 July 1910 – tensions were such that guests arriving at the church were asked by ushers 'Unionist or Liberal?', and seated accordingly.[13] Mary, inspired by dancers at the Hippodrome, had designed the bridesmaids' dresses: 'quasi-greek' drapery, belts of fine gold braid, and red gladioli in their arms – an 'authorized classical style', she told Hugo, anticipating criticism. She emphasized that she had not gone for the full fashion, which involved a rope tied around the ankles: 'it is too ugly the fat brides-maids would look like tubs', she said, illustrating her words with a sketch – doleful tub next to her reed-like counterpart, the latter waving her gladioli in triumph.[14] The following summer, Balfour was amused to be asked by one concerned hostess whether he would object to being at a dinner where Cincie and Beb were present.[15] Mary's early fears proved sadly well founded. By the 1920s, with Beb debilitated by shell-shock and alcoholism, Cynthia was more or less singlehandedly supporting their family as private secretary to the celebrated playwright J. M. Barrie and what she could earn as a freelance writer.

Percy and Madeline Wyndham celebrated their golden wedding at Clouds in October.[16] Only Mananai was absent, from illness.[17] They held a large, celebratory tea as was customary. Their tenantry gave them a silver-gilt Tudor rose bowl, East Knoyle's schoolchildren a pair of fountain pens. In 1904, Percy had commissioned William Orpen to paint both their portraits.[18] Now a series of photographs marked the occasion, in front of Clouds' great doorway. In one, Percy and Madeline stand, strangely formal, shaking hands, a curious dachshund by Madeline's feet. In another, seated, they gaze at one another, Percy clutching a cane, Madeline swathed in shawls, her hand to her throat. Fifty years after they had married, the Wyndhams' relationship was still strong. Madeline's infidelities of the past had never diminished Percy's devotion.

Percy is dapper as ever in these portraits, but his health was slipping. He complained to Webb of 'various distressing infirmities'.[19] He was consumed by anxiety at the direction of the country, his class's apparently firm foundations turning to quicksand before his eyes. Had he known of the 'secret understanding' which George V 'reluctantly' gave Asquith in November, Percy would have been more splenetic still. In November, Asquith informed the King that, no cross-party resolution having been reached, the only solution was Parliament's dissolution, and an election fought on the question. He asked George V for a guarantee that if his government should win that election, then the King would use his prerogative 'to make Peers if asked for'. Without that guarantee, Asquith told him, he and his entire Cabinet would resign at once.

Faced with this ultimatum, George V sought the advice of his secretary Knollys. Knollys had told Edward VII of Balfour's offer of that spring, but he had concealed it from his successor, fearing, presumably, that the novice King might seek to take up Balfour's offer. Now Knollys assured his monarch (with no evidence that this was the case) that Balfour would decline to form a government; and that George V's only option was to give Asquith the guarantee. He told George V that this was the advice he would have given Edward VII, who would have taken it. Pressed by Asquith, deceived by Knollys, the King reluctantly assented. 'I disliked having to do this very much, but agreed that this was the only alternative to the Cabinet resigning, which at this moment would be disastrous,' he explained to his diary on 16 November 1910.[20]

The campaign itself was muted. Lloyd George did his best to keep the fires of class enmity burning, revisiting Limehouse to liken the aristocracy to cheese ('the older it is the higher it becomes'). At the Albert Hall, Balfour appeared to move slightly from the fence on tariff reform by announcing that he had no 'objection' to putting the matter to a referendum – immediately alienating tariff reformers, furious that he would not adopt it outright.[21] By and large apathy reigned. Candidates rehashed speeches made just a few months before. Poor weather kept people indoors. One-sixth of the men who had voted in January – over a million in all – declined to do so in December. The results, after a year of haggling, debating and gambling, were near identical. The Unionists had lost one seat, the Liberals three, and the Irish Nationalists and Labour Party each gained two. As Christmas approached, Percy wrote to Mary in anticipation of his daughter's visit to Clouds: 'Arthur is very welcome here especially if accompanied by yourself. The door is closed to Socialists, Fabians or other and I cannot say Radicals are welcome unless near connections by marriage,' he added mean-ingfully.[22]

TWENTY-SEVEN

Revolution?

On Monday 13 March 1911, Percy died in his bedroom at Clouds. He had been declining for days. His wife and four of his five children were with him, only Guy, summoned by telegram back from St Petersburg where he was military attaché, did not arrive in time. Percy's children agreed that their father was 'absolutely himself to the very end . . . his mind clear as crystal'.[1] He was 'ready for either alternative. He did not surrender weakly but neither did he struggle to live,' said George.[2] His friends were saddened, but not surprised. His frailty had been apparent at his last social appearance, Ego Charteris's wedding to Letty Manners the month before.

Percy, whose religious faith had wavered ever since he had read Darwin as a young man, appeared to have had some sort of deathbed enlightenment. '"God" *revealed* himself to Percy & gave him such a vision OF LOVE & HAPPINESS & glory that I can never forget it,' Madeline Wyndham told Wilfrid Blunt.[3] Her ardent polyglot faith gave her comfort. '[T]he feeling that He *has left us*, never makes me *unhappy*, not half as unhappy as seeing Him suffering & *miserable Here* – that was *wretchedness*,' she told Mary, some six months later from Clouds as she passed her first birthday for fifty years without her husband on 'a Heavenly day almost too Hot with a Peacock with head turned up to heaven piercing the air with his Cries'.[4]

Percy's body was cremated at Woking. His ashes, in an oak casket made from trees grown on the estate, were buried after a funeral held at East Knoyle church on Saturday 18 March,[5] and marked by a green sandstone cross.[6] Percy's obituaries mourned the passing of a man who was the last of an age: the independent-minded aristocrat dutifully undertaking the responsibility of paternalistic rule.[7] Pamela immediately placed an order with the milliners Maison St Louis in Halkin Street for a black straw quatre corn with chiffon veil, a coarse black straw and feather toque with veil, a widow's hat with crêpe veil, two chiffon hats, a black tagel picture hat with grey feather mount, a mercury in black straw-lined velvet with velvet trimming, and a grey straw with velvet lining and grey wing – £26 16s 6d in total.[8]

Percy's estate was valued at £241,162 gross.[9] He left Madeline Wyndham a lifetime interest in 44 Belgrave Square, his household effects and her jewellery, all to revert to George on her death. She received absolutely a lump sum of £1,000 and an annuity of £3,100 and his horses, carriages, personal effects and 'consumable stores'. Guy received £5,000 and a further annuity of £850 during his mother's lifetime. Percy's daughters received nothing – nor did Dorothy Carleton (on whom he had intended to settle £300) – for all, so he wrote in his will, were sufficiently provided for by settlement. The governess Bun received £100, so did Percy's agent Edward Miles. Various other members of staff received small bequests. Everything else went to George.[10] Increasingly, Madeline Wyndham divided her time between Clouds, Stanway, Babraham and Wilsford, a shawl-clad, mob-capped expansive figure, beloved of her grandchildren, known to them as 'Gan-Gan'.

George turned his substantial energy towards making his own mark upon Clouds. He arranged for electricity to be installed, and commissioned Detmar Blow to turn the old nursery into a large library for himself. The now redundant lamp room was made into a chapel for Sibell, panelled in old Italian dark wood with a red-brick floor and an arching whitewashed ceiling overhead.[11] George assumed with relish, and a certain humility, the role of squire for which he had been preparing all his life: 'All the work I have to do here only increases – if that were possible – my deep respect for his [Percy's] definite character and my admiration of his justice and generosity,' he wrote to a friend.[12] For the present, his full energies were focused on securing the future of his class.

For almost two decades the Souls had managed to separate politics from friendship. In 1900, Arthur had written to Mary recounting a heated 'passage of arms' with Asquith in the Commons over Irish landlords which took place directly after Arthur had dined with the Asquiths: 'Asquith was the challenger, but I felt a mild awkwardness replying to a man in the strength of his own champagne!'[13] Now the situation was forcing underhand behaviour. In January 1911, Arthur dined with Lord Knollys and fell into the trap of giving him his views on the constitutional position and the creation of peers, not knowing either of the secret guarantee or that the dinner was approved by Asquith, to whom Knollys was reporting back. At the same time, Margot, who almost certainly had some idea of the guarantee, was leading Mary astray. Visiting her at Gosford, she came to her room for a talk after tea. While claiming to know no real details, she urged magnanimity from the Unionists with regard to the Parliament Bill about to be put before the Commons. As Mary wrote to Arthur:

> She was practically making a great appeal to 'trust Henry' . . . I said but supposing we are disposed to trust Henry and accept the veto bill as the best way out, trusting to amendments and Henry's conscience or moderation, how can we tell that Henry would not be pushed much further than he wanted to go . . . She said Henry's not a bit afraid of his own party. She is horrified at the idea of having to create peers.[14]

The Parliament Bill had its first reading in the Commons on 22 February. During three readings over three months, 900 amendments were tabled – almost all from the Opposition – only the most minor of which succeeded. All knew that the real action was to come in the Lords, where a tribe of backwoods peers, who had never hitherto troubled the Upper House with their presence, were mustering under the leadership of Lord Willoughby de Broke, given encouragement by more senior figures, including George Wyndham, Curzon and Lord Lansdowne, the Leader in the Lords. It was shaping up to be a sweltering summer. George V's coronation, held on 22 June, was one of the few cool, cloudy days of the Season. Whenever he could, Balfour adopted flannels and straw hats;[15] after work, Edward Grey and Winston Churchill splashed about in the marbled swimming baths at the Automobile Club on Pall Mall.[16] At a fancy-dress ball at Claridge's given by Lord Winterton and the rising Unionist star F. E. Smith on 24 May, to general merriment Waldorf Astor, son of William Astor and a Unionist MP, appeared clad in a peer's robes of state and a tinsel coronet on which was balanced a placard: '499' read one side; 'still one more vacancy' read the other. Both Asquith and Balfour were present.[17]

It was no laughing matter when the Lords massacred the Parliament Bill with amendments in July, and the news of the King's secret guarantee was finally leaked. It was a 'shocking scandal', Arthur said to Mary. 'I expect an anxious, but not a laborious week . . .'[18] In fact, he was furious at Asquith's and Knollys's underhand behaviour in securing and concealing the guarantee. For more rational Unionists, the guarantee's existence made it impossible to continue to obstruct the Bill, since a House flooded with Liberal peers would destroy any remaining Unionist power in the Lords. Yet when on 21 July Balfour called his Shadow Cabinet to Carlton Gardens to vote on what course the peers should take, there was no agreement: 'indeed most violent differences', he told Mary.[19] Standing against the 'Hedgers', like Arthur, who recommended capitulation, were 'Ditchers', like George, in a phrase of his own coining, determined 'to die in the last ditch' defending the Lords.[20]

For the first time in their long friendship, Arthur and George were on opposing sides, although that is to misrepresent their relative positions somewhat. George was zealous, and Arthur expressed almost no position at all. Privately Arthur thought resistance would only 'advertise . . . the fact that we are the victims of a revolution. Their policy may be a wise one, but there is nothing heroic about it.'[21] Publicly, he said only that he would stand and fall by Lord Lansdowne.[22] Lansdowne, the most reluctant of 'Hedgers', only advocated but did not demand from his peers the capitulation that privately he too found 'unpalatable'.[23] Passivity had settled like a blanket over the party leadership. The Ditchers were in full revolt.

The Commons was scheduled to address the Lords' wrecking amendments on 24 July. It was confounded by the 'Cecil Scene', as Asquith, rising to speak, was drowned out by a full half-hour of cat-calls, jeers and howls of 'Traitor', 'Who killed the King', 'Let Redmond speak' (an allusion to the fact that the Lords was considered the last bastion against Home Rule) and, more obliquely, 'American Dollars'. Eventually, without uttering a word, Asquith sat down. When Balfour rose, the Chamber fell embarrassingly silent. Nothing comparable to this had been seen since MPs brawled on the floor of the Commons over Home Rule in 1893, but that had been born out of momentary passion. This was a plot organized by Balfour's Cecil relations: 'as usual the leading lunatics are my own kith and kin,' he admitted to Mary wearily.[24]

By tacit agreement, neither Mary nor Arthur mentioned George's part in events. The next day, Wilfrid Blunt stopped in at Belgrave Square to find George, F. E. Smith and George's stepson Bend'Or Westminster ebullient at the Cecil Scene's success and planning their next line of attack. 'Here you see the conspirators,' cried George as his cousin poked his head round the door. 'They are all in the highest possible spirits at the commotion they have caused and consider they have forced Balfour's hand,' Wilfrid recorded in his diary; '. . . they are going to give a banquet to old Halsbury . . . as the saviour of the Constitution.'[25]

The 'Halsbury Banquet' – in honour of the eighty-seven-year-old Lord Halsbury, the Diehards' designated figurehead – took place at the Hotel Cecil on the Strand two days later. Tickets were advertised by a circular issued from the Carlton Club and signed by George, Edward Carson, Austen Chamberlain and F. E. Smith.[26] Spirits among the 600-strong crowd ran dangerously high. 'They [the Government] have been playing, and they are playing a game of gigantic bluff . . .' declared Austen Chamberlain. It is hard not to see George's hand in the hastily devised plan at the evening's end for the banqueters to draw Halsbury in triumph from the Strand to his house in Ennismore Gardens. Halsbury's family stymied the plan, fearing the octogenarian might expire from the excitement.[27]

The Ditchers resembled nothing so much as over-excited schoolboys, grandstanding in the face of irrefutable facts. 'The country is in revolt,' George told Wilfrid. 'They are ready for actual armed resistance, or rather, they would like that,' Wilfrid told his diary, with certain disbelief.[28] Later George sent to Arthur, via Mary, a letter explaining his conduct. '[Y]ou felt I believe it was . . . very involved & obscure . . . you couldn't really fathom his meaning,' Mary reminded Arthur. Having read it, she believed that 'that letter places him apart from many others of the die hard who behaved quite differently!' – but she never explained to Arthur or anyone else why.[29] The presence within the Ditchers' ranks of serious political figures – Austen Chamberlain and F. E. Smith to name just two – indicates serious dissatisfaction within the party ranks not just with their leaders' position, but with their failure to lead, and a belief, however faint, that the guarantee must be a bluff.

The final reckoning began at half-past four on the afternoon of 9 August, when the Lords convened to discuss the Commons' amendments made to the Parliament Bill. It was the final round of pass the parcel. If the Lords considered themselves 'Content' with those amendments, the Bill would pass. If 'Not Content', it was time for the guarantee – the precise terms of which were still unclear – to be put into action. After almost eight hours, the debate was adjourned just after midnight.

As it reconvened the next morning, 10 August, Balfour was making his way in baking heat to Paris, on the first leg of his journey to Bad Gastein. That the final act of a two-year saga was even now playing out at Westminster could not convince him to alter train fares booked some time back. He had washed his hands of the affair which, he told Mary, was more 'odious' to him 'from the personal point of view' than any other episode in his public life.[30] Asquith was also out of London, having gone to Wallingford to recover from a bout of laryngitis. But Asquith's party was not mutinous, and he had made contingency plans for an emergency Cabinet meeting the following day in the event that it was required.[31]

When the session recommenced in the Lords that morning, the atmosphere on the Opposition benches was electric, on the Government benches calm. The real fight, everyone knew, was not between the Government and the Opposition, but between Hedgers (many with buttonholes of white heather) and Ditchers (sporting red roses). On the Government side, Lord Morley sat quietly, glancing frequently at a small piece of paper that he kept in the pocket of his frock-coat. The debate recommenced. Lord Midleton began, taunting the Government that the proceedings were a sham. The call was taken up by Rosebery and Lansdowne for a clear statement by the Government about the nature of the guarantee.

At that point, Lord Morley stood up and read from the paper that he held in his hand: 'If the Bill should be defeated tonight His Majesty could assent – I say this on my full responsibility as the spokesman of the Government – to the creation of Peers sufficient in number to guard against any possible combination of the different Parties in Opposition by which the Parliament Bill might again be exposed a second time to defeat.'

Morley had barely finished speaking when a cheer rose up from the Government side. From the Opposition, Hedgers and Ditchers alike, there was dead silence. By request, Morley read the statement out one more time. It was the clearest possible answer to dispel any delusions the Diehards might have cherished. If they voted against the Bill, their number would be swamped until the Upper Chamber was so pliable as to vote through anything the Government might desire. In case anyone had not quite understood the implications of his words, Morley added helpfully, 'every vote given to-night against my Motion not to insist on what is called Lord Lansdowne's Amendment is a vote given in favour of a large and prompt creation of peers'.[32]

Outside, heat shimmered above warped railway lines; tarmac melted on the roads. It was the hottest day recorded in seventy years. In the East End, the dockers were on strike. Inside the neo-gothic splendour of the Upper Chamber, Rosebery attacked the Government for taking advantage of a 'young and inexperienced' King; others denounced the Bill as sheer 'revolution'.[33] But they knew they faced a choice of evils. As Lord Selborne put it, 'shall we perish in the dark, slain by our own hand, or in the light, killed by our own enemies . . .?'[34] At twenty to eleven at night, the division was called. As peers thronged the lobbies, a desperate Willoughby de Broke hid the top hat and coat of one duke to keep him in the Lords to vote. The duke bolted, preferring to commit the cardinal sin of appearing in public hatless and in shirtsleeves rather than make an impossible choice.[35] In any event, one duke would not have made a victory. The final vote was as follows: Contents, 131; Not Contents, 114. The Government had won by seventeen votes, thanks to the support of thirty-seven Unionist peers and thirteen prelates, or, as George Wyndham termed them, 'the Bishops and the Rats' – men, including George Curzon, who were henceforth hissed upon entering the Carlton Club by the hysterical Diehards.

From the Ritz in Paris, Balfour wrote to Mary: 'You must not ask me to tell anything about the last ten days. I am trying to forget it all.' Mary replied immediately and sympathetically from St Moritz: 'I feel I do not understand [the situation] and I suppose never shall! This letter is only to remind you of what perhaps you know ... that my heart goes out to you ... I longed and longed to be able to come and comfort you – not by talking over the situation but by quite other means – a good smacking would brace you up I think!'[36] Arthur's leadership would not survive the crisis. Succumbing to Leo Maxse's campaign in the *National Review* that 'Balfour Must Go' – staccatoed to 'B.M.G.' – he resigned in November. The night before the announcement, he visited Mary, one of very few to have known his plans from the first,[37] at Cadogan Square. Tired, sad, finding it difficult to speak, Mary stood on the steps of no. 62 to watch the motor 'turn away with you buried inside, not looking!, and I had a serrement de Coeur as the car drove away for the last time – with you as Leader – after so long'.[38]

That August, both kept silent about George, who himself wrote to Sibell, incoherent from tiredness and emotion, mourning the death of his age:

> Many things that I loved are shattered and some friendships gone ... Now we are finished with the cosmopolitan press – and the American duchesses and the Saturday to Mondays at Taplow – and all the degrading shams. When the King wants loyal men, he will find us ready to die for him. He may want us. For the House of Lords today – tho' they did not know it – voted for Revolution.[39]

TWENTY-EIGHT

1911–1914

As news of the vote reached India, F. W. Bain wrote to Pamela: 'I suppose that you and your "mountain-top" have been full of politics, rejoicing over the downfall of the Peers.'[1] In fact at the time of the Liberal triumph Pamela was face down on her bed in her darkened room, pillows sodden with tears, crumpled-up handkerchiefs strewn across the counterpane, succumbing to the grip of 'the Glen mood', a mixture of 'neuralgia', self-pity, depression and self-loathing that besieged her each year for several days on arrival at Glen, a place where even the weather seemed bent on victimizing her with 'hard metallic sunshine' and 'whipping wind'.[2]

'When I am in my Hinterland,' Pamela explained to Charlie Tennant, 'the chief feeling of it is a longing to be of use . . . not to spend so much money on the trivial things, and to do some tangible good. If you knew what a World there is in one, of a need to give . . . Money doesn't express it, I'm giving that away with both hands . . . & always will, so long as I have it, but that kind of giving doesn't express my need.'[3] Charlie was one of several confidants to whom she revealed at length her darkest feelings of worthlessness and despair. She drew for them comical pictures of herself, tear-stained, in her darkened room; recounted her imagined dialogues with God defending the insatiable need for affection and praise that He had bestowed on her; bemoaned her selfishness and vanity; complained how Eddy did not afford her 'the smallest little sayings of praise'; and vowed to make the best of her life through the futures of her children: 'if only I may make a good success of that, I shouldn't mind about my own rubbishy life. But sometimes the fear of failing, or the responsibility of it all floods over me, & I feel as if I were out on an open Sea – in the dinghi [sic] – . . .with a hair-pin for a paddle,' she said, writing to another, unnamed recipient.[4]

Pamela had a magpie's knack for the picturesque image or phrase. Her 'hair-pin' line seems to have been inspired by a Sanskrit translation sent to her by Bain from 'the great Hindoo Poet' Kalidasa earlier that year: 'I am desirous of crossing the impassable ocean, in my infatuation, in a tiny boat' ('You can remember the words when I am in India,' Bain said).[5] Pamela tweaked it in her letter to Charlie Tennant ('sometimes it seems to me as if I were on a great Sea, alone in a little boat; & all my love of poetry & books & great ideas, avail nothing. I only feel utterly useless, & of no value anywhere . . .')[6] and to better effect here. The brilliant transposition is an indication of her flashes of real talent as a writer, but so easily did she lay her soul bare to numerous correspondents that her letters, ostensibly so anguished, become almost glib. It is hard not to agree with Elizabeth Asquith, sharp-tongued daughter of Margot, that Pamela gave her 'essence . . . cheaply'.[7]

In March 1911, Eddy had been raised to the peerage as Baron Glenconner and appointed Lord High Commissioner to the General Assembly of the Church of Scotland. He was now the sovereign's personal representative to the Scottish Kirk's governing body.[8] Edward Grey began to address him, affectionately, as 'Your Grace'. The Glenconners' official residence in Scotland was Holyrood, but Eddy's post required them to spend ever more time at Glen. In print, Pamela described Glen as a 'paradise' for children: with parties and lawn tennis, acting, charades and camping parties at Loch Eddy.[9] She invited her Adeane nieces to parties of young people that she took to Peebles Ball,[10] insisting on giving Mananai 'money presents' (kept secret from Charlie) for their ballgowns.[11] Privately, she never ceased to hate it.

Eddy's appointment reflected the considerable financial support provided by the Tennants to the Asquiths as well as the Liberal party, although he never sent Margot a cheque without an accompanying homily and protestations that he too needed to 'be careful'. Margot gave this short shrift – 'I wish I felt he & Pamela wd ever be in debt!' she scrawled on one such letter of 1910.[12] 'Highly characteristic of my brother on the subject of money', she wrote on another envelope from Eddy. 'They both owe Henry *everything*.'[13]

For over a decade, Margot had been devising ways to exploit her brother's finances and his wife's social appeal to the party's end. From the start, she tried to use the aristocratic Pamela to make the party 'more socially attractive'. 'I shall have a "day"', she told Eddy in 1900, '& with Pamela's beauty . . . I'll show our party what we can do', planning also to recruit Mananai to the cause. At the time, Margot bemoaned the failure of the Liberal leadership, except the Asquiths, 'ever [to] do anything of this sort Ly Harcourt & Ly C.B. do nothing at all . . .'.[14] The construction of the gallery at Queen Anne's Gate in 1910 facilitated the hosting Margot wanted Pamela to take on. She still complained that the Tennants entertained far too little.[15]

Pamela thought they entertained far too much. '[T]he world of Books . . . is more to me than any other', she told Sidney Cockerell, drawing a little crown above the capitalized word to emphasize her point.[16] In 1912, her compendium, *The White Wallet*, was published, the title a reference to her vellum commonplace folder. She included her poem 'Fantasia – of a London House Closed', in which she wanders through the shut-up great houses of London, lamenting time spent in 'tedious revelry', haunted by ghosts of 'murdered Summers' that:

speak of Mays, strangled in Rotten Row,
Of massacred Julys, whose glowing heads
Hung on the lances of red-cloth Bazaars – ('Society Bazaars' that
kill the soul . . .)[17]

Pamela refused to let the demands of her official engagements impinge upon time spent devoted to the things she thought most worthwhile – 'her children, her village friends, poetry, the cultivation of her own considerable literary gift, and that life-long enthralling interest . . . her love for, and study of, wild birds'.[18] It resulted in a certain ruthlessness where everyone else was concerned. On occasion Mary became distressed by how little the sisters saw of each other. She wrote to Pamela expressing this sentiment. 'It is quite all right about you and me. I find I am able to love *operatively* (the italics are mine) from a distance,' Pamela replied. Mary's children thought it 'wonderfully typical' of their aunt, and urged their mother to 'love operatively from a distance' whenever she proposed inviting disliked guests to Stanway.[19]

When Pamela did entertain, she did it on her own terms. The rest of the family had long turned away from Bosie Douglas, on account not of scandal but of his character: 'the kind . . . I most despise', Mary told Arthur privately – weak, vitriolic, aimless, a conspiracy theorist quick to exercise his vitriol against the world.[20] Bosie had 'converted' to heterosexuality and married Olive Custance in 1902. Pamela persuaded Eddy to give the Douglases a cottage on the Wilsford estate; and to offer Bosie, in 1907, the editorship of the *Academy*, a literary monthly recently bought by Eddy. Bosie used it as a vehicle to attack the Asquiths until his attacks became so extreme – he described Margot as 'bound with lesbian fillets' (the intent of which statement to offend being undiminished by its being unintelligible) – that Eddy, unable to fire him for fear of Pamela's fury, cut all ties with the publication, giving the entire enterprise to Bosie as a gift.[21] In 1912, Bosie prompted another scandal when he came face to face with Robbie Ross, the executor

of Wilde's literary estate, at a reception held by the Tennants at
Queen Anne's Gate, and launched himself at him, shouting abuse.
Ross hid behind a large table, and Bosie, sliding across the polished
oak in pursuit, was hauled back by other guests, allowing Ross to
dodge into the drawing room and bar the door. Roaring impotently
with rage, Bosie remained glowering and huffing in the gallery's
corner until Sibyl Queensberry persuaded him out by requesting
he escort her to her carriage. Meanwhile, Eddy Tennant moved
quietly among his female guests, apologizing in his understated
manner for the unseemly disturbance to which they had been
subjected.[22]

Pamela's regal indifference to convention provoked a certain
cattiness – 'an Olympian character, she floated to and fro between
Wilsford and the Glen, appreciating their different beauties, and
so well buttressed by wealth that she never had to catch a bus or
think about the price of fish', said Elizabeth Buchan, wife of the
writer John[23] – and provided ample anecdotage beloved of
the press. She stopped her carriage in the middle of a state procession through Edinburgh, to buy up all the birds caged in a pet
shop, ordering them to be delivered to Holyrood, then setting them
free in King's Park.[24] Mary recalled a visit by the sisters to London
Zoo to visit a cockatoo of Pamela's from which she had 'parted . . .
because its language was too shocking for words!' At the Zoo she
'outraged the authorities by taking her dog Roly into the gardens,
she hitched the dog under her arm and disregarded the complaints
and threats of the officials, who followed her protesting, and at last
withdrew in despair!'[25] When they found the disreputable bird, it
recognized Pamela.[26] 'What would you think if I told you that I
knew of a family of which the eldest son walks up to his waist in
water when going out to dinner, & of which the mother, when she
dines out, burns her pocket handkerchief in the dining room fire?'
teased Edward Grey.[27]

Each New Year's Eve – Pamela told Sibell – she trysted with the
memory of her doomed love for Harry Cust, sobbing as she reread

all his letters stored in her keepsake box.[28] There are hints in Bain's letters that he and Pamela had some form of physical relationship – 'when I die, Stonehenge will be found printed on my heart', he said – and Pamela always made clear to Bain that her invitations to Wilsford did not include his wife.[29] But Grey was the constant, providing Pamela with the attention and reassurance that she needed, meeting her mind in the truest fashion. At Queen Anne's Gate, they shared firelight 'knitting suppers', at which Grey read aloud to Pamela as she knitted, needles clacking furiously beneath her serene face.[30] 'Are you not more than Mary-Queen-of-Scots beautiful?' he asked her, and Pamela, mollified, receded from her hysteria.[31] 'Emma, You are very perverse in supposing that when I tell you of having refused bridge I do so with the object of conveying to you that I make sacrifices when I spend an evening with you. I tell you of these refusals to convince you how very much I prefer a K.S. [knitting supper] evening to other attractions,' he wrote, addressing her as Emma Woodhouse, and signing off as her fictional lover Mr Knightley, after a stormy one-sided row in which Pamela had accused him of being motivated to see her by duty rather than desire.[32]

On an early-summer Sunday in 1912, Grey wrote to Eddy from Wilsford, a beautiful day, with missel thrushes out in force, and the river flowing strongly and full. He recounted his anxious journey from London, transporting in a slopping can of water six giant orfes ordered by Pamela for Dingley Cut, the pond at the bottom of the garden; the sight, at breakfast, of a stoat proceeding at stately pace across the lawn, its mouth full of prey; and a long afternoon's walk with Pamela across the Downs featuring 'the usual adventures; finding & negotiating precarious planks in unfamiliar water meadows'. All the children were well, he continued, Clare reluctant to return to school in Salisbury the next day, six-year-old Stephen satisfied with his new gardening method: digging up the crocuses flowering in the other children's gardens and replanting them in his own plot. '"Rousing up the bulbs" he called it.'[33] One would think that this letter came from the father of this family, such is Edward Grey's familiarity with the Tennants' quiet domesticity. Eddy, kept in Scotland by business and a mistress – a sweet-natured local woman about whom no one ever spoke – was an increasingly shadowy presence in that family's life,[34] even to the extent that Bim was sent to Winchester, Grey's alma mater, rather than Eddy's Eton, with Grey making the necessary introductions to the suggested housemaster. It must be this which provoked Stephen's acidic claim in adulthood that he could scarcely remember what his dull father looked like.[35]

The Glenconners' houses provided Grey with respite from his tussles at the Foreign Office. The Great Powers were aligning themselves on opposing sides in a tangle of ententes and alliances: in 1911, France's designs on Fez in Morocco brought England within a whisper of war against Germany; in 1912, the frighteningly fast disintegration of the Balkans brought together the Great Powers in London at a conference of eight interminable months of petty disagreements and squabbles. Domestically, the bloody revolution that George had predicted, perhaps hoped for, had not come to pass, but the seeds of social unrest seemed everywhere. Bills proposing Home Rule for Ireland and the disestablishment of the Welsh Church were progressing through Parliament, their eventual legislative force apparently now only a matter of time. Suffragettes poured acid on to golf courses in green suburbia or chained themselves to the railings of Buckingham Palace; and, in front of dumb-struck crowds at the Epsom Derby, Emily Davison, with a return train ticket in her pocket, stepped out in front of the King's horse, and died four days later from the injuries sustained. The sympathy of many was for the horse. At Wilsford, Nanny Trussler read out to her charges at breakfast the *Daily Mail*'s dire warnings about the consequences of the coal strikes breaking out across the North Country;[36] in East London, the dockers continued their protests.

The discordant strains of Stravinsky's music filled the air; Chekhov's languid characters appeared on West End stages; Society dressed in exotic costumes inspired by Sergei Diaghilev's astonishing Ballets Russes. Time seemed to be slipping ever faster past. Roger Fry's exhibition 'Manet and the Post-Impressionists' opened to public outrage at the Grafton Gallery in the winter of 1910. Two years later, a second exhibition of Post-Impressionism (now containing contributions from English artists inspired by the first) barely raised an eyebrow. Everything seemed fragile. The *Titanic*'s sinking in April 1912 blindsided a society that thought itself technologically invincible, and the disaster, remembered Cincie Asquith, 'loomed . . . large in one's life for months'.[37] Invasion fears blossomed: Lord Roberts began campaigning for a Home Defence Army to protect England against the Germans. Summering at Baden-Baden in 1912 with Cincie, Mary noted with unease the effect of such speeches when reported in the German press. Only that morning, her German doctor had asked her in a truculent tone 'if there was going to be a war in the spring . . . they are persistently, and absolutely convincing themselves that we want to fight them', she reported to Arthur.[38]

In Baden-Baden, Cincie showed Mary a passage in the memoirs of Charles Greville, the celebrated diarist of the Regency and early Victorian years, concerning their ancestor the 'Third Earl'. Mary was thrilled to recognize in Egremont's patronage and open-handed hospitality qualities that 'are me!', surprised that they stemmed 'from my paternal English (stiff shy English) and not from my Franco-Irish (Celtic! Red rag to Balf) side!'[39] Mary was fifty, with married children, and now with grandchildren (Cincie's son John was born in 1911 and Ego and Letty's son David in 1912). In 1913 Guy Charteris became engaged to Eddy's niece, Frances Tennant, another example, commented Mary, of the way in which 'we Wyndhams . . . have dipped into the Tennant family as our marriage Lucky Bag'.[40]

Over the years, Mary and Stanway had melded into one another: the house was 'a kind of material envelope – a shell – exactly fitted to your personality', declared Arthur;[41] 'a golden beehive of mellow stone and yellow grass with beautiful children and grandchildren swarming in and out', said Detmar Blow.[42] 'I am simply absorbed in happiness over my family!' Mary told Arthur on a September's afternoon in 1912, writing from the warmth of her 'boudoir' as rain beat against the windowpanes. The fire was crackling in the hall, where Mary had arranged chairs for the 'young females' to work and read; the boys were playing stump cricket in the barn; her mother was writing letters in her bedroom. As the house hummed with quiet activity, Stanway seemed to Mary 'a wonderful centre of Love and Vitality (Life) Radiance and Harmony, and I begin to see dimly that I have done something, or that to speak more humbly and truly . . . something has been done thro' me, for to have built up this home life is something and to have the radiating centre from which people can draw something and pass it on, is like having founded a watering place!'[43]

The house was short on creature comforts, even cleanliness: 'every horizontal object wears a coat of dust, like a chinchilla. It's a wonder the inmates look as clean as they do,' commented Letty's sister Lady Diana Manners in 1909,[44] and Mary was constantly battling to find enough space for all her guests. 'When a man's tired he rests, when Mary Elcho['s] tired she moves furniture,' Mary told Arthur.[45] In 1913, Lord Wemyss (under some pressure from Connor, Gosford's agent, whom Mary called 'my Scotch champion')[46] agreed to install electricity at Stanway and increase the Elchos' annual income to £1,000. When Connor telephoned to tell her the good news, Mary, at first so relieved she could only weep, then poured all her energies into cajoling, bludgeoning and wheedling her husband, father-in-law and agent into agreeing to build Stanway a new wing, frantic not to let this dreamlike opportunity slip out of her grasp.[47] The resulting extension, built by Detmar Blow, was torn down by Mary's prescient grandson shortly after the Second World War, realizing it to be the only way the house might survive as a private residence.

Looking down over the assorted scrum of people at breakfast at these weekends, Mary was fond of saying that Stanway was like a lunatic asylum, although 'sometimes . . . and this is probably true, I think it's I who am a mad woman keeping house for the sane . . .' she wrote.[48] Certainly she anticipated this reaction from her 'worldly' friends (Ettie Desborough and the like) when, in the spring of 1913, she hosted Hugo's latest mistress, Lady Angela Forbes,[49] and her two young daughters at Stanway for several weeks, even going so far as to help Angela enrol the elder, Marigold, in the same Malvern girls' boarding school attended by her own daughters Mary Charteris and Bibs.[50] Angela was a chain-smoking, brash, hard-living divorcée. Mary could not resist the challenge – 'this is a very hard nut ahead', she said, with an ill-concealed glimmer of excitement.[51] Even so, she recognized the difficulties her instinct could lead her into. 'It's very awkward living with a leg in each world. Some day I shall split and shriek like a mandrake!' she admitted to Arthur.[52]

In the same letter, Mary reported the 'great excitement' of the engagement of George and Sibell's son Percy 'Perf' Wyndham to Diana Lister, daughter of Tommy and Charty Ribblesdale, just two weeks after they met. The wedding six weeks later was remarkable as a grand convention of 'the Wyndham clan – all so beautiful and so well pleased with each other', commented an onlooker.[53] The great hope was that Perf's marriage would restore life to Clouds. Percy's death had left Clouds 'awful – haunted by vivid memories, presences you may almost say of Papa and Mama, myself! You! My children, Madeline, Pamela, Guy and all', Mary told Arthur.[54] Madeline Wyndham, having handed over the reins to Sibell, 'naturally won't' play the chatelaine 'and Sibell apparently can't!' said Mary. 'Let the young people in I say and give them their heads.'[55]

Six weeks after Perf's wedding George took a trip to Paris, accompanied by his mistress Gay Plymouth and her daughter, and planning to meet up with Hilaire Belloc while he was there. George's time in Paris was nigh perfect: he hunted through antiquarian bookshops for books for his library (which needed only the inscriptions on the walls to be complete); and enjoyed the late-spring sunshine on walks with Gay and Phyllis in the gardens of Fontainebleau.

At the Ledoyen he dined, quite alone, on potage Saint-Germain – a fresh pea soup; a whole brill in mushroom sauce; a cold quail stuffed with truffles, garnished with aspic and parsley, with a salad; hot green asparagus, as thick and fat as the white ones, with a sauce mousseline; a cold salade russe, without ham but with a 'perfect' mayonnaise; and the best strawberries that he could ever remember eating. The wine was a Richebourg of 1890 that was to other wines, George told Belloc, 'in the relation of Homer and Shakespeare to other poets'. He considered it a perfect evening: 'No Jew was there. No American. No Englishman but myself. I had struck an oasis of civilization. There were few women, and that was fit. For how few women understand?'[56]

With hindsight, George might have avoided the mousseline. Four days later, he was dead of a heart attack. The official version, in his *Life*, is of an entirely respectable demise, nagging heart pains, morphine injections by a nurse, a turn for the worse. The unofficial version is that George died not in the arms of a nurse in the Hôtel Lotti but in those of a prostitute in a brothel.[57] Perf Wyndham went to bring his father's body back to England. 'He looks very peaceful and very beautiful,' he told Sibell. 'England has lost someone as valuable and precious to Her, as He was dear to us – it is an unfathomable callamity [sic] – but callamities must be borne and endured.'[58]

Wilfrid Blunt dedicated his poem 'To a Happy Warrior' to George, sending copies to the Wyndhams. It immortalized George as poet, warrior, lover, chivalric knight of old, 'the ultimate man . . . Whose keener sight / Grasped the full vision of Time's masterplan'. Mary wrote to Wilfrid immediately, excusing the scrappy paper that was all she had to hand:

I think yr poem to George most beautiful – quite magnificent &
very fine – I am *so glad* you have done it . . . you speak of God
& Paradise but it's *the* most gloriously Pagan thing that I've ever
read but then I feel that *you* & George and I *are* pagans really . . .
there is no mawkish sentiment about you, no cloying & seeing
thro coloured glass – but the broad horizon & the big sweep . . .[59]

In the last decade of his life, George had separated from his party's
leadership, moving ever rightwards. Yet his campaigns for tariff
reform, naval reform and as a Ditcher had shown what influence
the crusading knight could still wield. Wilfrid Blunt considered
'George's politics . . . the least creditable part of him . . . it was
George's other side that I loved and admired'.[60] But among his
wider circle there was genuine disbelief that George, barely fifty,
would not return from political exile to a second act. 'I think all
must feel that he has been cut off at a time of life when there was
still before him the hope and promise of greater things in the future
than ever in the past. These are the great tragedies of life,'[61] said
Arthur in a eulogy delivered to a hushed House of Commons.
Hilaire Belloc thought George's death the 'end of honesty in public
life'.[62]

Clouds and almost £20,000 of death duties still owing from
Percy Wyndham's death passed to Perf Wyndham, although George's
foresight in insuring his own life for £30,000 meant that the estate
was not financially crippled from the start. A stained-glass window
in St Mary's Church in East Knoyle was dedicated to George by
his erstwhile parliamentary colleagues. In just two years, the
charmed circle of the Wyndhams had suffered two shattering blows.
Sending Mary '*fondest* Love' on her birthday that year, Mananai
added: 'These anniversaries make one *sad* yet one can be grateful
& look back on happy times all of us together in the past.'[63]

More change came a year later when Lord Wemyss died, aged
ninety-five, on 30 June 1914. He had tied up almost everything in
trusts, even Gosford and Stanway's household effects. Almost the

only thing that Hugo received outright was his father's London house, 23 St James's Place. He promptly sold it.[64] Mary's 'General Account' was raised to £4,500 a year and Hugo's personal allowance to £2,000.[65] But death duties which obliged the estate to pay out £28,000 a year for eight years[66] and personal legacies (Lord Wemyss's will had over twenty codicils) made Hugo, paradoxically, feel more insecure financially than he had ever done before. He threatened to let Stanway at once and move to Gosford. '[A]t present the Change of name seems only to have brought Trouble & the sense of fresh responsibilities & burdens and less freedom. . .!' Mary told Wilfrid, adding, 'I simply *hate* my new name I feel that Romance & Poetry have fled with my old *pretty* name!'[67] It took Lady Elcho of Stanway years to become accustomed to the cold, hard grandeur of the Countess of Wemyss of Gosford, and she often found herself absentmindedly signing off letters as 'Melcho'.

Stanway's reprieve came at a greater cost to Mary than she could possibly have imagined. Two days before Lord Wemyss's death came the news of the assassination of Archduke Franz Ferdinand, in the faraway crumbling Balkans. On 23 July 1914, Austria-Hungary issued an impossible ultimatum to Serbia. The house of cards built on secrecy and paranoia began tumbling down. The ten days that followed were a blur of ultimatums; crisis talks between the diplomats of the Great Powers; mobilization orders issued, halted, partially revoked, reissued. Germany came out in support of Austria, Russia in support of Serbia, France in support of Russia. Sir Edward Grey appealed to Germany, through its Ambassador Prince Lichnowsky, for peace; the Germans tried to persuade Sir Edward Goschen, Britain's Ambassador in Berlin, to stay neutral if an attack on France was routed through Belgium. For this was the basis of Germany's Schlieffen Plan, which was intended to wipe out French resistance in a matter of weeks. And Britain, since the 1839 Treaty of London, had sworn to uphold Belgian neutrality at all costs. So, suddenly, war went from a remote possibility, which allowed Grey to spend his usual Sunday in Wiltshire on 26 July, to a probability in the week that followed, to a certainty, as Grey left the Foreign Office, brushing off in the doorway Prince Lichnowsky who had come to make a final appeal, and went to address the Commons in an historic speech on 3 August. 'Mr. Speaker,' he said, as the cheers around him died down, 'Last week I stated that we were working for peace not only for this country, but to preserve the peace of Europe. Today – but events move so rapidly that it is exceedingly difficult to state with technical accuracy the actual state of affairs – it is clear that the peace of Europe cannot be preserved.'

Slowly and clearly, Grey laid out before the Commons the ententes and alliances to which Britain was party. He stressed that no secret engagement was to be sprung upon the country. He sketched for the MPs massed around him the nature of the 1839 Treaty by which Britain had promised to defend Belgium's neutrality, reminding them that Gladstone himself had upheld it some fifty years before:

> We worked for peace up to the last moment, and beyond the last moment. How hard, how persistently and how earnestly we strove for peace last week, the House will see from the papers that are before it. But that is over so far as the peace of Europe is concerned. We are now face to face with a situation and all the consequences which it may yet have to unfold.[68]

The only step that Britain could take was to issue Germany with an ultimatum: unless Germany guaranteed Belgian neutrality by midnight the following night, Britain would declare war. So Britain did. That evening, so it was said, an exhausted Edward Grey stood at the window of his room in the Foreign Office. The dusk was gathering, and the gloaming pierced by the fireflies of warm yellow gas as the lamp-lighters moved steadily from one streetlight to the next. 'The lamps are going out all over Europe,' Grey said, turning to the man who stood beside him. 'We shall not see them lit again in our lifetime.'[69]

TWENTY-NINE

MCMXIV

Early in the evening of 4 August 1914, as news of the British ultimatum spread, crowds began to mass in London's political heartland. Motor-cars carrying men and women in evening dress waving
the Union Jack wound their way slowly among the crowds
thronging Whitehall, Parliament Street, Trafalgar Square and the
Mall. People scaled the plinth of Nelson's Column and pedestals
of Whitehall's statues; spectators eagerly leant out of the windows
of Government offices. Outside Buckingham Palace, where the
Victoria Memorial was 'black with people', the cheering and singing
reached fever pitch at 7 p.m., and again at half-past nine when the
Royal Family appeared on the balcony. In Trafalgar Square, where
two days before Keir Hardie had been shouted down attempting
to address a socialist anti-war convention, the ebullient crowd was
provoked to fresh heights of enthusiasm as the occasional field
gun or ammunition wagon lumbered by. But, as the hour of the
ultimatum approached, a 'profound silence fell upon the crowd
. . . Then as the first strokes rang out from the Clock Tower, a vast
cheer burst out and echoed and re-echoed for nearly twenty
minutes. The National Anthem was then sung with an emotion

and solemnity which manifested the gravity and sense of responsibility with which the people regard the great issues before them,'
reported *The Times*.[1]

At 10.45 the following morning, George V signed a formal
proclamation of war against Germany. It is trite but accurate to
say that most people truly thought the war would be 'over by
Christmas'. Earl Kitchener, the hastily appointed War Secretary,
discomfited the Cabinet when he predicted an engagement of
several years. Mary had lunched with Kitchener the day war broke
out. She and Ettie were at Alice Salisbury's house and Kitchener
stopped by, having been urgently recalled from Dover – where
he had been about to depart for Egypt – to Downing Street. In
other times, the Souls' talk would all have been of this dramatic
development. But as mothers of adult sons their main preoccupation was with their children.[2] That afternoon, Mary made her way
back to Stanway. At Oxford station she bumped into Sibell
Grosvenor on the platform. 'Perf is getting ready,' said Sibell,
ashen-faced.[3]

As a lieutenant in the Coldstream Guards, Perf was a member
of Britain's Regular Army, of which six infantry divisions and five
cavalry brigades were deployed to the Western Front as part of the
British Expeditionary Force (the BEF)[4] in the late summer of 1914.
These professional soldiers termed themselves 'the Old
Contemptibles', after an apocryphal story that the Kaiser had vowed
to wipe out Field Marshal Sir John French's 'contemptible little
army'. By the end of the year the Old Contemptibles had nearly all
been mown down at the battles of Mons, Le Cateau, the Aisne and
Ypres. The BEF was now composed of the Territorial Army's
yeomanry and Kitchener's volunteers, who flocked in their thousands to his imperious finger. Three hundred thousand men enlisted
in the first month of the war, exceeding by 50 per cent Kitchener's
target. The total number of volunteers for the first week of
September 1914 alone was 174,901.[5]

Conscription was not introduced until 1916, when all men

between the ages of eighteen and forty-one were called up. Instinctively, the British revolted against it. 'It is repugnant to the mental constitution of a freedom-loving people and the British nation would never stand it,' Eddy Tennant declared, addressing Liverpool's Liberal Reform Club on the subject of Home Defence in 1913.[6] Hugo, blinded by patriotic fervour, was not of this mind. The day after war broke out, Mary breakfasted with him in Stanway's dining room. He was silent behind his newspaper, except for the occasional snort of disgust. After an hour or so, Angela Forbes came into the room. Hugo looked up. 'I'm afraid I've done something rather rash,' he told his mistress. 'I've dismissed all the servants.'[7]

Hugo had told his male household staff they must join the army, or be sacked. Mary was horrified: beyond Hugo's typical disregard for her and for the obvious logistical difficulties ('I shall have no chauffeur, no stableman, no odd man to carry the coals! I may have 100 parlour maids but someone must carry the coals!' she protested to Balfour, helplessly, seeking his advice),[8] she felt that it smacked of the chain-gang. Her footman's elderly father had 'begged' his son not to go,[9] but both Stanway's footmen, the odd-man, two gardeners, one carpenter and four keepers enlisted in that first wave.[10]

All over the country, aristocrats and squires were vigorously enjoining their tenants to fight, with generous terms: promising to keep jobs open; to house families rent free; even to pay them part of their wages. Charlie Adeane threw himself into the campaign at Babraham.[11] 'Are you a man or a mouse?' asked Lord Lonsdale in a recruiting poster of his own devising distributed throughout the Lake District. 'If I had twenty sons, I should be ashamed if every one of them did not go to the front when his time came,' said Lord Derby, the chairman of the West Lancashire Territorial Association.[12]

This was doubtless true. The sons of the elite who were not already, like Ego, part of the armed forces – Ego had held a commission in the Gloucester Yeomanry, a Territorial Army cavalry regiment, since 1912, and left Stanway to join them on 6 August 1914 – mostly joined up as soon as they could. Bim Tennant, who had quit Winchester in June, planning to spend several months in Germany before entering the Diplomatic Service, joined the Grenadier Guards at the age of seventeen – having, said Pamela, 'the distinction of being the youngest Wykehamist to take up arms in defence of his country', and still a year below the official age for enlistment.[13] Guy Charteris was gazetted into the Shropshire Light Infantry, subsequently moving to the Scots Guards. With difficulty Mary persuaded Yvo Charteris – who on 4 August had stood in a London street with shining eyes, reading the proclamation of war pasted to a lamppost[14] – to see out his final term at Eton. In the early spring of 1915 he joined the King's Royal Regiment, and then the Grenadier Guards. Raymond Asquith's initial decision not to join up was seen as a dereliction of duty. By 1915 the pressure of the metaphorical white feather was such that he joined the Grenadier Guards as well.[15]

War offered the patricians an opportunity to lead the country that half a century of political reform, ideological advancement and agricultural crisis had taken away. They had been abused by the radical press and politicians for their reactionary attitudes, their idleness, their parasitical lifestyles. This was 'the supreme opportunity' for an embattled class 'to prove themselves and to justify their existence . . . to demonstrate conclusively that they were not the redundant reactionaries of radical propaganda, but the patriotic class of knightly crusaders and chivalric heroes, who would defend the national honour and the national interest in the hour of its greatest trial'.[16] All their years of hunting and shooting, and controlling and caring for their tenantry, had equipped them to perfection. And so, infamously, Ettie's son Julian Grenfell, a professional soldier, and a warrior so bloodthirsty that it would not be a surprise to discover him cannibalistic, declared from Ypres in October 1914: 'I *adore* war. It is like a big picnic . . .'[17]

Aristocratic women were also enthusiastic about their war effort.

They besieged the London hospitals, asking for positions as probationers. Shops selling domestic uniforms experienced a run on caps and aprons.[18] First-aid classes were set up in the ballrooms of the great houses of London; plans were made to turn stately homes into convalescent homes and hospitals; and at Charing Cross Station a line of Rolls-Royces idled as the ladies inside them waited to greet and transport Belgian refugees arriving on the trains.[19] Stanway's Belgian refugees, Monsieur Beyart, his wife, his mother-in-law and his three-year-old twin girls, were installed above the stables, to the disgruntlement of the coachman Prew and his wife, who were induced to move.[20] Mary described M. Beyart as a 'charming Belgian notaire',[21] but in fact the Beyarts became notable for their 'ingratitude', said Angela Forbes.[22]

Angela herself used Stanway as a dumping ground for her children while she made her way to France to volunteer in a hospital. A few months later, armed with £8 worth of provisions from Fortnum & Mason, and, in her own words, 'hardly' able to 'make a cup of tea',[23] she set up a canteen in the waiting room of Boulogne's railway station, which became known as Angelina's, and its proprietor as 'la dame avec la cigarette' for her largesse with her Woodbines.[24] Angelina's was totally shambolic – for some time, washing up was done in one tin pail, in which Angela also washed her hair – and a roaring success.[25] Angela's raucous *Memories and Base Details* records the throb and thrum of wartime Boulogne – the 'gigantic hub of the war machine' – where hospitals and canteens mushroomed and trainloads of soldiers rattled in at odd hours. There was red tape to battle, generals to wheedle, the Red Cross to be prevailed upon for more supplies and petrol. Angela found the war invigorating – better for her than the days of peace.[26]

Angela was one of many women previously accustomed to hopping across the Channel for gambling at Biarritz or golf at Le Touquet who now made the journey equipped with bandages and tin cups, setting up makeshift hospitals, ambulance units and

canteens.[27] The Duchess of Westminster and Lady Dudley established field hospitals at Le Touquet; the dowager Duchess of
Sutherland, whose ambulance unit was driven out of Belgium by
the German advance, set up a 160-bed hospital in Calais. Further
afield, Lady Muriel Paget, wife of Arthur, organized an Anglo-
Russian hospital on the Eastern Front. These redoubtable grandes
dames, accustomed to getting their own way through influence and
charm, were wearisome to the authorities in their aristocratic disregard for rules. They were also shameless: in the earliest weeks when
nurses still outnumbered patients, 'body-snatching' was common
as ambulances from competing hospitals vied to get the best cases.[28]
France was not considered suitable for their daughters: the injuries,
fresh from the battlefield, too gruesome for them, their virginity
too precious to risk. Publicly prim reference was made to men 'not
being able to control themselves'. Privately, there must have been
concern that young women, freed from the confines of their
upbringing, might throw off their own moral code.

Stanway was turned down by the authorities as unsuitable for a
hospital.[29] A Voluntary Aid Detachment hospital was set up at
nearby Winchcombe. The VAD's volunteers, who provided field
nursing services, were predominantly middle- and upper-class
women. Medical professionals were initially sceptical, believing
them to be 'playing' at a serious job, but many volunteers disproved
them, and did excellent service in England and in France. The
Winchcombe Hospital was a short drive from Stanway in the pony-
trap. Eliza Wedgwood, a nearby neighbour, was Commandant. Mary
and her daughters (including Bibs, just twelve in 1914) all volun-
teered, as did Mananai's eldest, twenty-five-year-old Pamela Adeane,
who stayed at Stanway for several months before being reluctantly
dissuaded from going out to France ('I think everybody thinks
France is too much for me, perhaps so'). She moved to the Queen's
Hospital, a military hospital in Frognal, North London specializing
in 'heads & jaws'. It was hard work, requiring immense courage
and a stomach of steel. Pamela thrived there: 'I believe one is more

useful in a military hospital . . . they do wonderful things here.'[30] She lost a lover in the war, spent it nursing and did not marry until 1919, when she was nearly thirty.

Winchcombe's atmosphere was informal and convivial. Cynthia chatted to Sister Awde as she stirred porridge on night duty; Bibs peeled potatoes in the kitchen, sulking at not being considered old enough to help in the wards. When funds ran low, Mrs Patrick Campbell organized a charity matinee in London that raised £400, enough to keep the hospital going until the end of the war.[31] In *Family Record*, Mary presented a rose-tinted view of the hospital as the family's second home, with Hugo taking convalescents for drives.[32] In fact, Hugo was mostly with Angela in France, while Angela's daughters remained at Stanway: 'he told me that he didn't care when I went to London[,] that he didn't mean to be there much!' Mary told Arthur in the spring of 1915.[33] On the rare occasions he returned, he was 'carping' and 'critical' about efforts at Winchcombe and Stanway, conducting small feuds with Eliza Wedgwood.[34] Mary reproached him for his behaviour when he was 'so full of admiration & sympathy about everything Angela does'.[35] She felt keenly that Stanway's war effort was less glamorous than Angela's.[36]

Pamela Tennant recalled the war's opening months as possessing a curious sense of unreality, like 'the early morning, before the world was numb with pain and broken, before things were stale and tired as they became'.[37] Both Bim and fifteen-year-old Kit, a naval cadet at Dartmouth, were still too young for combat – an officer could not officially go to the Front until the age of nineteen. There is a stillness to Pamela's descriptions of herself at the time, almost as if she were frozen. Reading her account in her memoirs of the mothers who 'lay awake' at night and 'listened' to 'the quiet sound of feet, the measured beat of soldiers going by, company after company', thinking of what lay ahead, the sense is that she was speaking of her own experience.[38]

In this limbo, one of the most curious incidents of Pamela's life took place. In October 1914, she wrote to Mary of 'The adopted baby': 'very good and nice – as far as he goes', in some ways even 'better than [a baby] of my own . . . for one thing, it is such a relief . . . to be able to hear with perfect equanimity of a Baby having a rise of temperature!' Joking aside, Pamela said, 'he is a great solace. I love babies – I like their ways & their ridiculous hands, & perfect feet', and he had 'incidental value' for her 'in deflecting some of dear [Nanny] Trussler's zeal from Stephen'.[39] This is Pamela's only letter to Mary mentioning this child, whose name was Oliver Hope.

Pamela had long had a habit of scooping up children. Bim's 'village boys' were often more frequently at Wilsford than in their own homes. Pamela's granddaughter, the author Emma Tennant, has recounted her surprise on hearing from an elderly villager that her grandmother had 'adopted four children in all: Mary and Tossie and Roger', in addition to Oliver.[40] In Pamela's relatively few surviving letters to Eddy, she mentions at least two instances of taking in a child when their parents could not cope – the bigamous curate's son,[41] and after the war a small South African girl whose mother, abandoned by her husband, was struggling to maintain her family and hold down her job at the War Office.[42] Oliver was different. He was the only one of Pamela's patchwork assortment of strays who actually lived full-time at Wilsford, and the only one left an annuity in her will – £50 per annum.[43]

Wilsford School – which Oliver attended briefly from summer 1918 to winter 1919 – records in its register his birth date as 7 July 1912, meaning he was just over two when he was adopted.[44] The official story, insofar as there is one, is that Oliver was the son of a 'tinker woman' named Hope who died giving birth in Salisbury Infirmary.[45] A search for boys born to a woman of that name between 1910 and 1915 yields no results in the England and Wales birth registers. While it is not impossible that the birth simply escaped registration (particularly in a Gypsy community), the hospital element makes a record more likely. It adds to the mystery surrounding this child, whose very name sounds like a fairytale,

and whose story peters out into a welter of rumour. He entered
the Merchant Navy at a very young age (either running away, or
being sent by Christopher, according to who is telling the story),[46]
and then disappeared so effectively that most of Pamela's descendants did not know of his existence.[47] The surmise, by Emma Tennant,
is that round-faced, dark-haired Oliver, similar in looks to both
Bim and Pamela, was in fact Bim's illegitimate son, from a fling
with an artist's model when he was little more than fifteen,[48] already
very good looking and advanced for his years.[49] While unproven,
it is entirely plausible that Pamela would have scooped up her son's
illegitimate child. A decade on, she tried to do exactly that with an
illegitimate daughter born to her son David with the actress
Hermione Baddeley.[50] The timing – taking on this child exactly as
Bim faced danger – may be coincidental, but it lends force to the
supposition.

In September, when the war was barely a month old, Perf
Wyndham was 'shot *dead* through the head',[51] leading his men on
a charge out of a wood at the battle of the Aisne. 'How *glorious*
the death is,' said Mananai, '*no* suffering, no *knowing* he must die.'[52]
Bim echoed these sentiments in a poem that Pamela distributed
to all the family:

> Father and son have not been long asunder
> And joy in heaven leaves mortals sad and wan
> His death-salute was the artillery thunder
> Praise be to God for such an Englishman![53]

Balfour heard the news from an acquaintance while lunching at
the Travellers Club. He waited to see confirmation in the casualty
lists published daily in *The Times* before writing to Mary. 'We live
in the perpetual knowledge that our friends are in hourly peril . . .
and we bear the news [of their deaths] as best as we can,' he said.[54]
In those early days, when death was still a shock, not yet a near
inevitability, it was strangely easy to believe in its heroic glamour.

Cynthia Asquith later wondered how she had mourned these losses so intensely while still swallowing 'the rather high-faluting platitude that it was all right for them – that they were not to be pitied, but were safe, unassailable, young, and glamorous for ever'.[55] Mary found it difficult from the start. After hours writing to her family in sorrow and loss over Perf's death, she wrote to Arthur last of all, with 'a pen made of lead', unable to dissemble further:

> it doesn't seem like sending youths to war, it seems more like a shambles . . . despite one's feelings of pride that they should 'die in their glory' the lads that will never grow old . . . there are times when the feeling of 'exaltation' ebbs and fades away and leaves one feeling utterly blank and flat and miserable and grim. It seems such a sickening waste . . .[56]

In a devastating postscript, Perf Wyndham's will provided that if he died without issue his heir would be Dick Wyndham, the younger of Guy Wyndham's two sons. He thus doubly disinherited Guy on the one hand and on the other Dick's elder brother George – whom, the family presumed, he had overlooked simply because he got on better with Dick, and never thought this provision in the will would come into effect. 'Dear Percy never realized that when a will is made it is facing the possibility of death at *any* time . . .' said Mananai. Clouds now belonged to Dick – barely eighteen years old. Guy and Minnie, who moved into Clouds with their teenage son (George was already serving in the army), were merely housekeepers until Dick came of age. It was a 'crushing sadness . . . a mistake & absolutely contrary to the spirit of Papa's & George's Wills & in direct opposition to their wishes', lamented Mananai, who of all the sisters felt Guy's misfortune the most keenly. 'I cannot bear to think that people might think this had been done intentionally & that there had been a split in our *united* family,' she told Mary.[57]

Mary busied herself, moving between London, where Yvo's

Grenadier Guards were stationed in Chelsea Barracks – and Ego and Guy Charteris's billets around the country. 'I am living – here there & everywhere, like a soldier,' Mary reported to Wilfrid Blunt in an undated letter written from Cadogan Square,[58] recently returned from seeing Ego in Newbury, where Letty had taken 'tiny little lodgings . . . like a dolls house' near by. The night before Mary and Mary Charteris had dined with them, Ego 'so *beautiful* in his khaki', and George Vernon, a member of the Coterie and like another son to the family. Mary had brought down a picnic of 'grouse! & *roses & champagne* . . . we had leopard skins stretched on a sofa, the piano acted as a sideboard . . . & we had a *feast* & talked camp shop – the arrival of transport, horses rifles – & the death of all the young friends who are giving their lives in France – it was a wonderful evening.'[59] A few months later, Mary and Bibs visited Ego in Hunstanton, staying at the Le Strange Arms. This time (in a turn of events that seems delightfully apposite given the du Maurieresque name of the inn), Bibs was suspected by locals of signalling to the enemy when she left her window open, the light on in her bedroom and the blind flapping in the wind.[60]

At Cadogan Square, Mary started a 'War Salon' to amuse Yvo,[61] filling the house with interesting guests – Hilaire Belloc, the *Observer*'s editor J. L. Garvin, Curzon and Balfour. At one of these gatherings in 1915, Cincie invented a new game: to discover everyone's secret complex. To general hilarity, she decided that Balfour, now advising Asquith's government on defence, and attending meetings of the War Council, formed in November 1914, 'was obsessed with the notion that he had caused the War and was feeling, secretly, very worried about it'.[62] At another, the Elchos, Charles Whibley and Lord Hugh Cecil debated Grey's Commons speech that had brought England into the war. Whibley attacked Grey 'for shilly-shallying . . . he didn't even know himself which way his own speech was going to sum up'; Lord Hugh maintained that the war was 'the inevitable, logical conclusion of the Entente Cordiale', the speech 'an absolute masterpiece' of 'Mark Antony oratory' which was the only way Grey could secure the support of the Radicals for the war. Cincie agreed with Lord Hugh on every point.[63]

Mary found it difficult to engage in such discussions. From the war's very beginning, she had felt desolate. 'Hopeless' reports of the war alarmed her – the 'parallell [sic] lines & the germans [sic] living like trapdoor spiders – with the hills armed with Howitzers on cement floors!'[64] She worried about Britain's shortage of artillery shells which had been apparent almost from the war's outbreak, and fretted that she was not doing enough war work, which might serve as talismanic protection for her own sons.[65] More than ever, she was drawn to her boxes of papers, but this correspondence was capable of making her break down, sounding 'so still and small a note, so faint and futile in the midst of the bloody horrors and the Hellish Din'. 'Are all letters flattery?' she asked Arthur. 'If not, they have built me a pretty monument, but are they worth keeping? Who cares? And does anything matter? Except explosive *Big* artillery! The one thing we have not got.'[66]

In the early spring of 1915, with Mary '"out of sorts" mentally and physically',[67] her doctor, Halliwell, prescribed a rest cure at Stanway. For three weeks, she was confined to her room in total isolation. Yvo was highly amused to hear of this latest development: 'How is your languid self', he wrote to his sister Mary,

and how is Stanway, and how pray is that strange recluse or unspeakable monster, whom none may look on, closeted and communing with her spirit, dwelling on the heights until she emerge a full Mahatma? I suppose in the silence of the night the house echoes to the sound of beds, wardrobes and all manner of furniture being trundled round the room, and again to the rustlings of many sheet and blanket 'manias'. She will awake after a month and find Mockett [the butler] waiting with a sheaf of telegrams to the effect that her three sons are at the Front, her eldest daughter doing time for card-sharping, her second eloped with a young cavalry officer, her youngest truant from school and God knows where. But she will have forgotten them, so what matter? With renewed zest she will wheel the grand piano round in the drawing room and wander off over the hills with a pack of wild and aggravated chows, till Stanway falls in ruins about her. What a curious sight Halliwell must be, entering the forbidden room like the Steward of Glamis?[68]

Shortly afterwards, on a cool April night, Mary, Mary Charteris, Bibs and Letty waved off 'the Gallant Glittering Gloucesters'[69] to Egypt in preparation for the Allied naval attack on Turkish forces in the Dardanelles. Allied control of the strategically vital strait would allow munitions to be shipped through to Russia. Britain's Government also hoped that victory in the Dardanelles might persuade the neutral states of Greece, Bulgaria and Romania to join the Allied side, and provoke the collapse of the tottering Ottoman Empire. The night before the Gloucesters left, the two Marys, Bibs and Letty had dined with Ego and his friend and fellow officer Tom Strickland.[70] As part of their kit, the two had been issued with 'little bottles of iodine' with instructions to apply instantly 'to a fresh wound'. 'It would hurt a great deal to paint all round a very large wound,' remarked Ego wryly.[71] Letty followed them out a week later, taking nineteen-year-old Mary Charteris with her as a companion, ostensibly to do VAD work. Two months later, Mary returned from Egypt to announce that she was engaged to Tom Strickland. They married in Egypt, in December 1915. The coincidence that their daughter should be married in Egypt was not lost on either Mary or Wilfrid.[72]

A week after Ego's departure, Mary wrote to Arthur, distressed about the Gloucesters' shambolic artillery:

these men have been mobilized since the very day war broke out, they contain the flower of England's nobility (what a flowery Daily Mail phrase) . . . and the flower of the darling yeoman men who

left their crops – and their sheep at the most critical moment . . .
they go with guns bought from (scrapped by?) the Germans after
the Boer War. Now my dear! You are in with everything . . . all
their councils and hob nob and gossip with Kitchener the God of
War and with all the Bosses, just you order some nice little (or
big) right little tight little guns to be dispatched at once, to reach
them before their horses are fit.[73]

Balfour had been on the Shell Committee, as the Cabinet Munitions
of War Committee was known, since Easter, working with Lloyd
George to rectify the 'deplorable' munitions output.[74] Within weeks
the 'Shell Crisis' and disaster at Gallipoli would force Asquith into
a Coalition government. Balfour was brought back into office
proper, as First Lord of the Admiralty, replacing Winston Churchill,
disgraced after the Dardanelles.[75]

Arthur had always held the political fates of Mary's male family
members in his hands. Now, in a sense, he held their lives. Yet the
tenor of Mary's relationship with him during the war years was
not markedly different to that of the decade preceding. At Downing
Street, shut out by Asquith's infatuation with the young Venetia
Stanley, a close friend of Asquith's daughter Violet, who had become
the Prime Minister's confidante and obsession, Margot agitated to
be told official secrets in order to boost her own sense of self. Mary
discussed developments with Arthur and was honest in her views.
She only ever pressed him for information when it directly
concerned her sons, and even then her tone was measured and
humorous. She understood if Arthur could not give her information. She knew that, if he were able, he would.

Many women – and men – were capable of compartmental-
izing to mourn loved ones lost in a war negligently handled by
generals that they nonetheless believed was just and necessary.
Looking back, it is incredible, near impossible, that women of
this generation and class watched their sons being sacrificed in
a war governed by their husbands and lovers without ever once

breaking faith. Pamela and Mary were two of these women. Yet, for different reasons, they did not. For Mary, Balfour was only ever trying to improve a situation rendered parlous by the neglect of others, drawn back into service by the need of the country. She mourned when he was brought back to the Admiralty: 'so weary, reluctantly obliged to shoulder a heavy burden because all the nation trusts him'.[76]

After the war, Pamela helped Grey write *Twenty-Five Years*, his staunch, quiet defence of his conduct as Foreign Minister that took Britain into the war. That she seems never once to have considered Grey culpable is unsurprising; even had such thoughts occurred to her, she would have excised them before they took root. She defended her own, even down to rubbishing Margot's criticisms of Grey's and Eddy's wartime fishing habit. Margot proposed they should use the time in visiting the war wounded instead. Pamela replied, 'I admit that the surface appearance of this fishing business, now, in Wartime, is ridiculous . . . I used to think the same as you – till I realized what a conventional view it was. It is not self-indulgence on his part, but relaxation – & [Eddy] needs relaxation . . . his way is in fishing, yours is in buying new clothes, mine is studying Psychological aspect of things.' Unsurprisingly, Margot underlined the section alluding to her love of clothes in red ink.[77]

In her own published works after the war Pamela maintained that the conflict had been glorious. 'War . . . meant for Bim Romance,' she wrote. 'He had been playing at it, and dreaming of it, and writing about it . . . now it was his, and it brought him freedom, and self-expression, and joy . . . it was this that met him on the threshold of manhood, something as great as this. Not only illusive pleasure and the empty tyranny of little things . . .'[78] If her private façade differed, it was only that Pamela did not engage with the war at all: not the munitions crisis; the changeovers in power; or the failings of the generals. She kept aloof, within her own world, frozen until her son came back.

Both Yvo – 'a joy-dispenser', said Cincie[79] – and Bim were part of a frenetic youth, squeezing out every moment of their lives. Pamela recalled that time as days of 'colour and purpose' for Bim,[80] bombing around town in a two-seater crammed with people;[81] arriving at Queen Anne's Gate in a flurry of hairdressers, tailors, buttonholes of white gardenias 'in silver-foil and cotton wool', telephone ringing off the hook as he made plans for the next dance, the next dinner, the next play.[82] They attended parties thrown by the American George Gordon Moore, nicknamed the 'Dances of Death', dancing all night to jazz and Hawaiian bands, fuelled by 'rivers of champagne' and surrounded by 'mountains of red and white camellias', believing, as Iris Tree, another Coterie member, wrote, that there was 'something of myth and legendary revival, the glory of Greece, the grandeur of Rome' in their antics.[83] By night Diana Manners and Raymond Asquith's wife Katharine doped themselves on morphine and 'chlorers' (chloroform).[84] The Coterie's brittle vivacity and grim humour appalled Cincie. 'I'm sure there is an insidiously corruptive poison in their minds . . . I don't care a damn about their morals and manners, but I do think . . . their anti-cant is really suicidal to happiness,' she said. But Cincie was unusual in her sympathy for her parents' generation, who were 'an object of ridicule' to the Coterie.[85]

Time took on double speed. Within a space of ten months two of Mananai's daughters, Sibell and Madeline Adeane, clad in silk charmeuse and lacy veils progressed up the aisle towards a khaki-clad groom in St Peter's Church, near Babraham.[86] Nineteen-year-old Clare Tennant married Adrian Bethell, an officer she had met barely weeks before in 1915. She was divorced, and remarried to Lionel Tennyson, before the war was out. Margot complained to Pamela that the young were 'uncultivated' and immodest. Pamela defended them:

I think the 'young females' of the present day *as a whole* have shown good quality. They have set to work & they go cheerfully

without the gaieties of the world, which at 17 & 18 are, or might
be looked on, as their right. Clare & her particular little world are
exceptional, thank goodness, & she has a certain little exuberance
of folly & [irreverence] of nature that must bubble to the top, like
scum on ham.[87]

In July 1915, worn out by his exertions, Bim came down to Wilsford
on sick leave. He stayed for a fortnight, quietly recuperating. Pamela
read aloud to her convalescent son. 'Seeing him there again,' she
said, 'among all the serene flowing of the currents of home life
. . . it seemed to his Mother as if there must be some mistake,
there could be no War . . . this must be the Summer Holidays, just
beginning . . .'[88] She took the opportunity to update the weight
chart on which she recorded her family's growth: Bim, David, Kit,
Gan-Gan (for Madeline Wyndham was staying with the family at
the time), Eddy (a mere 9 stone 8 pounds, the same weight as
Madeline Wyndham), Roly, the family dog, and at the bottom,
'Oliver – 2st 4lb'.[89]

A month later, Bim was specially selected to serve at the Front,
despite being just eighteen. Edward Grey was honest with Eddy
Tennant: 'The selection of Bimbo . . . is a great honour & compliment but a great trial for you & Pamela. There is no way out of
the trial & I pray that all may be well.'[90] The drumbeat was
growing ever faster with George Vernon, Guy Wyndham's elder
son George, Julian and Billy Grenfell, Violet Rutland's son John
Manners and Charles Lister, son of the Ribblesdales, all among
the recent dead. Bim left for France barely a week later, with a
photograph of Pamela in his breast pocket. Less than a month
after that, Mary suffered the same blow. She had stayed in London
to be with Yvo, whose leave had been cancelled. In the late afternoon, Yvo, 'dog-tired', took himself to bed for a nap. Mary went
to see Evelyn de Vesci for tea. When she got back to Cadogan
Square at about 7, Yvo answered the door. Still in his 'flame-
coloured, Turkish' dressing gown, his hair tousled with sleep, he

The young officer: a charcoal of Bim in khaki,
by John Singer Sargent.

held a scrap of paper in his hand. 'I've got my warning,' he said 'in a voice tense with suppressed excitement'. All Mary could think was how young her son looked. She telephoned Evelyn. 'Don't let him out of your sight,' said Evelyn, 'not even for a moment.'[91]

Plans were made for a fleeting visit to Gosford, where the rest of the family were making a last visit before the house shut up for the duration of the war; that summer, Connor the agent had made it clear that this was the only way to meet death duties on Lord Wemyss's estate, and that it was 'out of the question' to attempt 'living in two houses'.[92] The night that Mary and Yvo were due to leave, London was cast into confusion by a Zeppelin raid. Mary was dining with Arthur when 'the row' began. 'I am responsible, and the guns are quite inadequate,' said Arthur.[93]

Zeppelins were still an awesome and eerie novelty, their strange beauty illuminated by the copper glow cast across the sky by flaming buildings and the boom of the defensive guns. King's Cross Station was pitch black and plunged into confusion as Mary waited for Yvo, who had been at the theatre with friends.[94] They missed the sleeper, managing to get on a train that left at 4.55 a.m. Yvo slept on the train. Mary could not. '[H]e looked so white and still,' she later recalled, 'and though I said to myself, he is still safe, he is still alive and under my wing, yet all the time as I watched him sleeping so peacefully there lurked beneath the shallow safety of the moment a haunting dreadful fear, and the vision of him, lying stretched out cold and dead.'[95]

They were at Gosford for just hours – arriving late afternoon and leaving at eleven that night. The party was avid for details of the 'Zep' raid. Angela Forbes asked Yvo whether he had been scared. 'Not a bit, after all why should one be presumptuous enough to imagine one would be killed?' Angela thought the reply typical of Yvo: 'he was born with the rare gift of seeing things in perspective'.[96] That afternoon, Yvo went for a walk with Mary Charteris in the woods. The two were close as twins, and Yvo could speak to Mary

more frankly than anyone. 'You know I probably shan't come back?'
he said. 'Oh *don't* say that!' she replied. They both knew the odds[97]
– as everyone there did, and the atmosphere of forced gaiety could
not conceal it. 'Poor Bibs looked too desperately miserable, never
taking her eyes off his face,' said Cincie. That night she slept with
her little sister in their mother's bed.[98] Recollecting Yvo's brief visit
Angela Forbes later spoke of the 'Spartan' courage of parents 'who
did nothing to thwart the enthusiasm of their boys'.[99] It epitomizes
how insensitive Angela could be. For, short of pulling strings to
get them out of combat and into a staff position – which would
be considered a dishonourable and deplorable dereliction of one's
patriotic duty – there was nothing these parents could do to stop
their sons going.

Almost before Mary knew it, the day of Yvo's departure came.
His train was scheduled to leave at 8.30 a.m., and they had a hurried,
early breakfast at Cadogan Square, before making their way through
the crisp autumn morning to Charing Cross. The station was a
scrum, packed with English and Belgian soldiers, nurses in their
starched white uniforms, luggage underfoot, and friends and family
hanging over barriers to see their loved ones off. There Guy Charteris
joined them, and friends of Yvo's, including the 'hell-kitten' and
Coterie member Nancy Cunard. Yvo's kitbag was stuffed so full that
they had had to stand on it to squash it all in, and his mess-tin was
crammed with coffee, sugar and tea. In the mêlée, Mary spotted a
doctor she knew. 'I flew to him and said "Yvo is here,"' she recalled.
'Dr. Atkyns spoke most kindly and said I was to tell Yvo to go to
him if he was ill or if he wanted anything.'[100] Mary was entrusting
her tall fair son, still just eighteen, to the care of anyone she could
find. Just before Yvo stepped up into the carriage, 'he took out of
his pocket the grenade [the ornamental badge worn by the
Grenadiers] off his uniform, which was taken off when the less
conspicuous ones were put on, and thrust it into my hand'.

Mary stood among the waving throng, her arms hanging by her
sides, the grenade clutched in her hand, and watched the train

move slowly off amid clouds of steam. As the train picked up pace, the other officers in Yvo's carriage crowded to the windows to wave goodbye. For a moment Yvo was lost from sight. Then, wrote Mary, 'Yvo leapt high into the air,' allowing Mary 'one more last glimpse of his beloved face'.[101]

THIRTY

The Front

Madeline Wyndham spent the war shuttling between Clouds, Stanway, Babraham and Wilsford to stay with her four surviving children; 'the anxiety is almost more than I sometimes *can bear* . . . all *those* that I love best in the world Mary, Guy, Madeline & Pamela *all* & *each* one on the *rack* of anxiety & of *torture of heart & mind* . . .,' she wrote to Wilfrid Blunt in October 1915, shortly after Yvo's departure.[1] That spring, Mary had visited Clouds, arriving with Guy Wyndham to find their mother 'waiting in the dusky hall; her darling eyes as big as an owl's with anxiety. Two telegrams lay waiting, she had watched them for hours without daring to open them, they were of no importance but I realized from the gulp in Guy's throat, after he had read them, what a strain it is nowadays to get a telegram.'[2]

Half a century later and in a different world, Tommy Lascelles, a Coterie member who considered the Charteris and Tennant families 'the salt of my earth',[3] wrote a cautionary note to his grandsons:[4]

> If you read any of my war letters, you may feel that it wasn't as bad as it has been painted. Don't get that idea. In our letters, most

of us deliberately omitted references to the many horrors and cruelties of war – to the dreadful sights one saw, to the hideous discomforts one had to endure, and the never-ending pain of the casualty lists. Such things were, obviously, better not talked about to friends who understood them well enough; but they were there all right. So in letters home, one tried to recount only the lighter happenings, which, thank God, were there too.[5]

To Yvo and Bim, war at first still did seem really like a great game. Yvo wrote to his family of having 'one's legs swung onwards by a thousand singing men' on night marches, and forays under darkness across no man's land to look at the German trenches returning with puttees torn from the barbed wire.[6] He joked that, like a child waiting for Christmas, he could not wait for the cold weather to require him to use his new waterproof kit. He met up with Bim for 'tea', and the cousins compared notes on their experiences thus far, enjoying the contents of the hampers from Fortnum & Mason ('the soldiers' twin saints', said Bim) that Pamela sent her son along with almost daily letters.[7]

For the first month in France, Bim, known to his men as 'the Boy Wonder', was well behind the lines of combat, digging trenches and learning how to set traps out of barbed wire. 'It is rather fun making these entanglements and imagining the Germans coming along in the dark and falling over these things and starting to shout whereupon you immediately send up a flare . . . and turn a machine gun on to them as they struggle in the wire. It sounds cruel, but it is War,' he wrote to his thirteen-year-old brother David in September.[8]

Yvo likened war to a fairground. The German rockets were 'as good as any Roman Candles I have seen on the 4th of June', he said.[9] But it was a grotesque hall of mirrors that he evoked when he wrote to Cynthia from the ruins of Vermelles after a three-day stint in the trenches near Loos. A shell had landed on his billet that morning, almost burying him with falling earth and brickwork; and the town itself was little more than rubble. 'I think one of the

effects of this war will be that people will give up their feelings for
ruins, qua ruins . . . there will be no more parties to Wardour Castle
from Clouds,' he predicted. He had a good mind to buy up the
whole town and turn it into an amusement park like London's
White City: 'with flying-boats from the ruined shaft-heads – a maze
made out of the trenches and rifle-ranges with dummy Huns
peeping from the windows and ruined walls – shells filled with
chocolate bursting at intervals throughout the grounds. I shall lay
the suggestion before George [Gordon] Moore.'[10]

The devastation of the landscape had shocked Charlie Adeane
when he visited France that summer in his capacity as Honorary
Treasurer of the Royal Agricultural Society, investigating how agriculture in war-ravaged areas might be restored. The blasted landscape was even more desolate than he had anticipated. What shells
had failed to bring to rubble, the Germans had burnt. Charlie found
villages deserted, only a few survivors living underground or huddled
in the corners of a ruin. 'The marvel is that cultivation should be
carried on,' he said, describing the sight of old men, women and
children stoically loading carts and driving reapers through fields
in which 'the soldiers' red kepis [caps] hang on wooden crosses . . .
where they fell, and show like red poppies above the corn'. In a
sun-bleached landscape, Charlie found himself outside a small
church, almost the only building left standing, listening to the lusty
singing of a congregation of French soldiers within. The service
ended, the men streamed out, surrounding Charlie and his companions, while the shout rang out 'Mort aux Boches!'[11]

The trenches were still worse. Trench life was 'an exact inversion
of what is natural to man,' said Yvo.[12] Men lived underground,
worked through the night, and slept, with interruptions for meals,
at what intervals they could during the day.[13] Their hours were
punctuated by the sickening boom of shellfire ('an incomparably
dreary sound, rather human – as though it loathed its mission')
and the sinister death-rattle of machine guns.[14] Yvo, who turned
nineteen while he was at the Front, was a platoon commander, the

lowest officer's rank. He, like most, had already grasped the disparity between the shallow, stinking, swampy Allied trenches and those of the enemy. 'The Germans have dug-outs 27 feet deep, with a long periscope going up the trench with a machine-gun run up and down on a winch and fired by means of a periscope at the bottom (at least so they tell me), so they don't stand to lose many men, even in a bombardment,' he told Cincie. He had also grasped the essential futility of trench warfare. 'I don't see that there is any military advantage in the line being a mile nearer Berlin, unless a gap is made through which troops can be poured to stop the enemy establishing himself in a second line,' he said.[15] 'This war . . . seems weary of its own melodrama and does not know how to give up.'[16]

Still, ten days later, when Yvo was ordered to rally his men, holed up in a shallow trench, into a fresh – and clearly suicidal – attack, he did not demur. He led his men 'over the top' and died in a fusillade of bullets: instantly, so his commanding officer said.[17] He had been at the Front for not quite five weeks. Bim heard the rumour of his cousin's death the next day. 'Osbert [Sitwell] and I are miserable about it, for no more lovable person ever stepped,' he wrote to his mother, hoping against hope it might not be true.

But Bim himself was holed up in a front-line trench, under heavy bombardment from shellfire. He had had no more than four hours' sleep in seventy-two hours, and was sufficiently discomposed, as the ground around him shook and rumbled and debris showered over him, to allow his nerves to show, if only momentarily:

I used to think I was fairly impervious to noise, but the crash upon crash, and their accompanying pillar of black smoke simply upset me, as they pitched repeatedly within 30 or 40 yards, and some even nearer. I don't think I showed I was any more frightened than anyone else. Perhaps I wasn't . . . I was very glad to get a letter from Daddy which seemed cheerful about the war. Please thank him for it . . .[18]

Bim appears to have been entirely unconscious of the irony of this juxtaposition.[19]

The news of Yvo's death reached his family the next day. Hugo's brother Evan Charteris, hearing the news at the War Office, had arranged that the Elchos be informed by telephone rather than telegram. It took Cincie several moments to comprehend the full import of the blurred voice at the other end of the receiver telling her the call was 'about Yvo Charteris . . . you must be prepared for the very worst'.

Cincie's diary entry of that long, awful day records a family devastated: Bibs, huge-eyed, 'petrified' and disbelieving; Mary Charteris, for whom Yvo was 'practically her life', 'frozen' at her dressing table, 'mechanically greasing' her face with cold cream as she prepared to leave with Letty for Egypt the next day; 'Poor Papa . . . most piteous – heartbroken and just like a child – tears pouring down his cheeks and so naively *astonished* . . . I think he really loved Yvo far the most of his children, and was so proud and hopeful about him';[20] and Mary, who had missed the telephone call while 'closeted' in confabulation with Sockie, Bibs's governess, but guessed the news as soon as she saw Cynthia's face. '. . . I think she really expected it . . . She was wonderful, quite calm after the first moment of horror. About five minutes afterwards she said something so sweet and natural, just what one feels when one is dazed: "What a bore!"'[21]

Ego wrote to Mary from Egypt, a frank letter that acknowledged in bald terms what this war had become:

Darling Mum,

I have absolutely nothing to say. When your own mother and brother are concerned it is futile to talk about sympathy, and the one consolation for me is that – if any comfort is to be extracted, or if the best thought is of any use, which of course it is – your soul is big enough, large enough for that purpose

. . . The only sound thing is to hope the best for one's country and to expect absolutely nothing for oneself in the future. To write down everyone one loves as dead – and then if any of us are left we shall be surprised. To think of one's country's future and one's own happy past. The first is capable of vast improvement – as for the second, when all is said and done, we were a damned good family. Qua *family* as good as Clouds . . . I am so awfully sorry for Papa who loved him . . . He must write his sons off and concentrate upon his grand-children who thank God exist . . .

Goodbye darling – I love you till all is blue.[22]

For his family, Yvo's death was the point of no return. Whatever happened in the war, they could never go back to the lives they had lived before. For Cincie, it destroyed the familiar platitudes of glamour: 'I am haunted by the feeling that [Yvo] is disappointed. It hurts me physically,' she wrote in her diary.[23] 'Not little Yvo,' Ettie Desborough wrote to Balfour.[24] The following months felt to Mary as though 'all the universe was rocking round one'.[25] She bore the return of Yvo's kit, his empty clothes 'the most poignantly pathetic of all the heartbreaking angles & sharp turnings one has wearily to take', she told Wilfrid Blunt.[26] 'Mary has a lion-heart, it will make her able to triumph even over this, & prove herself indestructible,' Ettie had written, but Yvo's death had eviscerated Mary,[27] had 'taken . . . all that I ever had of high worldly hopes & aspirations', as she put it to Blunt.[28]

Mary refused to dissemble. 'No one can maintain that it is not tragedy,' she told Arthur from Stanway as the family faced its first Christmas without Yvo:

– pure and unadulterated, that it is draped in all the glamour of romance . . . does not mean the price is less to pay . . . and although the houses are not ruined or the harvests burnt here in England,

still the long cruel tentacles of this deadly war has stretched its
icy claw and reached each house and hearth . . . if you hold yr
breath you hear the sound of widows weeping, sisters sobbing and
the ceaseless falling falling of the mothers' tears, the whole air is
stifled, surcharged with sadness, which eats into the soul . . . I will
not believe that sadness is not sadness – or say it is God's will and
all is for the best![29]

In the autumn of 1915, in her mid-forties, Pamela fell pregnant.
She rejoiced in this late, unexpected pregnancy. It gave her 'new
courage & joy & hope – & bridged one over an Autumn & winter
of [illegible] anxiety about Bim & Xtopher', she told Mary.[30] In her
poem 'Hester', describing this time, she is Demeter-like, fecund, as
the land around her during:

nine months' joy of happy life,
Of quiet dreams and blessed days,
Of peace that even calmed the Strife,
And steeped her in a golden haze . . .[31]

Pamela was no longer frozen while the world moved around her.
Now she was blooming while the world held its breath. Strings had
been pulled and for the duration of Pamela's pregnancy, Bim was
given a staff position under Brigadier John Ponsonby (commanding
the 2nd Guards Brigade), away from action.[32] The decision was
justified by concerns about Pamela's health. Nonetheless, Bim took
the position reluctantly. 'My duties are to copy out recommenda-
tions for medals into books, and to check figures . . . Also I inspect
the billets and rifles and gas-helmets of the Orderlies, telephone
clerks and cyclists. Quite a large portion of my work is telling the
General the date,' he told his mother.[33] He whiled away his time
performing in shows for the troops: two-hour rowdy affairs each
evening involving 'Pierrot business', 'Sketches' and songs. He
procured a motorcycle and 'tiff-tiff-ed' his way across the

countryside; read the large packages of books Pamela sent him; and prepared his own poems for publication – *Worple Flit*, a slight, forty-page volume, published by Pamela's publishers Blackwell later that year. Pamela's son was safe, her child was about to be born. But the moment was to prove as fleeting as she might have feared. Hester was born on 24 May 1916, and died a few hours later.

'It has been dreadful – so overwhelming a sense of loss – at times I can hardly stand up against it,' Pamela confessed to Mary.[34] She had Hester photographed by H. C. Messer's studio in Castle Street, Salisbury – the waxen child, eyes shut, nestled among broderie anglaise – and sent the image to all her family and friends. Photographing the dead was not in itself uncommon: Percy Wyndham was photographed in his bed after death, surrounded by his favourite books and pictures.[35] Pamela's widespread dissemination of the image at a time of mass grieving was.

Pamela had always established a monopoly on loss. During the Harry Cust episode, she never spoke, nor apparently thought, once of Nina. When Drummy died, she acted as though she alone could have saved him, almost entirely ignoring the fact that he had been engaged to another woman. But her behaviour on Hester's death, as her own family's sons died around her, tries the empathy of the biographer most. Pamela had suffered a terrible loss. She reacted as though she were the only person to have suffered loss in the world. She bombarded grieving families with pictures of her own dead child, and everyone who would listen, including Bim, in France, with pages about her grief. Perhaps the most difficult element is that Pamela paid lip-service to self-awareness. 'I try to dwell on how much all the World is suffering now – & how deep the sorrows of others,' she said to Mary, but she employed these thoughts as consolation, not as perspective.[36] It is doubtless this behaviour that gave rise to another myth surrounding Oliver Hope's origins – disseminated, among others, by Susan Lowndes – that having buried Hester at Queen Anne's Gate Pamela made her way to Salisbury Infirmary, saying to the Matron: 'I've lost my baby,

have you any orphans?'[37] The Lowndes family had a strange fascination with laying claim to and denigrating Pamela's memory. This,
as is evident from Pamela's earlier references to Oliver, is no more
than a florid romance. But such was her behaviour that the story
of a high-handed aristocrat mad with grief could almost be true.
Pamela was not the monster of myth. She had simply been so long
spoiled that she could not see anyone else as more than a circling
planet and herself the sun. But as she dwelt at length on her grief
and pain in her letter to Mary she did rouse herself enough to
recognize her sister's 'anxiety – & dear Letty's' and add, 'I long for
you both to get good news.'[38]

Some six weeks previously, Mary had spent Easter at Stanway
with a large group of family and friends. They had good weather,
and games of tennis. But the 'parliaments' in Mary's boudoir
focused almost exclusively on the war; and a flippant discussion at
lunch on the necessity of post-war polygamy now that all the young
men of their acquaintance were being wiped out left thirteen-year-
old Bibs, recorded Cincie, 'seriously distressed'. A further blow was
struck at both sisters' hearts that afternoon on receipt of letters
from Connor the agent enclosing the sum of ninety-seven pounds:
their shares 'of Ickey's [Yvo's] little fortune'. In the gloaming, Cincie
walked with a desolate Bibs up to the Pyramid. Stanway, as always,
was magical in the dusk. But 'Mamma is *miserable* – it's really like
a broken heart. What *can* one do?' said Cincie.[39]

That night Mary had a 'dream-vision': 'The atmosphere of the
room seemed to quiver with excitement – I felt the stress and strain
and *saw* as if thrown on a magic-lantern sheet, a confused mass of
black smoke splashed with crimson flame . . . like a child's picture
of a battle or an explosion.' Among these 'flames and smoke' she 'saw
Ego standing, straight and tall'. His profiled face was set and stern,
his eyebrows and moustache dark against his pale face. It seemed as
though 'he was exercising his forces with all his might and main'. A
brilliant golden banner swathed his chest in spiral folds, and 'seemed
to protect him'. 'I felt that something had happened,' Mary said later,

'but I knew not what, it was below the level of consciousness.'[40] She spent the rest of the weekend in a reverie.

Mary's dream was on the night of Saturday 22 April 1916. Three days later *The Times* reported a small battle at Katia, in the Sinai, after a surprise attack by hostile forces at 5 a.m. on Easter Sunday. The day after that, Mary received a cable from Letty: the Gloucesters had been involved, Ego slightly wounded, and both he and Tom Strickland captured. 'I can't bear it for Mamma,' said a dismayed Cincie, knowing that Ego himself would be 'miserable' at having been 'captured at his very first engagement' – 'so like his pathetic luck'.[41]

But, despite best efforts, the details that trickled through over the next few days did not add up to any coherent story. *The Times* reported a 'Stiff Fight' by British cavalry against enemy forces of up to 3,000 – Germans, and Turks on camelback, in conditions of mist and fog.[42] But the war correspondents' conjecture could not be confirmed because, as Mary said, '*all*' at Katia that day 'were killed & taken',[43] their fates obscured as much as the battleground that day. The trickle of news guttered out, to be replaced by 'lots of confusing Egyptian rumours', prismed through the Chinese whispers of the well-meaning and those for whom Lord Elcho's fate was simply bavardage. At a dinner party in London Mary overheard Mrs Keppel say that a syce (an Arab servant) had sworn that after the battle he had watched by Lord Elcho's body for hours.[44]

Mary later said of her 'dream-vision' that 'it helped me to *wait* and kept me outwardly calm'.[45] But inwardly she was 'terribly worried, over-tired and nervy'.[46] She pressed Balfour for 'the private account of what happened to the Yeomanry (Glos. Worcs. and Warwicks.) on Easter Sunday . . . it's so maddening not knowing'.[47] Almost a month after the battle the Elchos were 'inexpressibly relieved' to receive confirmation through the American Embassy that Tom Strickland was a prisoner in Jerusalem and being taken to Damascus. But the cable was silent about Ego. The next day, in early May, Mary went to Truro to stay in Miss Jourdain's Anglican convent 'for a rest', taking with her a crucifix as an offering (the former governess had become a nun).[48]

The uncertainty continued. A list procured by Hugo of prisoners at Constantinople did not bear Ego's name. More frustratingly still, Tom Strickland's letters to his wife Mary, delivered by the Red Cross, made no mention of Ego. On 10 June the Red Cross telephoned with the message 'Lord Elcho at Damascus. No details', which rendered the family 'wild with joy'.[49] Two weeks later the message was countermanded: the Red Cross had sent the wrong name.[50]

The final news came on 1 July. The French Red Cross confirmed Lord Elcho's death at Katia. He had been twice wounded, had had the wounds dressed and, despite his batman's entreaties, had gone back into battle. A shell had blown out his chest, killing him instantly. 'Oh God – Oh God, my beautiful brother that I have loved so since I was a baby – so beautiful *through* and *through*! Can it be true that he'll never come back?' asked Cincie.[51] Mary was at Clouds.[52] Hugo wired through, asking Guy Wyndham to break the news to his wife. For Mary it was confirmation of a still, small feeling in her deepest heart: 'Ego told me – when he died . . . for I saw him in my dream,' she told her mother. 'I never really *felt* that he'd come home – from the War – but of course I didn't *know*.'[53] But so cataclysmic was the final confirmation of Ego's death that, ever afterwards, Mary could not remember whether it came on the 1st or the 2nd of July.[54]

Instances of people sensing a loved one's death from many miles away are not uncommon. It can be felt as a shift of energy, a tickertape of images running through the mind, an inexplicable sense of discombobulation and loss. There is no rational explanation; many will think it simply imagination. But Mary thought that the vision – which seems to have coincided exactly with the time of battle – was the product of 'a strenuous love'. Ego had reached her at his time of greatest 'mental stress and strain'. She clung to that, determined 'not to fail' Ego and to create for his sons the life that he now could not.[55] 'I'm *not* going to be wonderful! I'm sick of the word,' she told Arthur.[56] '[B]ut there is no other word for it,' Cynthia said.[57]

After Ego's death, Mary struggled – though she would never say it – with the fact that he had died in such a small battle, with no medals or mentions in dispatches to prove his valour. In a further wrench, General Sir Archibald Murray's official report of the battle, published in *The Times* in September 1916,[58] did not even mention Ego's name. The baldest account of Ego's death gave Mary the most comfort: a wire received from Hyatt, Ego's sergeant, now a prisoner of war, several months after Ego's death: 'Lord Elcho twice wounded – then shell carried away chest. Acted magnificently.' '*Acted magnificently*' Mary underlined, immediately sending to Ettie and Evelyn this last shred of news. Such words, from a 'simple, unsuperlative sergeant', must mean something.[59]

The day confirmation of Ego's death was received was – although this must have been reduced to the periphery of the family's thought – the first day of the battle of the Somme. It is strangely apposite: both such monumental tragedies, the difference only one of scale. Mary had heard the rumours of a new campaign back in January. 'I suppose you know (I'm not asking you!) that there'll be heavy fighting in March or April,' she wrote to Balfour at the time.[60] Intended for spring, the campaign, a concerted Anglo-French offensive, devised, in the wake of Gallipoli and the British attack on the Eastern Front, to end the war on the Western Front once and for all, was delayed until July by the German offensive at Verdun. For a week beforehand the Allied forces had bombarded the German trenches with artillery. The sound was so loud that Asquith heard it in Downing Street. So confident were the generals that, as Raymond Asquith wryly wrote to his wife Katharine shortly before, 'An order has just come to say that there is to be no cheering in the trenches when peace is declared. No-one can say that our Generals don't look ahead.'[61]

At 7.30 a.m. on 1 July 1916 the first troops went over the top. They were assured by their generals that they could make their way across no man's land 'with a walking stick', that not even a rat could have survived the bombardment of the German trenches.[62] At Angelina's, Angela fried 800 eggs in three hours.[63] A short distance away, wave after wave of soldiers, weighed down by 60-pound packs, walked steadily into a line of German fire, mown down, toppled like ninepins, entangled and shredded by barbed wire, pulped under the feet of the men who came up behind them only to fall themselves. A total of 19,249 British soldiers, including 993 officers, died that day; almost 40,000 more were wounded. The battle, which the generals had so confidently expected to be a rout, lasted in total 140 days. Nothing illustrates the generals' failure of intelligence and apparent disregard for human life more than the catastrophic Somme.

Bim turned nineteen on that first day of the Somme. His battalion was posted nearby, and in combat, on and off, that summer. But his letters home dwelt on 'do you remembers', literary discussions and his anxiety about *Worple Flit*'s publication (Bim knew that his work was not 'fashionable' and feared the critical response: 'I daresay if I wore black shirts . . . and wrote verse that was quite incomprehensible, the reviewers would take it for genuine "poesie"').[64] He wrote to Pamela, leaning on one elbow while lying on a blanket in a field surrounded by poplars, telling her about a nice new company commander who 'laughs at my jokes', and alluding to a brief love affair with a young, 'very pretty and very well-dressed' French woman called Ninette, promising to send his mother a photograph of her.[65]

Bim's letters that summer were love letters, reassuring Pamela of her youth and beauty, mourning with her Hester's loss, marvelling at her courage and strength. There are only brief hints at a darker truth, a pointedly casual reference to a corporal in his battalion who had received a 'Blighty' wound only that morning ('He was hit in the ankle and fore-arm, and was simply jubilant.

The other chaps envied him a good deal, and so did I');[66] a passing reference to the difficulty of sending mail ('We are moving around a lot'); a capitulation at the end of a long letter ('I would give the last ten years of my life for six months' rest now');[67] and, in August, a plea ('I do wish you would tell me what the High Brows think? The P.M. and sic-like . . .').[68]

The war drove a rift between the generation that fought and those who sent them there, nowhere more so than among the elite. The mechanistic chain of command and incomprehensible orders gave the upper classes serving a glimpse for the first time of the impotence felt on a daily basis by most of Britain's populace. Suddenly there was a 'They': generals and politicians who made decisions with no regard to what the men – even officers – thought.[69] Those fighting were part of an anonymized mass, aristocrat and common man alike, buried where they fell. Many of those officers felt angered at the betrayal of their generation by their parents, and for the children of the Souls this was in many cases a literal statement – none more so than Raymond Asquith. The Coterie's acknowledged leader wrote to Diana Manners, savagely tearing apart the Souls who continued to chatter and talk:

> Their minds are almshouses . . . We do not hunt the carted hares of 30 years ago. We do not ask ourselves and one another and every poor devil we meet 'How do you define Imagination?' or 'What is the difference between talent and genius?', and score an easy triumph by anticipating the answer with some text-book formula, originally misconceived by George Wyndham in the early eighties at Glen, and almost certainly misquoted by Margot at the borrowed house of a Frankfort baronet, not because it was either true or witty or even understood, but because it was a sacred obligation to respect whatever struck the late Sir Charles Tennant as a cut above what he had heard in the night school at Paisley where they taught him double-entry . . .[70]

Raymond's cousin Bim could not say this – he could not yet comprehend this. But he was no longer the child who had gone to war
and who wrote to his mother, 'I think I shot a German the other
day; if I did, God rest his soul.'[71] In the dog-eared *Oxford Book of
English Verse* that he carried always with him, the poems underlined
all dwell on farewell and longing. In June, while at Poperinghe, he
wrote 'The Mad Soldier'. Written in the vernacular, it is the voice
of a dead soldier, decaying beneath a heap of bodies in the trenches
where 'rats eat Body-meat!'

> It's a sin . . .
> To say that Hell is hot 'cause it's not:
> Mind you, I know very well we're in hell.
> In a twisted hump we lie heaping high,
> Yes ! an' higher every day . . .[72]

Bim's innocence had been corrupted – although it has been rightly
noted that he could still only express this horror in a voice very
different to his own. He sent it to Pamela, with anxious enquiries
about whether she liked it. He had to ask her view several times
before she gave it. Eventually, she appears to have replied with
praise: but the delay is indicative. To read 'The Mad Soldier' would
be a shock for any mother. For Pamela it must have been a striking
blow to her world view.[73]

Bim's battalion was sent up to the front line of the Somme on
9 September. His first three days in the trenches were spent under
intense shelling: 'We have had all the kicks and none of the ha'pence
in this show, as other batt[alion]s had the fun of repulsing attacks
and killing hundreds, while we had to just sit and be shelled . . .
the C.O. is very envious of what he calls the "other chaps' hellish
good shoot", he wrote home.[74] After three days behind the front
line, his battalion returned to the trenches again as support. This
time Bim was shaken – or wired – enough to reveal details he
normally kept hidden. He had been directed to follow the Guards

to their new location and then bring his battalion, which was in support, alongside. It required three trips back and forth along no man's land. During the first, he was 'shot at by Boches on the high ground with rifles . . . with bullets that scuffed up dust all around with a wicked little "zump"'. The second was 'an unpleasant journey' of 'about half a mile over nothing but shell-holes full of dead and dying, with any amount of shells flying about' and with only an orderly beside him. Intercepted during the third, he spent 'that afternoon, evening, and night in a large rocky shell-hole' with his commanding officer, the adjutant and the battalion's doctor under severe shelling; 'about four men were done in in the very next shell-hole a couple of yards away. That night was one of the coldest and most uncomfortable it has ever been my fortune to spend with the stars to see.'

There was another day still of leading, dodging, weaving to go. 'My worst job was that of taking messages down the line of trenches to different captains. The trenches were full of men, so I had to go over the open. Several people who were in the trench say they expected every shell to blow me to bits.' His battalion were relieved at midnight, and got back behind the lines at 2.30 a.m., 'dog-tired', to 'Soup, meat, champagne, and cake . . . That is the time one really does want champagne, when one comes in at 3 a.m. after no sleep for fifty hours. It gives one the strength to undress.' Already, from along the lines had come rumours of the dead: 'Guy Baring, Raymond Asquith, Sloper Mackenzie, and many others . . . Death and decomposition strew the ground . . . I must tell you of other things.'

And so Bim retreated into memory. He told his mother of a pleasant walk of a few hundred yards taken a few days earlier with a Corporal Jukes who, it transpired, was the son of a former keeper at Clouds. Corporal Jukes remembered Pamela's wedding; remembered when Icke the butler was a mere footman – his sister had been housemaid at Glen under the Bart: 'And so he is altogether a great family friend . . . We had a very good talk about people like Mr. Mallet, Mrs. Vine and suchlike hench-folk. Do write and tell me if you remember him?' So Bim ends an account of forty-eight hours of hell with an enquiry more suited to a polite dinner-party.[75]

Raymond Asquith's death – shot in the chest as he led his men out in an advance from Ginchy, lighting a cigarette to reassure them, and dying before he reached the dressing station – made headlines in England.[76] 'It seems to take away one's last remains of courage,' said Cincie.[77] Everyone had thought that Raymond would be the man to lead his country into a new era. 'What a glorious company they are by now, recruited every week from our best and most radiant,' Asquith said to Ettie, 'those who, we fondly imagined, were going to make & guide the future here.'[78] If Asquith regretted not once writing to his eldest son while he was at the Front, he did not show it. It appears he did not, for he never once wrote to Beb either.

Four days later, Bim's battalion were ordered back into the trenches. They were to go 'over the top' the next day in an attack over 1,200 yards. Bim wrote to Pamela. He knew, in all likelihood, it would be his last letter. 'Our Brigade has suffered less than either of the other two Brigades in Friday's biff (15th), so we shall be in the forefront of the battle,' he explained. He had taken Communion that morning, slept 'like a top' the night before, and was 'full of hope and trust'. He invoked the spirit of his 'fighting ancestors', buoyed up by the thought of 'all the old men . . . in the London clubs . . . thinking and hoping about what we are doing here!' 'I have never been prouder of anything, except your love for me, than I am of being a Grenadier,' he added. Bim told Pamela that on going into action he would carry as always 'four photies [sic]' of her, and that 'that line of Harry's' from 'Non Nobis' rang through his head: 'High heart, high speech, high deeds 'mid honouring eyes'. 'Today is a great day for me,' he ended. 'Your love for me and my love for you, have made my whole life one of the happiest there has ever been . . .'[79]

Bim played the role expected of him by Pamela to the last, even invoking lines written about her own great romance with Harry Cust. Doubtless puppy-doggish, sweet-natured Bim genuinely believed the sentiments he invoked: the aristocrat worthy of his ancestors and the Guards who went before him. But this was also the officer who had dodged bullets and cowered inwardly in shell holes through long, freezing nights while trying outwardly to appear unmoved; who wrote 'The Mad Soldier', and who in 'À Bas la Gloire', another poem from that time, mocked the stout generals in their gleaming cars behind the lines. This is the generous spirit of the boy who on first getting a motorcycle drove along Wiltshire lanes with a cardboard placard attached to the back on which was written, in letters three inches high, 'Apologies for the dust',[80] one who feels, as Bim wrote in his letter, 'rather like saying "If it be possible let this cup pass from me"' but then invokes God's will and the 'triumphant finish . . . [that] steels my heart and sends me into this battle with a heart of triple bronze'.[81]

On 22 September, Bim was among his company, sniping in a 'sap' – a short trench dug from the front line into no man's land – when he was killed by a German sniper: 'absolutely instantaneously', said his commanding officer.[82] He was buried in the Guillemont Road Cemetery, a few graves along from Raymond Asquith, two of 400,000 British casualties lost in the 140 days of the battle of the Somme.[83] A total of 1.3 million men died on both sides in all. At the end of it, the British had advanced 6 miles.[84]

The death of 'Lord Glenconner's heir', 'the 55th heir to a peerage who has lost his life in the war', headed *The Times*'s list of casualties the next day. The paper, noting that his death came just a week after that of his cousin Lieutenant Mark Tennant, reprinted lines from Bim's final letter: 'your love for me and my love for you have made my whole life one of the happiest there has ever been. This is a great day for me.'[85] Two days later, at Pamela's behest, *The Times* published Bim's 'Home Thoughts in Laventie', a gentle, wistful poem in which a soldier buries his head in flowers found growing in the ruins of a blasted, shattered town. Inhaling their scent, he steps back on to the Downs: 'Home, what a perfect place!'[86]

THIRTY-ONE

The Remainder

It has been forcibly demonstrated by statistics that the legend of 'the flower of England's aristocracy' falling in the war was no mere myth. One in five of the British and Irish peers and their sons who fought in the war died, compared with one in eight for all members of the fighting services.[1] There is no mystery to this: junior officers, leading their troops into battle, were the first in the line of fire; concepts of honour meant patrician males were among the first to join up or were already in the forces when war broke out, when casualties were proportionately at their worst. The Upper Ten Thousand's exclusivity meant that such losses were almost as acutely felt as in the decimated communities of the 'Pals' Battalions' – for when these specially constituted units that allowed the men of a locality to serve alongside each other were wiped out in battle, so too was the male population of entire towns. Out of the Coterie of some thirty or forty men and women in total, fourteen died.[2] 'Oh why was I born for this time? Before one is thirty to know more dead than living people? Really, one hardly knows who is alive and who is dead,' Cynthia wrote in her diary, expressing the sentiment that every woman of her acquaintance felt.[3]

The historian David Cannadine has said that 'it is not necessary to join the clichéd cult of the Wyndhams, the Grenfells, and the Charterises, to recognize that they were uncommonly gifted and promising young men, whose greatness had been predicted before they died and was not just invented afterwards'.[4] Enough Souls had demonstrated that predicted greatness could come to disappointing ends. Yet to an extent the mythologization of the 'Golden Generation' by their mothers has done them a disservice. This generation had wit and talent. Many had integrity. '[H]e had George's cleverness plus – great scholarly learning & absolute freshness, I looked to him to save the world!' said Mary of Yvo.[5] Their true gold is rendered almost indiscernible under the thick layer of gilt. In 1916, Ettie Desborough's Pages from a Family Journal, 1888–1915 was privately published (250 copies by Spottiswoode of Eton High Street at a total cost of £375). It was a scrapbook of reminiscence and letters, saccharine and utterly sanitized.[6] 'I find Ettie's book thrilling, it tells of our children's (the children of the Souls!) Golden Age,' Mary told Balfour.[7] Yet Raymond Asquith, receiving a copy at the Front, was weary of the Souls' cant, and criticized the way Ettie doctored the book to remove all trace of her sons' undoubted insolence, arrogance and aggression. 'Ettie is a snob in [a] harmless sense . . . She meant to give her sons the best mise-en-scène from a worldly point of view which could be had . . .'[8] Eleven days later, Raymond was killed on the Somme and became mythologized himself as 'this star of England'. The words, from Henry V, are inscribed on his tombstone.

Edward Wyndham Tennant, Pamela's memoir of Bim, was published in 1919. She first began sending chapters to her publisher, John Lane, in 1917. Writing her son's life was 'like bearing him over again, a moral parturition', she said.[9] She did not have to edit too much to provide the mise-en-scène she wished for Bim. 'The Mad Soldier' and 'À Bas la Gloire' were included – quite possibly Pamela was trying to show that Bim, in 1916, was already moving towards work worthy of the greatest war poetry, and would have achieved work similar to Wilfred Owen's 'Dulce et Decorum Est' and that of Siegfried Sassoon had he lived. She maintained that 'War' was, for Bim, 'Romance', and that he had died in the best, most fitting way, too exalted for the life of an ordinary mortal.

Mary first began collating material for her own memoir in January 1917. Sitting on the floor, 'amongst heaps of "dead leaves" fluttering papers of the past . . . has almost killed me with misery', she told Balfour. 'I know I ought to feel grateful for the many happy years, but . . . I see . . . life's hopes and aspirations – and incidentally one's own heart! – lie bleeding in the dust.'[10] Rereading all these letters, Ego's times from school to university, 'the sweet short track of little Yvo',[11] Mary could see only 'the long years of preparation leading up to the holocaust'.[12]

Lacking Pamela's facility for writing for publication and Ettie's facility with emotion, Mary laboured over *Family Record* for fifteen years, looking up to the Pyramid for inspiration from her boudoir at Stanway, struggling to avoid the 'dragon's teeth' of cliché and hyperbole.[13] She was terrified she might not do justice to her sons – worse still, might expose them inadvertently to criticism.[14] It was written, so she told Ettie, 'in heart's blood. . .!',[15] and was published privately in 1932. Of the three memoirs, Mary's is the most painful, truthful reading. Her sons 'emerge luminous', as she had hoped.[16]

Since the war's start Mary had questioned the assumption of a glorious death. Yet, except to Arthur, it took courage to give voice to the heresy. When she first began working on the memoir she had asked Ettie to write a tribute to Yvo for inclusion. This was fairly common. Ettie did so willingly and ended by proclaiming Yvo's death 'the only end worthy of his beginning'. Revisiting these words in 1931 Mary baulked. 'Lovely as every word of it is,' she wrote, tiptoeing carefully towards her point, '. . . during the passage of years does not one slightly change not one[']s point of view – but perhaps the manner of expressing it?. . . I only feel that . . . (altho' we know that it was wholly glorious right and noble what they *did*) we do not quite think that any other way (their darling lives, lived out here) would have been *unworthy of their beginning*? Perhaps you'll think me mad . . . but they *might*, as thank God, many did – they might have fought & lived?. . .'[17]

In December 1916, Asquith's Coalition collapsed. Balfour replaced Edward Grey as Foreign Secretary in Lloyd George's ministry – although without a seat in the new Prime Minister's streamlined War Cabinet. Grey, since July Viscount Grey of Fallodon, retreated gratefully to his Northumberland estate. 'I read nothing remotely connected with the war except the newspapers,' he told Eddy Tennant, expressing his relief at being able to share 'general anxiety' without feeling personal responsibility for the events that took place.[18]

Grey had worried daily about Bim's welfare when at the Front, and was devastated by his death. On first hearing the 'terrible news', he sent Eddy two letters in as many hours: 'I will come to you at a word whenever you want me . . .'[19] In April 1917, a fire at Fallodon all but destroyed the house, and all Grey's papers. It was 'a melancholy business' – although he was the first to admit that it was nothing to compare with that suffered by the Glenconners. There was no question of rebuilding until after the war. In the interim, Grey stayed with the Glenconners at Queen Anne's Gate, and at Itchen Abbas.[20]

It is still debated how far Grey, a Foreign Secretary who spoke no French and never once visited Germany, could have avoided Britain's entry into the war. Diana Bethell, Clare Tennant's daughter who more or less lived at Wilsford in the post-war years, remembered as a small girl tugging at Grey's sleeve asking, 'Will there be another war? Will there be another war?' 'The subject always made him shake, and brought the same answer: "There will never ever be another war" he would repeat.'[21] What is clear is that neither Pamela nor Eddy ever held Grey responsible for the war that caused their son's death. Perhaps that was also because, to Pamela, Bim was not lost. As she explained in *The Earthen Vessel*, published by John Lane in 1921: 'When the time came to need the comfort offered by Spiritualism, I turned to it . . . in just as common-sense and practical a manner as I would have gone about to book a passage or to send a cable to New Zealand, had it so chanced that my son had gone to that quarter of the globe.'[22]

The spiritualist craze that arose in the war years and continued throughout the 1920s was a bereaved society's response to incomprehensible loss. In post-Reformation England, people began to believe in witchcraft when Puritan austerity stripped them of Catholicism's amuletic defences against evil. Now, a society shorn of its husbands, brothers and sons reached out for mediums, book tests and séances as solace in its pain. In 1915, Cincie had predicted that the great numbers of casualties would force a change in the way society treated its dead. 'Now they are so many one *must* talk of them naturally and humanly, not banish them by only alluding to them as if it were almost indelicate.'[23] Instead, society began talking to them.

The Earthen Vessel, its subtitle *A Volume Dealing with Spirit-Communication Received in the Form of Book-Tests*, records the results of Pamela's book tests carried out between 1917 and 1920 with Mrs Leonard, a medium on a salaried position with the Society for Psychical Research who communicated through her spirit guide, Feda.[24] From January 1918, the sittings were paid for by the SPR, who sent a professional notetaker to attend the sittings 'in the interests of investigation!', said Pamela, thrilled to have the accuracy of 'dear Bim's book tests & messages' recognized in this way, happier than at any point since Bim had died. As a child, 'Step fearless into the dark' had been one of Bim's favourite expressions. Now Pamela found the phrase running round her head. 'It seems to match the endeavour somehow,' she said.[25]

A book test involved a medium, acting on spirit information, directing the sitter to a line of a page of a book in a room in a house. The sittings were conducted mostly at Clouds, Wilsford and Queen Anne's Gate, attended by Pamela and Eddy, their sons, bereaved cousins and close friends. Chief among those friends was Oliver

Lodge, whose longstanding interest in spiritualism had become obsessive since the death of his own son, Raymond, in the war in 1915. Lodge and his wife Mary, devotees of Mrs Leonard, lived in close proximity to the Glenconners. They rented from Eddy Normanton House, a property just across the way from Wilsford, and Lodge wrote the preface to *The Earthen Vessel*.[26] Pamela recounts an intensely loaded atmosphere: the receipt of the message from Feda, the hunt for meaning, the triumph when a book corresponding to the description was found, the relief and joy when the extract produced a message. Later Stephen recalled Pamela's face when she received a book test that worked: 'so wonderful, so uplifted & happy'.[27]

Pamela claimed always to have held spiritualist beliefs. But there is little evidence of her ever employing them until she was confronted with death. Her early letters dwelt long on Christ, those in her middle years on her children. Only when Hester died did Pamela seize upon Lady Betty Balfour's suggestion that Hester's touching 'Earth through me' might have been 'necessary to her development in another life', as giving her hope.[28] After Bim's death, spiritualism became an obsession for her: scarcely a letter goes by without Pamela recommending the latest spiritualist tract or recounting a message received.

As the number of mediums and sittings proliferated (by 1918, Mrs Leonard had a three-month waiting list for sittings),[29] the War Office became concerned, fearing that officers, caught off-guard, were leaking confidential material in sittings. The *Daily Mail*'s Harold Ashton began a campaign to expose fraudulent mystics. Pamela appeared as a witness for the defence in one of the first trials, that of the American Mrs Brockway charged with pretending to tell fortunes in December 1916. It was a sensation, ending in a furore when the defence counsel, Ernest Wild KC, came to verbal blows with the sceptical magistrate and stormed out of court.[30] At Pamela's behest Eddy exerted his influence to have Mrs Brockway's deportation order sending her back to the United States commuted to one to Paris, a safer journey than across the submarine-infested Atlantic.[31]

Margot was scathing: 'Pamela, poor dear, has reached her religion through spiritualism . . . a random slap on the ear in a dark room has convinced her of the existence of God.'[32] Yet reports of these trials, in which magistrates tried to get to grips with whether 'spirits' might be 'lying' to the mediums who were their conduits, showed the ambiguity of society's attitude towards spiritualism. It suspected it was nonsense – but it could not quite be sure. Pamela, seeing herself as a guide for others, wanting to allow them to enjoy the 'supreme joy' she found in this communication, encouraged those still unsure.[33] In November 1916 she took Mary to a séance with a man in Tavistock Square. Mary told Cincie she was 'agnostical', thinking 'perhaps one ought just to give a chance to the theory that the middle-man may still be necessary for communication – more on account of Yvo than Ego'.[34] In fact, Mary wanted to believe far more than she let on to her cynical daughter. In December, she took Cincie to a further session at Tavistock Square. It was disastrous. The medium accused a mistrustful, uneasy Cincie of acting as a mental 'screen' and 'got hopelessly on the wrong track about me, thinking my husband had been killed', said Cincie.[35] Mary could not stretch her credulity further. Pamela indefatigably continued to send her reports of sittings with Mrs Leonard whenever Ego and Yvo made an appearance.[36]

In 1914, Pamela had responded to war's outbreak by scooping up another child. An exchange from 1918 suggests that she responded to Bim's death in a similar way. In 1918, Marie Stopes published *Married Love*, and shortly afterwards *Wise Parenthood*, a birth-control manual popularizing the contraceptive diaphragm. One of *Married Love*'s controversial propositions concerned artificial insemination. Stopes believed that for many reasons – 'the husband's actual sterility or the lack of mutual adjustment in their organs, or from an ill-understood lack of chemical affinity' – an otherwise loving couple might not be able to have a child. Since husbands might object to their wives 'yielding' their bodies to another man,

Stopes's solution was artificial insemination: 'there are sufficient records in the medical profession of success . . . for it to offer much hope'.[37] She added, helpfully, that 'Where the injection is undertaken by a woman doctor, the husband need have no feeling that his wife has been violated' at all.[38] Her theories were contested in the preface by her editor, William J. Robinson, informing readers that successful artificial insemination was so rare that the method 'is never likely to acquire a great vogue'.[39]

Among Stopes's papers in the British Library is a tantalizingly brief exchange of just two letters between her and Pamela in July 1918, shortly after publication. In the first, Stopes refers to an intimate conversation between the women the day before:

the more I think of it, the more undecided I am. You ask a thing I could only do for a most *intimate* friend, as *so* much is involved – I really do think you should find the right person *yourself* because you know *heredity* is a very very important factor – & how could I take such a responsibility? Supposing you were ever to regret any developing trait how would you prevent a feeling that you trusted me & I was somehow responsible?[40]

Pamela replied that day:

I quite see that you might view the matter we discussed *as you do*. It is worthy of you – and as I might expect . . . Thank you with all my heart . . . I don't yet fully know how much tension I am undergoing in keeping this longing in control, because I have a strong will! I must just wait & see. Meanwhile because of my talk with you I have felt much helped, & happier . . . I have never spoken to anyone as I did to you. I believe I was not misguided in my confidence?[41]

With Pamela, almost nothing is too strange. These letters fit exactly a surmise that she had, however tentatively, suggested that Stopes should artificially inseminate her with sperm from a donor of Stopes's choosing, and Stopes shrank from being responsible for determining the paternity of any child Lady Glenconner might bear. So far as it is possible to tell, the idea was dropped, but there remained an understanding between the two women, and a deep gratefulness towards Stopes on Pamela's part.

The young continued to die – and the old. Harry Cust succumbed, suddenly, to pneumonia in 1917, and a death that once would have been seismic for the Souls passed almost unnoticed in the context of seas of crosses in France. Pamela placed memorials to Bim in Salisbury Cathedral, in the church at Wilsford and in the kirk at Traquair near Glen.[42] Madeline Wyndham raised a plaque in East Knoyle church 'In Memory of my Five Grandsons who were killed in the Great War'. Her faith had become ever more determined in the war's bleak years. She now lived, said Pamela, 'in close communion with all those who had gone before'.[43]

Mary suffered the evisceration of public appearances, laying foundation stones for a Garden City for disabled soldiers at Longniddry and memorial stones to her sons at Stanway and Gosford. Solace for her was Stanway – a place saturated with her sons' spirits[44] – playing over 'might-have-beens', trying to work out what would have happened with better scouting at Katia, or if Yvo had never switched from the Rifles to the Guards. She and Ego's widow Letty cherished David and Martin, Ego's two small sons.[45] 'I get through *bit by bit* (and nobody *need* ask one how, because one cannot tell them),' she told her mother. But after 1916 everything was an afterthought.[46]

At 11 a.m. on 11 November 1918 came the Armistice and the guns finally fell silent. Once again raucous crowds filled the streets. For those who had fought, the forced celebration was far removed from the innocence of four years before. 'This was the moment to which I had looked forward for four years, and now that it had arrived I was overcome by melancholy. Amid the dancing, the cheering, the waving of flags, I could think only of my friends who were dead,' said Duff Cooper, one of the few Coterie members to survive, who married Diana Manners the following year;[47] 'I had expected riotous excitement, but the reaction of everyone, officers and men, seemed the same – flat depression,' said Oliver Lyttelton, son of Alfred and D.D.[48] 'Even when you win a war you cannot forget that you have lost your generation,' said Tommy Lascelles, who, like Duff Cooper, had seen most of his friends die.[49]

So these officers stood frozen among the celebrating crowds, and the mothers of the dead thought only of the sons they had lost. 'All day the thought of you has burnt in my innermost heart. Victory, & you & I look in vain for our Victors,' Ettie wrote to Mary.[50] 'No one can feel light of heart ... we miss our shining victors in the hour of victory,' echoed Mary in her diary.[51] The survivors had now to endure the peace, which Cincie thought 'will require more courage than anything that has gone before. It isn't until one leaves off spinning round that one realizes how giddy one is. One will have to look at long vistas again, instead of short ones, and one will at last fully recognize that the dead are not only dead for the duration of the war.'[52]

THIRTY-TWO

The Grey Dawn

Among Pamela's papers is a printed pamphlet from July 1920 issued by F. S. Graham, a North Yorkshire game dealer. Mr Graham was pleased to announce that he would be importing Hungarian partridge from Czechoslovakia, and French partridge eggs. The widespread shortage of wild duck eggs – the result of farmers having to kill off wild ducks during the war – was also being put right. There was one further message: 'The late war has brought about such a wonderful change in the titles and names of proprietors and tenants of shootings, and in gamekeepers names that it is necessary for me to revise my list of customers names and addresses . . . therefore my annual booklet will, this year, reach many addresses for the last time, unless I hear of a desire to have it continued.'[1] In 1918, Mary was fifty-six, Mananai and Pamela in their late forties. The war had brought an end to their way of life as conclusively, and briskly, as shutting the covers of an old hardback book.

Dick Wyndham, Clouds' heir, survived the war, although his elder brother George did not. In 1919, his mother Minnie died in the Spanish Influenza epidemic. Guy was bereft. 'Bitter waters have rolled over Clouds,' said Mary. 'It began with the death of a little child – my Colin – then Papa George Percy – and four other grandsons of mamma – and now Minnie – most unexpected (and I venture to say uncalled for!) & soon we shall have to lay here the tired heart & body of darling Mamma,' Mary told Arthur.[2]

Madeline Wyndham was now over eighty, and ever more living in another world. Weeks before, Mary had spent '2 nights holding my mother's hands, talking of people long since dead and roaming with her through strange realms of phantasy and delirium in what *seemed* a *death chamber*, or birth into *another* world'.[3] It was decided that she should live permanently at Babraham, since the Adeanes, with ever increasing duties within the county, were the most frequently at home. In 1915, Charlie had been appointed Lord Lieutenant of Cambridgeshire, and in 1917 President of the Royal Agricultural Society, thus turning his energies towards 'matters concerned with food production'.[4] Mananai proved herself indefatigable in her work throughout the war, always conscious that what had caused her such pain for so long – her inability to bear a son who lived – had saved her from seeing a grown son die. Nonetheless, the Adeanes still visited London, and could no longer afford to keep two houses running full time. The sisters agreed that when their mother was in sole residence she would pay for the kitchen staff, and her guests would pay their own way. Charlie, who had darkly visualized his house being turned into a permanent rest home for his mother-in-law's multitude of elderly relations and friends, was relieved. Mananai was scrupulously fair: 'When I come down to see Mamma I will pay my Board as she will be running the kitchen,' she explained to Mary.[5]

A decade before, such a proposal would have been unthinkable. But now death and taxes, which had risen throughout the war and were increasing once again, seemed to herald the break-up of estates everywhere one looked. The wrecking ball was a familiar sight in the streets of Mayfair and Piccadilly, demolishing the private palaces in which the Wyndhams had danced to make way for natty blocks of flats with en-suite bathrooms and all mod cons.[6] 'England is changing hands . . . Will a profiteer buy it? Will it be turned into a school or an institution? Has the mansion house electric light and modern drainage?' asked *The Times* in 1920.[7] Even Eddy was feeling the pinch. 'I could afford to give you a large allowance when taxation was upon a more moderate scale than it is now . . . [but] income tax and super tax are for me about 11/- in the pound so you will see . . . how I am financially situated,' he said to Margot in 1919, explaining why he could no longer accede to her persistent requests for more money. '[U]nfortunately everyone thinks that I am very rich and forget the obligations under which I stand . . .'[8] The Glenconners' charitable obligations and benefactions were considerable. Most recently, in 1918 Eddy had gifted to the nation Dryburgh Abbey, the monastic ruins where Sir Walter Scott is buried. The only condition was that an existing annual service of thanksgiving be maintained. Scott was one of Pamela's favourite writers, and the decision was undoubtedly precipitated by her.[9]

Mary spent the post-war years fighting for her past. From the moment the war had ended, Hugo was itching to reopen Gosford.[10] In the autumn of 1919, Stanway was let for the first time. Mary spent a fortnight there prior to the letting, 'working like a galley slave a charwoman and a cabinet minister all in one' to prepare the house; 'now poor Stanway is swept and garnished and the people come in October', she told Arthur.[11] During the war, and in reflection of her greater responsibilities as Countess of Wemyss, Mary had begun to employ a personal assistant, Miss Wilkinson, known (like her maternity nurse) as 'Wilkie', who stayed with her for the next twenty years.[12] Wilkie became invaluable to Mary as she struggled with the Sisyphean task of trying to maintain 62 Cadogan Square, Stanway and Gosford. 'Three houses in these days, will take every drop out of my body, every grain of energy out of my soul I never go out of my office, night or day,' Mary complained to Arthur in 1920, contemplating an American let of Gosford for five weeks in August that would allow the Wemysses to live there for September and October, but required Mary to supply the servants: 'an awful task – but not I think quite imposs [sic] if one puts one's back to it'.[13]

Now that she was Countess of Wemyss, and no longer had to kowtow to a difficult father-in-law, Mary refused to stay at Gosford. She rented instead Craigielaw, a small house a short way down the coast. She justified her 'bungalow' on financial grounds.[14] It allowed one wing of Gosford to be let, and 'even the most ill-natured cannot pretend that Hugo & I have quarrelled if we lunch or tea together every day!'[15] Craigielaw made East Lothian just bearable, limiting her exposure to 'Hugo (the biggest child of them all)', the 'Angel in the house!' as she called Angela, 'the dull neighbour and the clergy, the disgruntled farmer or the Beggar at the Gate'. Mary left Frances Charteris, Guy's wife, to keep the peace. 'She is the only woman I could count on to do everything in the home exactly as I would have it done only a great deal better!' Mary told Arthur.[16]

In 1921, Stanway was redeemed. J. M. Barrie, to whom Cincie had been indispensable as a private secretary since 1918,[17] would take it each August, with Cincie acting as his hostess,[18] allowing Mary to live there for the rest of the year. The system continued for over a decade, and brought further artists and writers to Stanway. Mary returned to Stanway that autumn, at the time that the Anglo-Irish Treaty ending the bitter War of Independence was signed. She wrote to Arthur while unpacking her 'household Gods' of photographs and trinkets: 'now our home will be here', she said staunchly.[19] She recounted her previous night's drive in her 'pony shay' with Wilkie and Eliza Wedgwood from a musical party back to Stanway: 'the stars shining brightly out of the velvety deep blue black & so far away sky & the Didbrook church bells ringing for Peace between England & Ireland . . . All the many different times the bells have pealed or tolled – I feel that I shall hear them when they peal I hope (not toll!) for me . . . I felt very near to all I loved both those who have gone – so many & the precious few that are left . . .'[20] It is a love letter to Stanway and to her past.

By the 1920s Arthur, author of the 1917 Balfour Declaration
promising a national home to Jews in Palestine, and negotiator of
the 1919 Treaty of Versailles, had been propelled to international
statesman: 'you are the World's Chef making an apple pie of the
universe', Mary wrote proudly as he attended the World Disarmament
Conference in Washington DC in 1921.[21] She made light of the
contract with herself, 'all hoary and moss grown in Gloucestershire
struggling with my Village Women's Institutes and War Memorials
and looking after my . . . grandchildren'.[22] She remained mischievous and irreverent. At the birth of Mary Strickland's first child in
1919, Mary, summoned from her bed at Cadogan Square at 3 a.m.,
was, to her delight, permitted by the doctor to administer the
chloroform. 'I had the time of my life,' she said.[23] At Stanway she
composed melodramas for her grandchildren's Christmas theatricals in which she appeared as a pirate in turban, 'Moorish coat &
riding boots'.[24] She redoubtably sat down on the stairs at the formal
reopening of Westminster Hall in 1923 when she was tired – the
only one with common sense enough to do it, she told Arthur
stoutly,[25] and Mary Strickland recalled her kneeling on Paddington
platform to finish writing a letter begun on the train while all about
her streamed the disembarking hordes.[26] Mary hustled to provide
the funds she needed to keep up Stanway, importuning her friends
to provide her with their old finery for a rummage sale to raise
the £50 required for electric lighting in Stanway's barn. 'Ettie sent
me 20 old Hats – & 16 prs of shoes!' she triumphantly informed
Arthur of the event where the servants manned the stalls and Hugo's
valet was auctioneer.[27] In 1923, cautioned by Cincie's experience,
Mary echoed history and shepherded a reluctant Bibs into a match
with Ivor Windsor-Clive, a shy, awkward man, thirteen years Bibs's
senior.[28] Ivor was heir to the earldom of Plymouth, the eldest
surviving son of George's mistress Gay. '[I]t warms my heart to
think how George would have rejoiced – and my mother . . .' said
Mary.[29]

Madeline Wyndham had died at Babraham on 8 March 1920 at

the age of eighty-four. Mary and Mananai were with her in her final weeks as she slipped in and out of consciousness, and her mind wandered through her past. 'She has gone even further away into the borderland & only returns for short intervals, she still knows Madeline & me but no one else for long,' Mary wrote to Dorothy Carleton. Dorothy had sent Madeline Wyndham a letter: 'she held it in her hands all day together with some things I cut out for her . . . She has no anxiety now & says "I am quite well" & she has no pain just . . . grows steadily weaker.' Dorothy had also sent a message from Wilfrid Blunt. Whatever it was, it pulled Madeline Wyndham momentarily back half a century to a handsome cousin's flattery, for on receiving it 'she said "he means it!" her smile has been too wonderful', Mary reported to Dorothy.[30]

Madeline Wyndham's body was cremated at Golders Green Crematorium, her ashes buried in the family plot at East Knoyle on 12 March. She was the last Wyndham to be buried there. Pamela was not among the large crowd of mourners. For several months the Glenconners had been touring America, visiting Grey, who had come out of near retirement to serve as Ambassador to the United States. Pamela decided not to cut short their trip. 'I was absolutely convinced she was going to die before I returned so it was no extra grief to me,' she explained to Mary from the Biltmore Hotel in New York, adding that she had taken the precautionary step of leaving an obituary she had written with Frederick Lowndes, who edited *The Times* obituary section, so that he could publish it if her mother died while she was away. Pamela's spiritualism had rendered her strangely impervious to grief. She had sought out mediums in every place the Glenconners visited, from Chicago to California (Eddy had privately chartered a Pullman to make the journey).[31] Her first act upon hearing the news of her mother's death – in Boston – had been to go, anonymously, to a medium named Mrs Chenoweth. It was a 'very beautiful' sitting, she told Mary, 'and the very first person who came was darling Mamma, it gave me such a great comfort . . . I can truly say I am thankful she is released – into the fuller Life, which I *know* is now hers!. . . I dwell in the thought of her joy.'[32]

America had given the spectacularly wealthy Glenconners a rapturous reception. '. . . I never knew I was so delightful! or could be so clever! – how overlooked I have been until now! What have the people in London been thinking about? – didn't they know that when I was with them?. . . my room is a bower of roses, the table groans under cards . . .' Pamela wrote in her diary as they arrived in New York.[33] They were fulfilling a semi-ambassadorial role, helping promote relations between the nations (the subject of an address made by Eddy to New York's Sulgrave Institution).[34] Their every step was followed by pressmen, fascinated by the 'Scottish Magnate' and his eccentrically beautiful wife, who organized her thirteen-year-old son to give dance recitals at their hotels.[35]

In England the work of the press barons – both Lords Beaverbrook and Northcliffe were friends of Pamela's – was coming to fruition. The public was avid for tales of upper-class eccentricity. Pamela and her family provided it to perfection. Less than six months after their return to England Eddy died, aged sixty-one, in a private nursing home after suffering complications from what was intended to be a routine operation.[36] He left Wilsford and Queen Anne's Gate in trust to Pamela. Christopher, now the second Baron Glenconner, inherited Glen. The remainder, valued at £814,479 gross (a sum of over £17 million in today's money), was divided predominantly between David and Stephen, with a large lump sum to Clare, a bequest to Edward Grey and an annuity to Nanny Trussler.[37]

Pamela, a widow not yet fifty, proved her mettle. She let out Queen Anne's Gate to a shipbuilding magnate and his wife on a rolling seven-year lease, so that Christopher could move back in when he married, and took 4 Buckingham Street, a 'dear little house' two doors down from Guy and Frances Charteris on a street 'like Quality Street in its prettiness'. Pamela decorated the house with cream-coloured walls, 'dark Columbine blue' curtains and carpet, and chintz sofas and chairs; the 'dark red roses & pink roses look so lovely against the . . . blue curtains', she told Dorothy Carleton. The magnate and his wife had been happy to caretake the larger pictures in the Gallery, so Pamela had brought '*only* a picked few of the smaller canvassed pictures' with her to the new house. She listed them for Dorothy and Wilfrid: two Turners, two Bonningtons, a Constable, three Nasmyths ('great favourites'), two Lancrets, two Hogarths, one Floris, the Orpen of Madeline Wyndham, the Lawrence crayon of Charles Dickens, *The Leslie Boy* by Raeburn, Mignard's portrait of Colbert, the Reynolds of 'the dew bird', *Miss Stephens* by Zoffany, *The Widow Wadham* and *The Uncle Toby* by Leslie, a woman's head by Angelica Kauffmann, the Millais of Lady Millais as Marguerite, the Natier of the Duc de Guise, Morland's *Industry* and *Idleness* 'and a Fragonard'.[38]

From the moment of Eddy's death, Margot had scrutinized the Tennants, hawk-like, for sufficient distress. Mary described to Ettie Margot's behaviour during a fraught visit to the Tennants at Glen, where they had repaired immediately after Eddy's death; 'no tears, no heart, the dry-eyed are relegated to an everlasting limbo of callousness & cruelty,' she added wryly. As for Pamela, who refused to break down in front of Margot: 'I think one may as well . . . be thought "to have done one's husband to death".'[39] Shortly afterwards, Pamela began to hear reports from friends of a 'story of falsehood' and neglect reeled out by Margot at dinner parties[40] – that Pamela and her children had shamefully abandoned Eddy to die alone in his nursing home.

Pamela confronted her sister-in-law: 'Margot, I do not open my letter with the conventional term of endearment, as I cordially dislike you. Will you write me your apology for perverting the truth of my conduct towards Eddy on his death bed? I do not require a long letter; having neither time nor inclination for anything beyond the apology for which I ask. Yours, in utter sincerity . . .'[41] Pamela subsequently explained that she had been with Eddy on the day of his death for almost fourteen hours straight, from '4 a.m. till about

6.30 (or 6 . . . I cannot recall accurately)'. She was only absent at the moment of death because she had 'fainted through anguish and lack of food' and been taken back to Queen Anne's Gate by Eddy's brother Jack to eat and change.[42] Margot backtracked enough to give a semblance of apology, and Pamela graciously accepted it as though it were fulsome: 'we will not quarrel for Eddy's sake', she told her sister-in-law.[43]

To Pamela's mind this was still very much a present obligation, as she remained in close contact with her dead husband. 'I have received two most excellent Messages in Book Tests from Bim & Eddy together . . . they are singularly *Good* and made me happy', she wrote to Mary three months after Eddy's death.[44] She spoke of her dead as though she had just put down the telephone to them, encouraged by Oliver Lodge, so nearby at Normanton House, where he had built a large room to serve as a laboratory for further psychical experiments.[45] Her granddaughter Dinah Bethell remembered her sitting on her bed each morning, recounting the previous night's conversations with Bim.[46] More bitterly, Stephen recalled arriving back at Wilsford, having been taken by his friend (and lover) Siegfried Sassoon to meet the elderly Thomas Hardy. He burst into the house, eager to tell his mother about the encounter. Pamela, according to Stephen, barely looked up from her spiritualist tract.[47]

In February 1922, *The Times* reported that it was 'authorised' to announce that Pamela and Grey would marry in the early summer of that year.[48] At half-past eight on the morning of Sunday 4 June, Pamela and Grey were married at St Michael's Church in Wilsford. Christopher Tennant gave Pamela away; Edward's sister Mrs Curtis was the only other witness. The ceremony was kept so secret that the villagers of Wilsford did not even know of it until it was over.[49] Grey had in fact proposed on Whitsunday a full year before, cycling over to Wilsford after an 'odious paragraph' of speculation in the press. Then, Pamela had refused. At the time she told Lucy Graham Smith that it was because her sons still needed her, and expressly

asked Lucy to tell 'your immediate circle' – meaning Margot – that
Grey 'would not have suggested a thing so early had he not thought
that the paragraph in the Press had worried me'.[50] A year later,
Pamela had decided to bow to her sisters-in-law no longer. '[T]he
great step was taken, at last, by me,' she told Wilfrid.

> I had no really valid reason for refusing any longer, and now that
> it is taken, I am quite certain it was right. Edward is so very fond
> of me, and I can be of use to him: and he is a wonderful LOVER
> and makes me very happy in a hundred ways . . . I feel – like
> Philip Sydney's mother – who made her second marriage so late
> in life that, like her, I could inscribe inside my wedding ring 'NO
> Spring till now' . . .[51]

The press leapt on the news. *The Times* on 6 June reported 'A
"Marriage of the Minds"', talking of the newlyweds' many shared
interests (the correspondent is anonymous, but the tone smacks of
Marie Belloc Lowndes). A double-page spread in the American
press, on 'The Romantic Miracle of England's Loneliest Man',
claimed that Grey's sight had been cured by his nuptials: 'Now all
of England is saying that the healing touch of the woman he loved
brought life to the stricken nerves that had been pronounced dead
by surgery.'[52]

Grey's sight had continued to deteriorate to the point that he
was practically blind, and neither operation (which he tried) nor
love (which he had) was going to fix it. But the marriage was very
happy. The Greys moved, in London, to Mulberry House, an elegant
Lutyens house on gas-lit Smith Square in Westminster,[53] but on the
whole they divided their time between Wilsford and Fallodon.
Pamela was spotted shopping in Newcastle with a green parrot on
her shoulder (the same parrot was walking on her bed at Mulberry
House the last time that Mary saw her sister).[54] 'He was sometimes
a long-suffering husband,' recalled David Tennant's wife, Hermione
– but the example she gave was simply of Pamela, 'not renowned

for her punctuality', keeping a resigned Grey waiting by the car,[55] a far cry from the tales of Pamela terrorizing Eddy. A 'very perfect friendship' had become still better a marriage.[56] 'I feel I can write to you . . . telling you that I am happy, I was going to say – *at last*,' Pamela told Wilfrid, remembering distant Stockton days when her cousin had asked her if she was happy, and she had been unable to reply.[57]

Pamela and Grey undoubtedly had a sexual relationship. Marie Belloc Lowndes, who never left a confidence unrevealed, said in her memoirs that Pamela had a miscarriage shortly after her marriage, which she attributed to an overlong drive to a political meeting.[58] This was in the early spring of 1923. At fifty-two, older than what is now the average age for menopause, Pamela's chances of miscarriage were extremely high. Her doctor prescribed three weeks of bed-rest, and no exertion for a further three months: 'a holiday for 3 months! A lovely prescription!. . . I believe Dr Aarons is going to combine a douching or ichth[y]ol treatment during the 3 weeks to increase the slender hope for the future,' Pamela explained to Marie Stopes from Wilsford in March.[59]

Pamela had not forgotten her debt of gratitude to Stopes. She agreed with pleasure (when most other grandees who were approached regretfully declined) to become a patron of Stopes's first birth-control clinic, the Mothers' Clinic, in Holloway, North London, on its opening in 1921. She even hoped to connect that 'fine work' with her Home for Working Mothers in Westminster, where 'I have the Infant Welfare scheme . . . The mothers who attend there, & they are continually increasing, would benefit by your work being made known to them.'[60] Throughout the 1920s, Pamela arranged for contraceptive devices to be provided to Wilsford's villagers. In some instances, this was to help women who already had large families. 'I want to help [her] to feel secure . . . can I get one of the little rubber fitments you invented? If so where –' she said of one early case.[61] Yet Pamela, like Stopes (and many more, including John Maynard Keynes, Havelock Ellis and Balfour),[62] was an advocate of eugenic theory, then part of a progressive ideology. Eugenics applied in this context meant the use of birth control to prevent breeding among, in Stopes's words, the 'inferior, the depraved, and the feeble-minded'.[63] In an undated letter to the Stopes Society, Pamela asked for 'some appliances' that she could 'take down . . . & explain . . . the use of' to a woman in Wilsford village: 'She is not of very high intelligence, & it is really of importance that she should not bear a child. She has just married . . . I should be glad to be of use to her.'[64]

Despite her belief in Stopes's work, Pamela always gracefully resisted appearing on platforms at Stopes's meetings. Possibly this was her old fear of public speaking. She was probably also reluctant to become the controversial movement's figurehead that Stopes clearly wished her to be. On her remarriage, she gave up public support entirely. 'I have been a breaking reed, I fear: not in conviction, but in supporting you in public,' she told Stopes, explaining that 'Lord Grey is averse to my taking up public work, though he knows & admires your work . . .'[65] It is most likely that Grey could not countenance Pamela having public involvement in this work.

Pamela was not to have another child. In 1925, she wrote to Mananai recounting another prolonged period of bed-rest, with troublesome heart and raised blood pressure. She explained that the underlying cause was 'the change' – the menopause. '[S]he has had to give up doing everything & live the life of an invalid,' Mananai told Mary.[66] The Greys and Stephen spent the winter in Madeira and the spring in Vernet-les-Bains.

Grey's *Twenty-Five Years* had just been published, to remarkable commercial success (six impressions in six months) and critical acclaim. It was widely considered to vindicate Britain's entry into the war. Grey's dedication to Pamela explained that she had read over what he had written each day, offering suggestions and improvements. It seems that this amounted, in some cases, to rewriting. *Twenty-Five Years* contains an anecdote of Grey, as a child, seeing the Northern Lights and thinking them Paris burning in the 1870 Siege. It replicates almost exactly a supposed childhood memory of the Wyndhams, published in George's *Life and Letters* that same year.[67] In one biography of Grey Pamela has been presented as a society dalliance who had no impact on his life and work.[68] This is emphatically not so.

An added frisson of interest for the popular press was that this elder statesman breakfasted with stepchildren who were leading lights of the Bright Young Things. Immense wealth, good looks ('Of course, we have the fatal gift of beauty, darling,' Stephen commented)[69] and utter disdain for convention made Clare, David and Stephen irresistible to the press. David founded the notorious Gargoyle Club, a louche Soho nightspot that drew into its mirrored rooms everyone from the Prince of Wales to Tallulah Bankhead and the Bloomsbury Group. He married, in 1927, the pint-size revue star Hermione Baddeley, famous for her rendition of Noël Coward's 'Poor Little Rich Girl', written especially for her.[70] Stephen was the androgynous beauty immortalized by Cecil Beaton, whose 'Silver Room' in Mulberry House, wallpapered in silver foil, with a polar-bearskin rug on the floor, was the subject of a *Vogue* spread (Pamela said it looked like an iceberg).[71] Several of Beaton's most famous photographs of the Bright Young Things were taken at Wilsford, including that, in Pamela's drawing room, of Beaton, Stephen, Baby and Zita Jungman, Osbert and Sacheverell Sitwell, Rex Whistler, Elinor Wylie and Rosamond Lehmann lying on a rug underneath a tigerskin. In another, on the bridge over the Avon, men and women alike are dressed as Regency dandies in breeches with powdered faces, the river still as glass below them. Clare was an icy Society beauty, regularly featured in the press.

In *Broken Blood*, a family biography, Pamela's descendant Simon Blow alleged the corruption of an industrious, Presbyterian line by Pamela's blue blood. Certainly her extraordinary self-possession infected her children, but the way that David and Stephen Tennant, in particular, fascinated, titillated and outraged the press is redolent of the impact Eddy's sisters had had when launching themselves upon Society forty years before. Perhaps Wyndham blood melded with generation-skipping Tennant insouciance.

Moving in and out of their circle was Dick Wyndham, who had lived at Clouds for only a couple of years, during a disastrous early marriage. After his divorce in 1924, Dick, a playboy with artistic pretensions, moved to the French Riviera and let Clouds, first to Sibell's son Bend'Or, then to a wealthy Dutch couple, Adriaan and Nancy Mosselman. Despite a substantial income, Dick had developed a habit of selling off a painting a year to keep his funds buoyant. In 1927 it was *The Wyndham Sisters*.

Dick justified the sale as providing an annuity for Guy Wyndham, who had remarried in 1923 and had two small sons with his wife Violet (née Leverson). Sargent was rapidly falling out of fashion, but Dick thought he could get £20,000 for the painting – 'an entirely artificial value over and above what Grandpapa payed [sic] for it' – which, invested, would provide an income of £1,200 a year. He explained to Mary:

> I look upon this painting as really belonging to you and Aunt Madeline & Pamela, so would do nothing without your consent. Personally I feel very strongly that it ought to be sold . . . The alternative is keeping a picture in a house, where neither I nor any heirs will ever be able to live. I feel sure that Grandpapa would have been the first to chuckle at his good buy – the painting is 'sentiment' and I feel that Father's income is a more practical sentiment, particularly as none of the family get any advantage from the picture.[72]

The Wyndham Sisters was sold to New York's Metropolitan Museum of Art in 1927 for £20,000. There is no evidence that any of the money did go towards supporting Guy.[73] Pamela later heard from the Mosselmans that Dick had not even bothered to tell his tenants that he was intending to remove the painting. 'The first they knew of the matter was the men trampling in to unhook it! What a lack of *touch*,' she commented to Mary.[74]

Pamela in later life was as ripe for anecdote as ever. She appears in Hermione Baddeley's memoirs as an imperious grande dame, whisking David off on Alpine tours with more suitable young women, and recruiting the press baron Lord Beaverbrook to have a quiet word with Hermione over lunch. 'Marriage is not for a clever young actress like you . . .' he advised. 'You keep your mind right there on your career. Don't get married. D'you hear me?'[75] In Hermione's account, on discovering that David and Hermione had had an illegitimate daughter, Pauline, Pamela swoops in: '"By the way", said David, "you know how fond she is of babies. She asks if you'd like Pauline and her nanny to live at Wilsford?" I couldn't believe my ears. Not only was she trying to marry David off to some suitable girl, but she wanted my baby too . . .'[76] The story has a happy ending. After pitching up at David and Hermione's low-key wedding at Chelsea Registry Office in April 1928, draped in fox, with a feathered toque and Christopher and Stephen in morning suits, Pamela softened. She approached Hermione at the reception held at the Gargoyle 'and pressed the most beautiful pearl, emerald and diamond ring into my hand. "This is something very precious from me to you" she said. "The first man I ever loved gave it to me."'[77]

Hermione and David threw a party to celebrate their marriage, requiring their guests to dress in nightwear. The press went to town.[78] 'Hasn't all this racket about poor Hermione's "Bottle & Pyjama Party" been silly?' Pamela said to Mary, 'the occasion really being nothing different to an ordinary Fancy Dress Party – & "bringing a bottle" being one of the rather good "short-cuts" I think of modern days, that facillitates [sic] impromptu entertaining! But the Press *must* have copy – so they invent long interviews.'[79] A month later, the long interviews were about Stephen, one of the

protagonists in the 'Great Mayfair War' in which he brought unin-
vited guests to a ball given by Lady Ellesmere, who then threw the
'gate-crashers' out. The Old Guard were fighting a rearguard action.
Society had changed irrevocably since the pre-war years. But
Pamela's concern was for Stephen. Shortly afterwards, Edith Olivier
found her at Wilsford 'in a panic, quite broken . . . She and Lord
Grey have been warned that it's the beginning of a "Round-Up" of
Stephen and his foppish friends,' and Pamela was afraid that Stephen
'would be suspected of real immorality if he continues to be written
of in the papers in this company'.[80]

Pamela's concerns for Stephen were amplified by those about
Clare, who was in the throes of a second divorce and lining up
James Beck, her co-respondent, to be her third husband:[81] 'they
quarrel as if they had been already married for ten years (!) cynical
this – but you know what I mean . . . poor little Clare she looks
so worn and cross and miserable that I am anguished for her,'
Pamela told Mary. For some time Pamela's doctor had told her that
she had a 'hard patch in my Aorta . . . [which] gets affected by any
emotional strain'.[82] In May 1928 she suffered a bout of illness after
a 'gruelling week' in London in which she presented two young
cousins at court (the Queensberrys' girls), gave a paper on spiritualism at the Forum Club and chaired a Sunlight League meeting
in a stiflingly hot room at Sunderland House: 'I really did too much
and my heart cried out against me.'[83] The following month, further
anxiety about Clare 'threw' her 'back again [with] rather heightened
B.P. and a sense of troubled circulation in my breast'. She assured
Mary that she was at Wilsford, 'happily, *wisely resting* – & holding
as well as I can a quiet Centre of my own – in the midst of these
troubles'. She had adopted a raw diet, and was enjoying the latest
biography of Emily Brontë, written with a fashionably new psycho-
analytical slant.[84]

Some five months later, on a Sunday afternoon in November,
Pamela was alone in her garden at Wilsford when she suffered a
stroke. She died a few hours later without regaining consciousness.

She was fifty-seven. David and Christopher reached Wilsford in time. Stephen, who was summoned back from France where he had been holidaying with Siegfried Sassoon, and Clare, now married to Beck (she had sobbed, 'it's the end of my childhood' when told the news),[85] were both too late. So was Edward Grey. He had been at Fallodon when he was telephoned on Sunday evening. Just before 10 p.m. that night the Edinburgh–London express train was stopped at the little private railway station on the estate and Edward Grey boarded. He reached King's Cross at 5.15 a.m., ashen-faced, to be met by Christopher with the news that Pamela was dead.[86]

Mananai would never forget the ghastly shock of the telephone call the next morning. In the days after their sister's death the three remaining Wyndham children, the survivors of Percy's 'remarkable quintette', cleaved together for 'heavenly days of *healing* and *comfort*' at Babraham.[87] The Bishop of Salisbury conducted a bleak funeral at Wilsford, and a grim memorial service was held at St Margaret's Church in London, at which those attending had to fight their way through pouring rain and packs of pressmen eager to catch sight of the Bright Young Things in mourning, and the widowed Elder Statesman.[88]

Pamela did not cease to demand attention even in death. At Glen that Christmas, Stephen said that his mother had 'rained messages on me!'[89] Shortly after she died, headlines were splashed across the popular press. Hermione had told friends of a ghostly experience the night Pamela died, and they had leaked it to the press. The press tenor is exemplified by Utah's *Ogden Standard-Examiner* which asked, referencing David's rakish lifestyle, 'Did the Ghost of Viscountess Grey Return to Rebuke Her "Naughty Boy"?' with a mock-up of Hermione with hair standing on end.[90] Yet the incident, recounted in Hermione's memoirs, is curiously touching. She described being woken in the night by the sound of her bedroom door opening, and someone walking over to David's side of the bed:

'Is that you, Stephen?' I whispered. No one answered. There was complete quietness in the room. I sat up terrified . . . 'David,' I said hoarsely, 'someone's been in here.' My heart was thumping. 'There's someone in the room . . . whoever it was bent over you.' David lay back. 'Don't worry darling,' he said sleepily. 'It must have been Mummy coming to wish us goodnight.'[91]

THIRTY-THREE

The End

The force of Pamela's personality made it difficult for her sisters to believe that she was really gone. '[I]t seems . . . so bewildering & less easy to realize somehow to me now than when the blow first fell,' Mananai wrote to Mary, three weeks after Pamela's death.[1] For years, her instinct was to write to 'Darling Pamela' with every piece of family news: '[she] still seems here to share as I know she would our family happenings'.[2]

The lives of the Adeane children – albeit without the column inches – reflected how dramatically the war had changed their class's ways. Mananai rejoiced when Sibell Adeane and her second husband Charles Lyttelton (brother of Pamela Adeane's husband George) moved out of Hawarden, 'the huge cold gaunt house with miles of basement!', into the recently deceased Helen Gladstone's 'lovely sunny central heated – lit – modern house The Rectory'.[3] She mourned when Sibell, four and a half months pregnant, was obliged to undergo an induced miscarriage in 'a little absolutely new & up to date Maternity Home' after the doctor said that she would never carry the child to full term.[4] In 1929, Robert Adeane married Joyce Burnett. That November, Mananai was overwhelmed, even tearful when she found out that they were to have a baby: 'isn't it *wonderful*? it seems so somehow to me I don't know why – *Robert's* child', she wrote to Mary.[5]

As that Christmas approached, Mananai was wrestling with the implications of the impending Local Government Act for her county council business. It was to come into force on April Fools' Day 1930, and had given her 'much extra . . . work . . . but *most* interesting'. She was also carrying on her Red Cross work, trying to launch an 'Orthopoedic [sic] scheme' to add to that of massage already existing.[6] Mananai's letters were, as always, enthusiastically loving and short on reflection. She had escaped, by disposition, the fragility and nerviness of her sisters: she had also been helped by a happy marriage, and finding work that she loved.

From the late 1920s, Mary frequently asserted that she had not long to live.[7] Crippling arthritis in both hips required her to walk with the aid of sticks, and left her in near-constant pain. She had been crushed by the sudden, early death, in 1925, of Frances Charteris, Guy's wife. 'With Frances there . . . I felt "safe" about them ALL and could have died tomorrow without a tremor,' she told Arthur.[8] Now, 'I feel I must – – more broken-winged than ever – trudge on like a snarling wrinkled charwoman, old and harsh with years! A crippled witch groping about with the Fairy Princess gone who ruled us with her gentle gracious sway.'[9] Others disagreed. An anonymous correspondent, paying tribute to Mary in *The Times* after her death, wrote:

> Many who remember with admiration and love the brilliant, vivid woman portrayed in Sargent's 'Three Graces' may think that the last phase was the loveliest of all: the frail, shrunken, halting figure, dependent on the two sticks which were always losing themselves, and the monkey-headed hot-water bottle Pongo: the laces and muslin, fastened with little glimmering brooches, framing the finely modelled, deep-lined, ivory face in which the eyes of a young girl shone with inexhaustible fun.[10]

Throughout the decade, the publication of memoirs sporadically flung the Souls back into the public eye. The first occasion was early on in the decade, when Margot released the first volume of her autobiography. Gossipy, indiscreet and ludicrously self-important, it provoked a 'controversial maelstrom', in Balfour's words.[11] 'All the things that people quote to me from it as containing observations of mine seem to be quite untrue but not intentionally malevolent,' he said to Mary, declining to even read it.[12] There was another flurry in January 1929, when *The Times* serialized extracts from Richard Haldane's forthcoming memoirs which criticized the Souls for taking themselves on occasion 'much too seriously . . . on the whole it is doubtful whether their influence was on balance good'.[13] A number, including Ettie Desborough, wrote anonymously to the Editor to protest. 'When Lord Haldane says that . . . he is taking himself too seriously. [The Souls] were not concerned with chaperoning the conscience of anybody. They shared different ideas, different ambitions and different politics,' said 'Q' in a forthright riposte.[14] All these letters emphasized the cross-party nature of the group, their lifelong devotion and loyalty to one another. The Souls continued to deny that they were a 'set', maintaining, in a distinction perhaps only they could see, that they were simply a group of good friends. It left them in the somewhat awkward position of defending the character of a clique they claimed had never existed.[15]

The previous spring had been the longest period Mary and Balfour ever spent under one roof, when Balfour came to Stanway for five weeks to recover from a mild stroke. Ettie was also there: a trinity of Souls, as of old.[16] That year, Mary wrote to Arthur imagining what people might say about them: 'How pathetic to see Arthur and Mary Wemyss. How sad is the end of life – the necessary onslaught of illness and old age. How sad to outlive Romance. I believe they were lovers once, tho' nobody knows the truth about these things!'[17]

Arthur died at Whittingehame in 1930. Mary was at Hyères. Two days before that, she had woken feeling out of sorts, edgy, nervous and tearful. From Hyères she sent a bunch of rosemary and thyme, the only flowers, besides family flowers, thrown into his grave.[18] 'I cannot yet realize how great the blank will be,'[19] she wrote, upon the loss of her 'unfailing friend'.[20] Her lifelong confidant had gone. With the publication of *Family Record* in 1932, she began work on her Souls memoir in earnest.[21] Ettie and Evelyn de Vesci, friends spanning fifty years, continued to marvel at Mary's energy. She was as 'Napoleon-like' as ever, said Ettie, as Mary planned a day that involved leaving Stanway after breakfast, lunching in London and dining at Taplow Court, after stopping off in Surrey for tea.[22] Yet Mary was also prone to fits of depression and gloom, and mental demons could drive her into fits of anxiety. She reached such a crisis in 1936.

In 1932 Dick had put Clouds – estate and contents – up for sale. Only the most precious objects – the Orpens of Madeline and Percy, the Watts of Madeline, George Wyndham's bust by Rodin – were kept in the family. Everything else – from eighteenth-century Italian cabinets to a pair of ice-skates – was auctioned off over the following months. 'The prices weren't too good – but not *too* bad,' Dick Wyndham told his father.[23] It took four years for Knight, Frank & Rutley, the estate agents, to find a buyer for the 'dignified mansion' and its 3,000 acres. In 1936 it was sold for a little over £39,000 to a property developer, who parcelled it up. The eventual buyer of Clouds – now marooned on just 26 acres – demolished a third of the house before the Second World War, just to make it manageable.[24]

Mary, adrift without Balfour, the *Family Record* that had accompanied her for fifteen years complete, Clouds sold, and agitated by Margot's prolific publications, began to try to pin down her past. Her progress on her memoir of the Souls had been faltering. Now she reattempted it, as an article which she intended for publication under the title 'Friendship's Garland'.[25] Becoming frantic at her inability to capture it properly, she sought the help of Evelyn and her brother-in-law Evan Charteris. The manuscript horrified them. The article was meant to be 'character sketches' of 'ball throwers' that Mary had admired,[26] but in reality it was full of titles, names and 'unsubstantiated assertions', said Evan.[27] 'I think it is an *impossible* document for the *public* to play about with,' said Evelyn. She thought it could attract only 'unkind derision & criticism . . . a *saddening* document'.[28] Yet their attempts to dissuade Mary – now 'verging on a nervous breakdown' in their view – failed. Evan agreed to go to Gosford to help her edit the work. Mary had told him that she would 'go mad' if he did not help her, '& she looks a wraith – & agonized & distracted', he explained to Evelyn.[29]

On arriving at East Lothian, Evan was dismayed by what he saw. Gosford had reached its nadir with Angela and Hugo's decision to turn it into a hotel of sorts, taking in paying guests. Evan's description is redolent of Fawlty Towers: 'the little dining room (marble hall end) – now a gaudy cocktail bar – with a rather pretty barmaid – cheap little tables – & cheaper chairs – disposed in the true bar manner', Hugo 'sulky as a bear' striding the corridors, barking at a man in plus-fours turning into the saloon to ask him what he was doing there. Angela was 'always in the house – usually in the Bar – following guests about, spying what she can & giving them fits with a monster Alsatian which barks & bays along the corridors'; while Connor, 'in great distress about the situation financial & social . . . weeps for the good name of the Brigadier & Mumsey [the tenth Earl and Countess of Wemyss]'. There was only one guest when Evan arrived, '& it has now got so bad a name locally & I believe universally that it is commonly regarded as doomed'.[30] No one escaped Evan's furious eye: 'Guy [Charteris] with no more manners than a fish hook . . . wraps – papers – cards – bridge scores strewn about – dogs fighting and being screamed at – never a moments serenity or peace – everyone snapping & scrapping. I have paid my last visit there.'[31]

Evan's attempts to help with editing had been futile. 'M is incorrigible . . . she concedes an exclusion of a name or the alteration of a sentence or paragraph & the next day it is returned – she is a naughty child up to every sort of subterfuge & dodge secretly determined to get her own way.'[32] He was more concerned about Mary's mental state:

[she] has been undone by coming here . . . the Souls & Moby Dick [Wyndham] have played havoc – & her state of mental agitation is worse than I can recall it to have ever been . . . I wonder if she ought not to try psycho-analysis. . .? I know nothing about it beyond its claim to reduce complexes – & here at any rate are the complexes allright [sic] – complexes which are biting into her reason – dominating her outlook & blotting out all other considerations.[33]

The article was never finished. The following February, Mary's children and grandchildren held a 'Family Banquet' for her at her club, the Albemarle, on Dover Street as her seventy-fifth birthday approached. The Adeanes did not attend, Mananai was recovering from the flu and Charlie had duties as Lord Lieutenant which he could not miss. 'We don't want to complicate things (which leaving things open does) so I feel we ought to say no,' said Mananai.[34] Two months later, Mary had a small house party at Stanway: five or six of her oldest friends, and a new young writer and his artist sister whom 'she had newly taken to her heart'. To her guests she seemed as vibrant as ever – although she confided to one of them that she did not think she had long to live. This time she was right. She died a week later on 29 April 1937, at the age of seventy-four. She had been taken ill at Stanway in the afternoon, and died that night with 'a swiftness merciful to her', wrote the anonymous correspondent in *The Times*: 'a rare spirit has passed away'.[35] Hugo lived another two months, rivalrous to the end, and died in his sleep at Gosford, in his eightieth year.

Mananai and Guy, the two quietest of Percy's 'remarkable quintette', lived long enough to experience the sadness of seeing the world once more descend into war. Guy Wyndham died in the darkest days of the Blitz, on 17 April 1941, peacefully in his sleep in Wiltshire. Two months later, on 31 July, Madeline Adeane at the age of seventy-two suffered a fatal heart attack at Babraham, cheated of her hope to live long enough to see what became of Adolf Hitler. She had been engaged 'literally' to the very day of her death in her county council and charity work. 'The gap she leaves there . . . cannot be filled,' wrote a correspondent in anonymous tribute.[36] Under the headline, 'One of "The Three Graces"', *The Times* noted the passing of a dynasty: 'She was the last survivor of the gifted family of the Hon. Percy and Mrs. Wyndham, whose home at Clouds in Wiltshire, was, during the 30 years before the last War, a delightful social and intellectual centre.'[37]

And so it ends. But not, perhaps, if one takes Pamela's word for it. In 1928 she had made a 'pilgrimage' back to Clouds, taking David, bearing wreaths for the graves of her parents and George. They had found the graveyard 'profoundly beautiful & peaceful'. Except that the rosemary on Madeline Wyndham's grave was overgrown, everything was as it should be. David had read aloud from Shelley's *Adonais* for George; Pamela had recited lines for her parents: a 'little Persian rhyme' that Madeline Wyndham had loved, and for her father Proverbs 4:18 – 'But the path of the just is as the shining light, that shineth more and more unto the perfect day.'[38]

Pamela and David had gone into the house, to be greeted kindly by Mrs Mosselman, and wandered around the place. The house was warm and lived in, Pamela told Mary, and scattered with children's toys. In the library, Pamela had stood by the Rodin bust of George and 'received a fine, and convincing RAP (– one of my *raps* that are so astonishingly apposite!) . . . I laughed, & said "*All Right!* – Message received!"' The atmosphere of the house was still overpowering 'like a tangible, all encompassing actuality! Just like great mid-summer Lilies or Honeysuckle, come towards you . . . on the air in Summer evenings'.

Walking through the house, Pamela felt like Kay in *The Snow Queen*, a fairytale she had read with her sisters long ago, in which dreams and vapours passed the boy that only he could see.[39] She relived the sight of Madeline Wyndham, making her way across the hall, arms piled high with shawls for music listeners, of Percy in his flapping slipper-heels slip-slopping his way across. She heard the sound of herself on her guitar. She saw themselves as children impatiently tapping the weather glass, longing for snow and ice to go tobogganing; saw the great teas where thirty or more sat and waited for toast, always cold and curling after the servants' trek down miles of corridor. She saw Mary and Madeline Wyndham, desperately trying to battle up the narrow stone staircase through gathering smoke, thinking the children still above on that January night that Clouds was ablaze; she saw too in the empty, rebuilt hall herself and Harry Cust standing on the hearthstone in that final interview at the end of the summer – the end of their affair. Clouds' atmosphere, like the scent of the wild flowers that once filled it, was still strong.

'Just as there are long strands of Time, here, on the Earth Plane which we live through & then fold up & lay away, so I believe, in the next phase of Consciousness, there are long sweeps of Earth Life, to be lived over again, to be more fully realized perhaps,' Pamela told Mary. The only difference she thought likely was that 'sad facts' might be hidden from 'dead eyes'. 'And so', Pamela concluded, 'it might be that Mamma may quite well be happily unconscious of any disturbing or chilling factors in the present history of Clouds, and be – possibly – safely and joyously tucked away again into a nest of lovely sisters, and visiting Mrs Curragh with Lord Odo Fitzgerald [sic] . . . or shining in an equipage of old Lord Carlisle's, with outriders, driving through the gates of Dublin Castle . . .'[40] – on her way to meet, perhaps, for the first time, the young, uncertain Percy Wyndham, and let the whole story unfurl once more.

Acknowledgements

Writing thanks for a project that has taken some eight years from inception to publication is a daunting prospect. My first debts are to Anthony Cheetham, who came up with the idea for this book, and to my incomparable agent Georgina Capel, who with extra-ordinary tenacity has brought that idea to fruition. Without them, this book would never have come into being. Then thanks are to my clear-sighted editor Arabella Pike at William Collins, whose incisive comments have immeasurably improved the work; to all her team for their hard work and endless patience, in particular Stephen Guise, Joseph Zigmond and Katherine Patrick; and to Peter James, for his sympathetic copy-editing.

The research for this book has taken me to libraries, archives, record offices and private homes all over the country. The following institutions and archives generously gave me access to, and permission to quote from, their collections, and their staff were unfailingly helpful: the Bodleian Library; British Library; Fitzwilliam Museum, Cambridge; Hertford Archives; National Records of Scotland; National Library of Scotland; and Somerset Record Office. Thanks also to the staff of the Cheshire Record Office and the West Sussex County Council Record Office for allowing me to read private collections on site, and to the staff of the London Library. For access to private collections, I am grateful to the Earl of Egremont; Hugo Vickers; the Whittingehame Estate; Francis Wyndham; and others. Lord Wemyss has been generous beyond measure in allowing me access to the Stanway archives, and granting me permission to reproduce images in the Stanway Collection. James and Olinda Adeane have been extraordinarily helpful and kind. The Bonham Carter Trustee and Christopher Osborn were kind enough to grant me permission to quote copyright work of Margot Asquith. Others to whom I am grateful are the Earl and Countess of Oxford and Asquith for showing me material relating to Raymond Asquith and Frances, Lady Horner; Lady Glenconner; Philip Hoare for answering last-minute, anxious requests; and Melissa Wyndham and Suzanne Lobel for their enthusiasm for the project.

Certain people have helped this book immeasurably along its way. Philippa Brewster, Dan Jones and Hugo Vickers have all been the most sympathetic and helpful of ears in various times of crisis. Juggling writing with my other career as a barrister has been possible only thanks to the support of those at Essex Court Chambers, in particular my clerks David Grief and Jack Wood; and my erstwhile pupil supervisor Nathan Pillow. To all my friends: especially Will Gresford, who encouraged me to take on the project and whose connections set me on the way; Laura Hamm, my wingman in every coffee shop in New York; Lauren Aguilar, who lived with the book for two months across Sri Lanka; Ollie Marre, Joanna Buckley and Henry Day, my life-lines through law school; Lucy Davis; Maggie Asquith; Phoebe Barran; and Charlotte Evans, whose support has been unfailing since we were eighteen years old. To my godparents David and Angela Neuberger and Alex Gordon Shute; Jonny and Gabrielle Levy for their immediate, overwhelming support in the darkest of times. To all those who have lived with me and my boxes of books (in chronological order): Sarah O'Reilly, Sophie Elmhirst, Raya al Bader, Patrick Hennessey, Viva van Loock, Becca Ratcliffe and Nicky Sayers: thanks for listening to me bang on and I'm sorry about the mess. To Mark Lobel, who has now so gracefully taken on their mantle – thank you.

To list my myriad, ever-expanding family requires a deep breath, so here goes: my father Simon Renton, stepmother Rachel Smith and sister Izzy Renton; my grandmother Lavinia Hankinson; my stepfather Derek J. Content; Judy Englender; my sister Philippa Content and her clan, Chris, Arlo and Nina Winterbourne; my South African family, Jonathan, Gail, Kate, Nicky and Matty Schrire; Toby Colegate-Stone, the most patient and tolerant of brothers-in-law; and Imi and Mabel, the next generation of (head) strong women. Thank you all beyond measure.

Finally, I come to the hardest, and the easiest, thanks of all. To my brilliant, bold and beloved mother Amanda Content, who died in October 2009, as I was halfway through this book, and my sister Julia Colegate-Stone, who has helped me every step of the way before and since. I could not have begun to understand the ties that bound the Wyndham women together without my own experience to draw on. To my mother and my sister, this is for, and because of, you.

Claudia Renton
Lincoln's Inn Fields
December 2013

Notes

A note on the references:

The correspondence between Mary Elcho and Arthur Balfour lies principally in the Stanway archives, at Stanway House in Gloucestershire, and the Whittingehame archives. Professor Jane Ridley and Clayre Percy have edited a wonderful collection of this correspondence in *Letters of Arthur Balfour and Lady Elcho 1887–1917* (Hamish Hamilton, 1992). For the reader's ease, where the letter I have referred to also appears in this published collection, I have referenced it according to the page at which it may be found in the *Letters*.

A note on the values:

Where I provide calculations of money values in today's terms, I provide three values for the sum. For income or wealth: the simple RPI calculation (RPI), the economic status value, which may be described as the 'prestige value' of that income or wealth (ESV), and the economic power value, which measures the amount of income or wealth relative to the total output of the economy (EPV). Both these latter calculations are based on GDP, and help to give a better idea of relative wealth within contemporary society. For commodity values I give the real price; the labour value, which is measured by using the relative wage for a worker to buy that commodity; and the income value, which measures the relative average income that would be used to buy the commodity. All calculations are from www.measuringworth.com.

Epigram

J. W. Mackail and Guy Wyndham, *Life and Letters of George Wyndham*, 2 vols (Hutchinson, 1925), 2.723.

Prologue

1. Pamela Glenconner, 'Fantasia – of a London House Closed', in Pamela Glenconner, *The White Wallet* (T. Fisher Unwin, 1912), pp. 211–12.
2. Frances, Lady Horner to Edward Burne-Jones, quoted in Caroline Dakers, *Clouds: The Biography of a Country House* (New Haven and London, Yale University Press, 1993), p. 163.
3. The phrase is that of William Lethaby, the architectural historian, and friend and biographer of Philip Webb, cited in Dakers, *Clouds*, p. 83.
4. Percy Wyndham to Pamela Tennant, 7 February 1900, Glenconner Papers, NRS GD510/1/26.
5. Pamela Tennant to Percy Wyndham, quoted in Dakers, *Clouds*, pp. 164–5.
6. Pamela Tennant to Percy Wyndham, quoted in ibid., p. 164.
7. Ibid.
8. Mary Elcho to Madeline Wyndham, 18 January 1899, Stanway Papers.
9. Ibid.
10. Madeline Wyndham to Pamela Tennant, 16 February 1900, Glenconner Papers, NRS GD510/1/26.
11. William Howe Downes, *John S. Sargent: His Life and Work* (Thornton Butterworth, 1926), p. 17.
12. James Lomax and Richard Ormond, *John Singer Sargent and the Edwardian Age: An Exhibition Organized Jointly by the Leeds Art Galleries, the National Portrait Gallery, London, and the Detroit Institute of Arts* (Leeds, Leeds Art Galleries, 1979), p. 53.
13. Pamela Tennant to Percy Wyndham, quoted in Dakers, *Clouds*, pp. 164–5.
14. Arthur Balfour to Mary Elcho, 22 September 1900, quoted in Jane Ridley and Clayre Percy (eds), *The Letters of Arthur Balfour and Lady Elcho 1885–1917* (Hamish Hamilton, 1992), p. 176.

15. Quoted in Downes, *John S. Sargent*, pp. 188–9.
16. Quoted in ibid., p. 50.
17. Quoted in ibid., pp. 109–10.
18. Quoted in Lomax and Ormond, *John Singer Sargent and the Edwardian Age*, p. 55.

Chapter 1: 'Worse than 100 Boys'

1. Constance Leconfield to Madeline Wyndham, 15 March 1909, Petworth Papers.
2. Emily Eden, *Miss Eden's Letters*, ed. Violet Dickinson (Macmillan, 1919), pp. 250–1 n. 423.
3. Quoted in Fiona MacCarthy, *The Last Pre-Raphaelite: Edward Burne-Jones and the Victorian Imagination* (Faber & Faber, 2011), p. 324.
4. Percy Wyndham to Madeline Wyndham, 31 July 1860, Petworth Papers.
5. Percy Wyndham to Fanny Montgomery, 3 August 1862, cited in Dakers, *Clouds*, p. 20.
6. Quoted in D. G. Boyce, *The Irish Question and British Politics 1868–1996* (2nd edn, Macmillan, 1996), p. 1.
7. Lawrence James, *Aristocrats: Power, Grace and Decadence – Britain's Great Ruling Classes from 1066 to the Present* (Little, Brown, 2009), p. 314.
8. Katharine Tynan Hinkson, *The Years of the Shadow* (Constable, 1919), p. 256.
9. Ibid., p. 257.
10. Max Egremont, *The Cousins* (Collins, 1977), p. 21.
11. John Darwin, *The Empire Project: The Rise and Fall of the British World System 1830–1970* (Cambridge, Cambridge University Press, 2009), p. 26 n.1.
12. Mackail and Wyndham, *Life and Letters*, 1.153.
13. Percy Wyndham to Madeline Wyndham, 1 August 1860, Petworth Papers.
14. Percy Wyndham to Madeline Wyndham, 5 August 1860, Petworth Papers.
15. Conversation with Mrs James Adeane, *c.*2008.
16. Lady Campbell to Lord Leconfield, 12 July 1860, quoted in Mackail and Wyndham, *Life and Letters*, 1.17.
17. See the correspondence between Henry Brydon, the lawyer responsible for the transaction, Percy Wyndham and Lord Leconfield in September and

October 1860, Petworth Papers. The money, £35,727 16s 5d in consols, was transferred from Lord Leconfield's account at the Bank of England on 19 September 1860. Lord Leconfield was charged £1 1s 6d for the transaction. On 10 October, it was transferred to the trustees of the marriage settlement – Percy's elder brother Henry, and Adolphus Liddell, a lifelong friend of Percy and Madeline's, and in time a close friend of their children. The equivalent in today's money is £2,754,000 in RPI, £30,250,000 in ESV and £66,340,000 in EPV. The settlement was signed by Percy and Madeline either the day before or the morning of their marriage.

18. 'Heads of Settlement by the Honourable Percy Scawen Wyndham on his marriage with Miss Campbell of Woodview, Stillorgan near Dublin, daughter of the late Sir Guy Campbell, Bart., of £35,000 consols', Petworth Papers. When Percy's brother Henry married Constance Primrose, granddaughter of the Earl of Rosebery, some seven years later, Lord Leconfield provided the same amount for her. However, Constance matched this with the dowry she brought to the marriage herself.

19. Madeline Wyndham to Pamela Tennant, 14 January 1898, Glenconner Papers, NRS GD510/1/32 f. 24r.

20. Mary, Countess of Wemyss, *A Family Record* (Plaistow, Curwen Press, 1932), pp. 19–20.

21. Nancy Waters Ellenberger, 'Constructing George Wyndham: Narratives of Aristocracy in Fin-de-Siècle England', *Journal of British Studies* 39:4 (October 2000): 487–517, 496.

22. Bernard Cracroft, 'The Analysis of the House of Commons, or Indirect Representation', in *Essays on Reform*, quoted in Lawrence Stone and Jeanne C. Fawtier Stone, *An Open Elite? England 1500–1880* (Oxford, Clarendon Press, 1984), p. 422.

23. Quoted in Leonore Davidoff, *The Best Circles: Society, Etiquette and the Season* (Croom Helm, 1974), p. 64.

24. Ridley and Percy (eds), *Letters of Arthur Balfour and Lady Elcho*, p. 11.

25. G. F. Watts to Madeline Wyndham, quoted in Mary S. Watts, *George Frederic Watts: The Annals of an Artist's Life*, 2 vols (Macmillan, 1912), 1.239–41.

26. Mackail and Wyndham, *Life and Letters*, 1.20–1.

27. Dakers, *Clouds*, p. 35.

28. Mary Elcho to Wilfrid Scawen Blunt, 16 August 1921, Blunt Papers, FM 225-1976.

29. Ibid.

30. Lady Campbell to Percy Wyndham, quoted in Dakers, *Clouds*, p. 20.

31. Mary Elcho to Madeline Wyndham, 7 December 1899, Stanway Papers.

32. Mary Elcho to Madeline Wyndham, 17 February 1871, Petworth Papers.

33. Mary Elcho to Madeline Wyndham, 8 October 1874, Petworth Papers.

34. Mary Elcho to Madeline Wyndham, n.d. [1874], Petworth Papers.

35. Mackail and Wyndham, *Life and Letters*, 1.21.

36. Ibid., 1.19.

37. Mary Elcho to Arthur Balfour, 16 August 1895 (*Letters*, pp. 138–9).

38. Christine Kinealy, *This Great Calamity: The Irish Famine 1845–52* (Dublin, Gill & Macmillan, 1994), p. 357.

39. Edith Olivier, *Four Victorian Ladies of Wiltshire* (Faber & Faber, 1940), p. 92.

40. Ibid., p. 93.

41. George Wyndham to Edward Clifford, September 1895, quoted in Mackail and Wyndham, *Life and Letters*, 1.287.

42. Percy Wyndham to Madeline Wyndham, 12 August 1860, Petworth Papers.

43. Ellenberger, 'Constructing George Wyndham', p. 497.

44. Mary Elcho to Margot Asquith, 3 May 1911, Bodleian, Asquith Papers, MS. Eng. d. 3283.

45. As she grew older, the Wyndhams' second daughter more frequently used 'Madeline'. In order, however, to distinguish between mother and daughter, I refer throughout to Madeline (daughter) as Mananai, except where I use her married name, Madeline Adeane. Doubtless Mananai would have understood, as even she was capable of being caught out on occasion by the family's faithful adherence to a mere handful of names: '[T]here were two Madelines in the house, two Pamelas, two Percys . . . three Guys . . . so it was rather confusing' Mananai commented of a visit by Campbell cousins to Wilbury in 1883 (Madeline Adeane to Mary Elcho, 16 September 1883, Stanway Papers).

46. Dakers, *Clouds*, p. 36.

47. Ibid.

48. Mackail and Wyndham, *Life and Letters*, 1.16.

49. Mary Elcho to Madeline Wyndham, n.d. [November, 1869], Petworth Papers.

50. Madeline Wyndham to Mary Elcho, 25 October [1869], Stanway Papers.

51. Jerry White, *London in the Nineteenth Century* (Vintage, 2008), pp. 371–2.

52. Quoted in David Marquand, *Britain since 1918: The Strange Career of British Democracy* (Orion, 2008), p. 33.

53. White, *London in the Nineteenth Century*, p. 137.

54. Marquand, *Britain since 1918*, p. 53.

55. See G. F. Watts to Madeline Wyndham in Watts, *George Frederic Watts*, 1.239–41, 325–6.

56. Quoted in Dakers, *Clouds*, p. 57.

57. Madeline Wyndham to Mary Elcho, c.September 1884, Stanway Papers.

58. Philip Burne-Jones to Lady Frances Balfour, 15 October 1889, Whittingehame Papers, NRS GD433/2/301 f. 72.

59. For the suggestion that this is so, see Dakers, *Clouds*, p. 129; and Jane Abdy and Charlotte Gere, *The Souls* (Sidgwick & Jackson, 1984), pp. 90–1.

60. Cynthia Asquith, *Haply I May Remember* (James Barrie, 1950), p. 138.

61. See Pamela Tennant's recollection in her letter to Mary Elcho, 13 March 1928, Stanway Papers.

62. See Madeline Wyndham's response to Mary Elcho's miscarriage in 1884 and Madeline Adeane's stillborn child in 1899.

63. Elizabeth Longford, *Pilgrimage of Passion: The Life of Wilfrid Scawen Blunt* (Weidenfeld & Nicolson, 1979), p. 172.

64. Frederic Harrison, *Autobiographic Memoirs*, 2 vols (Macmillan, 1911), 2.166, 173.

65. Katherine Tynan Hinkson, *Twenty-Five Years: Reminiscences* (John Murray, 1913), pp. 302–3.

66. Wilfrid Scawen Blunt, diaries, quoted in Longford, *A Pilgrimage of Passion*, p. 102.

67. Wilfrid Scawen Blunt, 'Alms to Oblivion', Part V, Chapter III, Blunt Papers, FM 311-1975.

68. Blunt Papers, K6115.

69. Dakers, *Clouds*, p. 45; Mackail and Wyndham, *Life and Letters*, 1.24.

70. Wilfrid Scawen Blunt, diaries, quoted in Longford, *Pilgrimage of Passion*, p. 102.

71. Wilfrid Scawen Blunt, 'Alms to Oblivion', Part V, Chapter III, Blunt Papers, FM 311-1975.

72. Madeline Wyndham to Pamela Tennant, 1 June 1896, Glenconner Papers, NRS GD510/1/30.

Chapter 2: Wilbury

1. Longford, *Pilgrimage of Passion*, pp. 157, 310.
2. Percy Wyndham to Mary Elcho, 22 November 1900, Stanway Papers.
3. George Wyndham to Pamela Tennant, 23 December 1896, Glenconner Papers, NRS GD510/1/32.
4. Cynthia Asquith, *Remember and Be Glad* (James Barrie, 1952), p. 192.
5. Wemyss, *Family Record*, p. 20.
6. Richard Davenport-Hines, *Ettie: The Intimate Life and Dauntless Spirit of Lady Desborough* (Weidenfeld & Nicolson, 2008), p. 83.
7. Mary Elcho to Guy Wyndham, 11 May 1877, Stanway Papers. For Mary's recollection of herself at this time see Mary Elcho to Arthur Balfour, 16 August 1895 (*Letters*, pp. 138–9).
8. MacCarthy, *The Last Pre-Raphaelite*, p. 308.
9. Mackail and Wyndham, *Life and Letters*, 1.21.
10. Mary Elcho to Arthur Balfour, 16 August 1895 (*Letters*, pp. 138–9).
11. Mary Elcho to Madeline Wyndham, 14 October 1880, Stanway Papers.
12. Mary Elcho to Madeline Wyndham, 3 June 1885, Stanway Papers.
13. Wilfrid Scawen Blunt, diary entry, 9 January 1895, quoted in Longford, *Pilgrimage of Passion*, p. 310.
14. Asquith, *Haply I May Remember*, p. 135.
15. Alfred Lyttelton to Mary Gladstone, 31 December 1886, quoted in Nancy Waters Ellenberger, 'The Souls: High Society and Politics in Late Victorian England', PhD thesis, University of Oregon, 1982, pp. 62–3.
16. Mabell, Countess of Airlie, *Thatched with Gold: The Memoirs of Mabell, Countess of Airlie*, ed. and arranged by Jennifer Ellis (Hutchinson, 1962), p. 40.
17. George Wyndham to Madeline Wyndham, 15 October 1874, Petworth Papers.
18. Mary Elcho to Madeline Wyndham, 4 September 1883, Stanway Papers.
19. Mary Elcho to Madeline Wyndham, 19 November 1876, Petworth Papers.

20. Mary Elcho to Madeline Wyndham, 7 December 1889, Stanway Papers.

21. Mackail and Wyndham, *Life and Letters*, 1.26.

22. Ibid., 1.24.

23. Dakers, *Clouds*, p. 45; Mackail and Wyndham, *Life and Letters*, 1.24.

24. Philip Burne-Jones to Mary Elcho quoted in Dakers, *Clouds*, p. 176.

25. Mackail and Wyndham, *Life and Letters*, 1.21.

26. Walter Crane in *Transactions of the National Association for the Advancement of Art and its Application to Industry*, quoted in Mary Greensted (ed.), *An Anthology of the Arts and Crafts Movement: Writings by Ashbee, Lethaby, Gimson and their Contemporaries* (Aldershot, Lund Humphries, 2005), p. 18.

27. See, for example, the Victoria and Albert Museum's résumé of Beerbohm Tree at http://www.vam.ac.uk/users/node/8593.

28. Mackail and Wyndham, *Life and Letters*, 1.27–8.

29. Mary Elcho to Madeline Wyndham, 6 October 1880, Stanway Papers.

30. Dakers, *Clouds*, p. 42.

31. Ibid., p. 47.

32. Ibid., p. 48. The equivalent in RPI is £7,719,000; in ESV £64,500,00; and in EPV £122,700,000.

33. Mackail and Wyndham, *Life and Letters*, 1.31.

34. Dakers, *Clouds*, p. 44.

35. Ibid., p. 48.

36. Mary Elcho, diary entry, 16 September 1878, quoted in Dakers, *Clouds*, p. 114.

37. Quoted in Geoffrey Wheatcroft, *The Strange Death of Tory England* (Penguin Books, 2005), p. 31.

38. Lawrence James, *The Rise and Fall of the British Empire* (Abacus, 1995), p. 196.

39. Ibid., p. 198.

40. Ibid., pp. 196–7.

41. Ibid., pp. 196–9.

42. Mackail and Wyndham, *Life and Letters*, 1.11.

43. Mackail and Wyndham, *Life and Letters*, 1.32.

44. Ellenberger, 'Constructing George Wyndham', pp. 487, 496.

45. Dakers, *Clouds*, pp. 67–8.

46. Ibid., p. 64.

47. Mary Elcho to Guy Wyndham, 11 May 1877, Stanway Papers.

48. Mary Elcho, diary entry, 30 June 1878, Stanway Papers.

49. Mary Elcho to Madeline Wyndham, 15 July 1898, Stanway Papers.

50. Madeline Adeane to Madeline Wyndham, 26 July 1878, Petworth Papers.

51. Pamela Tennant to Madeline Wyndham, 11 December 1878, Petworth Papers.

52. Pamela Tennant to Percy Wyndham, 13 November 1878, Petworth Papers.

53. *The Times*, 10 May 1887.

54. MacCarthy, *The Last Pre-Raphaelite*, p. 281.

55. *The Times*, 1 May 1877.

56. *The Times*, 10 May 1887.

57. MacCarthy, *The Last Pre-Raphaelite*, p. 281.

58. For a fuller account of the Aesthetic movement and its impact upon society, see Charlotte Gere, *Artistic Circles: Design & Decoration in the Aesthetic Movement* (V&A Publishing, 2010), and Stephen Calloway and Lynn Federle Orr (eds), *The Cult of Beauty: The Aesthetic Movement 1860–1900* (V&A Publishing, 2011).

59. Mary Elcho, diary entry, quoted in Dakers, *Clouds*, p. 57.

60. Mary Gladstone, quoted in R. J. Q. Adams, *Balfour: The Last Grandee* (John Murray, 2008), p. 29.

61. Harold Begbie (as 'A Gentleman with a Duster'), *Mirrors of Downing Street: Some Political Reflections* (Mills & Boon, 1920), pp. 76–9.

62. Laura Tennant to Lady Frances Balfour, 9 October [1885], Whittingehame Papers, NRS GD433/2/477.

63. See Arthur James Balfour, *Chapters of Autobiography*, ed. Blanche Dugdale (Cassell, 1930), p. 234. *Chapters of Autobiography* has seventeen chapters. The first sixteen concern Balfour's political youth. The final words of this section recollect his meeting Mary, Madeline and George Wyndham at Sir Frederic Leighton's studio. The seventeenth chapter, tacked on somewhat incongruously, covers Balfour's first trip to the United States in 1917, and his subsequent diplomatic work there.

Chapter 3: 'The Little Hunter'

1. Mary Elcho, diary entry, 12 May 1880, Stanway Papers.
2. Davidoff, *The Best Circles*, p. 25.
3. Dakers, *Clouds*, p. 59.
4. Quoted in Max Egremont, *The Cousins: The Friendship, Opinions and Activities of Wilfrid Scawen Blunt and George Wyndham* (Collins, 1977), p. 33.
5. See, in particular, David Cannadine, 'The Context, Performance and Meaning of Ritual: The British Monarchy and the "Invention of Tradition" circa 1820–1977', in Eric Hobsbawm and Terence Ranger (eds), *The Invention of Tradition* (Cambridge, Cambridge University Press, 1992).
6. Piers Brendon, *The Decline and Fall of the British Empire 1781–1997* (Jonathan Cape, 2007), pp. 165–6.
7. Christopher Hibbert, *Queen Victoria: A Personal History* (HarperCollins, 2000), pp. 320, 362, 367.
8. Quoted in A. N. Wilson, *The Victorians* (Hutchinson, 2002), p. 449.
9. *The Times*, 14 March 1911.
10. White, *London in the Nineteenth Century*, pp. 373–4.
11. David Cannadine, *The Decline and Fall of the British Aristocracy* (rev. edn, Penguin Books, 2005), p. 347.
12. Quoted in Ellenberger, 'The Souls: High Society and Politics', p. 72.
13. Cannadine, *Decline and Fall*, p. 346.
14. Davidoff, *The Best Circles*, p. 49.
15. Ibid., p. 25.
16. Margot Asquith, *More Memories* (Cassell, 1933), pp. 219–22.
17. Mary Elcho, 'The Souls', unpublished memoir, quoted in Ellenberger, 'The Souls: High Society and Politics', p. 45.
18. Mary Elcho, diary entry, 8 October 1884, Stanway Papers.
19. Mary Elcho, sketches, n.d., Stanway Papers.
20. Phrenological Reports, n.d. [*c.*1880 and 1883], Stanway Papers.
21. Airlie, *Thatched with Gold*, p. 40.
22. Mary Elcho to Arthur Balfour, 14 February 1905 (*Letters*, p. 218).
23. Mary Elcho to Madeline Wyndham, 3 October 1883, Stanway Papers.
24. Ridley and Percy, *Letters of Arthur Balfour and Lady Elcho*, p. 13.

25. Mary Elcho to Arthur Balfour, 14 February 1905 (*Letters*, p. 218).

26. Ibid.

27. The claim was famously made by Lord Beaverbrook: see Ruddock F. Mackay, *Balfour: Intellectual Statesman* (Oxford, Oxford University Press, 1985), p. 8; Davenport-Hines, *Ettie*, p. 54.

28. Balfour was close friends with May (a niece of Gladstone, and cousin of Mary Gladstone), who died in 1875, and he mourned her all his life. He was a keen spiritualist (later in life, he became President of the Society for Psychical Research, a body founded in 1882 to use scientific analysis to 'prove' the existence of a spirit world), and he tried several times to contact May through a medium. R.J.Q. Adams has said there is no evidence that Balfour and May, who by all accounts had a tomboy charm not dissimilar to Mary's in her youth, were secretly engaged – or, whatever Blanche said, that Balfour asked for a ring to be put in her coffin (see Adams, *The Last Grandee*, pp. 29–31). However, certainly contemporaries believed the story to be true: see Maud Wyndham to Ettie Desborough, n.d. (1944), Desborough Papers, HALS DE/Rv/C2806 f.2, recalling at length the affair: 'He [Balfour] put what I believe had been his mother's engag[ement] ring into May's coffin, saying "she wd [sic] have been my wife" . . . it's impossible to make out all the "ins & outs" of the whole situation . . .'

29. Begbie, *Mirrors of Downing Street*, pp. 76–9.

30. Arthur Balfour to Mary Elcho, January 1894 (*Letters*, pp. 98–9).

31. Mary Elcho to Madeline Wyndham, 7 December 1880, Stanway Papers.

32. Lord Elcho invented an Elcho boot, bayonet and military shovel and was a founder of the Volunteer Rifle Force, a forerunner of the Territorial Army, established in the late 1850s in response to invasion scares in the wake of the Crimean War (Wemyss, *Family Record*, p. 11).

33. Ibid., p. 10.

34. Hugo Elcho to Mary Elcho, 12 October 1887, Stanway Papers.

35. Mary Elcho to Madeline Wyndham, 23 February 1881, Stanway Papers.

36. Mary Elcho to Hugo Elcho, n.d. (Summer 1887), Stanway Papers.

37. Mary Elcho to Hugo Elcho, 3 August 1881, Stanway Papers.

38. Quoted in James, *Aristocrats*, p. 307.

39. Evan Charteris to Hugo Elcho, 1 October [1881], Stanway Papers.

40. Hugo Elcho to Mary Elcho, 31 August 1887, Stanway Papers.

41. Mary Elcho to Hugo Elcho, n.d. [summer 1887], Stanway Papers.

42. Quoted in Simon Blow, *Broken Blood: The Rise and Fall of the Tennant Family* (Faber & Faber, 1987), p. 42; Abdy and Gere, *The Souls*, p. 11.

43. Hugo Elcho to Madeline Wyndham, 1 November 1881, Stanway Papers.

44. Mary Elcho to Madeline Wyndham, 1 April 1882, Stanway Papers.

45. Mary Elcho to Hugo Elcho, n.d. [summer 1887], Stanway Papers.

46. Adams, *The Last Grandee*, p. 55.

47. Quoted in Longford, *Pilgrimage of Passion*, p. 180.

48. Ibid., p. 190.

49. *The Times*, 27 November 1882.

50. Quoted in Hugh Cunningham, *The Challenge of Democracy: Britain, 1832–1918* (Harlow, Longman, 2001), p. 122.

51. Mary Elcho to Hugo Elcho, 28 June 1883, Stanway Papers.

52. Percy Wyndham to Hugo Elcho, 2 July 1883, Stanway Papers.

53. Unknown correspondent to Percy Wyndham, 11 July 1883, Stanway Papers.

54. Hugo Elcho to Mary Elcho, n.d. [July 1883], Stanway Papers.

55. Mary Elcho to Arthur Balfour, 6 December 1913 (*Letters*, p. 307).

56. See, for example, the letters of Godfrey Webb to Percy Wyndham, and Constance Mure to Percy Wyndham, both n.d. [July 1883], Stanway Papers.

57. Mary Elcho to Arthur Balfour, 6 December 1913 (*Letters*, p. 307).

58. Mary Elcho to Madeline Wyndham, 11 August 1883, Stanway Papers.

59. Mary Elcho to Hugo Elcho, n.d. [July 1883], Stanway Papers.

60. Hugo Elcho to Mary Elcho, n.d. [July 1883], Stanway Papers.

61. Mary Elcho to Hugo Elcho, 2 July 1883, Stanway Papers.

62. Hugo Elcho to Mary Elcho, 1 July 1883, Stanway Papers.

63. Mary Elcho to Hugo Elcho, 18 July 1883, Stanway Papers.

64. Ibid.

65. Mary Elcho to Hugo Elcho, n.d. [*c.*17 July 1883], Stanway Papers.

66. George Wyndham to Mary Elcho, 15 February 1913, quoted in Mackail and Wyndham, *Life and Letters*, 2.737–8.

67. Maud Wyndham to Ettie Desborough, 3 March 1944, Desborough Papers, HALS DE/rv c2806 f.3.

68. Mary Elcho to Hugo Elcho, 31 July 1883 [sic], Stanway Papers

69. Hugo Elcho to Mary Elcho, 9 August 1883, Stanway Papers.

70. *The Times*, 10 August 1883.

71. Madeline Wyndham to Mary Elcho, 10 August 1883, Stanway Papers.

72. Ibid.

Chapter 4: Honeymoon

1. Madeline Wyndham to Mary Elcho, n.d. (*c.*August 1885), Stanway Papers.

2. Mary Elcho to Guy Wyndham, n.d. [1883], Stanway Papers.

3. Andrew Marr, *The Making of Modern Britain* (Macmillan, 2009), pp. 74–5.

4. Mary Elcho to Madeline Wyndham, 11 August 1883, Stanway Papers.

5. Mary Elcho to Hugo Elcho, n.d. [*c.*1903], Stanway Papers.

6. Lambert, *Unquiet Souls*, p. 143.

7. Mary Elcho to Hugo Elcho, n.d., Stanway Papers; Mary Elcho to Madeline Wyndham, 7 September 1884, Stanway Papers.

8. Hugo Elcho to Percy Wyndham, 14 August 1883, Stanway Papers.

9. Pat Jalland, *Women, Marriage and Politics 1860–1914* (Oxford, Oxford University Press, 1988), pp. 59–64.

10. The equivalent in ESV is £9,881,000 and in EPV £17,600,00.

11. Asquith, *Haply I May Remember*, p. 21.

12. Percy Wyndham to Mary Elcho, 13 and 18 May 1888, Stanway Papers.

13. Mary Elcho to Arthur Balfour, 6 December 1913 (*Letters*, p. 308).

14. Daker, *Clouds*, pp. 136–7.

15. Mary Elcho to Madeline Wyndham, 27 September 1888, Stanway Papers.

16. Wemyss, *Family Record*, p. 16.

17. Mary Elcho to Wilfrid Scawen Blunt, 11 August 1915, Blunt Papers, FM 758-1975.

18. Cynthia Asquith, diary entry, 1 August 1918, quoted in Cynthia Asquith, *Diaries, 1915–1918*, ed. E. M. Horsley (New York, Alfred A. Knopf, 1969), p. 464.

19. Dakers, *Clouds*, pp. 136–7.

20. Mary Elcho to Hugo Elcho, 16 October 1883, Stanway Papers.

21. Mary Elcho to Madeline Wyndham, 17 October 1883, Stanway Papers.

22. Mary Elcho to Madeline Wyndham, 19 April 1884, Stanway Papers. Until mid-March 1884, Mary's letters from London are written on writing paper

headed 44 Belgrave Square. After that, they are headed 12 North Audley Street (see, for example, Mary Elcho to Madeline Wyndham, 10 and 27 March 1884, Stanway Papers).

23. Laura Lyttelton to Arthur Balfour, n.d. (*c.*1885), Whittingehame Papers, NRS GD433/2/477/4.

24. Abdy and Gere, *The Souls*, p. 150.

25. Hugo Elcho to Mary Elcho, 31 August 1887, Stanway Papers.

26. Mary Elcho to Hugo Elcho, 28 January 1886, Stanway Papers.

27. Mary Elcho to Madeline Wyndham, 10 March 1884, Stanway Papers.

28. Madeline Adeane to Madeline Wyndham, *c.*1902, Adeane Papers.

29. Mary Elcho to Madeline Wyndham, 1 August 1884, Stanway Papers.

30. Wemyss, *Family Record*, p. 35.

31. Mary Elcho to Madeline Wyndham, 5 September 1884, Stanway Papers; Wemyss, *Family Record*, p. 7.

32. Madeline Wyndham to Mary Elcho, September 1884, Stanway Papers.

33. Ibid.

34. Quoted in Kenneth Young, *Arthur James Balfour: The Happy Life of the Politician, Prime Minister, Statesman and Philosopher, 1848–1930* (G. Bell, 1963), pp. 81–2.

35. Mary Elcho to Percy Wyndham, 30 November 1884, Stanway Papers.

36. Mary Elcho, diary entry, 23 November 1884, Stanway Papers.

37. Ellenberger, 'The Souls: High Society and Politics', p. 53.

38. Ibid., p. 50.

Chapter 5: The Gang

1. The dates suggest that Ego was a 'new thread', and that Mary fell pregnant almost immediately after she miscarried in the spring of 1884.

2. Pamela Tennant to Mary Elcho, n.d. [*c.*January 1905], Stanway Papers.

3. For a full account see Jan Morris, *Heaven's Command: An Imperial Progress* (Harmondsworth, Penguin, 1979), pp. 491–513.

4. *The Times*, 24 December 1884.

5. *The Times*, 31 December 1884.

6. Longford, *Pilgrimage of Passion*, p. 212.

7. Mary Elcho, diary entries, December 1884, Stanway Papers.

8. Mary Elcho to Madeline Wyndham, 30 July 1889, Stanway Papers.

9. Madeline Wyndham to Mary Elcho, February 1885, Stanway Papers.

10. Mary Elcho to Arthur Balfour, 15 March 1899 (*Letters*, pp. 60–1).

11. Mary Elcho to Madeline Wyndham, 13 February 1885, Stanway Papers.

12. Madeline Wyndham to Mary Elcho, February 1885, Stanway Papers.

13. Madeline Wyndham to Mary Elcho, February 1885, Stanway Papers.

14. Percy Wyndham to George Wyndham, 19 February 1885, quoted in Mackail and Wyndham, *Life and Letters*, 1.29.

15. Madeline Wyndham to Mary Elcho, February 1885, Stanway Papers.

16. Madeline Adeane to Mary Elcho, 18 February 1885, Stanway Papers.

17. Madeline Wyndham to Mary Elcho, February 1885, Stanway Papers.

18. Madeline Wyndham to Mary Elcho, March 1885, Stanway Papers.

19. Pamela Tennant to Mary Elcho, 6 March 1885, Stanway Papers.

20. Madeline Wyndham to Mary Elcho, March 1885, Stanway Papers.

21. Margot Asquith, *An Autobiography*, 2 vols (Thornton Butterworth, 1920–2), 1.60.

22. Mary Elcho to Percy Wyndham, 12 April 1885, Stanway Papers.

23. Mary Elcho, 'The Souls', unpublished memoir, cited in Ellenberger, 'The Souls: High Society and Politics', pp. 49–50.

24. Quoted in Blow, *Broken Blood*, p. 88.

25. Ellenberger, 'The Souls: High Society and Politics', p. 53.

26. Quoted in ibid., p. 51.

27. Mary Elcho to Percy Wyndham, 12 April 1884, Stanway Papers.

28. Mary Elcho to Arthur Balfour, 26 May 1905 (*Letters*, p. 223).

29. Ibid.

30. Mary Elcho to Hugo Elcho, 14 August 1887, Stanway Papers.

31. Mary Elcho to Hugo Elcho, December 1886, quoted in Ellenberger, 'The Souls: High Society and Politics', p. 201.

32. Laura Lyttelton to Lady Frances Balfour, 9 October [1885], Whittingehame Papers, NRS GD433/2/477 f. 10:13r.

33. Ibid.; and see also Laura Lyttelton to Arthur Balfour, n.d. [*c*.1885], Whittingehame Papers, NRS GD433/2/477 f. 8r, in which Laura declined,

on behalf of herself and Mary, Arthur's suggestion that they dine at the New Club, with Hugo Elcho and Arthur Lyttelton out of town: 'dear Mr. Arthur I wd not go to the new Club anyhow with the awful protection of 10 Alfreds & 15 Hugos because it is full of gratuituous gossip & I think it wd be idiotic ...'.

34. Mary Elcho to Madeline Wyndham, 3 June 1885, Stanway Papers.

35. Laura Lyttelton to Lady Frances Balfour, 9 October [1885], Whittingehame Papers, NRS GD433/2/477. f. 10.13r.

36. Madeline Wyndham to Mary Elcho, May 1885, Stanway Papers.

37. Mary Elcho to Madeline Wyndham, 3 June 1885, Stanway Papers.

38. Ellenberger, 'The Souls: High Society and Politics', p. 244.

39. Laura Lyttelton to Lady Frances Balfour, n.d. [autumn 1885], Whittingehame Papers, NRS GD433/2/477/4 f. 17r.

40. Madeline Wyndham to Mary Elcho, August 1885, Stanway Papers.

41. Madeline Wyndham to Mary Elcho, 10 August 1885, Stanway Papers.

42. Mary Elcho to Madeline Wyndham, n.d. [August 1885], Stanway Papers.

43. Laura Lyttelton to Lady Frances Balfour, n.d. [autumn 1885], Whittingehame Papers, NRS GD433/2/477/4 f. 17r.

Chapter 6: Clouds

1. Quoted in Dakers, *Clouds*, p. 81.

2. Ibid.

3. Georgiana Burne-Jones to Mary Elcho, November 1885, quoted in Dakers, *Clouds*, p. 81.

4. Dakers, *Clouds*, p. 225.

5. Ibid., p. 106.

6. Ibid., p. 104.

7. Ibid., pp. 87–9.

8. Percy Wyndham to Mary Elcho, September 1886, quoted in ibid., p. 82.

9. Quoted in Dakers, *Clouds*, p. 81.

10. Asquith, *Haply I May Remember*, pp. 40–1.

11. The auction was of the collection of William Graham, Frances Horner's

father and an eminent art collector. In fact, the painting was by Pseudo Pier Francesco Fiorentino. This was only discovered later. Dakers, *Clouds*, p. 142.

12. Ibid., p. 94.

13. Pamela Adeane, daughter of Madeline and Charles Adeane, quoted in ibid., p. 91.

14. Dakers, *Clouds*, p. 130.

15. Wemyss, *Family Record*, pp. 20–1.

16. Asquith, *Haply I May Remember*, pp. 40–1.

17. Madeline Wyndham to Pamela Tennant, 19 August 1897, Glenconner Papers, NRS GD510/1/26 f. 33r.

18. Mackail and Wyndham, *Life and Letters*, 1.31.

19. Dakers, *Clouds*, p. 81.

20. Ibid., p. 119.

21. Ibid., p. 107.

22. Percy Wyndham to Philip Webb, c.January 1886, quoted in ibid., p. 82.

23. Quoted in Dakers, *Clouds*, p. 83.

24. Ibid., p. 81.

25. Violet Bradby, *A Family Chronicle*, quoted in ibid., p. 116.

26. Madeline Adeane to Mary Elcho, 18 December 1885, Stanway Papers.

27. Dakers, *Clouds*, p. 119.

28. Fiona MacCarthy, 'Lethaby, William Richard (1857–1931)', *Oxford Dictionary of National Biography*, Oxford, Oxford University Press, 2004; online edn, May 2008 [http://www.oxforddnb.com/view/article/34503, accessed 22 October 2013].

29. Wemyss, *Family Record*, pp. 21–2.

30. Madeline Adeane to Mary Elcho, 16 September (1883), Stanway Papers.

31. Dakers, *Clouds*, p. 94; Asquith, *Haply I May Remember*, p. 42.

32. Mary Elcho to Evelyn de Vesci, 24 September 1889, De Vesci Papers, DD/DRU/87/3.

33. Mary Elcho to Madeline Wyndham, 15 September 1884, Stanway Papers.

34. Pamela Glenconner, *The Earthen Vessel: A Volume Dealing with Spirit-Communication Received in the Form of Book-Tests* (New York, John Lane, 1921), p. 138.

35. Walburga, Lady Paget, *In my Tower*, 2 vols (Hutchinson, 1924), 1.5–6.

36. Samuel Hynes, *The Edwardian Turn of Mind: First World War and English Culture* (Pimlico, 1991), pp. 134–5.

37. Ibid., p. 139.

38. Ibid.

39. Madeline Wyndham to Mary Elcho, September 1884, Stanway Papers.

40. Glenconner, *The Earthen Vessel*, pp. 136–7.

41. Dakers, *Clouds*, p. 78.

42. Ibid., p. 105.

43. Angela Lambert, *Unquiet Souls: The Indian Summer of the British Aristocracy* (Macmillan, 1984), p. 144.

44. Ibid.

45. Madeline Wyndham to Mary Elcho, *c.*September 1884, Stanway Papers.

46. Percy Wyndham to Mary Elcho, 14 March 1892, Stanway Papers.

47. Petworth Papers; Jeremy Musson, *Up and Down Stairs* (John Murray, 2009), pp. 148–9.

48. Ibid., p. 245. Horne's memoir was splendidly titled *What the Butler Winked At* (T. Werner Laurie, 1923), confirmation for suspicious employers of just how much their staff knew about their most intimate lives.

49. Dakers, *Clouds*, p. 107.

Chapter 7: The Birth of the Souls

1. Marquand, *Britain since 1918*, p. 32.

2. White, *London in the Nineteenth Century*, p. 375.

3. Marquand, *Britain since 1918*, p. 58.

4. Mary Elcho to Hugo Elcho, n.d., Stanway Papers.

5. Mary Elcho to Hugo Elcho, 28 January 1886, Stanway Papers.

6. See Mary Elcho to Madeline Wyndham, 21 March 1885 and 6 January 1886, Stanway Papers. The Cadogan Square house was originally numbered 36, and then renumbered 62 as the square expanded. Hugo's initial objection – that the house did not come with stables – was overcome when Mary found stables nearby that the Elchos could buy.

7. Mary Elcho to Madeline Wyndham, 20 March 1883, Stanway Papers.

8. Mary Elcho to Madeline Wyndham, 7 February 1886, Stanway Papers.

9. White, *London in the Nineteenth Century*, p. 376.

10. Mary Elcho to Madeline Wyndham, dated 7 February 1886 (in fact, the riots were on 8 February), Stanway Papers.

11. Mary Elcho to Madeline Wyndham, 21 February 1886, Stanway Papers.

12. Mary Elcho to Arthur Balfour, 1 February 1906 (*Letters*, p. 231).

13. Mary Elcho to Hugo Elcho, 27 February 1886, Stanway Papers.

14. Mary Elcho to Madeline Wyndham, 21 February 1886, Stanway Papers.

15. Laura Lyttelton to Arthur Balfour, 2 April 1886, Whittingehame Papers, NRS GD433/2/479/1 f. 6r.

16. Margot Asquith to Wilfrid Scawen Blunt, 10 and 28 May 1906, 27 January 1911, quoted in Longford, *Pilgrimage of Passion*, p. 375.

17. Mary Elcho, diary entry, 24 April 1886, Stanway Papers.

18. Laura Lyttelton to Arthur Balfour, 2 April 1886, Whittingehame Papers, NRS GD433/2/479/1 f. 6r.

19. Asquith, *An Autobiography*, 1.63–4.

20. Spencer Lyttelton to Mary Gladstone, 22 April 1886, quoted in Ellenberger, 'The Souls: High Society and Politics', p. 54.

21. Mary Elcho to Madeline Wyndham, 26 April 1886, Stanway Papers.

22. Quoted in Ridley and Percy (eds), *Letters of Arthur Balfour and Lady Elcho*, p. 24.

23. Mary Elcho to Arthur Balfour, 8 May 1886 (*Letters*, pp. 24–5).

24. Ellenberger, 'The Souls: High Society and Politics', p. 54.

25. Ibid.

26. Mary Elcho to Arthur Balfour, 8 May 1886 (*Letters*, pp. 24–5).

27. Wheatcroft, *The Strange Death of Tory England*, p. 33; Marquand, *Britain since 1918*, p. 57; James, *Aristocrats*, p. 337.

28. Asquith, *An Autobiography*, 1.203–4.

29. Ibid., 1.207.

30. Ibid.

31. Asquith, *An Autobiography*, 1.217; 2.14–15.

32. Robert Blake, quoted in Ellenberger, 'The Souls: High Society and Politics', p. 1.

33. Frances Horner, *Times Remembered*, quoted in ibid., p. 5.

34. Quoted in Blow, *Broken Blood*, p. 202.

35. Quoted in Longford, *Pilgrimage of Passion*, p. 297.

36. Mary Elcho to Hugo Elcho, 28 October 1886, Stanway Papers.

37. Quoted in Abdy and Gere, *The Souls*, p. 12.

38. Arthur Balfour to Mary Elcho, 29 April 1890 (*Letters*, p. 69).

39. Abdy and Gere, *The Souls*, p. 11.

40. See MacCarthy, *The Last Pre-Raphaelite*, p. 478. Burne-Jones described Poynter, his brother-in-law, as filled with 'dull excellencies'.

41. Cynthia Asquith, quoted in Abdy and Gere, *The Souls*, p. 108.

42. Quoted in ibid., p. 11.

43. Ibid., p. 12.

44. Lambert, *Unquiet Souls*, p. 93.

45. Nancy Waters Ellenberger, 'The Souls and London "Society" at the End of the Nineteenth Century', *Victorian Society* 25:2 (Winter 1982): 133–60, 146 n. 43; Robert, Lord Vansittart, *The Mist Procession: The Autobiography of Lord Vansittart* (Hutchinson, 1958), p. 90.

46. Edith Lyttelton, quoted in Ellenberger, 'The Souls: High Society and Politics', p. 83.

47. Ellenberger, 'The Souls: High Society and Politics', p. 5, and 'The Souls and London "Society"', p. 133; see also Abdy and Gere, *The Souls*, p. 10.

48. Arthur Balfour to Mary Elcho, [10 April] 1890 (*Letters*, pp. 67–8); also quoted in Ellenberger, 'The Souls: High Society and Politics', p. 84.

49. Mary Elcho, diaries, 30 May 1887, Stanway Papers.

50. Ibid., 20, 25 June 1887.

51. Ellenberger, 'The Souls: High Society and Politics', p. 85.

52. Lady Sibyl Lubbock, quoted in Abdy and Gere, *The Souls*, p. 169.

53. Quoted in ibid., p. 15.

54. Ridley and Percy (eds), *Letters of Arthur Balfour and Lady Elcho*, p. 19; Blanche Dugdale, *Family Homespun* (John Murray, 1940), pp. 72–3.

55. Lady Frances Balfour to Lady Betty Balfour, June 1889, Whittingehame Papers, NRS GD433/2/301.

56. Mary Elcho to Ettie Grenfell, 19 November 1890, Desborough Papers, HALS DE/Rv/C477.

57. Mary Elcho to Ettie Grenfell, n.d. [*c.*1929], Desborough Papers, HALS DE/Rv/C477/101.

58. See, for example, Arthur Balfour to Mary Elcho, 28 February [1894] (*Letters*, p. 102), and Mary Elcho to Arthur Balfour, 15 May 1895 (*Letters*, pp. 124–5).

59. Margot Asquith, *Off the Record* (Frederick Muller, 1944), p. 52.

60. Ellenberger, 'Constructing George Wyndham', p. 497.

61. Elizabeth, Countess of Fingall, *Seventy Years Young: Memories of Elizabeth, Countess of Fingall* (Dublin, The Lilliput Press, 1991), p. 273.

62. Quoted in Egremont, *The Cousins*, p. 141.

63. Paget, *In my Tower*, 1.110.

64. Fingall, *Seventy Years Young*, p. 271.

65. Abdy and Gere, *The Souls*, p. 92.

66. For an account of the episode see Egremont, *The Cousins*, pp. 78–9.

67. Alfred Lyttelton to Mary Gladstone, 31 December 1886, quoted in Ellenberger, 'The Souls: High Society and Politics', pp. 62–3.

Chapter 8: The Summer of 1887

1. Mary Elcho to Hugo Elcho, 13 January 1887, Stanway Papers.

2. Ibid.

3. Ridley and Percy (eds), *Letters of Arthur Balfour and Lady Elcho*, p. 17.

4. Mary Elcho to Hugo Elcho, 12 January 1887, Stanway Papers.

5. Mary Elcho to Hugo Elcho, 13 January 1887, Stanway Papers.

6. *The Times*, 8 February 1887.

7. Dakers, *Clouds*, p. 119.

8. Ibid.

9. Patrick Jackson, 'Sir George Trevelyan', *Oxford Dictionary of National Biography*.

10. Lambert, *Unquiet Souls*, p. 59; Ridley and Percy (eds), *Letters of Arthur Balfour and Lady Elcho*, p. 33.

11. For the suggestion, see Adams, *The Last Grandee*, p. 71. However, there does not appear to be an example in print of this phrase until Eric Partridge's *Dictionary of Slang and Unconventional English* (George Routledge, 1937), which would make it surprising if the phrase really dated back to 1887.

12. Mackail and Wyndham, *Life and Letters*, p. 37.

13. Adams, *The Last Grandee*, p. 76.

14. Mary Elcho to Arthur Balfour, 8 December 1921, Whittingehame Papers, NRS GD433/2/229/1 f. 29.

15. Mary Elcho to Arthur Balfour, 7 March 1929 (*Letters*, p. 353).

16. Quoted in Davenport-Hines, *Ettie*, p. 62.

17. Quoted in Longford, *Pilgrimage of Passion*, p. 297.

18. Arthur Balfour to Lady Frances Balfour, 6 March 1887, quoted in Ridley and Percy (eds), *Letters of Arthur Balfour and Lady Elcho*, pp. 33–4.

19. Mary Elcho, diary entry, 8 July 1887, Stanway Papers.

20. Mary Elcho to Madeline Wyndham, 4 July 1887, Stanway Papers.

21. Mary Elcho to Hugo Elcho, 12 August 1887, Stanway Papers.

22. Mary Elcho to Hugo Elcho, 26 August 1887, Stanway Papers.

23. Mary Elcho to Hugo Elcho, 12 August 1887, Stanway Papers.

24. Mary Elcho to Hugo Elcho, 29 August 1887, Stanway Papers.

25. Asquith, *An Autobiography*, 2.83.

26. Abdy and Gere, *The Souls*, p. 145.

27. Quoted in Longford, *Pilgrimage of Passion*, p. 303.

28. Mary Elcho to Hugo Elcho, 18 August 1887, Stanway Papers.

29. Ibid.

30. Marie Adeane married, in 1891, Sir Bernard Mallet. Her recollections of her life with Queen Victoria were published under her married name.

31. Mary Elcho to Wilfrid Scawen Blunt, 27 March 1899, Blunt Papers, FM 492-1975.

32. MA vol 10.

33. Madeline jokingly adopted the name herself: see her signature in a letter to Wilfrid Scawen Blunt, 21 February 1901, Blunt Papers, FM 258-1975.

34. Madeline Adeane to Madeline Wyndham, 19 August 1899, Adeane Papers.

35. Madeline Adeane to Madeline Wyndham, 15 November 1887, Adeane Papers.

36. Hibbert, *Queen Victoria*, p. 467.

37. Mary Elcho to Hugo Elcho, 18 August 1887, Stanway Papers; Pamela Tennant to Mary Elcho, 27 September 1903, Stanway Papers.

38. Hugo Elcho to Mary Elcho, 29 August 1887, Stanway Papers.

39. Hugo was born on 25 August 1857, making him just short of five years older

than Mary. Charles Adeane was born on 2 November 1863, making him about five and a half years older than Mananai, born on 31 March 1869.

40. Charles Adeane to Madeline Wyndham, 29 August 1887, Adeane Papers.
41. Percy Wyndham to Mary Elcho, 18 May 1888, Stanway Papers.
42. Quoted in Brendan, *Decline and Fall*, p. 295.
43. Ibid.
44. Tynan Hinkson, *Years of the Shadow*, p. 256.
45. See Constance Leconfield to Madeline Wyndham, 30 March 1898, 7 April 1898, Petworth Papers.
46. Longford, *Pilgrimage of Passion*, pp. 228–9.
47. Quoted in ibid., p. 246.
48. Quoted in Dakers, *Clouds*, pp. 126–7.
49. Quoted in Longford, *Pilgrimage of Passion*, p. 247.
50. Ibid.
51. Quoted in Lambert, *Unquiet Souls*, p. 62.
52. Mary Elcho to Hugo Elcho, 3 September 1887, Stanway Papers.
53. Lambert, *Unquiet Souls*, p. 63.
54. Madeline Adeane to Madeline Wyndham, 15 November 1887, Adeane Papers.
55. Madeline Adeane to Madeline Wyndham, 10 November 1887, Adeane Papers.
56. White, *London in the Nineteenth Century*, pp. 377–9.
57. Brendon, *Decline and Fall*, p. 295.
58. Arthur Balfour to Mary Elcho, 24 December 1887 (*Letters*, p. 46).
59. Pamela Tennant to Mary Elcho, 13 August 1888, Stanway Papers.
60. Longford, *Pilgrimage of Passion*, pp. 259–61.
61. Quoted in ibid., p. 252.
62. Quoted in Egremont, *The Cousins*, p. 130; Lambert, *Unquiet Souls*, p. 63.
63. Longford, *Pilgrimage of Passion*, p. 261.

Chapter 9: Mananai

1. Pamela Tennant to Mary Elcho, Good Friday (30 March 1888), Stanway Papers.
2. Percy Wyndham to Mary Elcho, 30 March 1888, Stanway Papers.
3. Madeline Adeane to Mary Elcho, 26 November 1887, Adeane Papers.

4. Percy Wyndham to Mary Elcho, 18 May 1888, Stanway Papers.
5. Ibid.
6. *Modern Society*, 4 August 1888, Adeane Papers.
7. Charles Adeane to Madeline Wyndham, 26 July 1888, Adeane Papers.
8. Madeline Adeane to Mary Elcho, 1 August 1888, Stanway Papers.
9. Madeline Adeane to Madeline Wyndham, 4 August 1888, Adeane Papers.
10. Charles Adeane to Madeline Wyndham, 26 July 1888, Adeane Papers.
11. Madeline Adeane to Madeline Wyndham, 12 August 1888, Adeane Papers.
12. Madeline Adeane to George Wyndham, 25 August 1888, George Wyndham Papers.
13. George Wyndham to Madeline Adeane, 31 August 1888, quoted in Mackail and Wyndham, *Life and Letters*, 1.226.
14. Madeline Adeane to George Wyndham, 25 August 1888, George Wyndham Papers.
15. Marie Mallet, *Life with Queen Victoria: Marie Mallet's Letters from Court 1887–1901*, ed. Victor Mallet (John Murray, 1968), p. xiv; Madeline Adeane to Mary Elcho, 27 March 1889, Stanway Papers.
16. Madeline Adeane to Percy Wyndham, 8 October 1889, Adeane Papers.
17. Madeline Adeane to Madeline Wyndham, 28 March 1889, Adeane Papers.
18. Charles Adeane to Madeline Wyndham, 6 September 1893, Adeane Papers.
19. Madeline Adeane to Madeline Wyndham, 17 July 1889, Adeane Papers.

Chapter 10: Conflagration

1. Pamela Tennant to Mary Elcho, 17 September 1893, Stanway Papers.
2. Percy Wyndham to Mary Elcho, 8 March 1887, Stanway Papers.
3. Pamela Tennant to Mary Elcho, 21 September 1888, Stanway Papers.
4. Ibid.
5. Dakers, *Clouds*, p. 134.
6. Mary Elcho to Lady Frances Balfour, 21 January 1889, Whittingehame Papers, NRS GD433/2/301 f. 11r.
7. Dakers, *Clouds*, p. 130.
8. Ibid., p. 131.
9. Wemyss, *Family Record*, p. 23.
10. Olivier, *Four Victorian Ladies*, p. 89.

11. Ridley and Percy (eds), *Letters of Arthur Balfour and Lady Elcho*, p. 58.

12. Abdy and Gere, *The Souls*, pp. 160–1; and see Mary Elcho to Arthur Balfour, 3 April 1905 (*Letters*, p. 221).

13. Mary Elcho to Arthur Balfour, 23 January 1889 (*Letters*, p. 56).

14. Ibid. (*Letters*, p. 55).

15. Mary Elcho to Arthur Balfour, 13 January 1889 (*Letters*, p. 55).

16. Mary Elcho to Arthur Balfour, 23 January 1889 (*Letters*, p. 56).

17. Mary Elcho to Frances Balfour, 21 January 1889, Whittingehame Papers, NRS GD433/2/301 f. 11r.

18. George Wyndham to Madeline Wyndham, 7 January 1889, Mackail and Wyndham, *Life and Letters*, 1.231.

19. Pamela Tennant to Mary Elcho, 15 March 1889 and 7 February 1905, Stanway Papers.

20. Quoted in Dakers, *Clouds*, p. 134.

21. Ibid.

22. Lady Betty Balfour to Lady Frances Balfour, 14 January 1899, Whittingehame Papers, NRS GD433/2/301 f. 10r.

23. Ibid.

24. Quoted in Dakers, *Clouds*, p. 131.

25. Mackail and Wyndham, *Life and Letters*, 1.231.

26. Mary Elcho to Arthur Balfour, 13 January 1889 (*Letters*, p. 55).

27. Dakers, *Clouds*, pp. 132–3.

28. Quoted in ibid., p. 135.

29. Ibid.

Chapter 11: The Season of 1889

1. Madeline Adeane to Madeline Wyndham, 17 July 1889, Adeane Papers.

2. Percy Wyndham to Mary Elcho, 14 September 1888, Stanway Papers.

3. Mary Elcho to Wilfrid Scawen Blunt, 27 March 1899, Blunt Papers, FM 492-1975.

4. Quoted in Philip Hoare, *Serious Pleasures: The Life of Stephen Tennant* (Hamish Hamilton, 1990), p. 8.

5. Pamela Tennant to Mary Elcho, 14 June 1928, Stanway Papers.

6. Pamela Tennant to Mary Elcho, 23 November 1891, Stanway Papers.

7. Mary Elcho to Wilfrid Scawen Blunt, 16 November 1893, Blunt Papers, FM 1592-1976.

8. Pamela Tennant to Mary Elcho, 10 February 1889, Stanway Papers.

9. Quoted in Hoare, *Serious Pleasures*, p. 22.

10. Percy Wyndham to Mary Elcho, 14 September 1888, Stanway Papers.

11. Lady Frances Balfour to Lady Betty Balfour, 13 July 1889, Whittingehame Papers, NRS GD433/2/301 f. 42r.

12. Arthur Balfour to Mary Elcho, 16 August 1893 (*Letters*, p. 95).

13. *The World*, 16 July 1890, quoted in Ellenberger, 'The Souls: High Society and Politics', p. 55; and in Lambert, *Unquiet Souls*, p. 10.

14. Ellenberger, 'The Souls and London "Society"', pp. 146–7.

15. Ibid.

16. Lady Frances Balfour to Lady Betty Balfour, June 1889, Whittingehame Papers, NRS GD433/2/301 f. 32r.

17. Mary Elcho to Madeline Wyndham, 3 July 1889, Stanway Papers.

18. Mary Elcho to Evelyn de Vesci, 28 April 1891, De Vesci Papers, DD/DRU/87/3.

19. Madeline Adeane to Madeline Wyndham, 3 December 1899, Adeane Papers.

20. Mary Elcho to Evelyn de Vesci, 2 July 1889, De Vesci Papers, DD/DRU 87/3.

21. Mary Elcho to Evelyn de Vesci, 28 April 1891, De Vesci Papers, DD/DRU/87/3.

22. Mary Elcho to Hugo Elcho, 27 July 1900, Stanway Papers.

23. Pamela Tennant to Mary Elcho, 28 July 1889, Stanway Papers.

24. Pamela Tennant to Mary Elcho, 17 September 1890, Stanway Papers.

25. Pamela Tennant to Mary Elcho, 28 July 1889, Stanway Papers.

26. Ibid.

27. Mary Elcho to Madeline Wyndham, 3 August 1889, Stanway Papers.

28. Mary Elcho to Evelyn de Vesci, 7 August 1889, De Vesci Papers, DD/DRU/87/3.

29. Ibid.

30. Madeline Adeane to Madeline Wyndham, 3 April 1889, Adeane Papers.

31. Madeline Adeane to Madeline Wyndham, 25 September 1889, Adeane Papers.

32. Madeline Adeane to Madeline Wyndham, 4 October 1889, Adeane Papers.

33. Pamela Tennant to Mary Elcho, 17 September 1893, Stanway Papers.

34. Madeline Adeane to Pamela Tennant, 8 October 1889, Adeane Papers.

35. Marie Mallet to Lady Elizabeth Biddulph, 8 November 1889, quoted in Mallet, *Life with Queen Victoria*, p. 35.

Chapter 12: The Mad and their Keepers

1. Neil McKenna, *The Secret Life of Oscar Wilde* (Arrow Books, 2004), pp. 185–6.
2. Curzon's reference is presumably to the quintessential false god of the Old Testament: see 2 Kings 5:18: 'In this thing the LORD pardon thy servant, *that* when my master goeth into the house of Rimmon to worship there, and he leaneth on my hand, and I bow myself in the house of Rimmon: when I bow down myself in the house of Rimmon, the LORD pardon thy servant in this thing.'
3. Helen Kelsall Melland, Asquith's first wife, was the daughter of a Manchester doctor. The Asquiths married in 1877 and had five children: Raymond, Herbert, Arthur, Violet and Cyril. Helen died a few months after this visit, in the autumn of 1891, from typhoid fever.
4. Quoted in Davenport-Hines, *Ettie*, pp. 57–8.
5. Mary Elcho to Evelyn de Vesci, 28 April 1891, De Vesci Papers, DD/DRU/87/3.
6. Wilfrid Scawen Blunt, Secret Memoirs XVI, 1 July 1893 to 3 July 1893, Blunt Papers, FM 33-1975.
7. Quoted in David Gilmour, *Curzon: Imperial Statesman* (John Murray, 2003), pp. 103–4.
8. Quoted in Longford, *Pilgrimage of Passion*, p. 293.
9. Vansittart, *The Mist Procession*, p. 90.
10. Arthur Balfour to Mary Elcho, 16 August 1893 (*Letters*, p. 14).
11. Quoted in Ellenberger, 'The Souls: High Society and Politics', p. 187. If rumours are to be believed, Harry's affair with a housemaid at Belton House, home of his uncle and aunt, the Earl and Countess Brownlow, resulted in the child named Beatrice Stephenson, whose own daughter was Margaret Roberts, later Thatcher. Certainly Lady Diana Cooper, Harry's daughter by Violet Granby, maintained that Mrs Thatcher was her niece. See the *Telegraph*, 4 June 2008 and the *Express*, 21 April 2013.

12. Laura Tennant to Lady Frances Balfour, October (1885), Whittingehame Papers, NRS GD433/2/477/4 f. 10:13r. Laura's reference is to a man armed 'cap-à-pie': meaning from head to foot.

13. Pamela Tennant to Mary Elcho, 16 August 1892, Stanway Papers.

14. Ibid.

15. Osbert Sitwell, *Laughter in the Next Room* (Macmillan, 1949), p. 100.

16. Pamela Tennant to Mary Elcho, 25 August 1893, Stanway Papers.

17. Pamela Tennant to Mary Elcho, 16 August 1892, Stanway Papers.

18. Paget is remembered now as the inventor of sign language for the deaf and dumb, but his 'engaging personal qualities' – his geniality, sympathy and 'deep affection for the young and old alike' – as well as his eccentricity receive almost as much attention as his achievements in the *Oxford Dictionary of National Biography*: see Harry Lowery, 'Paget, Sir Richard Arthur Surtees, second baronet (1869–1955)', rev. John Bosnell, *Oxford Dictionary of National Biography*, online edn, May 2008 [http://www.oxforddnb.com/view/article/35358, accessed 23 October 2013].

19. Pamela Tennant to Mary Elcho, 31 August 1892, Stanway Papers.

20. Ibid.

21. Mary Elcho to Madeline Wyndham, 5 September 1892, Stanway Papers.

22. Percy Wyndham to Mary Elcho, 30 November 1892, Stanway Papers.

23. Ibid.

Chapter 13: Crisis

1. Nicola Beauman, *Cynthia Asquith* (Hamish Hamilton, 1987), p. 6.

2. Asquith, *Haply May I Remember*, p. 59.

3. Mary Elcho to Evelyn de Vesci, 16 January 1891, De Vesci Papers, DD/DRU/87.

4. Ellenberger, 'The Souls: High Society and Politics', p. 216.

5. Lambert, *Unquiet Souls*, p. 78.

6. Fingall, *Seventy Years Young*, pp. 179, 182.

7. Hugo Elcho to Evelyn de Vesci, 20 March 1895, De Vesci Papers, DD/DRU/102.

8. Ettie Grenfell to Constance, Lady Wenlock, 8 December 1892, quoted in Davenport-Hines, *Ettie*, p. 54.

9. Tynan Hinkson, *Years of the Shadow*, p. 15.

10. Mary Elcho to Arthur Balfour, 13 August 1890 (*Letters*, pp. 71–2).

11. Ibid.

12. Ibid.

13. Arthur Balfour to Mary Elcho, 16 July 1891 (*Letters*, pp. 73–4).

14. Mary Elcho to Arthur Balfour, 30 October 1912 (*Letters*, p. 291).

15. Asquith, *Haply I May Remember*, p. 134.

16. Beauman, *Cynthia Asquith*, pp. 6–7; Mary Elcho to George Wyndham, 3 January 1892, George Wyndham Papers.

17. Pamela Tennant to Sibell, Countess Grosvenor, 28 December 1892, George Wyndham Papers.

18. Madeline Adeane to Madeline Wyndham, 28 December 1892, Adeane Papers.

19. Jalland, *Women, Marriage and Politics*, p. 181.

20. Asquith, *Haply I May Remember*, p. 135.

21. Arthur Balfour to Mary Elcho, 9 January 1893 (*Letters*, pp. 89–90); see also Mary Elcho to George Wyndham, 3 January 1893, George Wyndham Papers.

22. Mary Elcho to Madeline Wyndham, 21 April 1893, Stanway Papers.

23. Wemyss, *Family Record*, pp. 50–2.

24. Lambert, *Unquiet Souls*, pp. 64–5, 78; Beauman, *Cynthia Asquith*, p. 15.

25. Adams, *The Last Grandee*, pp. 34, 126.

26. Arthur Balfour to Mary Elcho, 16 August 1893 (*Letters*, p. 14).

27. Madeline Wyndham to Mary Elcho, quoted in Dakers, *Clouds*, p. 160.

28. Percy Wyndham to Mary Elcho, 6 September 1893, Stanway Papers.

29. Wilfrid Scawen Blunt, Secret Memoirs XVI, 9 November 1893.

30. Pamela Tennant to Mary Elcho, 25 August 1893, Stanway Papers.

31. Pamela Tennant to Mary Elcho, 16 August 1893, Stanway Papers.

32. Pamela Tennant to Mary Elcho, 25 August 1893, Stanway Papers.

33. Paget, *In my Tower*, 1.5–6.

34. Pamela Tennant to Mary Elcho, 25 August 1893, Stanway Papers.

35. Wilfrid Blunt, Secret Memoirs XVI, 16 October 1893.

36. See Mary Lovell, *The Churchills: A Family at the Heart of History – from the Duke of Marlborough to Winston Churchill* (Little, Brown, 2011), pp. 49–50.

37. Longford, *Pilgrimage of Passion*, p. 298.

38. Wilfrid Blunt, Secret Memoirs XVI, 9 November 1893.

39. George Wyndham to Ettie Grenfell, 30 September 1893, Desborough Papers, HALS DE/Rv/C2800/39. All others found in NRS GD433/2/482 ff. 1–19r.

40. Wilfrid Blunt heard the story from two different sources. Once the immediacy of the crisis had passed, George Wyndham gave him the fundamentals of the entanglement. Shortly afterwards, at what was doubtless a gossipy lunch with Lewis ('Loulou') Harcourt at 11 Downing Street (Loulou being the son of the Chancellor, Sir William Harcourt), Loulou, who had been present at the Derwent house party, told Blunt that George Curzon, upon receiving anonymous telegrams at the Derwent house party from a lady in distress, 'very foolishly shewed [them] around', thinking they signified a crisis in Violet Granby's marriage. On then receiving a telegram from Harry Cust, at Sheffield, who had just seen the pregnancy certificate sent to him by Nina and Violet Granby, Curzon hastened to him, returning only briefly to enlist George Wyndham's help, before the two hared off again to Harry (Secret Memoirs, 16 October 1893 and 9 November 1893). Ridley and Percy have Harry himself receiving letters from Nina Welby and showing them around as a joke (*Letters of Arthur Balfour and Lady Elcho*, p. 103), but it is likely that this is an example of the way in which the tale mutated as it filtered through society. Harry could be cruel, but he was surely not foolish enough to incriminate himself so completely as that. As subsequent events demonstrated, the Souls' morality could not extend to seducing unmarried women.

41. George Wyndham to Ettie Grenfell, 27 September 1893, Desborough Papers, HALS DE/Rv/C2800/38.

42. Pamela Tennant to Sibell, Countess Grosvenor, n.d. (September 1893), George Wyndham Papers.

43. Mary Elcho to Madeline Wyndham, 20, 21 November 1893, Stanway Papers.

44. Harry Cust to Arthur Balfour, 15 October 1893, Whittingehame Papers, NRS GD433/2/482 f. 4r.

45. Pamela Tennant to Mary Elcho, 13 March 1928, Stanway Papers.

46. Harry Cust to Arthur Balfour, 15 October 1893, Whittingehame Papers, NRS GD433/2/482 f. 4r.

47. Madeline Adeane to Madeline Wyndham, 19 November 1893, Adeane Papers;

see also Madeline Adeane to George Wyndham, 4 October 1893, George Wyndham Papers.

48. Sitwell, *Laughter in the Next Room*, p. 99.

49. Wilfrid Scawen Blunt, Secret Memoirs XVI, 7 October 1893.

50. Ibid.

51. Ibid., 16 October 1893.

52. *The Times*, 16 October 1893.

53. George Curzon to Arthur Balfour, 16 October 1893, Whittingehame Papers, NRS GD433/2/482 f. 6r.

54. Charles Welby to Arthur Balfour, 16 October 1893, Whittingehame Papers, NRS GD433/2/482 f. 8r.

55. Quoted in Ellenberger, 'The Souls: High Society and Politics', p. 214.

56. Wilfrid Scawen Blunt, Secret Memoirs XVI, 27 June 1894.

57. Harry Cust to Arthur Balfour, n.d., f. 5r; Charles Welby to Arthur Balfour, 31 October 1893, f. 14r, and 3 November 1893, f. 15r, all Whittingehame Papers, NRS GD433/2/482.

58. Quoted in Ellenberger, 'The Souls: High Society and Politics', p. 214.

Chapter 14: India

1. Pamela Tennant to Mary Drew, 13 January 1894, BL Mary Gladstone Papers, vol. XXXIII, Add. MSS. 46251.

2. Percy Wyndham to Mary Elcho, 20 October 1893, Stanway Papers.

3. Ibid.

4. Harry Cust to Sibell, Countess Grosvenor, quoted in Egremont, *The Cousins*, p. 164.

5. Pamela Tennant to Madeline Adeane, n.d. [October 1893], Stanway Papers.

6. Pamela Tennant to Sibell, Countess Grosvenor, 12 November 1893, George Wyndham Papers.

7. Ibid.

8. Madeline Adeane to Madeline Wyndham, 19 November 1893, Adeane Papers.

9. Pamela Tennant to Mary Drew, 13 January 1894, BL Mary Gladstone Papers, vol. XXXIII, Add. MSS. 46251.

10. Madeline Adeane to Mary Elcho, 19 December 1893, Stanway Papers.

11. James, *Rise and Fall*, pp. 233–4.

12. Pamela Tennant to Mary Drew, 13 January 1894, BL Mary Gladstone Papers, vol. XXXIII, Add. MSS. 46251.

13. Madeline Adeane to Madeline Wyndham, 7 December 1893, Adeane Papers.

14. Ibid.

15. Madeline Adeane to Madeline Wyndham, 14 March 1894, Adeane Papers.

16. Quoted in Hoare, *Serious Pleasures*, p. 4.

17. Ibid., p. 17.

18. Madeline Adeane to Madeline Wyndham, 14 March 1894, Adeane Papers.

19. Arthur Balfour to Mary Elcho, January 1894 (*Letters*, p. 94).

20. Pamela Tennant to Sibell Grosvenor, 1 February 1894, George Wyndham Papers.

21. Pamela Tennant to Sibell Grosvenor, October 1894, George Wyndham Papers.

22. Pamela Tennant to Mary Elcho, 28 August 1916, Stanway Papers.

23. Pamela Tennant to Sibell, Countess Grosvenor, 1 February 1894, George Wyndham Papers.

24. Ibid.

25. Wilfrid Scawen Blunt, Secret Memoirs XVI, 4 May 1894.

26. 'Testament of Millicent Fawcett', 19 March 1894, Whittingehame Papers, NRS GD433/2/482 f. 23r.

27. Millicent Fawcett to Arthur Balfour, 26 March 1894, Whittingehame Papers, NRS GD433/2/482 f. 27–8r.

28. Arthur Balfour to Millicent Fawcett, copy, n.d., Whittingehame Papers, NRS GD433/2/482 f. 25–6r.

29. 'Testament of Millicent Fawcett', 19 March 1894, Whittingehame Papers, NRS GD433/2/482 f. 23r.

30. Arthur Balfour to Harry Cust, 1 June 1894, Whittingehame Papers, NRS GD433/2/482 f. 41r.

31. Madeline Adeane to Madeline Wyndham, n.d. [spring 1894], Adeane Papers.

32. Madeline Adeane to Madeline Wyndham, 14 March 1894, Adeane Papers.

33. Madeline Adeane to Madeline Wyndham, 5 May 1894, Adeane Papers.

Chapter 15: Rumour

1. Roy Hattersley, *David Lloyd George: The Great Outsider* (Little, Brown, 2010), p. 72.
2. Cannadine, *Decline and Fall*, p. 45.
3. The letter that the Queen wrote to Gladstone after their meeting was scarcely warmer. Victoria told her erstwhile Prime Minister that she would confer a peerage on him, except that she knew he would not accept it: Hibbert, *Queen Victoria*, pp. 368, 376.
4. Ibid., p. 376.
5. Patrick Jackson, 'Harcourt, Lewis Vernon, First Viscount Harcourt (1863–1922)', *Oxford Dictionary of National Biography*, Oxford University Press, 2004; online edn, January 2008, www.oxforddnb.com/view/article/33692, accessed 14 November 2013.
6. McKenna, *Secret Life of Oscar Wilde*, pp. 332–3.
7. Ibid., pp. 342–3.
8. Pamela Tennant to Mary Elcho, 30 October 1894, Stanway Papers.
9. Ibid.
10. Pamela Tennant to Sibell, Countess Grosvenor, 29 September 1894, George Wyndham Papers.
11. Pamela Tennant to Sibell, Countess Grosvenor, n.d. [October 1894]. 'Percy's policy for dealing with misfortunes had not changed since he outlined it to Madeline Wyndham thirty years before, and would not change thereafter. Some five years later, he briskly, albeit sympathetically, reproved his eldest daughter when she made reference to domestic troubles: 'I know well all your trials and difficulties but don't allude to them as it only makes things worse putting them down in *black* and *white* and *underlining* them' (Percy Wyndham to Mary Elcho, 22 November 1900, Stanway Papers).
12. Pamela Tennant to Mary Elcho, 30 October 1894, Stanway Papers.
13. McKenna, *Secret Life of Oscar Wilde*, p. 422.
14. Ibid., p. 421.
15. Pamela Tennant to Mary Elcho, 30 October 1894, Stanway Papers.
16. Ibid.
17. Madeline Adeane to Madeline Wyndham, 14 December 1894, Adeane Papers.

18. Madeline Adeane to Madeline Wyndham, 10 December 1894, Adeane Papers.

19. Pamela Tennant to Mary Elcho, 30 October 1894, Stanway Papers.

Chapter 16: Egypt

1. For discussion of the play, see Hynes, *Edwardian Turn of Mind*, pp. 174–8.

2. Ibid., pp. 177–8.

3. Longford, *Pilgrimage of Passion*, p. 295.

4. Fingall, *70 Years Young*, p. 184.

5. Mary Elcho to Wilfrid Scawen Blunt, 16 November 1893, Blunt Papers, FM 1529-1976.

6. Longford, *Pilgrimage of Passion*, p. 308.

7. Ibid., p. 307.

8. Wilfrid Scawen Blunt, Secret Memoirs XVI, 10 to 13 August and 5 October 1894.

9. Mary Elcho to Madeline Wyndham, 22 November 1894, Stanway Papers.

10. Annie, Countess of Wemyss and March to Mary Elcho, 30 September 1894, Stanway Papers.

11. Ibid.

12. Wilfrid Scawen Blunt, diary entry, 5 January 1895, Blunt Papers, FM 343-1975.

13. Mary Elcho to Evelyn de Vesci, 17 January 1895, De Vesci Papers, DD/DRU/87.

14. Ibid.

15. Quoted in Longford, *Pilgrimage of Passion*, p. 311.

16. Arthur Balfour to Mary Elcho, 27 February 1895 (*Letters*, p. 120).

17. Wilfrid Scawen Blunt, diary entry, 14/15 January 1895, FM 344-1975.

18. Ibid.

19. Longford, *Pilgrimage of Passion*, p. 311; Mary Elcho to Wilfrid Scawen Blunt, 27 March 1899, Blunt Papers, FM 492-1975; and 5 May 1906, Blunt Papers, FM 559-1975.

20. Quoted in Longford, *Pilgrimage of Passion*, p. 313.

21. Mary Elcho to Wilfrid Scawen Blunt, 6 April 1899, Blunt Papers, FM 493-1975.

22. Ibid.

23. Quoted in Longford, *Pilgrimage of Passion*, p. 311.

24. Beauman, *Cynthia Asquith*, pp. 26, 30, 292–3.

25. Mary Elcho to Wilfrid Scawen Blunt, 6 April 1899, Blunt Papers, FM 493-1975.

26. Mary Elcho to Evelyn de Vesci, 13 February 1895, De Vesci Papers, DD/DRU/87.

27. Quoted in Longford, *Pilgrimage of Passion*, p. 312.

28. Ibid., p. 313.

29. Hugo Elcho to Evelyn de Vesci, n.d. [1895], De Vesci Papers, DD/DRU/102.

30. Ibid.

31. Longford, *Pilgrimage of Passion*, p. 313.

32. Mary Elcho to Wilfrid Scawen Blunt, 6 April 1899, Blunt Papers, FM 493-1975.

33. Harrison, *Autobiographic Memoirs*, 2.173–9.

34. Longford, *Pilgrimage of Passion*, p. 313.

35. Hugo Elcho to Mary Elcho, n.d. [February 1895], Stanway Papers.

36. Mary Elcho to Wilfrid Scawen Blunt, 6 April 1899, Blunt Papers, FM 493-1975.

37. Wilfrid Scawen Blunt, diary entries, 5 March 1895 to 13 March 1895, Blunt Papers, FM 344-1975.

38. Mary Elcho to Wilfrid Scawen Blunt, 6 April 1899, Blunt Papers, FM 493-1975.

39. Hugo Elcho to Evelyn de Vesci, 20 March 1895, De Vesci Papers, DD/DRU/102.

40. Telegram from Hugo Elcho to Mary Elcho, 20 March 1895, Stanway Papers. It had been arranged in Hugo's previous letter to Mary that the two would meet in Rome: Hugo Elcho to Mary Elcho, 14 March 1895, Stanway Papers.

41. Hugo Elcho to Evelyn de Vesci, 20 March 1895, De Vesci Papers, DD/DRU/102.

42. Mary Elcho to Hugo Elcho, 21 March 1895, Stanway Papers.

43. Mary Elcho to Madeline Wyndham, 9 April 1895, Stanway Papers.

44. Mary Elcho to Madeline Wyndham, 9 July 1895, Stanway Papers.

45. Wilfrid Scawen Blunt, Secret Memoirs XVII, diary entry, 13 May 1895 (transcript of a letter from Mary Elcho), Blunt Papers, FM 34-1975; Mary Elcho to Madeline Wyndham, 9 July 1895, Stanway Papers.

46. Wilfrid Scawen Blunt, Secret Memoirs XVII, diary entry, May 1895.

Chapter 17: The Florentine Drama

1. Madeline Adeane to Madeline Wyndham, 6 April 1895, Adeane Papers.
2. George Wyndham to Percy Wyndham, 7 April 1895, BL Eccles Bequest (unbound), vol. CXIV, Add. MSS. 81732.
3. Ibid.
4. Arthur Balfour to Mary Elcho, 20 March 1895 (*Letters*, p. 123).
5. Madeline Adeane to Mary Elcho, 6 May 1895, Stanway Papers.
6. Paget, *In my Tower*, 25 April 1895, 1.136–9.
7. Blow, *Broken Blood*, p. 113.
8. Quoted in Ellenberger, 'The Souls: High Society and Politics', p. 51.
9. E. F. Benson, *Dodo – A Detail of the Day* (Lightning Source UK, [n.d.]), p. 27.
10. Quoted in Ellenberger., 'The Souls: High Society and Politics', p. 64.
11. Pamela Tennant to George Wyndham, 21 August 1895, George Wyndham Papers; Madeline Adeane to Mary Elcho, 6 May 1895, Stanway Papers.
12. Edward Tennant to Charlotte, Lady Ribblesdale, 7 May 1895, Bodleian, Asquith Papers, MS. Eng. c. 6697 f. 156.
13. Madeline Adeane to Mary Elcho, 6 May 1895, Stanway Papers.
14. Mary Elcho to Arthur Balfour, quoted in Dakers, *Clouds*, p. 163.
15. Edward Tennant to Charlotte, Lady Ribblesdale, 7 May 1895, Bodleian, Asquith Papers, MS. Eng. c. 6697 f. 156.
16. Wilfrid Blunt, diary entry, 12 May 1895, Blunt Papers, FM 345-1975.
17. George Wyndham to Mary Drew, May 1895, quoted in Mackail and Wyndham, *Life and Letters*, 1.330–1.
18. Mary Elcho to Madeline Wyndham, 18 July 1895, Stanway Papers.
19. Mary Elcho to Madeline Wyndham, 16 May 1895, Stanway Papers.
20. Ibid.
21. Mary Elcho to Arthur Balfour, n.d. [spring 1895] (*Letters*, p. 124).
22. Percy Wyndham to Guy Wyndham, 23 May 1895, Stanway Papers.
23. George Wyndham to Mary Drew, May 1895, quoted in Mackail and Wyndham, *Life and Letters*, 1.330–1.
24. Mary Elcho to Madeline Wyndham, 9 July 1895, Stanway Papers.
25. Mary Elcho to Arthur Balfour, 31 August 1895 (*Letters*, pp. 128–9).
26. Wilfrid Scawen Blunt, Secret Memoirs XVII, 16 August 1895.

27. Ibid., 11 and 27 April 1895.

28. Ibid., 13 May 1895.

29. Ibid., 28 June 1895.

30. Longford, *Pilgrimage of Passion*, p. 315.

31. Wilfrid Scawen Blunt, Secret Memoirs XVII, 14 and 19 July 1895.

32. Order of Service for Pamela and Edward Tennant, kept and decorated by Mary Elcho, Stanway Papers.

33. *The Lady*, 18 July 1895; and quoted in Blow, *Broken Blood*, p. 114.

34. Wilfrid Scawen Blunt, Secret Memoirs XVII, 14 and 19 July 1895.

35. Ibid., 16 August 1895.

36. Ibid.

37. Ibid., 9 December 1895.

38. Edward Burne-Jones to Madeline Wyndham, 25 October 1895; unknown correspondent to Madeline Wyndham, 26 October 1895, Stanway Papers.

39. Wilfrid Scawen Blunt, Secret Memoirs XVII, 9 December 1895.

40. Longford, *Pilgrimage of Passion*, pp. 318–19.

41. Mary Elcho to Wilfrid Scawen Blunt, 29 April 1896, Blunt Papers, FM 281-1975.

42. Mary Elcho to Wilfrid Scawen Blunt, 27 March 1899, Blunt Papers, FM 492-175.

43. Mary Elcho to Wilfrid Scawen Blunt, 26 September 1901, Blunt Papers, FM 518-1975.

44. Mary Elcho to Wilfrid Scawen Blunt, 1 February 1906, Blunt Papers, FM 554-1975.

45. Ibid.

46. A full account of this is given in Longford, *Pilgrimage of Passion*, chapters 17 to 19.

47. Mary Elcho to Arthur Balfour, 6 June 1893 (*Letters* pp. 135–6).

Chapter 18: Glen

1. Quoted in Blow, *Broken Blood*, p. 116.

2. Wilfrid Scawen Blunt, Secret Memoirs XVII, 19 July 1895.

3. Pamela Tennant to George Wyndham, 22 October 1895, George Wyndham Papers.

4.   Pamela Tennant to Marie Stopes, 14 July 1918, BL Stopes Papers, vol. CCXXXVIII, Add. MS. 58684.

5.   Pamela Tennant to George Wyndham, 21 August 1895, George Wyndham Papers.

6.   Pamela Tennant to George Wyndham, 21 August 1895 and 24 August 1898, George Wyndham Papers.

7.   Pamela Tennant to Mary Elcho, 23 October 1897, Stanway Papers.

8.   Pamela Tennant to Mary Elcho, n.d. [c.1900], Stanway Papers.

9.   Pamela Tennant to Mary Elcho, 23 October 1897, Stanway Papers.

10. Edward Tennant to Pamela Tennant, 19 February 1896, Glenconner Papers, NRS GD510/1/30 f. 34.

11. See correspondence between Pamela Tennant and Edward Tennant in the course of autumn 1895 and spring 1896, Glenconner Papers, NRS GD510/26, 30, 31.

12. Edward Tennant to Pamela Tennant, spring 1896, Glenconner Papers, NRS GD510/1/30 f. 17.

13. Edward Tennant to Pamela Tennant, 17 January 1896, Glenconner Papers, NRS GD510/1/31 f. 20.

14. Edward Tennant to Pamela Tennant, 26 April 1896, Glenconner Papers, NRS GD510/1/31 f. 26.

15. Edward Tennant to Pamela Tennant, 10 January 1896, Glenconner Papers, NRS GD510/1/30 f. 38.

16. Edward Tennant to Pamela Tennant, n.d. [c.Easter 1896], Glenconner Papers, NRS GD510/1/30 f. 20.

17. Madeline Wyndham to Pamela Tennant, 9 August 1897, Glenconner Papers, NRS GD510/1/26 f. 33.

18. Mary Elcho to Arthur Balfour, n.d. [c.November 1920], Whittingehame Papers, NRS GD433/2/229/1 f. 19.

19. Blow, *Broken Blood*, pp. 132–3.

20. Harry Cust to Pamela Tennant, n.d., Tennant Papers, NLS 12143/4.

21. Mary Elcho to Madeline Wyndham, 6 January 1886, Stanway Papers.

22. Madeline Wyndham to Pamela Tennant, 9 August 1897, Glenconner Papers, NRS GD510/1/26 f. 33.

23. Pamela Tennant to Wilfrid Scawen Blunt, 11 June 1922, Blunt Papers, FM 286-1976.

24. Pamela Tennant to Mary Elcho, 23 October 1897, Stanway Papers.

25. Madeline Wyndham to Pamela Tennant, 9 August 1897, Glenconner Papers, NRS GD510/1/26 f. 33.

26. Brendon, *Decline and Fall*, pp. 207, 209–10.

27. Pamela Tennant to Mary Elcho, 7 June 1895, Stanway Papers.

28. George Wyndham to Pamela Tennant, 19 January 1898, quoted in Mackail and Wyndham, *Life and Letters*, 1.323.

29. George Wyndham to Pamela Tennant, 5 March 1898, quoted in ibid., 1.334; 11 February 1898, ibid., 1.333.

30. George Wyndham to Pamela Tennant, 11 February 1898, ibid., 1.333.

31. George Wyndham to Pamela Tennant, 10 January 1898, ibid., 1.320.

32. George Wyndham to Pamela Tennant, 23 April 1899, ibid., 1.352.

33. Cuttings all found in the Garden Book of Pamela Tennant, Stephen Tennant Papers.

34. Pamela Tennant to Mary Elcho, 20 June 1900, Stanway Papers.

35. *The Times*, 20 November 1928.

36. Pamela Glenconner, *Edward Wyndham Tennant: A Memoir* (John Lane, The Bodley Head, 1919), p. 11.

Chapter 19: The Portrait, War and Death

1. John Singer Sargent to Percy Wyndham, 20 December 1898, quoted in Dakers, *Clouds*, p. 163.

2. Percy Wyndham to Mary Elcho, n.d. [*c*.May 1895], Stanway Papers.

3. Mackail and Wyndham, *Life and Letters*, 1.67, 349–50.

4. Egremont, *The Cousins*, pp. 196, 198.

5. Mackail and Wyndham, *Life and Letters*, 1.66.

6. Quoted in Egremont, *The Cousins*, p. 193.

7. Mallet, *Life with Queen Victoria*, 21 October 1898, p. 141.

8. Mary Elcho to Madeline Wyndham, 18 January 1899, Stanway Papers.

9. Mary Elcho to Madeline Wyndham, 11 February 1899, Stanway Papers.

10. Mary Elcho to Madeline Wyndham, 1 February 1899, Stanway Papers.

11. Mary Elcho to Madeline Wyndham, 7 February 1899, Stanway Papers.

12. Mary Elcho to Madeline Wyndham, 14 February 1899, Stanway Papers.

13. Madeline Adeane to Madeline Wyndham, 17 March 1899, Adeane Papers.

14. Madeline Adeane to Percy Wyndham, 6 April 1899, Adeane Papers.

15. Mary Elcho to Madeline Wyndham, 28 February 1899, Stanway Papers.

16. Madeline Adeane to Madeline Wyndham, 29 March 1899, Adeane Papers.

17. Charles Adeane to Madeline Wyndham, 21 April 1899, Adeane Papers.

18. Charles Adeane to Madeline Wyndham, 24 March 1899, Adeane Papers.

19. Madeline Adeane to Madeline Wyndham, 16 August 1899, Adeane Papers.

20. Madeline Adeane to Madeline Wyndham, 28 September 1899, Adeane Papers.

21. Quoted in Egremont, *The Cousins*, p. 201.

22. Mackail and Wyndham, *Life and Letters*, 1.71.

23. Egremont, *The Cousins*, p. 201.

24. Quoted in ibid., p. 188.

25. Quoted in ibid., p. 201.

26. Madeline Adeane to Madeline Wyndham, 31 October 1899, Adeane Papers.

27. Madeline Adeane to Madeline Wyndham, 2 November 1899, Adeane Papers.

28. Charles Adeane to Madeline Wyndham, 3 November 1899, Adeane Papers.

29. Madeline Wyndham to Pamela Tennant, 4 November 1899, Glenconner Papers, NRS GD510/1/29 f. 38; 7 November 1899, Glenconner Papers, NRS GD510/1/29 f. 22.

30. Madeline Wyndham to Pamela Tennant, 7 November 1899, Glenconner Papers, NRS GD510/1/29 f. 22.

31. Ibid.

32. H. G. Wells, *The New Machiavelli* (Duffield, 1910), p. 122.

33. See Chapter 9 onwards of Arthur Conan Doyle, *The Great Boer War* (Smith, Elder, 1900).

34. Brendon, *Decline and Fall*, pp. 218–19.

35. Percy Wyndham to Mary Elcho, 16/17 December 1899, Stanway Papers.

Chapter 20: Plucking Triumph from Disaster

1. H. G. Wells, *The New Machiavelli*, p. 122.
2. Brendon, *Decline and Fall*, p. 219.
3. George Wyndham to Guy Wyndham, 6 January 1900, quoted in Mackail and Wyndham, *Life and Letters*, 1.386.
4. Margot Asquith to Edward Tennant, 17 January 1900, Glenconner Papers, NRS GD10/1/42 f. 8.
5. George Wyndham to Madeline Wyndham, 3 February 1900, quoted in Mackail and Wyndham, *Life and Letters*, 1.391.
6. Arthur Balfour to Mary Elcho, 1 February 1900 (*Letters*, p. 166).
7. Margot Asquith to Edward Tennant, n.d. [5 November 1900], Glenconner Papers, NRS GD510/1/42 f. 12.
8. Percy Wyndham to Mary Elcho, 5 February 1900, Stanway Papers.
9. Arthur Balfour to Mary Elcho, 16 March 1900 (*Letters*, p. 167).
10. Newspaper cutting, n.d., among Glenconner Papers, NRS GD510/1/29 f. 7.
11. Madeline Adeane to Madeline Wyndham, 29 March 1900, Adeane Papers.
12. Mackail and Wyndham, *Life and Letters*, 1.72.
13. *New York Times*, 14 December 1913.
14. Madeline Adeane to Madeline Wyndham, 18 March 1900, Adeane Papers.
15. George Wyndham to Pamela Tennant, 11 September 1900, quoted in Mackail and Wyndham, *Life and Letters*, 1.405.
16. Charles Adeane to Madeline Wyndham, 1 February 1900, Adeane Papers.
17. Madeline Adeane to Madeline Wyndham, 13 August 1900, Adeane Papers.
18. Madeline Adeane to Madeline Wyndham, 20 May 1900, Adeane Papers.
19. Brendon, *Decline and Fall*, p. 220.
20. Jan Morris, *Farewell the Trumpets: An Imperial Retreat* (London and Boston, Faber 1978), p. 86.
21. Downes, *John S. Sargent*, pp. 54, 188–9.
22. Dakers, *Clouds*, p. 97.
23. Quoted in ibid., p. 165.
24. Mary Elcho to Hugo Elcho, 1 August 1900, Stanway Papers.
25. Quoted in Mackail and Wyndham, *Life and Letters*, 1.72–3.

Chapter 21: The 1900 Election

1.   Mary Elcho to Hugo Elcho, 1 August 1900, Stanway Papers.

2.   Mary Elcho to Hugo Elcho, 13 September 1900, Stanway Papers.

3.   Quoted in Ellenberger, 'The Souls: High Society and Politics', p. 91; Dakers, *Clouds*, p. 158.

4.   Abdy and Gere, *The Souls*, p. 106.

5.   Mary Elcho to Madeline Wyndham, 16 July 1895, Stanway Papers.

6.   Wilfrid Scawen Blunt, Secret Memoirs XVII, 16 July 1895.

7.   Mary Elcho to Hugo Elcho, n.d. [*c*.1898], Stanway Papers.

8.   Mary Elcho to Hugo Elcho, 13 September 1900, Stanway Papers.

9.   Mary Elcho to Hugo Elcho, 25 September 1900, Stanway Papers.

10. Ellenberger, 'The Souls and London "Society"', p. 154. The equivalent in RPI is £7,389,000; in ESV £43,050,000; and in EPV £66,680,000.

11. Mary Elcho to Arthur Balfour, 30 August 1899 (*Letters*, pp. 158–9).

12. Abdy and Gere, *The Souls*, p. 105.

13. Arthur Balfour to Mary Elcho, n.d. [September 1896] (*Letters*, p. 146).

14. Mary Elcho to Percy Wyndham, 28 September 1899, Stanway Papers.

15. Mary Elcho to Arthur Balfour, 30 August 1899 (*Letters*, pp. 158–9).

16. Mary Elcho to Arthur Balfour, 20 September 1904 (*Letters*, pp. 216–17).

17. Margot Asquith to Edward Tennant, 10 October 1900, Glenconner Papers, NRS GD510/1/42 f. 9.

18. Margot Asquith to Edward Tennant, 31 July 1900, Glenconner Papers, NRS GD510/1/42 f. 11.

19. Pamela Tennant to Mary Elcho, n.d. [1900], Stanway Papers.

20. Quoted in Marquand, *Britain since 1918*, p. 56.

21. Pamela Tennant to Mary Elcho, n.d. [1900], Stanway Papers.

22. Ibid.

23. Jalland, *Women, Marriage and Politics*, pp. 206ff.

24. Ibid., quoted at pp. 209–10.

25. Ibid., pp. 209–14.

26. See, for example, Edward Tennant to Pamela Tennant, 27 May 1896, teasingly suggesting that Pamela should show a prominent suffragist guest at Clouds, Lady Grove (a niece of the Wyndhams' friend Rosalind Howard), a letter in

The Times presumably opposing women's suffrage, Glenconner Papers, NRS GD510/1/30 f. 32.2; and Clare Tennant to Edward Tennant, 15 November 1912, responding to her father's having sent her a printed copy of a recent speech he had made opposing women's suffrage: 'I'm sure the meeting will retard the "vote" & when I read your speech I couldn't think *what* the suffragets [sic] could find to contradict reasonably the things you said …', Glenconner Papers, NRS GD510/1/41 f. 21.

27. Madeline Adeane to Madeline Wyndham, 21 and 1 September 1900, Adeane Papers.

28. Madeline Adeane to Madeline Wyndham, 28 September 1900, Adeane Papers.

29. Quoted in Marr, *History of Modern Britain*, p. 27.

30. James, *Rise and Fall*, p. 321.

31. Margot Asquith to Edward Tennant, 31 July 1900, Glenconner Papers, NRS GD510/1/42 f. 11.

32. Madeline Adeane to Madeline Wyndham, 5 October 1900, Adeane Papers.

33. Pamela Tennant to Mary Elcho, n.d. (1900), Stanway Papers.

34. Margot Asquith to Edward Tennant, 5 November 1900, Glenconner Papers, NRS GD510/1/42 f. 12.

35. Antony MacDonnell to George Wyndham, 22 September 1902, quoted in Mackail and Wyndham, *Life and Letters*, 2.760–1.

Chapter 22: Growing Families

1. Asquith, *Remember and Be Glad*, p. 192.

2. Ibid.

3. Mary Elcho to Ettie Desborough, 23 June 1915, Desborough Papers, HALS DE/Rv/C479/1.

4. Margot Asquith to Mary Elcho, *c.*1900, quoted in Blow, *Broken Blood*, p. 142.

5. Mary Elcho to Ettie Desborough, n.d. [*c.*1918/19], Desborough Papers, HALS DE/Rv/C477/66.

6. Madeline Adeane to Percy Wyndham, 12 February 1901, Adeane Papers.

7. Madeline Adeane to Madeline Wyndham, 30 January 1901, Adeane Papers.

8. Pamela Tennant to Mary Elcho, n.d. [July 1902], Stanway Papers.

9. Mary Elcho to Arthur Balfour, 2 January 1903 (*Letters*, pp. 193–4).

10. Francis Oke Buckland, *Health Springs of Germany and Austria* (W. H. Allen, 1890), p. 71.

11. Madeline Adeane to Madeline Wyndham, 11 September 1900, Adeane Papers.

12. Pamela Tennant to Mary Elcho, n.d. [July 1902], Stanway Papers.

13. Madeline Adeane to Madeline Wyndham, 1 January 1901 and 20 December 1900; Charles Adeane to Madeline Wyndham, 21 December 1900, Adeane Papers.

14. Madeline Adeane to Madeline Wyndham, 17 January 1901, Adeane Papers.

15. Blow, *Broken Blood*, p. 134.

16. Viscount Grey of Fallodon, *Recreation* (New York, Houghton Mifflin, 1920). These essays were drawn from an address given at Harvard University in December 1919.

17. Their lengthy correspondence is in four large folders in the Glenconner Papers at NRS GD510/1/60.

18. See the picture of Edward Grey drawn by Prince Carl Lichnowsky, *My Mission to London, 1912–1914* (Toronto, Cassell, 1918), pp. 27–8.

19. Robert Eccleshall and Graham Walker (eds), *Biographical Dictionary of British Prime Ministers* (London and New York, Routledge, 1998), p. 229.

20. Pamela Tennant to Mary Elcho, December 1903, Stanway Papers; Pamela Tennant to Sidney Cockerell, 22 January 1904, BL Cockerell Papers, vol. CXLVII, Add. MSS. 52769 f. 157.

21. *The Times*, 5 February 1906.

22. Quoted in Marie Belloc Lowndes, *A Passing World* (Macmillan, 1948), p. 187.

23. Viscount Grey of Fallodon, *The Cottage Book: The Undiscovered Country Diary of an Edwardian Statesman*, ed. and introduced by Michael Waterhouse (Gollancz, 1999), p. 26.

24. Belloc Lowndes, *A Passing World*, p. 175.

25. Charles Adeane to Mary Elcho, 6 November 1905, Stanway Papers.

26. Sitwell, *Laughter in the Next Room*, p. 45.

27. Pamela Tennant to Charles Tennant, 25 March 1908, Glenconner Papers, NRS GD510/1/41 f. 3r.

28. Edward Wyndham Tennant to Pamela Tennant, 23 August 1916, quoted in Glenconner, *Edward Wyndham Tennant*, p. 221.

29. Ibid., p. 249.

30. Pamela Tennant to Mary Elcho, 9 June 1928, Stanway Papers.

31. Hoare, *Serious Pleasures*, p. 6.

32. Ibid., p. 14.

33. Blow, *Broken Blood*, p. 165.

34. Quoted in Hoare, *Serious Pleasures*, p. 7.

35. Ibid., p. 23.

36. Ibid., p. 7.

37. Mary Elcho to Hugo Elcho, 31 October 1909, Stanway Papers.

38. Fanny Cliffe to Mary Elcho, 6 July 1906, Stanway Papers.

39. Wemyss, *Family Record*, p. 204.

40. Asquith, *Remember and Be Glad*, p. 23.

41. Ibid., p. 20.

42. Ibid.

43. Ibid.

44. Asquith, *An Autobiography*, 2.44.

45. Asquith, *Remember and Be Glad*, pp. 42–3; *Haply I May Remember*, p. 14.

46. Beatrice Webb, *The Diary of Beatrice Webb: All the Good Things of Life*, vol. 2: 1892–1905, ed. Norman and Jeanne MacKenzie (Virago, 1986), p. 254.

47. Mary Elcho to Arthur Balfour, 1 October 1896 (*Letters*, p. 148).

48. Mary Elcho to Hugo Elcho, 30 November 1912, Stanway Papers.

49. Mary Elcho to Arthur Balfour, 18 February 1907 (*Letters*, p. 237).

50. Asquith, *Remember and Be Glad*, pp. 42–3; *Haply I May Remember*, p. 14.

51. Mary Elcho to Arthur Balfour, 18 February 1907 (*Letters*, p. 237).

52. Ridley and Percy (eds), *Letters of Arthur Balfour and Lady Elcho*, quoted at p. 17.

53. Asquith, *Haply I May Remember*, p. 13.

54. Madeline Adeane to Madeline Wyndham, 12 October 1905, Adeane Papers.

55. Charles Adeane to Madeline Wyndham, n.d. [November/December 1905], Adeane Papers.

56. Percy Wyndham to Madeline Wyndham, 3 November 1905, Stanway Papers.

57. Madeline Adeane to Madeline Wyndham, 1 December 1905, Adeane Papers.

58. Ibid.

59. Madeline Adeane to Mary Elcho, 21 November 1905, Stanway Papers.

60. Charles Adeane to Mary Elcho, 6 November 1905, Stanway Papers.

61. Madeline Adeane to Madeline Wyndham, 12 December 1905, Adeane Papers.

62. Madeline Adeane to Percy Wyndham, 31 December 1905, Adeane Papers.

Chapter 23: The Souls in Power

1. Mary Elcho to Arthur Balfour, 15 July 1902 (*Letters*, pp. 188–9).
2. Ibid.
3. Asquith, *Remember and Be Glad*, p. 3.
4. Mary Elcho to Arthur Balfour, 19 January 1904 (*Letters*, p. 210).
5. Ibid.
6. Mary Elcho to Arthur Balfour, 27 February 1904 (*Letters*, pp. 212–13). Lady Edward Cavendish was the widowed sister of Sir Frank and 'hostessed' for her brother in Berlin.
7. Ibid.
8. Nigel Nicolson, *Mary Curzon* (Weidenfeld & Nicolson, 1977), pp. 147–8.
9. Ibid.
10. Mary Elcho to Arthur Balfour, 1 August 1900 (*Letters*, p. 171).
11. Mary Elcho to Arthur Balfour, 19 January 1904 (*Letters*, p. 209).
12. Mary Elcho to Arthur Balfour, 14 February 1907 (*Letters*, p. 236).
13. Mary Elcho to Arthur Balfour, 19 January 1904 (*Letters*, p. 209).
14. Asquith, *An Autobiography*, 2.45.
15. Jalland, *Women, Marriage and Politics*, pp. 197, 204.
16. Arthur Balfour to Mary Elcho, 14 March 1894 (*Letters*, p. 105); Mary Elcho to Arthur Balfour, 23 September 1896 (*Letters*, p. 145).
17. Mary Elcho to Arthur Balfour, 15 July 1902 (*Letters*, p. 190).
18. Arthur Balfour to Mary Elcho, 12 July 1902 (*Letters*, p. 186); Mackail and Wyndham, *Life and Letters*, 1.79.
19. Ridley and Percy (eds), *Letters of Arthur Balfour and Lady Elcho*, p. 197.
20. Percy Wyndham to Mary Elcho, 3 September 1902, Stanway Papers.
21. Mary Elcho to Hugo Elcho, n.d. [1902], Stanway Papers.
22. Adams, *The Last Grandee*, p. 194.
23. Pamela Tennant to Mary Elcho, 17 February 1903, Stanway Papers.

24. Mary Elcho to Hugo Elcho, 20 February 1905, Stanway Papers.

25. Mary Elcho to Hugo Elcho, n.d. [1902], Stanway Papers.

26. Morris, *Farewell the Trumpets*, p. 114.

27. Pamela Tennant to Mary Elcho, 17 February 1902, Stanway Papers.

28. Arthur Balfour to Mary Elcho, 13 February 1903 (*Letters*, pp. 196–7).

29. Arthur Balfour to Mary Elcho, 27 February 1903 (*Letters*, pp. 197–8).

30. Mary Elcho to Arthur Balfour, 10 August 1903 (*Letters*, pp. 203–4).

31. Ibid.

32. Mary Elcho to Arthur Balfour, 18 September 1903 (*Letters*, p. 206).

33. Murray Hornibrook, in July 1924, quoted in Mackail and Wyndham, *Life and Letters*, 2.791.

34. Mackail and Wyndham, *Life and Letters*, 1.91.

35. Ibid., 1.92.

36. Ibid., 2.795.

37. Ibid.

38. Ibid., 1.93.

39. Antony MacDonnell to George Wyndham, 10 September 1904, quoted in Mackail and Wyndham, *Life and Letters*, 2.764–5.

40. Ibid., 1.97.

41. Mary Elcho to Wilfrid Scawen Blunt, n.d. [1913], Blunt Papers, FM 673-1975.

42. Mackail and Wyndham, *Life and Letters*, 1.102.

43. Ibid., 1.103.

44. Ibid., 1.105.

45. Ibid.

46. Pamela Tennant to Mary Elcho, 8 March 1905, Stanway Papers.

47. Mary Elcho to Arthur Balfour, 24 February 1905 (*Letters*, pp. 219–20).

48. Tynan Hinkson, *Years of the Shadow*, p. 257.

49. Mary Elcho to Arthur Balfour, 24 February 1905 (*Letters*, pp. 219–20).

50. Percy Wyndham to Mary Elcho, 14 January 1906, Stanway Papers.

51. Lambert, *Unquiet Souls*, pp. 128–9.

Chapter 24: Pamela at Wilsford

1. Hoare, *Serious Pleasures*, p. 4.
2. Percy Wyndham to Mary Elcho, 7 January 1906, Stanway Papers.
3. Pamela Tennant to Charles Tennant, 25 March 1908, Glenconner Papers, NRS GD510/1/41 f. 3r. The lines are from Wordsworth's 'Tintern Abbey'.
4. *The Times*, 5 February 1906.
5. Hoare, *Serious Pleasures*, p. 6.
6. *The Times*, 4 January 1921. The equivalent in RPI is £278,200,000; in ESV £1,605,000,000; and in EPV £2,338,000,000.
7. Ridley and Percy (eds), *Letters of Arthur Balfour and Lady Elcho*, p. 14.
8. *The Times*, 4 January 1921.
9. Pamela Tennant to Mary Elcho, 14 February 1901, Stanway Papers.
10. *The Times*, 9 May 1910.
11. Pamela Tennant to Charles Tennant, 26 May 1910, Glenconner Papers, NRS GD510/1/41 f. 9r.
12. Blow, *Broken Blood*, p. 124.
13. Hoare, *Serious Pleasures*, pp. 5–6.
14. Pamela Tennant to Wilfrid Scawen Blunt, 12 April 1905, Blunt Papers, FM 553-1975 .
15. Pamela Tennant to Sidney Cockerell, 22 April 1902, BL Cockerell Papers, vol. CXLVII, Add. MSS. 52769 ff. 150–1.
16. Ibid. The lines are a misquotation of Wordsworth's 'Lines Written in Early Spring': 'The budding twigs spread out their fan, / To catch the breezy air.'
17. *The Times*, 29 November 1920.
18. Quoted in Hoare, *Serious Pleasures*, pp. 88–9.
19. Ibid., p. 32.
20. James, *Rise and Fall*, p. 336.
21. John Biggs Davison, *George Wyndham: A Study in Toryism* (Hodder & Stoughton, 1951), p. 198; Egremont, *The Cousins*, p. 270.
22. George Wyndham to Sibell Grosvenor, 21 January 1906, quoted in Egremont, *The Cousins*, p. 259.
23. Ibid., p. 287.

24. Margot Asquith, diary entry, 14 July 1906, Bodleian, Asquith Papers, MS. Eng. d. 4204.

25. Raymond Asquith, diary entry of 1903, quoted in John Joliffe, *Raymond Asquith: Life and Letters* (Collins, 1980), p. 136.

26. Marriage Settlement of Margot Tennant, Glenconner Papers, NRS GD510/1/21 f. 4r.

27. Edward Glenconner to Margot Asquith, 6 August 1919, Bodleian, Asquith Papers, MS. Eng. c. 6697. The equivalent in RPI is £942,700; in ESV £3,657,000; and in EPV £6,873,000.

28. Margot Asquith, diary entry, 14 July 1906, Bodleian, Asquith Papers, MS. Eng. d. 4204.

29. Pamela Tennant to Sidney Cockerell, 26 February 1911, BL Cockerell Papers, vol. CXLVII, Add. MSS. 52769 f. 174.

30. Sidney Cockerell to Pamela Tennant, 27 February 1911, Glenconner Papers, NRS GD510/1/35 f. 3r; F. W. Bain to Sidney Cockerell, 24 February 1911, Glenconner Papers, NRS GD510/1/37.

31. N.d., Glenconner Papers, NRS GD510/1/32 f. 12r.

32. Asquith, *Remember and Be Glad*, pp. 191–2.

33. Pamela Tennant to Charles Tennant, 20 August 1908, Glenconner Papers, NRS GD510/1/41 f. 6r.

34. Belloc Lowndes, *A Passing World*, p. 181.

35. Hoare, *Serious Pleasures*, p. 7.

36. See Blow, *Broken Blood*; and Emma Tennant, *Strangers: A Family Romance* (Jonathan Cape, 1998); *Waiting for Princess Margaret* (Quartet Books, 2009).

37. Blow, *Broken Blood*, p. 188.

38. Ibid., p. 117.

39. Ibid., p. 124.

40. Pamela Tennant to Charles Tennant, 22 May 1908, Glenconner Papers, NRS GD510/1/41 f. 7r.

41. Pamela Tennant to Charles Tennant, 7 October 1908, Glenconner Papers, NRS GD510/1/41 f. 5r.

42. Pamela Tennant to Charles Tennant, 25 March 1908, Glenconner Papers, NRS GD510/1/41 f. 3r.

43. Pamela Tennant to Charles Tennant, 7 October 1908, Glenconner Papers, NRS GD510/1/41 f. 5r.

Chapter 25: Mr Balfour's Poodle

1. Mary Elcho to Arthur Balfour, 9 July 1907 (*Letters*, p. 238).
2. Mary Elcho to Arthur Balfour, 16 January 1906 (*Letters*, p. 229).
3. *The Times*, 7 July 1916.
4. Mary Elcho to Arthur Balfour, 16 January 1906 (*Letters*, p. 229).
5. Mary Elcho to Hugo Elcho, 26 July 1911, Stanway Papers.
6. Mary Elcho to Hugo Elcho, 31 October 1909, Stanway Papers.
7. See for example Mary Elcho to Arthur Balfour, n.d. [January 1916] (*Letters*, pp. 334–5); and 22 May 1920, Whittingehame Papers, NRS GD433/2/228/1 f. 7r.
8. Ridley and Percy (eds), *Letters of Arthur Balfour and Lady Elcho*, pp. 143–5.
9. Asquith, *Haply I May Remember*, pp. 210–11.
10. Ibid., pp. 2, 225–6.
11. Mary Elcho to Arthur Balfour, 9 July 1907 (*Letters*, pp. 238–9).
12. Mary Elcho to Hugo Elcho, 12 January 1906, Stanway Papers.
13. Mary Elcho to Arthur Balfour, 20 January 1906 (*Letters*, pp. 229–30).
14. Mary Elcho to Arthur Balfour, 15 October 1907 (*Letters*, pp. 242–3).
15. Mary Elcho to Arthur Balfour, 16 November 1907 (*Letters*, p. 244).
16. Quoted in Cannadine, *Decline and Fall*, p. 46.
17. *The Times*, 23 October 1906.
18. Hattersley, *Lloyd George*, p. 199.
19. Percy Wyndham to Mary Elcho, 14 January 1906, Stanway Papers.
20. Hansard 4, 176:1429, 26 June 1907.
21. *Hansard* 4, 188, 1908, col 47.
22. Asquith, *Remember and Be Glad*, p. 14.
23. George Wyndham to Percy Wyndham, 14 April 1908, quoted in Mackail and Wyndham, *Life and Letters*, 2.608.
24. Pamela Tennant to Charles Tennant, 25 February 1909, Glenconner Papers, NRS GD510/1/41 f. 8r.
25. Mary Elcho to Hugo Elcho, 26 Mary 1909, Stanway Papers.

26. Mary Elcho to Arthur Balfour, 31 January 1909 (*Letters*, p. 255).

27. Mary Elcho to Hugo Elcho, 26 March 1909, Stanway Papers.

28. Ibid.

29. Mary Elcho to Hugo Elcho, 7 March 1909, Stanway Papers.

30. The College, founded in 1907, was the brainchild of the reclusive Sir William Macdonald and his flamboyant sidekick James W. Robertson, the federal government's Commissioner of Agriculture and Dairying in the 1890s, who served as the College's first president. The College is now part of McGill University in Montreal.

31. Mary Elcho to Hugo Elcho, 2 March 1909, Stanway Papers.

32. Mary Elcho to Hugo Elcho, 7 March 1909, Stanway Papers.

33. Mary Elcho to Hugo Elcho, 13 March 1909, Stanway Papers.

34. Hansard, 5C, 4.548, 29 April 1909.

35. *The Times*, 22 June 1909.

36. Adams, *The Last Grandee*, p. 241.

37. Mary Elcho to Percy Wyndham, 21 January 1910, Stanway Papers.

38. Edward Tennant to Mr Allard, 27 June 1909, Tennant Papers, NLS 1.0172.

39. *The Times*, 24 June 1909.

40. *The Times*, 11 October 1909.

41. Ibid.

42. *The Times*, 31 July 1909.

43. *The Times*, 11 October 1909.

44. Percy Wyndham to Mary Elcho, 3 October 1909, Stanway Papers.

45. Mary Elcho to Hugo Elcho, 31 October 1909, Stanway Papers.

46. *The Times*, 3 December 1909.

Chapter 26: 1910

1. Adams, *The Last Grandee*, p. 241.

2. Mary Elcho to Percy Wyndham, 21 January 1910, Stanway Papers.

3. Ibid.

4. Ibid.

5. Ibid.

6. Percy Wyndham to Mary Elcho, 21 February 1910, Stanway Papers.

7. Mary Elcho to Arthur Balfour, 23 March 1910 (*Letters*, p. 261).

8. Ibid.

9. George Wyndham to Mary Elcho, 15 February 1913, quoted in Mackail and Wyndham, *Life and Letters*, 2.737–8.

10. Mary Elcho to Arthur Balfour, 23 March 1910 (*Letters*, p. 261).

11. Roy Jenkins, *Mr. Balfour's Poodle: Peers v. People* (Papermac, 1999), p. 146.

12. Ibid., p. 145.

13. Asquith, *Remember and Be Glad*, p. 127.

14. Mary Elcho to Hugo Elcho, 10 July 1910, Stanway Papers. Mary was right to anticipate objection. Her design was changed at the last minute, as Margot Asquith challenged Cynthia with the question: 'Do you want your bridesmaids to look like twelve loaves of bread?' (Asquith, *Remember and Be Glad*, p. 127).

15. Arthur Balfour to Mary Elcho, 26 July 1911 (*Letters*, p. 267).

16. George Wyndham to Mary Elcho, 6 October 1910, in Mackail and Wyndham, *Life and Letters*, 2.669.

17. Wemyss, *Family Record*, p. 208.

18. Dakers, *Clouds*, p. 172.

19. Quoted in ibid., p. 175.

20. Jenkins, *Mr. Balfour's Poodle*, p. 178.

21. Ibid., pp. 187, 190.

22. Percy Wyndham to Mary Elcho, 8 December 1910, Stanway Papers.

Chapter 27: Revolution?

1. George Wyndham to Philip Hanson, 5 April 1911, quoted in Mackail and Wyndham, *Life and Letters*, 2.687; Wemyss, *Family Record*, p. 209.

2. George Wyndham to Philip Hanson, 5 April 1911, quoted in Mackail and Wyndham, *Life and Letters*, 2.687.

3. Madeline Wyndham to Wilfrid Scawen Blunt, 6 December 1918, Blunt Papers, FM 894-1975.

4. Quoted in Dakers, *Clouds*, p. 176.

5. *The Times*, 20 March 1911.

6. George Wyndham to Madeline Wyndham, 11 December 1911, quoted in Mackail and Wyndham, *Life and Letters*, 2.710.

7. *The Times*, 14 March 1911.

8. Dated July 1911, Glenconner Papers, NRS GD510/1/21. In today's money the real price is £2,242; labour value £9,144; and income value £13,020.

9. The equivalent in RPI is £20,150,000; in ESV £117,000,000; and in EPV £163,300,000.

10. *The Times*, 11 April 1911.

11. George Wyndham to Madeline Wyndham, 1 October 1911, quoted in Mackail and Wyndham, *Life and Letters*, 2.707; and 21 December 1911, ibid., 2.712.

12. George Wyndham to Charles Gatty, 16 March 1911, ibid., 2.686.

13. Arthur Balfour to Mary Elcho, 19 July 1900 (*Letters*, pp.168–9).

14. Mary Elcho to Arthur Balfour, 12 January 1911 (*Letters*, pp. 263–4).

15. Arthur Balfour to Mary Elcho, 30 July 1911 (*Letters*, p. 269).

16. Viscount Grey of Fallodon, *Twenty-Five Years 1892–1916*, 2 vols (Hodder & Stoughton, 1926), 1.238.

17. Jenkins, *Mr. Balfour's Poodle*, p. 208.

18. Arthur Balfour to Mary Elcho, 16 July 1911 (*Letters*, p. 266).

19. Arthur Balfour to Mary Elcho, 23 July 1911 (*Letters*, pp. 266–7).

20. Adams, *The Last Grandee*, p. 252. The phrase has also been attributed to George Curzon: see David Gilmour, 'Curzon, George Nathaniel, Marquess Curzon of Kedleston (1859–1925)', *Oxford Dictionary of National Biography*, online edn, January 2011 [http://www.oxforddnb.com/view/article/32680, accessed 23 October 2013].

21. Jenkins, *Mr. Balfour's Poodle*, p. 226.

22. Ibid., p. 227.

23. Ibid., p. 223.

24. Arthur Balfour to Mary Elcho, 30 July 1911 (*Letters*, p. 268).

25. Jenkins, *Mr. Balfour's Poodle*, p. 233.

26. Ibid., p. 236.

27. Ibid., p. 238.

28. Ibid., p. 234.

29. Mary Elcho to Arthur Balfour, 10 October 1919, Whittingehame Papers, NRS GD433/2/229/1 f. 3r.

30. Arthur Balfour to Mary Elcho, n.d. [11 August 1911] (*Letters*, pp. 269–70); Mary Elcho to Arthur Balfour, 14 August 1911 (*Letters*, pp. 270–1).

31. Jenkins, *Mr. Balfour's Poodle*, pp. 252–3.

32. *The Times*, 11 August 1911; HL Deb. 10 August 1911, vol. 9, col. 1000.

33. HL Deb. 10 August 1911, vol. 9, cols 1003, 1014.

34. Quoted in Adams, *The Last Grandee*, p. 254.

35. Marr, *The Making of Modern Britain*, p. 113.

36. Arthur Balfour to Mary Elcho, n.d. [11 August 1911] (*Letters*, pp. 269–70); Mary Elcho to Arthur Balfour, 14 August 1911 (*Letters*, pp. 270–1).

37. Arthur Balfour to Mary Elcho, 8 October 1911 (*Letters*, p. 278).

38. Mary Elcho to Arthur Balfour, 7 November 1911 (*Letters*, p. 282).

39. George Wyndham to Sibell Grosvenor, 10 August 1911, quoted in Egremont, *The Cousins*, p. 278.

Chapter 28: 1911–1914

1. F. W. Bain to Pamela Tennant, 6 September 1911, Glenconner Papers, NRS GD510/1/37.

2. Pamela Tennant to unknown correspondent (as before), 3 August 1911, Glenconner Papers, NRS GD510/1/35 f. 22.3r.

3. Pamela Tennant to Charles Tennant, 3 August 1911, Glenconner Papers, NRS GD510/1/41 f. 14r.

4. Pamela Tennant to unknown (as before), 3 August 1911, Glenconner Papers, NRS GD510/1/35 f. 22.3r.

5. F. W. Bain to Pamela Tennant, 1 May 1911, Glenconner Papers, NRS GD/510/1/37.

6. Pamela Tennant to Charles Tennant, 3 August 1911, Glenconner Papers, NRS GD510/1/41 f. 14r; Pamela Tennant to unknown (as before), 3 August 1911, Glenconner Papers, NRS GD510/1/35 f. 22.3r.

7. Elizabeth Asquith to Mary Charteris, 27 December 1914, quoted in Blow, *Broken Blood*, p. 143.

8. *The Times*, 4 March 1911.

9. Glenconner, *Edward Wyndham Tennant*, p. 101.

10. Pamela Tennant to Charles Tennant, 7 October 1908, Glenconner Papers, NRS GD510/1/41 f. 5r.

11. Madeline Adeane to Mary Elcho, 22 March 1911, Stanway Papers.

12. Edward Tennant to Margot Asquith, 8 April 1910, Bodleian, Asquith Papers, MS. Eng. c. 6676 f. 160.

13. Bodleian, Asquith Papers, MS. Eng. 6676 f. 163 (n.d.).

14. Margot Asquith to Edward Tennant, 5 November 1911, Glenconner Papers, NRS GD510/1/42 f. 12r.

15. Edward Tennant to Margot Asquith, 15 January 1917, Bodleian, Asquith Papers, MS. Eng. c. 6697 ff. 164–5.

16. Pamela Tennant to Sidney Cockerell, 26 February 1911, BL Cockerell Papers, vol. CXLVII, Add. MSS. 52769 f. 174.

17. 'Fantasia – of a London House Closed', in Glenconner, *The White Wallet*, pp. 211–12.

18. Asquith, *Remember and Be Glad*, p. 192.

19. Ibid.

20. Mary Elcho to Arthur Balfour, 2 June 1923, Whittingehame Papers, NRS GD433/2/229/3 f. 4r.

21. Blow, *Broken Blood*, p. 125; and see *The Times* 13 June 1913, reporting on Bosie's bankruptcy that year, in which it is explained that, in 1907, Eddy had created a company, Wilsford Press Ltd, and had immediately then assigned all its shares to Bosie for a nominal sum.

22. Belloc Lowndes, *A Passing World*, p. 178; Philip Hoare, *Oscar Wilde's Last Stand* (New York, Arcade Publishing, 1998), pp. 20–1.

23. Susan, Lady Tweedsmuir, *The Edwardian Lady* (Duckworth, 1966), pp. 87–8.

24. Blow, *Broken Blood*, p. 172.

25. Wemyss, *Family Record*, p. 234.

26. Ibid., p. 235.

27. Edward Grey to Pamela Tennant, 18 December 1911, Glenconner Papers, NRS GD510/1/35 f. 12r.

28. Pamela Tennant to Sibell, Countess Grosvenor, 25 January 1912, George Wyndham Papers.

29. F. W. Bain to Pamela Tennant, 1 April and 18 August 1911, Glenconner Papers, NRS GD510/1/37.

30. Edward Grey to Pamela Tennant, 23 March 1913, Glenconner Papers, NRS GD510/1/60/3 f. 10r.

31. Edward Grey to Pamela Tennant, 8 December 1911, Glenconner Papers, NRS GD510/1/35 f. 12r.

32. Ibid., and 5 March 1913, ibid., f. 22.7r.

33. Edward Grey to Edward Tennant, 25 February 1912, Glenconner Papers, NRS GD510/1/60/2 f. 8r.

34. Tennant, *Waiting for Princess Margaret*, p. 72.

35. Hoare, *Serious Pleasures*, p. 17.

36. Clare Tennant to Edward Tennant, 25 February 1912, Glenconner Papers, NRS GD 510/1/42 f. 18r.

37. Asquith, *Diaries*, 8 May 1915, p. 17.

38. Mary Elcho to Arthur Balfour, 31 October 1912 (*Letters*, pp. 291–2).

39. Mary Elcho to Arthur Balfour, 30 October 1912 (*Letters*, pp. 290–1).

40. Mary Elcho to Arthur Balfour, 24 February 1913 (*Letters*, p. 294).

41. Arthur Balfour to Mary Elcho, 16 September 1912 (*Letters*, p. 288).

42. Mary Elcho to Arthur Balfour, 12 September 1912 (*Letters*, p. 287).

43. Ibid.

44. Philip Ziegler, *Diana Cooper* (Harmondsworth, Penguin Books, 1981), p. 41. Diana was the child of her mother's affair with Harry Cust, and was the infant born at the time that Harry first started courting Pamela in 1892.

45. Mary Elcho to Arthur Balfour, 15 October 1907 (*Letters*, p. 242).

46. Mary Elcho to Arthur Balfour, 29 March 1922, Whittingehame Papers, NRS GD433/2/229/2 f. 5r.

47. Mary Elcho to Arthur Balfour, 19 March 1913 (*Letters*, pp. 297–8).

48. Mary Elcho to Arthur Balfour, 12 September 1912 (*Letters*, pp. 286–7).

49. Mary Elcho to Arthur Balfour, 24 February 1913 (*Letters*, p. 294).

50. Mary Elcho to Hugo Elcho, 24 January 1913, Stanway Papers.

51. Ibid.

52. Mary Elcho to Arthur Balfour, 24 February 1913 (*Letters*, p. 295).

53. Kathleen Tynan Hinkson, *The Middle Years* (Constable, 1916), p. 233.

54. Mary Elcho to Arthur Balfour, 24 February 1913 (*Letters*, p. 294).

55. Ibid.

56. George Wyndham to Hilaire Belloc, 4 June 1913, quoted in Mackail and Wyndham, *Life and Letters*, 2.749.

57. Ellenberger, 'Constructing George Wyndham', p. 501. For a more colourful account see Joan Wyndham, *Dawn Chorus* (Virago, 2004), pp. 12–13.

58. Perf Wyndham to Sibell, Countess Grosvenor, 10 June 1913, Stanway Papers.

59. Mary Elcho to Wilfrid Scawen Blunt, n.d. [1913], Blunt Papers, FM 673-1975.

60. Longford, *Pilgrimage of Passion*, p. 390.

61. Mackail and Wyndham, *Life and Letters*, 1.126.

62. Longford, *Pilgrimage of Passion*, p. 390.

63. Madeline Adeane to Mary Elcho, 2 August 1914, Stanway Papers.

64. *The Times*, 29 July 1914.

65. Asquith, *Diaries*, 23 August 1915, p. 71.

66. Ibid.

67. Mary Elcho to Wilfrid Scawen Blunt, 28 September 1914, Blunt Papers, FM 719-1975.

68. *The Times*, 4 August 1914.

69. Simon Blow says that this was Eddy Tennant (see *Broken Blood*, p. 134). It seems more likely that it was, as claimed by himself, John Spender, Editor of the *Westminster Gazette* (see J. A. Spender, *Life, Journalism and Politics*, 2 vols (New York, Frederick A. Stokes, 1927), 2.14–15.

Chapter 29: MCMXIV

1. *The Times*, 5 August 1914.

2. Davenport-Hines, *Ettie*, p. 180; Wemyss, *Family Record*, p. 240.

3. Wemyss, *Family Record*, p. 241.

4. The terminology was alien to people at the time. In 1918, Pamela reminded Margot of 'your [Margot] exclaiming one early day in the War "'B.E.F.?' What does 'B.E.F.' mean?"' (Pamela Glenconner to Margot Asquith, Bodleian, Asquith Papers, MS. Eng. c. 6676 ff. 144–8).

5. Niall Ferguson, *The Pity of War* (Penguin Books, 1999), p. 198.

6. Newspaper cutting dated 1 December 1913, reporting Eddy's address to the

Liverpool Liberal Federal Council on Home Defence, Glenconner Papers, NRS GD510/1/51 f. 1r.

7.   Asquith, *Diaries*, p. xvi.

8.   Mary Elcho to Arthur Balfour, August 1914 (*Letters*, p. 311).

9.   Ibid.

10. Mary Elcho to Wilfrid Scawen Blunt, 28 September 1914, Blunt Papers, FM 719-1975.

11. Conversation with Mrs James Adeane, November 2013.

12. Cannadine, *Decline and Fall*, p. 72.

13. Glenconner, *Edward Wyndham Tennant*, p. vi.

14. Wemyss, *Family Record*, pp. 240, 242.

15. Asquith, *Diaries*, 16 October 1915, p. 88.

16. Cannadine, *Decline and Fall*, pp. 73–4.

17. Julian Grenfell to Ettie Desborough, 24 October 1914, quoted in Nicholas Mosley, *Julian Grenfell: His Life and the Times of his Death 1888–1915* (Weidenfeld & Nicolson, 1976), p. 239.

18. Lady Angela Forbes, *Memories and Base Details* (2nd edn, Hutchinson, 1922), p. 153.

19. Ibid., p. 171.

20. Mary Elcho to Arthur Balfour, 1 January 1915 (*Letters*, pp. 315–16).

21. Ibid.

22. Forbes, *Memories and Base Details*, p. 171.

23. Ibid., p. 76.

24. Ibid., pp. 174–5.

25. Ibid., p. 171.

26. Ibid., p. 161.

27. Cannadine, *Decline and Fall*, p. 73.

28. Forbes, *Memories and Base Details*, p. 161.

29. Mary Elcho to Arthur Balfour, August 1914 (*Letters*, p. 311).

30. Wemyss, *Family Record*, p. 285; Pamela Adeane to Mary Elcho, 1 October 1917, Stanway Papers.

31. Wemyss, *Family Record*, p. 286.

32. Ibid.

33. Mary Elcho to Arthur Balfour, 13 April 1915 (*Letters*, p. 323).

34. Mary Elcho to Hugo Elcho, 7 October 1915, Stanway Papers.

35. Ibid.

36. Ibid.

37. Glenconner, *Edward Wyndham Tennant*, pp. 119–20.

38. Ibid., p. 118.

39. Pamela Tennant to Mary Elcho, 9 October 1914, Stanway Papers.

40. Tennant, *Waiting for Princess Margaret*, p. 125.

41. Pamela Tennant to Charles Tennant, 25 February 1909, Glenconner Papers, NRS GD 510/1/41 f. 8r.

42. Pamela Tennant to Edward Tennant, n.d. [post-war], Glenconner Papers, NRS GD510/1/51 f. 16r. The child was an artistic prodigy – Pamela had hung some of her paintings in Queen Anne's Gate. Pamela took her down to Wilsford: 'my idea is to put the child at the Bishops school in Salisbury for the winter as her surroundings in London are very objectionable. She is a nice mannered quiet little child. She draws all day long,' she told Eddy.

43. Tennant, *Waiting for Princess Margaret*, pp. 115, 128.

44. Ibid., p. 120.

45. Hoare, *Serious Pleasures*, p. 13.

46. Ibid.; Blow, in *Broken Blood*, notes that his grandmother had adopted a child who 'had run away to sea in his early teens', but gives his date of adoption as nearer that of Stephen's birth, and his name as Barnaby (p. 173).

47. See Tennant, *Waiting for Princess Margaret*, and Blow's version in *Broken Blood*.

48. Tennant, *Waiting for Princess Margaret*, p. 128.

49. Glenconner, *Edward Wyndham Tennant*, p. 85.

50. For an account of this episode see Hermione Baddeley, *The Unsinkable Hermione Baddeley* (Collins, 1984), pp. 54–8.

51. Madeline Adeane to Mary Elcho, 18 September 1914, Stanway Papers.

52. Ibid.

53. Edward Wyndham Tennant, 'Percy Wyndham', Stanway Papers.

54. Arthur Balfour to Mary Elcho, 17 September 1914 (*Letters*, p. 312).

55. Asquith, *Diaries*, 20 October 1915, p. 91.

56. Mary Elcho to Arthur Balfour, September 1914 (*Letters*, p. 313).

57. Madeline Adeane to Mary Elcho, 29 September 1914, Stanway Papers.

58. Mary Elcho to Wilfrid Scawen Blunt, n.d., Blunt Papers, FM 724-1975.

59. Ibid.

60. Wemyss, *Family Record*, p. 256.

61. Mary Elcho to Arthur Balfour, 13 April 1915 (*Letters*, p. 323).

62. Wemyss, *Family Record*, p. 292.

63. Asquith, *Diaries*, 26 May 1915, pp. 29–30.

64. Mary Elcho to Wilfrid Scawen Blunt, 28 September 1914, Blunt Papers, FM 719-1975.

65. Mary Elcho to Hugo Elcho, 7 October 1915, Stanway Papers.

66. Mary Elcho to Arthur Balfour, 17 May 1915 (*Letters*, pp. 324–5).

67. Wemyss, *Family Record*, p. 287.

68. Ibid., p. 252; Asquith, *Diaries*, p. xvii.

69. Wemyss, *Family Record*, p. 264.

70. His real name was Algernon Walter, but he was known always as Tom.

71. Wemyss, *Family Record*, p. 263.

72. Mary Elcho to Wilfrid Scawen Blunt, 18 November 1915, Blunt Papers, FM778-1975.

73. Mary Elcho to Arthur Balfour, 13 April 1915 (*Letters*, p. 322).

74. Arthur Balfour to Mary Elcho, Easter Saturday 1915 (*Letters*, p. 320).

75. Ridley and Percy (eds), *Letters of Arthur Balfour and Lady Elcho*, p. 326.

76. Quoted in ibid., pp. 325–6.

77. Pamela Tennant to Margot Asquith, 12 March 1918, Bodleian, Asquith Papers, MS. Eng. c. 6676 ff. 144–8.

78. Glenconner, *Edward Wyndham Tennant*, pp. 119–20.

79. Asquith, *Diaries*, 19 October 1915, p. 90.

80. Glenconner, *Edward Wyndham Tennant*, p. 119.

81. Ibid., p. 118.

82. Ibid., pp. 157–8.

83. Quoted in Ziegler, *Diana Cooper*, p. 80.

84. Duff Cooper, *The Duff Cooper Diaries 1915–1951*, ed. John Julius Norwich (Phoenix, 2006), 9 January and 18 February 1916, pp. 24 and 25.

85. Asquith, *Diaries*, 15 September 1915, p. 79.

86. Sibell Adeane married Edward Kay-Shuttleworth in December 1914. Madeline Adeane married Denis Wigan in October 1915.

87. Pamela Tennant to Margot Asquith, 12 March 1918, Bodleian, Asquith Papers, Add. MS. Eng. c. 6676 ff. 144–8.

88. Glenconner, *Edward Wyndham Tennant*, pp. 121–2.

89. Tennant, *Waiting for Princess Margaret*, p. 119; see also Hoare, *Serious Pleasures*, p. 12.

90. Edward Grey to Edward Tennant, 7 August 1915, Glenconner Papers, NRS GD510/1/60/4 f. 18r.

91. Wemyss, *Family Record*, p. 303.

92. Asquith, *Diaries*, 23 August 1915, p. 71.

93. Ibid., 9 September 1915, p. 77.

94. Forbes, *Memories and Base Details*, p. 201.

95. Wemyss, *Family Record*, pp. 305–6.

96. Forbes, *Memories and Base Details*, p. 201.

97. Lambert, *Unquiet Souls*, p. 190.

98. Asquith, *Diaries*, 9 September 1915, p. 77.

99. Forbes, *Memories and Base Details*, p. 201.

100. Wemyss, *Family Record*, p. 307.

101. Ibid.

Chapter 30: The Front

1. Madeline Wyndham to Wilfrid Scawen Blunt, 6 October 1915, Blunt Papers, FM 772-1975.

2. Wemyss, *Family Record*, p. 281.

3. Sir Alan Lascelles, *End of an Era: Letters and Journals of Sir Alan Lascelles from 1887 to 1920*, ed. Duff Hart-Davis (Weidenfeld & Nicolson, 2006), 12 July 1912, p. 128.

4. Those grandsons include my father: his mother is Tommy's eldest daughter.

5. Lascelles, *End of an Era*, p. 162.

6. Wemyss, *Family Record*, p. 312.

7.   Ibid., pp. 315–16; Edward Wyndham Tennant to Pamela Tennant, 18 August 1915, quoted in Glenconner, *Edward Wyndham Tennant*, p. 127.

8.   Ibid., p. 130.

9.   Yvo Charteris to Hugo Elcho, 6 October 1915, quoted in Wemyss, *Family Record*, p. 322.

10. Yvo Charteris to Cynthia Asquith, 7 October 1915, ibid., p. 324.

11. *The Times*, 21 June and 7 August 1915.

12. Lambert, *Unquiet Souls*, p. 190.

13. Glenconner, *Edward Wyndham Tennant*, p. 172.

14. Lambert, *Unquiet Souls*, p. 190.

15. Wemyss, *Family Record*, p. 326.

16. Ibid., p. 312.

17. Lambert, *Unquiet Souls*, p. 191; Asquith, *Diaries*, 24 October 1915, p. 93.

18. Glenconner, *Edward Wyndham Tennant*, p. 145.

19. In September 1915, Bim had written to Pamela of the generals commanding his Guards brigade, division and army corps and the First Army, 'respectively … Brigadier General Hayworth, General Lord Cavan, General Haking, and Haig at the head of the list. They are all very fine generals and I could wish for no one else.' Just a month later, from Vermelles, Bim wrote in his poem 'Á Bas la Gloire' of those:

> who didn't die
> Although they were in France – these sat in cars,
> And whizzed about with red-band caps, awry,
> Exuding brandy and the best cigars,
> With bands and tabs of red, they could defy
> The many missives of explosive Mars

(Glenconner, *Edward Wyndham Tennant*, pp. 134, 151). The contrast shows the change wrought in Bim, or at least the extent to which he concealed his true thoughts from his parents in favour of the cheerful, trusting son they wished to see.

20. Asquith, *Diaries*, 22 October 1915, p. 92.

21. Ibid., 19 October 1915, pp. 90–1.

22. Ego Charteris to Mary Elcho, 25 October 1915, quoted in Wemyss, *Family Record*, p. 352; Asquith, *Diaries*, 3 July 1916, p. 186.

23. Asquith, *Diaries*, 20 October 1915, p. 91.

24. Davenport-Hines, *Ettie*, p. 202.

25. Mary Elcho to Arthur Balfour, 8 December 1921, Whittingehame Papers, NRS GD433/2/229/1 f. 29r.

26. Mary Elcho to Wilfrid Scawen Blunt, 5 December 1915, Blunt Papers, FM 779-1975.

27. Davenport-Hines, *Ettie*, p. 202.

28. Mary Elcho to Wilfrid Scawen Blunt, 5 December 1915, Blunt Papers, FM 779-1975.

29. Mary Elcho to Arthur Balfour, 22 December 1915 (*Letters*, p. 322).

30. Pamela Tennant to Mary Elcho, 9 June 1916, Stanway Papers.

31. Glenconner, *Edward Wyndham Tennant*, Appendix III.

32. Ibid., p. 184.

33. Ibid., p. 189.

34. Pamela Tennant to Mary Elcho, 9 June 1916, Stanway Papers.

35. For an illustration, see Dakers, *Clouds*, p. 175, plate 94.

36. Ibid.

37. Hoare, *Serious Pleasures*, p. 13.

38. Pamela Tennant to Mary Elcho, 9 June 1916, Stanway Papers.

39. Asquith, *Diaries*, 22 April 1916, p. 158.

40. Wemyss, *Family Record*, p. 372.

41. Asquith, *Diaries*, 22 April 1916, p. 160.

42. *The Times*, 25, 26, 27 April 1916.

43. Mary Elcho to Evelyn de Vesci, 26 September 1916, De Vesci Papers, DD/DRU/87.

44. Lambert, *Unquiet Souls*, p. 194.

45. Wemyss, *Family Record*, p. 372.

46. Asquith, *Diaries*, 19 May 1916, p. 166.

47. Mary Elcho to Arthur Balfour, 7 May 1916 (*Letters*, p. 337).

48. Asquith, *Diaries*, 20 May 1916, p. 167.

49. Wemyss, *Family Record*, p. 375.

50. Ridley and Percy (eds), *Letters of Arthur Balfour and Lady Elcho*, p. 339; Wemyss, *Family Record*, p. 373; Asquith, *Diaries*, 28 June 1916, p. 181.

51. Asquith, *Diaries*, 1 July 1916, p. 182.

52. Mary Elcho to Arthur Balfour, 3 July 1916 (*Letters*, p. 339).

53. Mary Elcho to Madeline Wyndham, July 1916, Stanway Papers.

54. Wemyss, *Family Record*, p. 373. In fact, as Cynthia's diary shows, the news came on 1 July 1916.

55. Mary Elcho to Arthur Balfour, 3 July 1916 (*Letters*, p. 339).

56. Ibid.

57. Asquith, *Diaries*, 4 July 1916, p. 187.

58. *The Times*, 26 September 1916.

59. Mary Elcho to Ettie Desborough, 26 September 1916, Desborough Papers, HALS DE/Rv/C477/49; see also Wemyss, *Family Record*, p. 376, where Mary recounts those words, asking, 'Could a finer epitaph be given by one soldier to another than these two words…?'

60. Mary Elcho to Arthur Balfour, January 1916 (*Letters*, pp. 334–5).

61. Quoted in Lambert, *Unquiet Souls*, p. 196.

62. Ibid., p. 198.

63. Cannadine, *Decline and Fall*, p. 76.

64. Glenconner, *Edward Wyndham Tennant*, p. 222.

65. Ibid.

66. Ibid., p. 210.

67. Ibid.

68. Ibid., p. 221.

69. Lambert, *Unquiet Souls*, p. 205.

70. Quoted in ibid., pp. 199–200.

71. Glenconner, *Edward Wyndham Tennant*, p. 166.

72. Ibid., p. 293.

73. Lambert, *Unquiet Souls*, p. 199.

74. Glenconner, *Edward Wyndham Tennant*, p. 229.

75. Ibid., p. 223.

76. Lambert, *Unquiet Souls*, p. 202.

77. Asquith, *Diaries*, 19 September 1916, p. 217.

78. Davenport-Hines, *Ettie*, p. 212.

79. Glenconner, *Edward Wyndham Tennant*, p. 234.

80. Ibid., p. 115.

81. Ibid., p. 234.

82. Ibid., p. 238.

83. Lambert, *Unquiet Souls*, p. 202.

84. Ibid., p. 199.

85. *The Times*, 27 September 1916.

86. Ibid.

Chapter 31: The Remainder

1. Cannadine, *Decline and Fall*, p. 83.

2. Quoted in ibid., p. 81; Lambert, *Unquiet Souls*, p. 221.

3. Asquith, *Diaries*, 11 November 1915, p. 97.

4. Cannadine, *Decline and Fall*, p. 80.

5. Mary Elcho to Wilfrid Scawen Blunt, 5 December 1915, Blunt Papers, FM 779-1975.

6. Davenport-Hines, *Ettie*, p. 209.

7. Mary Elcho to Arthur Balfour, 12 September 1916 (*Letters*, p. 341).

8. Quoted in Davenport-Hines, *Ettie*, p. 212.

9. Glenconner, *The Earthen Vessel*, p. 82.

10. Mary Elcho to Arthur Balfour, 21 January 1916 (*Letters*, pp. 342–3).

11. Ibid.

12. Ibid.

13. Mary Elcho to Ettie Desborough, 23 October 1931, Desborough Papers, HALS DE/Rv/C477/102.

14. Mary Elcho to Arthur Balfour, 21 January 1916 (*Letters*, pp. 342–3).

15. Mary Elcho to Ettie Desborough, 23 October 1931, Desborough Papers, HALS DE/Rv/C477/102.

16. Mary Elcho to Arthur Balfour, 21 January 1916 (*Letters*, pp. 342–3).

17. Mary Elcho to Ettie Desborough, 23 October 1931, Desborough Papers, HALS DE/Rv/C477/102.

18. Edward Grey to Edward Tennant, 22 January 1916, Glenconner Papers, NRS GD/510/1/60/4 f. 33r.

19. Edward Grey to Edward Tennant, 26 September 1916, Glenconner Papers, NRS GD/510/1/60/4 ff. 31, 32r.

20. Edward Grey to Edward Tennant, 27 April 1917, Glenconner Papers, NRS GD/510/1/60/2 f. 19r.

21. Blow, *Broken Blood*, p. 157.

22. Glenconner, *The Earthen Vessel*, p. 138.

23. Asquith, *Diaries*, 11 November 1915, p. 97.

24. Glenconner, *The Earthen Vessel*, p. 141.

25. Pamela Tennant to Mary Elcho, 23 January 1918, Stanway Papers; Glenconner, *The Earthen Vessel*, p. 79.

26. Hoare, *Serious Pleasures*, pp. 14–15.

27. Ibid., p. 129.

28. Pamela Tennant to Mary Elcho, 9 June 1916, Stanway Papers.

29. Glenconner, *The Earthen Vessel*, p. 79.

30. *The Times*, 8 January 1917. Pamela would appear as a witness for the defence in similar trials on subsequent occasions, such as the case of 'The Medium in the Mask' (*The Times*, 16 March 1920), and was one of those to attend the opening of *Earthbound*, an American motion picture dealing with spiritualism, at the Covent Garden Opera House, which was released early in the UK due to popular demand (*The Times*, 26 October 1920).

31. Barbara McKenzie, 'James Hewat McKenzie: November 11th 1869–August 29th 1929', *Quarterly Transactions of the British College of Psychic Science* 8:3 (October 1929): 159–68.

32. Quoted in Ellenberger, 'The Souls: High Society and Politics', p. 157.

33. Glenconner, *The Earthen Vessel*, p. 153.

34. Asquith, *Diaries*, 19 November 1916, p. 236.

35. Ibid., 16 December 1916, pp. 245–6.

36. Pamela Tennant to Mary Elcho, n.d., Stanway Papers.

37. Marie Stopes, *Married Love* (New York, The Critic and Guide Company, 1918), pp. 67–8.

38. Ibid.

39. Ibid., p. 68.

40. Marie Stopes to Pamela Tennant, 14 July 1918, BL Stopes Papers, vol. CCXXXVIII, Add. MS. 58684 f. 152.

41. Pamela Tennant to Marie Stopes, 14 July 1918, BL Stopes Papers, vol. CCXXXVIII, Add. MS. 58684 ff. 153–4.

42. Blow, *Broken Blood*, p. 150.

43. *The Times*, 9 March 1920.

44. Mary Elcho to Arthur Balfour, n.d. [spring 1917] (*Letters*, p. 344).

45. Mary Elcho to Madeline Wyndham, 22 September 1916, Stanway Papers.

46. Mary Elcho to Madeline Wyndham, July 1916, Stanway Papers.

47. Quoted in Lambert, *Unquiet Souls*, p. 222.

48. Ibid.

49. Quoted in Cannadine, *Decline and Fall*, p. 81; Lambert, *Unquiet Souls*, p. 221.

50. Davenport-Hines, *Ettie*, p. 229.

51. Quoted in Cannadine, *Decline and Fall*, p. 79.

52. Asquith, *Diaries*, 7 October 1918, p. 480.

Chapter 32: The Grey Dawn

1. Glenconner Papers, NRS GD 510/1/51 f. 24r.

2. Mary Elcho to Arthur Balfour, 10 October 1919, Whittingehame Papers, NRS GD433/2/229/1 ff. 3–6r.

3. Mary Elcho to Arthur Balfour, 23 September 1919, Whittingehame Papers, NRS GR433/2/229/1 f. 1r.

4. *The Times*, 28 November 1917.

5. Madeline Adeane to Mary Elcho, 18 January 1920, Stanway Papers.

6. Christopher Simon Sykes, *Private Palaces: Life in the Great London Houses* (Chatto & Windus, 1985), pp. 325–6.

7. Ibid., quoted at pp. 321, 322.

8. Edward Tennant to Margot Asquith, 6 August 1919, Bodleian, Asquith Papers, MS. Eng. c. 6697 ff. 152–3.

9. Earl Haig would also be buried there in 1928.

10. Mary Elcho to Arthur Balfour, 22 May 1920, Whittingehame Papers, NRS GD433/2/229/1 f. 7r.

11. Quoted in Ridley and Percy (eds), *Letters of Arthur Balfour and Lady Elcho*, p. 351.

12. Asquith, *Diaries*, 30 July 1918, p. 464.

13. Mary Elcho to Arthur Balfour, 22 May 1920, Whittingehame Papers, NRS GD433/2/229/1 f. 7r.

14. Ridley and Percy (eds), *Letters of Arthur Balfour and Lady Elcho*, p. 351; Beauman, *Cynthia Asquith*, p. 273.

15. Mary Elcho to Arthur Balfour, 13 May [1924], Whittingehame Papers, NRS GD433/2/229/3 f. 22r.

16. Quoted in Ridley and Percy (eds), *Letters of Arthur Balfour and Lady Elcho*, pp. 351–2.

17. Mary Elcho to Arthur Balfour, 22 May 1920, Whittingehame Papers, NRS GD433/2/229/1 f. 7r.

18. Ibid.

19. Mary Elcho to Arthur Balfour, 8 December 1921, Whittingehame Papers, NRS GD433/2/229/1 f. 29r.

20. Ibid.

21. Mary Elcho to Arthur Balfour, December 1921, Whittingehame Papers, NRS GD433/2/229/1 f. 28r.

22. Quoted in Ridley and Percy (eds), *Letters of Arthur Balfour and Lady Elcho*, p. 349.

23. Mary Elcho to Arthur Balfour, 23 September 1919, Whittingehame Papers, NRS GR433/2/229/1 f. 1r.

24. Mary Elcho to Arthur Balfour, 14 January 1922, Whittingehame Papers, NRS GD433/2/229/2 f. 1r.

25. Mary Elcho to Arthur Balfour, n.d. [1923], Whittingehame Papers, NRS GD433/2/229/3 f. 17r.

26. Lambert, *Unquiet Souls*, p. 57.

27. Mary Elcho to Arthur Balfour, n.d. [1921/2], Whittingehame Papers, NRS GD433/2/229/2 f. 27r.

28. See Mary Strickland to Wilfrid Scawen Blunt, 13 May 1921, commenting that the 'great question' had been whether Bibs and Ivor were in love with one

another, and that she, Mary Strickland, used to find Ivor 'rather a cold fish … but I expect Bibs will transform him'. Blunt Papers, FM 190-1975.

29. Mary Elcho to Wilfrid Scawen Blunt, n.d. [1921], Blunt Papers, FM 193-1976.

30. Mary Elcho to Dorothy Carleton, 1 March 1920, Blunt Papers, FM 988-1975.

31. Quoted in Hoare, *Serious Pleasures*, p. 16.

32. Pamela Tennant to Mary Elcho, 17 March 1920, Stanway Papers. Stephen had gone with Pamela, and was impressed by the reading. One medium had told them 'things unknown to us both, which we checked in England. She couldn't have read our minds.' Hoare, *Serious Pleasures*, p. 16.

33. Quoted in Hoare, *Serious Pleasures*, p. 16.

34. *New York Times*, 7 January 1920.

35. Quoted in Hoare, *Serious Pleasures*, p. 16.

36. Pamela Tennant to Margot Asquith, 13 January 1921, Bodleian, Asquith Papers, MS. Eng. c. 6676 f. 154.

37. Hoare, *Serious Pleasures*, pp. 17–18.

38. Pamela Tennant to Dorothy Carleton, 1 October 1921, Blunt Papers, FM 248-1976.

39. Mary Elcho to Ettie Desborough, 29 November 1920, Desborough Papers, HALS DE/Rv/C477.

40. Pamela Tennant to Margot Asquith, 17 January 1921, Bodleian, Asquith Papers, Add. MS. Eng. c. 6676 f. 155.

41. Pamela Tennant to Margot Asquith, 11 January 1921, Bodleian, Asquith Papers, Add. MS. Eng. c. 6676 f. 151.

42. Pamela Tennant to Margot Asquith, 17 January 1921, Bodleian, Asquith Papers, Add. MS. Eng. c. 6676 f. 155; Margot Asquith to Pamela Tennant, n.d., ff. 152–3.

43. Pamela Tennant to Margot Asquith, 17 January 1921, Bodleian, Asquith Papers, Add. MS. Eng. c. 6676 f. 155.

44. Pamela Tennant to Mary Elcho, 28 February 1921, Stanway Papers.

45. Hoare, *Serious Pleasures*, pp. 14–15.

46. Blow, *Broken Blood*, p. 164.

47. Hoare, *Serious Pleasures*, p. 97.

48. *The Times*, 17 February 1922.

49. *The Times*, 6 June 1922.

50. Pamela Tennant to Lucy Graham Smith, n.d. [summer 1921], Bodleian, Asquith Papers, Add. MS. Eng. c. 6676 f. 157.

51. Pamela Tennant to Wilfrid Scawen Blunt, 1 October 1921, Blunt Papers, FM 248-1976.

52. 'The Romantic Miracle of England's Loneliest Man', *American Feature Press*, 1922.

53. Hoare, *Serious Pleasures*, p. 63.

54. Wemyss, *Family Record*, p. 235.

55. Baddeley, *The Unsinkable Hermione Baddeley*, p. 47.

56. Pamela Tennant to Lucy Graham Smith, n.d. [summer 1921], Bodleian, Asquith Papers, Add. MS. Eng. c. 6676 f. 157.

57. Pamela Tennant to Wilfrid Scawen Blunt, 11 June 1922, Blunt Papers, FM 286-1976.

58. Belloc Lowndes, *A Passing World*, p. 175.

59. Pamela Tennant to Marie Stopes, 1 February 1923, BL Stopes Papers, Add. MSS. 58693 ff. 31–2.

60. Pamela Tennant to Marie Stopes, 9 February 1921, BL Stopes Papers, Add. MSS. 58688 f. 7; and see also letters of 27 May 1921, Add. MS. 58689 f. 69; and 27 June 1921, Add. MSS. 58689 f. 139.

61. Pamela Tennant to Marie Stopes, June 1922, BL Stopes Papers, Add. MSS. 58691 f. 224.

62. Founded as the Eugenics Education Society in 1906, it changed its name to the Eugenics Society in 1926.

63. Marie Stopes, *Radiant Motherhood* (G. B. Putnam's Sons, 1920), p. 220; *The Times*, 29 October 1918; Glenconner, *The White Wallet*, pp. 372–5.

64. Pamela Tennant to the Stopes Society, 10 November [post-1922], BL Stopes Papers, Add. MSS. 58702 f. 111.

65. Pamela Tennant to Marie Stopes, June 1922, BL Stopes Papers, Add. MSS. 58691 f. 224.

66. Madeline Adeane to Mary Elcho, 11 December 1925, Stanway Papers.

67. Grey of Fallodon, *Twenty-Five Years*, 1.xxii.

68. See Keith Robbins, *Sir Edward Grey: A Biography of Lord Grey of Fallodon* (Cassell, 1971).

69. Baddeley, *The Unsinkable Hermione Baddeley*, p. 13.

70. Ibid., pp. 44–9 and 53–4; Hoare, *Serious Pleasures*, p. 52. In this, David resisted Pamela's attempts to match-make him more successfully than Christopher, whom Pamela persuaded to marry her goddaughter Pamela Paget (offspring of her erstwhile suitor, Arthur). Stephen Tennant designed the bride and bridesmaids' medieval-themed dresses for the Paget–Glenconner wedding, which was billed by *Vogue* as one of the 'most important social events of 1925'. The marriage was a disaster and ended in divorce a decade later (see: Hoare, *Serious Pleasures*, p. 51).

71. Hoare, *Serious Pleasures*, p. 63.

72. Dakers, *Clouds*, p. 219.

73. Ibid., p. 220.

74. Pamela Tennant to Mary Elcho, 13 March 1928, Stanway Papers.

75. Baddeley, *The Unsinkable Hermione Baddeley*, p. 48.

76. Ibid., pp. 57–8.

77. Ibid., p. 62.

78. *Miami News*, 4 January 1931.

79. Pamela Tennant to Mary Elcho, 14 May 1928, Stanway Papers.

80. Quoted in Hoare, *Serious Pleasures*, p. 114.

81. Beck had been one of the speakers at the luncheon that Pamela and Eddy had attended on their American tour in 1920, promoting Anglo-American relations. It seems likely that when Pamela had advocated extending the arm of friendship, this was not quite what she had meant.

82. Pamela Tennant to Mary Elcho, 14 June 1928, Stanway Papers.

83. Pamela Tennant to Mary Elcho, 14 May 1928, Stanway Papers.

84. Pamela Tennant to Mary Elcho, 14 June 1928, Stanway Papers. Doubtless it was Romer Wilson's *All Alone: The Life and Private History of Emily Jane Brontë* (1928).

85. Blow, *Broken Blood*, p. 172.

86. *The Times*, 20 November 1928.

87. Madeline Adeane to Mary Elcho, 5 December 1928, Stanway Papers.

88. Hoare, *Serious Pleasures*, pp. 125–6.

89. Ibid., p. 128.

90. *Ogden Standard Examiner*, 17 February 1929.

91. Baddeley, *The Unsinkable Hermione Baddeley*, p. 68.

Chapter 33: The End

1. Madeline Adeane to Mary Elcho, 5 December 1928, Stanway Papers.
2. Madeline Adeane to Mary Elcho, 2 January 1929, Stanway Papers.
3. Madeline Adeane to Mary Elcho, 11 December 1925, Stanway Papers.
4. Ibid.
5. Madeline Adeane to Mary Elcho, 19 November 1929, Stanway Papers.
6. Ibid.
7. See, for example, Mary Elcho to Arthur Balfour, 7 March 1929 (*Letters*, p. 353).
8. Quoted in Ridley and Percy (eds), *Letters of Arthur Balfour and Lady Elcho*, pp. 351–2.
9. Ibid.
10. *The Times*, 3 May 1937.
11. Arthur Balfour to Mary Elcho, 17 November 1920, Whittingehame Papers, NRS GD433/2/229/1 f. 12r.
12. Ibid.
13. *The Times*, 17 January 1929.
14. *The Times*, 21 January 1929, letter from 'X'; 26 January 1929, letter from 'Q'; Ettie Desborough to Mary Elcho, 25 January 1930, Desborough Papers, HALS DE/Rv/C1100/257; and 9 November 1935, DE/Rv/C1100/166.
15. *The Times*, 21 January 1929, letter from 'X'; 26 January 1929, letter from 'Q'.
16. Ridley and Percy (eds), *Letters of Arthur Balfour and Lady Elcho*, p. 352.
17. Quoted in ibid., p. 353.
18. Ibid., p. 354.
19. Quoted in Abdy and Gere, *The Souls*, p. 41.
20. Mary Elcho to Arthur Balfour, 7 March 1929 (*Letters*, p. 353).
21. Ettie Desborough to Mary Elcho, 25 January 1930, Desborough Papers, HALS DE/Rv/C1100/257.
22. Ettie Desborough to Mary Elcho, 16 June 1936, Desborough Papers, HALS DE/Rv/C1100/176.
23. Dakers, *Clouds*, p. 226.
24. Ibid., pp. 225–7, 239–44.
25. Ettie Desborough to Mary Elcho, n.d. [1935], Desborough Papers, HALS DE/Rv/C1100/167.

26. Evelyn de Vesci to Evan Charteris, n.d. [summer 1936], De Vesci Papers, DD/DRU/5/3/2.

27. Evan Charteris to Evelyn de Vesci, n.d. [summer 1936], De Vesci Papers, DD/DRU/5/3/2.

28. Evelyn de Vesci to unknown correspondent, n.d., DD DRU 5/3/2.

29. Dorothy Charteris to Evelyn de Vesci, 18 August 1936, De Vesci Papers, DD/DRU/5/3/2.

30. Evan Charteris to Evelyn de Vesci, n.d. [summer 1936], De Vesci Papers, DD/DRU/5/3/2.

31. Ibid.

32. Ibid.

33. Ibid.

34. Madeline Adeane to Mary Elcho, 3 February 1937, Stanway Papers.

35. *The Times*, 3 May 1937.

36. Ibid., 4 August 1941.

37. Ibid., 2 August 1941.

38. Pamela slightly misquoted this, as she so often did, as 'the Light of the Just shineth more & more unto the perfect Day'.

39. Again, Pamela misquotes, giving the boy's name as 'Hans'.

40. Pamela Tennant to Mary Elcho, 13 March 1928, Stanway Papers.

Bibliography

MANUSCRIPT SOURCES

Where an abbreviation is used for a publicly accessible manuscript source in the
Notes, it is appended in square brackets.

Papers in publicly accessible archives

Bodleian Library: papers of Margot Asquith, Countess of Oxford and Asquith,
1862–1945 [Bodleian, Asquith Papers, MS. Eng.]

British Library:
Avebury Papers
Papers of Arthur James Balfour
Burns Papers
Cockerell Papers
Eccles Bequest of Manuscripts (Lady Eccles Oscar Wilde Collection)
Papers of Allan Fea
Papers of Viscount and Viscountess Gladstone
Papers of Mary Gladstone (Mrs Drew)
Letters to John Lane
Papers of Robert Ross
Society of Authors Archive
Stopes Papers
Watts-Dunton Papers
Papers of Douglas Young

Fitzwilliam Museum, Cambridge: papers of Wilfrid Scawen Blunt [FM]

Hertford Archives and Local Records Office: papers of Lady Desborough [HALS
DE/Rv]

National Records of Scotland (formerly the National Archives of Scotland):
Glenconner Papers: Papers of the Tennant Family of the Glen, Peebleshire,
Lords Glenconner [NRS GD510]

Whittingehame Papers: Papers of Arthur James Balfour, first Earl of Balfour, and Viscount Traprain of Whittingehame [NRS GD433]

National Library of Scotland: Tennant Papers [NLS 12143/4]

Somerset Records Office: Papers of Evelyn, Lady de Vesci [DD/DRU]

The Times Archive: http://www.thetimes.co.uk

National Census Archives: http://www.nationalarchives.gov.uk/records/census-records.htm

Papers in private collections

Adeane Papers: papers of Madeline and Charles Adeane

Petworth Papers: papers of Percy and Madeline Wyndham, by kind permission of Francis Wyndham and the Earl of Egremont

Stanway Papers: papers of Mary, Countess of Wemyss, held at Stanway House, Gloucestershire, in possession of the thirteenth Earl of Wemyss and March

Stephen Tennant Papers: formerly in the possession of Hugo Vickers, now predominantly at the Beinecke Rare Book and Manuscript Library, Yale University

George Wyndham Papers: papers of George Wyndham and Sibell, Countess Grosvenor

SECONDARY SOURCES

Books

Place of publication is London, unless otherwise stated.

Abdy, Jane and Gere, Charlotte, *The Souls* (Sidgwick & Jackson, 1984)

Adams, R. J. Q., *Balfour: The Last Grandee* (John Murray, 2008)

Adelman, Paul, *Great Britain and the Irish Question 1800–1922* (Hodder & Stoughton, 1996)

Adler, Kathleen, Hirshler, Erica and Weinberg, H. Barbara (eds), *Americans in Paris 1860–1900*, accompanying the exhibition *Americans in Paris 1860–1900* at the National Gallery, London; Museum of Fine Arts, Boston; and the Metropolitan Museum of Art, New York (National Gallery Company, 2006)

Airlie, Mabell, Countess of, *Thatched with Gold: The Memoirs of Mabell, Countess of Airlie*, ed. and arranged by Jennifer Ellis (Hutchinson, 1962)

Aldous, Richard, *The Lion and the Unicorn: Gladstone vs. Disraeli* (New York, W. W. Norton, 2007)

Appignanesi, Lisa, *Mad, Bad and Sad: A History of Women and the Mind Doctors from 1800 to the Present* (Virago, 2008)

Asquith, Lady Cynthia, *Diaries, 1915–1918*, ed. E. M. Horsley (New York, Alfred A. Knopf, 1969)

——, *Haply I May Remember* (James Barrie, 1950)

——, *Remember and Be Glad* (James Barrie, 1952)

Asquith, Margot, *An Autobiography*, 2 vols (Thornton Butterworth, 1920–2)

——, *The Autobiography of Margot Asquith*, ed. with an introduction by Mark Bonham Carter (Weidenfeld & Nicolson, 1995)

——, *More Memories* (Cassell, 1933)

——, *Myself When Young* (Frederick Muller, 1938)

——, *Off the Record* (Frederick Muller, 1944)

——, *Places and Persons* (Thornton Butterworth, 1922)

Baddeley, Hermione with Muriel Burgess, *The Unsinkable Hermione Baddeley* (Collins, 1984)

Bagehot, Walter, *The English Constitution*, ed. Miles Taylor (Oxford, Oxford University Press, 2001)

Balfour, Arthur James, *Chapters of Autobiography*, ed. Blanche Dugdale (Cassell, 1930)

Ball, Stuart, *The Conservative Party and British Politics 1902–1951* (London and New York, Longman, 1995)

Beauman, Nicola, *Cynthia Asquith* (Hamish Hamilton, 1987)

Begbie, Harold (as 'A Gentleman with a Duster'), *Mirrors of Downing Street: Some Political Reflections* (Mills & Boon, 1920)

Bell, Quentin, *A New and Noble School: The Pre-Raphaelites* (Macdonald, 1982)

——, *Victorian Artists* (Routledge & Kegan Paul, 1967)

Belloc Lowndes, Marie, *Diaries and Letters 1911–1947*, ed. Susan Lowndes (Chatto & Windus, 1971)

——, *I, Too, Have Lived in Arcadia: A Record of Love and Childhood* (Macmillan, 1941)

——, *A Passing World* (Macmillan, 1948)

——, *Where Love and Friendship Dwelt* (Macmillan, 1943)

Bennett, Alfred Rosling, *London and Londoners in the Eighteen-Fifties and Sixties* (T. Fisher Unwin, 1924)

Biggs Davison, John, *George Wyndham: A Study in Toryism* (Hodder & Stoughton, 1951)

Blow, Simon, *Broken Blood: The Rise and Fall of the Tennant Family* (Faber & Faber, 1987)

Boyce, D. G., *Decolonisation and the British Empire, 1775–1997* (Macmillan, 1999)

——, *The Irish Question and British Politics 1868–1996* (2nd edn, Macmillan, 1996)

Brandon, Ruth, *The Spiritualists: The Passion for the Occult in the Nineteenth and Twentieth Centuries* (Weidenfeld & Nicolson, 1983)

Brendon, Piers, *The Decline and Fall of the British Empire* (Jonathan Cape, 2007)

Brooke, Rupert, *1914 and Other Poems* (Solihull, Helion Books, 1993)

Bryant, Barbara (ed.), *G. F. Watts Portraits: Fame & Beauty in Victorian Society*, accompanying the exhibition *G. F. Watts Portraits: Fame & Beauty in Victorian Society* at the National Portrait Gallery (National Portrait Gallery Publications, 2004)

Buckland, Francis Oke, *Health Springs of Germany and Austria* (W. H. Allen, 1890)

Byatt, A. S., *The Children's Book* (Chatto & Windus, 2009)

Calloway, Stephen and Federle Orr, Lynn (eds) *The Cult of Beauty: The Aesthetic Movement 1860–1900*, accompanying the exhibition *The Cult of Beauty: The Aesthetic Movement 1860–1900* at the Victoria and Albert Museum (V&A Publishing, 2011)

Cannadine, David, *Class in Britain* (New Haven and London, Yale University Press, 1998)

——, *The Decline and Fall of the British Aristocracy* (rev. edn, Penguin Books, 2005)

Chesterton, G. K., *Autobiography* (Hamish Hamilton, 1986)

Clifford, Colin, *The Asquiths* (John Murray, 2002)

Colquhoun, Kate, *Taste: The Story of Britain through its Cooking* (Bloomsbury, 2007)

Conan Doyle, Sir Arthur, *The Great Boer War* (Smith, Elder, 1910).

Cooper, Duff, *The Duff Cooper Diaries 1915–1951*, ed. John Julius Norwich (Phoenix, 2006)

Crathorne, Nancy, *Tennant's Stalk: The Story of the Tennants of the Glen* (Macmillan, 1973)

Cunningham, Hugh, *The Challenge of Democracy: Britain, 1832–1918* (Harlow, Longman, 2001)

Dakers, Caroline, *Clouds: The Biography of a Country House* (New Haven and London, Yale University Press, 1993)

——, *The Holland Park Circle: Artists and Victorian Society* (New Haven and London, Yale University Press, 1999)

Dangerfield, George, *The Strange Death of Liberal England 1910–1914* (New York, Capricorn Books, 1961)

Darwin, John, *The Empire Project: The Rise and Fall of the British World System 1830–1970* (Cambridge, Cambridge University Press, 2009)

Davenport-Hines, Richard, *Ettie: The Intimate Life and Dauntless Spirit of Lady Desborough* (Weidenfeld & Nicolson, 2008)

Davidoff, Leonore, *The Best Circles: Society, Etiquette and the Season* (Croom Helm, 1974)

Davies, Philip, *Lost London 1870–1945* (Croxley Green, Transatlantic Press, 2009)

Downes, William Howe, *John S. Sargent: His Life and Work* (Thornton Butterworth, 1926)

Dugdale, Blanche E. C., *Arthur James Balfour: First Earl of Balfour, K.G., O.M., F.R.S.* (Hutchinson, 1936)

——, *Family Homespun* (John Murray, 1940)

Eccleshall, Robert and Walker, Graham, *Biographical Dictionary of British Prime Ministers* (London and New York, Routledge, 1998)

Eden, Emily, *Miss Eden's Letters*, ed. Violet Dickinson (Macmillan, 1919)

——, *The Semi-Attached Couple* and *The Semi-Detached House* (Virago, 1979)

Egremont, Max, *Balfour: A Life of Arthur James Balfour* (Collins, 1980)

——, *The Cousins: The Friendship, Opinions and Activities of Wilfrid Scawen Blunt and George Wyndham* (Collins, 1977)

——, *Siegfried Sassoon: A Biography* (Picador, 2005)

Ferguson, Niall, *The Pity of War* (Penguin Books, 1999)

Fingall, Elizabeth, Countess of, *Seventy Years Young: Memories of Elizabeth, Countess of Fingall* (Dublin, The Lilliput Press, 1991)

Fitzgerald, Penelope, *Edward Burne-Jones* (Stroud, Sutton Publishing, 2003)

Flanders, Judith, *A Circle of Sisters: Alice Kipling, Georgiana Burne-Jones, Agnes Poynter and Louisa Baldwin* (Viking, 2001)

——, *Consuming Passions: Leisure and Pleasure in Victorian Britain* (Harper Perennial, 2007)

Fletcher, Sheila, *Victorian Girls: Lord Lyttelton's Daughters* (Hambledon Press, 1997)

Forbes, Angela, Lady, *Memories and Base Details* (2nd edn, Hutchinson, 1922)

Foster, R. F., *Modern Ireland 1600–1972* (Penguin Books, 1989)

Gardiner, Juliet, *The Thirties: An Intimate History: Britain in the Thirties* (Harper Press, 2010)

Gere, Charlotte, *Artistic Circles, Design and Decoration in the Aesthetic Movement* (V&A Publishing, 2010)

Gilmour, David, *Curzon: Imperial Statesman* (John Murray, 2003)

Girouard, Mark, *Life in the English Country House* (New Haven and London, Yale University Press, 1978)

——, *The Victorian Country House* (New Haven and London, Yale University Press, 1979)

Glenconner, Pamela, *The Book of Peace: Made by Pamela Tennant* (Chiswick Press, 1900)

——, *The Children and the Pictures* (London, William Heinemann; New York, Macmillan, 1907)

——, *The Earthen Vessel: A Volume Dealing with Spirit-Communication Received in the Form of Book-Tests* (New York, John Lane, 1921)

——, *Edward Wyndham Tennant: A Memoir* (John Lane, The Bodley Head, 1919)

——, *The Sayings of the Children: Written down by their Mother* (Oxford, B. H. Blackwell, 1918)

——, *Shepherd's Crowns: A Volume of Essays* (Oxford, Basil Blackwell, 1923)

——, *Village Notes: and Some Other Papers* (William Heinemann, 1900)

——, *The White Wallet* (T. Fisher Unwin, 1912)

——, *Windlestraw: A Book of Verse with Legends in Rhyme of the Plants and Animals* (Chiswick Press, 1910)

Green, E. H. H., *The Crisis of Conservatism: The Politics, Economics and Ideology of the British Conservative Party 1880–1914* (London and New York, Routledge, 1995)

Greensted, Mary, *An Anthology of the Arts and Crafts Movement: Writings by Ashbee, Lethaby, Gimson and their Contemporaries* (Aldershot, Lund Humphries, 2005)

Grey of Fallodon, Viscount, *The Cottage Book: The Undiscovered Country Diary of an Edwardian Statesman*, ed. and introduced by Michael Waterhouse (Gollancz, 1999)

——, *Recreation* (New York, Houghton Mifflin, 1920)

——, *Twenty-Five Years 1892–1916*, 2 vols (Hodder & Stoughton, 1926)

Harris, José, *The Penguin Social History of Britain: Private Lives, Public Spirit: Britain 1870–1914* [**Kindle Edition]

Harrison, Frederic, *Autobiographic Memoirs*, 2 vols (Macmillan, 1911)

Hattersley, Roy, *David Lloyd George: The Great Outsider* (Little, Brown, 2010)

Hazelgrove, Jenny, *Spiritualism and British Society between the Wars* (Manchester, Manchester University Press, 2000)

Hibbert, Christopher, *Queen Victoria: A Personal History* (HarperCollins, 2000)

Higgin, Letitia, *Royal School of Needlework, Handbook of Embroidery (1880)* (East Molesley, Royal School of Needlework, 2010)

Hill, Georgiana, *A History of English Dress from the Saxon Period to the Present Day*, 2 vols (Richard Bentley, 1893)

Hoare, Philip, *England's Lost Eden: Adventures in a Victorian Utopia* (Harper Perennial, 2006)

——, *Oscar Wilde's Last Stand: Decadence, Conspiracy, and the Most Outrageous Trial of the Century* (New York, Arcade Publishing, 1998)

——, *Serious Pleasures: The Life of Stephen Tennant* (Hamish Hamilton, 1990)

Hobsbawm, Eric, *The Age of Empire 1875–1914* (Abacus, 1994)

Holmes, Richard, *Footsteps: Adventures of a Romantic Biographer* (Harmondsworth, Penguin Books, 1985)

——, *Sidetracks: Explorations of a Romantic Biographer* (Flamingo, 2001)

Hunt, Tristram, *Building Jerusalem: The Rise and Fall of the Victorian City* (New York, Metropolitan Books, Henry Holt, 2005)

Hynes, Samuel, *Edwardian Turn of Mind: First World War and English Culture* (Pimlico, 1991)

Illustrations of the Sargent Exhibition, Royal Academy, 1926 (Royal Academy of the Arts, 1926)

Jackson, Lee, *A Dictionary of Victorian London: An A–Z of the Great Metropolis* (Anthem Press, 2006)

Jackson, Margaret, *What They Wore: A History of Children's Dress* (Allen & Unwin, 1936)

Jalland, Pat, *Women, Marriage and Politics 1860–1914* (Oxford, Oxford University Press, 1988)

James, Henry, *The Ambassadors* (New York, Toronto, Signet Classic, 1960)

——, *The Awkward Age* (Macmillan, 1899)

——, *The Portable Henry James*, ed. John Auchard (Penguin Books, 2004)

——, *The Spoils of Poynton*, ed. David Lodge (Harmondsworth, Penguin, 1987)

James, Lawrence, *Aristocrats: Power, Grace and Decadence – Britain's Great Ruling Classes from 1066 to the Present* (Little, Brown, 2009)

——, *The Rise and Fall of the British Empire* (Abacus, 1995)

Jenkins, Roy, *Mr. Balfour's Poodle: Peers v. People* (Papermac, 1999)

Jennings, Humphrey, *Pandaemonium: The Coming of the Machine as Seen by Contemporary Observers 1660–1886* (Icon, 2012)

Joliffe, John, *Raymond Asquith: Life and Letters* (Collins, 1980).

Keating, Peter (ed.), *The Victorian Prophets: A Reader from Carlyle to Wells* (Fontana, 1981)

Keay, John, *India: A History* (HarperCollins, 2000)

Kinealy, Christine, *This Great Calamity: The Irish Famine 1845–52* (Dublin, Gill & Macmillan, 1994)

Kipling, Rudyard, *Plain Tales from the Hills*, ed. H. R. Woudhuysen (Harmondsworth, Penguin Books, 1987)

Lambert, Angela, *Unquiet Souls: The Indian Summer of the British Aristocracy* (Macmillan, 1984)

Lascelles, Sir Alan, *King's Counsellor: Abdication and War: The Diaries of Sir Alan Lascelles*, ed. Duff Hart-Davis (Weidenfeld & Nicolson, 2006)

——, *End of an Era: Letters and Journals of Sir Alan Lascelles from 1887 to 1920*, ed. Duff Hart-Davis (Hamish Hamilton, 1986)

Laver, James, *Taste and Fashion: From the French Revolution to the Present Day* (George G. Harrap, 1945)

Levine, Joshua, *Forgotten Voices of the Somme: The Most Devastating Battle of the Great War in the Words of Those Who Survived* (Ebury Press, 2008)

Lichnowsky, Prince Carl Max, *My Mission to London, 1912–1914* (Toronto, Cassell, 1918)

Liddell, Adolphus, *Notes from the Life of an Ordinary Mortal* (John Murray, 1911)

Lomax, James and Ormond, Richard, *John Singer Sargent and the Edwardian Age: An Exhibition Organized Jointly by the Leeds Art Galleries, the National Portrait Gallery, London, and the Detroit Institute of Arts* (Leeds, Leeds Art Galleries, 1979)

Longford, Elizabeth, *A Pilgrimage of Passion: The Life of Wilfrid Scawen Blunt* (Weidenfeld & Nicolson, 1979)

Lovell, Mary, *The Churchills: A Family at the Heart of History – from the Duke of Marlborough to Winston Churchill* (Little, Brown, 2011)

Luke, Michael, *David Tennant and the Gargoyle Years* (Weidenfeld & Nicolson, 1991)

MacCarthy, Fiona, *The Last Pre-Raphaelite: Edward Burne-Jones and the Victorian Imagination* (Faber & Faber, 2011)

——, *William Morris: A Life for our Time* (Faber & Faber, 1994)

Mackail, J. W. and Wyndham, Guy, *Life and Letters of George Wyndham*, 2 vols (Hutchinson, 1925)

Mackay, Ruddock F., *Balfour: Intellectual Statesman* (Oxford, Oxford University Press, 1985)

McKenna, Neil, *The Secret Life of Oscar Wilde* (Arrow Books, 2004)

MacKenzie, Jeanne, *The Children of the Souls: A Tragedy of the First World War* (Chatto & Windus, 1986)

Makari, George, *Revolution in Mind: The Creation of Psychoanalysis* (Duckworth, 2008)

Mallet, Marie, *Life with Queen Victoria: Marie Mallet's Letters from Court 1887–1901*, ed. Victor Mallet (John Murray, 1968)

Mansel, Philip, *The Levant: Splendour and Catastrophe on the Mediterranean* (John Murray, 2010)

——, *Paris between Empires 1814–1852: Monarchy and Revolution* (John Murray, 2001)

Marquand, David, *Britain since 1918: The Strange Career of British Democracy* (Orion, 2008)

Marr, Andrew, *The Making of Modern Britain* (Macmillan, 2009)

Masters, Brian, *Great Hostesses* (Constable, 1982)

Mayhew, Henry, *Mayhew's London: Being Selections from 'London Labour and the London Poor'*, ed. Peter Quennell (Pilot Press, 1949)

——, *London's Underworld*, ed. Peter Quennell (Feltham, Hamlyn, 1950)

Morris, Jan, *Farewell the Trumpets: An Imperial Retreat* (London and Boston, Faber, 1978)

——, *Heaven's Command: An Imperial Progress* (London and Boston, Faber 1978)

——, *Pax Britannica: The Climax of an Empire* (Harmondsworth, Penguin, 1979)

Mosley, Nicholas, *Julian Grenfell: His life and the Times of his Death 1888–1915* (Weidenfeld & Nicolson, 1976)

Moyle, Franny, *Constance: The Tragic and Scandalous Life of Mrs. Oscar Wilde* (John Murray, 2011)

Musson, Jeremy, *Up and Down Stairs* (John Murray, 2009)

Nevill, Lady Dorothy Fanny, *The Reminiscences of Lady Dorothy Nevill*, ed. Ralph Nevill (Edward Arnold, 1906)

Nicholson, Virginia, *Singled Out: How Two Million Women Survived without Men after the First World War* (Viking, 2007)

Nicolson, Juliet, *The Great Silence: 1918–1920, Living in the Shadow of the Great War* (John Murray, 2009)

——, *The Perfect Summer: Dancing into Shadow in 1911* (John Murray, 2007)

Nicolson, Nigel, *Mary Curzon* (Weidenfeld & Nicolson, 1977)

Olivier, Edith, *Four Victorian Ladies of Wiltshire* (Faber & Faber, 1940)

Oppenheim, Janet, *The Other World: Spiritualism and Psychic Research in England, 1850–1914* (Cambridge, Cambridge University Press, 1985)

Paget, Walburga, *In my Tower*, 2 vols (Hutchinson, 1924)

Pankhurst, E. Sylvia, *The Suffragette: The History of the Women's Militant Suffrage Movement, 1905–1910* (New York, Sturgis & Walton, 1911)

Pearce, Edward, *Lines of Most Resistance: The Lords, the Tories and Ireland 1886–1914* (Little, Brown, 1999)

Pearce, Malcolm and Stewart, Geoffrey, *British Political History 1867–1995: Democracy and Decline* (London and New York, Routledge, 1992)

Perkin, Joan, *Women and Marriage in Nineteenth-Century England* (Routledge, 1988)

Porter, Roy, *London: A Social History* (Penguin Books, 2000)

Powell, David, *The Edwardian Crisis: Britain 1901–1914* (London and New York, Macmillan, 1996)

Powell, Margaret, *Tales from Below Stairs* (Sidgwick & Jackson, 2012)

Pugh, Martin, *The Making of Modern British Politics, 1867–1939* (2nd edn, Oxford, Basil Blackwell, 1993)

Ridley, Jane and Percy, Clayre (eds), *The Letters of Arthur Balfour and Lady Elcho 1885–1917* (Hamish Hamilton, 1992)

Sackville-West, Vita, *The Edwardians* (Virago, 1983)

Seaman, L. C. B., *Victorian England: Aspects of English and Imperial History 1837–1901* (Methuen, 1973)

Sitwell, Osbert, *Left Hand, Right Hand! An Autobiography*. Vol. I (Macmillan, 1945)

——, *The Scarlet Tree: An Autobiography*. Vol. II (Macmillan, 1946)

——, *Great Morning: An Autobiography*. Vol. III (Macmillan, 1948)

——, *Laughter in the Next Room: An Autobiography*. Vol. IV (Macmillan, 1949)

Spender, John, *Life, Journalism and Politics*, 2 vols (New York, Frederick A. Stokes, 1927)

Steinbach, Susie, *Women in England 1760–1914: A Social History* (Weidenfeld & Nicolson, 2004)

Stevenson, David, *1914–1918: The History of the First World War* (Penguin Books, 2005)

Stone, Lawrence and Jeanne C. Fawtier, *An Open Elite? England 1500–1880* (Oxford, Clarendon Press, 1984)

Stone, Norman, *World War One: A Short History* (Allen Lane, 2007)

Stopes, Marie, *Married Love* (New York, The Critic and Guide Company, 1918)

——, *Radiant Motherhood* (G. B. Putnam's Sons, 1920)

Strachey, Lytton, *Eminent Victorians* (The Folio Press, 1979)

Sykes, Christopher Simon, *Private Palaces: Life in the Great London Houses* (Chatto & Windus, 1985)

Taylor, D. J., *Bright Young People: The Rise and Fall of a Generation 1918–1940* (Chatto & Windus, 2007)

Tennant, Emma, *Girlitude* (Jonathan Cape, 1999)

——, *Strangers: A Family Romance* (Jonathan Cape, 1998)

——, *Waiting for Princess Margaret* (Quartet Books, 2009)

Tennant, Harold John, *Sir Charles Tennant: His Forbears and Descendants* (Privately printed, 1932)

Thirkell, Angela, *Wild Strawberries: A Novel* (Hamish Hamilton, 1934)

Thorold, Peter, *The London Rich: The Creation of a Great City from 1666 to the Present* (Viking, 1999)

Thompson, Paul, *The Edwardians* (Paladin, 1979)

Tillyard, Stella, *Citizen Lord: Edward FitzGerald, 1763–1798* (Chatto & Windus, 1997)

Trevelyan, G. M., *English Social History* (Longmans, Green, 1944)

Tromans, Nicholas (ed.), *The Lure of the East: British Orientalist Painting*, accompanying the exhibition *The Lure of the East: British Orientalist Painting* at Tate Britain (Tate Publishing, 2008)

Tweedsmuir, Susan, *The Edwardian Lady* (Duckworth, 1966)

Tynan Hinkson, Katherine, *The Middle Years* (Constable, 1916)

——, *Twenty-five Years: Reminiscences* (John Murray, 1913)

——, *The Years of the Shadow* (Constable, 1919)

Vansittart, Robert, Lord, *The Mist Procession: The Autobiography of Lord Vansittart* (Hutchinson, 1958).

Walkley, Christina and Foster, Vanda, *Crinolines and Crimping Irons: Victorian Clothes: How They were Cleaned and Cared For* (Peter Owen, 1978)

Watts, Mary S., *George Frederic Watts: The Annals of an Artist's Life*, 2 vols (Macmillan, 1912)

Webb, Beatrice, *The Diary of Beatrice Webb: All the Good Things of Life*, vol. 2: *1892–1905*, ed. Norman and Jeanne MacKenzie (Virago, 1986)

Wells, H. G., *Ann Veronica: A Modern Love Story* (Virago, 1980)

——, *The Correspondence of H. G. Wells*, ed. David C. Smith (Pickering & Chatto, 1998)

——, *The New Machiavelli* (Duffield, 1910)

——, *Tono-Bungay* (Macmillan, 1914)

Wemyss, Mary, Countess of, *A Family Record* (Plaistow, Curwen Press, 1932)

West, Julius, *G. K. Chesterton: A Critical Study* (Martin Secker, 1915)

Wheatcroft, Geoffrey, *The Strange Death of Tory England* (Penguin Books, 2005)

White, Jerry, *London in the Nineteenth Century* (Vintage, 2008)

Wilde, Oscar, *The Complete Works of Oscar Wilde* (New Lanark, Geddes & Grosset, 2001)

Wilson, A. N., *The Victorians* (Hutchinson, 2002)

Wyndham, Joan, *Dawn Chorus* (Virago, 2004)

Wyndham, afterwards Adeane, Madeline Pamela Constance Blanche, *The Sad Story of a Pig and a Little Girl*, illustrated by Richard Doyle (Walker & Cockerell, 1901; reprinted from the 1st edn, Isel, Cumberland, 1876)

Young, Kenneth, *Arthur James Balfour: The Happy Life of the Politician, Prime Minister, Statesman and Philosopher, 1848–1930* (G. Bell, 1963)

Ziegler, Philip, *Diana Cooper* (Harmondsworth, Penguin Books, 1981)

Chapters, journal articles and unpublished theses

Cannadine, David, 'The Context, Performance and Meaning of Ritual: The British Monarchy and the "Invention of Tradition" circa 1820–1977', in Eric Hobsbawm and Terence Ranger (eds), *The Invention of Tradition* (Cambridge, Cambridge University Press, 1992)

Ellenberger, Nancy Waters, 'Constructing George Wyndham: Narratives of Aristocracy in Fin-de-Siècle England', *Journal of British Studies* 39:4 (October 2000): 487–517.

——, 'The Souls: High Society and Politics in Late Victorian England', PhD thesis, University of Oregon, 1982

——, 'The Souls and London "Society" at the end of the Nineteenth Century', *Victorian Society* 25:2 (Winter 1982): 133–60.

McKenzie, Barbara, 'James Hewat McKenzie: November 11th 1869–August 29th 1929', *Quarterly Transactions of the British College of Psychic Science* 8:3 (October 1929): 159–68.

List of Illustrations

Integrated

Picture section

Balfour, by London Stereoscopic & Photographic Company (albumen cabinet card, 1870s–1900s) © National Portrait Gallery; (bottom) George Wyndham, by Frank T. Foulsham, published by Underwood & Underwood (albumen stereoscopic card, 1900)

Page 6: (top) Mananai, Madeline, Sibell, Pamela and Charlie Adeane © Private Collection; (bottom) Madeline Wyndham and Madeline and Lettice Adeane © Private Collection

Page 7: (top left) Henry John Cockayne-Cust, by Sir Leslie Ward ('Spy'), 15 February 1894, *Vanity Fair* cartoon (colour litho), in Private Collection © Look and Learn/Peter Jackson Collection/The Bridgeman Art Library; (top right) The Hon. Percy Scawen Wyndham, by Sir Leslie Ward ('Spy'), 30 October 1880, *Vanity Fair* cartoon (colour litho), in Private Collection © Look and Learn/ Peter Jackson Collection/The Bridgeman Art Library; (bottom right) Lord Elcho, by Sir Leslie Ward ('Spy'), 26 March 1892, *Vanity Fair* cartoon (colour litho), in Private Collection © Look and Learn/Peter Jackson Collection / The Bridgeman Art Library; (bottom left) Sir Edward Tennant, 2 November 1910, *Vanity Fair* cartoon (colour litho), in Private Collection © Look and Learn/ Peter Jackson Collection/The Bridgeman Art Library

Page 8: (top) Arthur Balfour and Mary Charteris, by Lady Ottoline Morrell (vintage snapshot print, 1925) © National Portrait Gallery, London; (bottom) Pamela Grey, by unknown photographer (sepia-toned vintage bromide print on card mount, mid-1920s) © National Portrait Gallery, London

Index